DAVID BUSCH'S

NIKON D300 GUIDE TO DIGITAL SLR PHOTOGRAPHY

David D. Busch

Course Technology PTR
A part of Cengage Learning

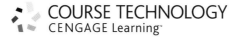

COURSE TECHNOLOGY
CENGAGE Learning

Australia, Brazil, Japan, Korea, Mexico, Singapore, Spain, United Kingdom, United States

COURSE TECHNOLOGY
CENGAGE Learning™

David Busch's Nikon D300
Guide to Digital SLR Photography
David D. Busch

Publisher and General Manager, Course Technology PTR: Stacy L. Hiquet

Associate Director of Marketing: Sarah Panella

Manager of Editorial Services: Heather Talbot

Marketing Manager: Jordan Casey

Executive Editor: Kevin Harreld

Project Editor: Jenny Davidson

Technical Reviewer: Michael D. Sullivan

PTR Editorial Services Coordinator: Erin Johnson

Interior Layout Tech: Bill Hartman

Cover Designer: Mike Tanamachi

Indexer: Sharon Shock

Proofreader: Sara Gullion

For product information and technology assistance, contact us at
Cengage Learning Customer & Sales Support Center, 1-800-354-9706

For permission to use material from this text or product, submit all requests online at **cengage.com/permissions**
Further permissions questions can be emailed to
permissionrequest@cengage.com

Library of Congress Control Number: 2008923824

ISBN-13: 978-1-59863-534-8

ISBN-10: 1-59863-534-4

Course Technology
25 Thomson Place
Boston, MA 02210
USA

Cengage Learning is a leading provider of customized learning solutions with office locations around the globe, including Singapore, the United Kingdom, Australia, Mexico, Brazil, and Japan. Locate your local office at: **international.cengage.com/region**

Cengage Learning products are represented in Canada by Nelson Education, Ltd.

For your lifelong learning solutions, visit **courseptr.com**

Visit our corporate website at **cengage.com**

Printed in the United States of America
4 5 6 7 11 10 09 08

For Mike Sullivan, friend and mentor.

Acknowledgments

Once again, thanks to the folks at Course Technology PTR, who recognized that a camera as advanced as the Nikon D300 deserves in-depth full-color coverage at a price anyone can afford. Special thanks to executive editor Kevin Harreld, who always gives me the freedom to let my imagination run free with a topic, as well as my veteran production team including project editor Jenny Davidson and technical editor Mike Sullivan. Also thanks to Bill Hartman, layout; Sharon Shock, indexing; Sara Gullion, proofreading; Mike Tanamachi, cover design; and my agent, Carole McClendon, who has the amazing ability to keep both publishers and authors happy.

About the Author

With more than a million books in print, **David D. Busch** is one of the best-selling authors of books on digital photography and imaging technology, and the originator of popular series like *David Busch's Pro Secrets* and *David Busch's Quick Snap Guides*. He has written five hugely successful guidebooks for Nikon digital SLR models, and five additional user guides for other camera models, as well as many popular books devoted to dSLRs, including *Mastering Digital SLR Photography, Second Edition* and *Digital SLR Pro Secrets*. As a roving photojournalist for more than 20 years, he illustrated his books, magazine articles, and newspaper reports with award-winning images. He's operated his own commercial studio, suffocated in formal dress while shooting weddings-for-hire, and shot sports for a daily newspaper and upstate New York college. His photos have been published in magazines as diverse as *Scientific American* and *Petersen's PhotoGraphic*, and his articles have appeared in *Popular Photography & Imaging, The Rangefinder, The Professional Photographer*, and hundreds of other publications. He's also reviewed dozens of digital cameras for CNet and *Computer Shopper*.

When About.com named its top five books on Beginning Digital Photography, debuting at the #1 and #2 slots were Busch's *Digital Photography All-In-One Desk Reference for Dummies* and *Mastering Digital Photography*. During the past year, he's had as many as five of his books listed in the Top 20 of Amazon.com's Digital Photography Bestseller list—simultaneously! Busch's 100-plus other books published since 1983 include bestsellers like *David Busch's QuickSnap Guide to Digital SLR Lenses*.

Busch earned top category honors in the Computer Press Awards the first two years they were given (for *Sorry About The Explosion* and *Secrets of MacWrite, MacPaint and MacDraw*), and he later served as Master of Ceremonies for the awards.

Contents

Chapter 3
Setup: Playback and Shooting Menus   77

Chapter 4
Setup: The Custom Setting Menu   133

Chapter 5
Setup: The Setup Menu, Retouch Menu, and My Menu   175

Chapter 6
Getting the Right Exposure   195

Chapter 7
Advanced Shooting Tips for Your
Nikon D300   227

Chapter 8
Working with Lenses 279

Chapter 9
Making Light Work for You   319

Chapter 10
Useful Software for the Nikon D300   361

Chapter 11
Nikon D300: Troubleshooting and Prevention   379

Glossary   405

Index   417

Preface

The Nikon D300 digital SLR is the most advanced intermediate camera for the professional or avid amateur photographer that Nikon has ever offered. Yet, the 400-plus page black-and-white manual packed in the box is almost impossible to wade through. Everything is in there, but how do you find it? And what does it all *mean?* What you really need is a comprehensive guide that explains the purpose and function of every one of the D300's controls, how you should use them in specific situations, and why.

You don't simply want to learn how to use Live View; you want to know how the ability to preview your picture on the D300's huge LCD can help you compose or take better photos. Before you spend a chunk of change on the Nikon MB-D10 vertical/battery grip, you'd like to know the exact benefits of this accessory. What's Active D-lighting, and when can using it actually *degrade* the quality of your images? You know that you can use certain older lenses with your D300—but why would you want to? This is the book that provides those answers.

If you want a quick introduction to the D300's focus controls, flash synchronization options, how to choose lenses, or which exposure modes are best, this book is for you. If you can't decide on what basic settings to use with your camera because you can't figure out how changing ISO or white balance or focus defaults will affect your pictures, you need this guide. I won't talk down to you, either; this book isn't padded with dozens of pages of checklists telling you how to take a travel picture, a sports photo, or how to take a snapshot of your kids in overly-simplistic terms. There are no recipes here. I give you all the information you need to cook up great photos on your own!

Introduction

Welcome back! It's good to see you again. I'm assuming, for the moment, that you bought this book because you benefited from one of my five previous guides to using Nikon digital SLRs, including my field guide to the D300's immediate predecessor, the Nikon D200. But if this is the first time you've given me the opportunity to introduce you to a Nikon dSLR, welcome aboard!

Whether you're a veteran of my previous books or a new convert, I think you'll find this introduction to the D300 quite different from the other books on the market. When Nikon introduced the long-awaited D300 on August 23, 2007, I scanned the new camera's list of features and realized that it deserved an entirely different approach. A compact "field guide" wouldn't hack it for such an advanced camera. Although many shrewd beginners will be buying the D300 as a first digital SLR, the vast majority of you will be advanced amateurs or professional photographers—or those who aspire to join those ranks as quickly as possible.

You don't need a book that devotes almost a third of its pages to little sections that provide the rudiments of shooting the most basic types of pictures. You don't need to be told that you ought to use a fast shutter speed when shooting sports—you probably already know a dozen different kinds of action situations when *slower* shutter speeds are superior (such as motor sports with spinning tires, or when panning to capture a long jumper speeding toward the pit). There's a good chance that telling you to use a large aperture when shooting a portrait is a bit simplistic for your skill level, too. If not, don't worry, I provide this kind of information, too. I just don't waste dozens of pages on these basic techniques when they can be covered in a few pages before jumping into the truly cool stuff.

Instead, I'm going to emphasize the exciting things you can do with the Nikon D300 digital SLR. After a couple introductory chapters that help you get your bearings with this innovative camera, we're going to explore dSLR photography using a significant new tool.

I've been using Nikon-based digital single lens reflex (SLR) cameras since before they had Nikon's name on them. That happy experience dates back to the previous millennium, when the wizards at Kodak began melding Nikon F3 film SLRs with 1.3 megapixel CCD sensors and a tethered 200MB *external* hard drive. Today, a decade and a half later, I'm convinced that the new Nikon D300 is the most significant digital SLR camera that Nikon has introduced, with the possible exception of the equally-new Nikon D3 (which is intended for a whole other class of shooter). The D300 is, in my mind, even more important than the Nikon D70, which first brought sub-$1,000 digital SLR photography within the reach of any serious photographer. Of course, I couldn't actually afford to buy any of the Nikon-platform Kodak DCS dSLRs, right up through the final Kodak DCS SLR 14/n model, but I was generously provided with several loaners and was allowed to shoot these ground-breaking cameras on research visits to Rochester. As a dedicated fan of the Japanese camera company for decades, I've owned all of the Nikon digital SLRs since the D70, and an alarming number of the company's lenses and accessories. And never before have I been blown away by a digital SLR as I was by the Nikon D300.

First and foremost, it's *affordable*, if you're serious about photography. Certainly, the sub-$1,000 price neighborhood is also important if you're in the early throes of passion for digital photography. Justifying even an entry-level digital SLR can be difficult for the beginner. But for those who are already (or soon to become) avid photographers, and for professionals looking for a solid main or backup camera body, when you consider the features and capabilities stuffed into the Nikon D300, its introductory price of $1,799 was a bargain. That's not chump change, of course, but when you realize that, before the D300, to get similar tools in any other Nikon dSLR, you'd be forced to spend more than twice as much.

The Nikon D300 is also more *expandable* than any previous Nikon dSLR at this price. Add the MB-D10 Multi-Power Battery Pack (which integrates much more solidly with the camera than did the MB-D200 pack for the D200 model), which gives you a longer-lasting power-source, a convenient vertical grip/shutter release for portrait-orientation shots, and the potential to fire off 8 frames per second with 12 megapixels of resolution. (The more expensive Nikon D2xs offers 8 fps only in High Speed Crop mode, and 6.8 megapixels of resolution.) You can now add a WT-4a wireless transmitter for WiFi remote operation and direct transfer of your photos to a laptop or other computer. That capability was previously solely within the realm of Nikon's top-of-the-line pro cameras. Want hi-res viewing? Your High Definition television can be used to savor the output of your camera, with only an HDMI cable required.

You'll find that the Nikon D300 also includes tons of *very cool features*, many of which it shares with Nikon's current flagship, the Nikon D3. These shared capabilities include a Live View capability that allows previewing the actual image on the camera's LCD screen before you snap a picture; a super-speedy 51-point autofocus system that's more accurate than anything this side of the D3 itself; and a metering system that works well with virtually every Nikon lens ever made, dating back to 1959 (although some require a $35 modification for compatibility). Indeed, the Nikon D300 provides 80-90 percent of the functionality of the D3 (except for the full frame sensor) at a fraction of the price, and, in many respects, it's a *better* camera than the nominal leader of the DX (cropped frame) class, the Nikon D2xs. The D300 even includes features not found on the D3, such as a built-in flash and automatic/manual sensor cleaning.

I sincerely believe that this book is your best bet for learning how to use your new camera, and for learning how to use it well. If you're a Nikon D300 owner who's looking to learn more about how to use this great camera, you've probably already explored your options. There are DVDs and online tutorials—but who can learn how to use a camera by sitting in front of a television or computer screen? Do you want to watch a movie or click on HTML links, or do you want to go out and take photos with your camera? Videos and web pages are fun, but not the best answer.

Of course, there's always the 400-plus page manual furnished with the camera. It's compact and filled with information, but there's really very little in there about *why* you should use particular settings or features, and its organization may make it difficult to find what you need. Multiple cross-references may send you flipping back and forth between two or three sections of the book to find what you need. The basic manual is also hobbled by black-and-white line drawings and tiny monochrome pictures that aren't very good examples of what you can do.

As I mentioned earlier, I haven't been happy with the third-party guidebooks to Nikon cameras, either, especially those written for advanced models like the D300. The existing books range from skimpy and illustrated by black-and-white photos to lushly illustrated in full color but too generic to do much good. Photography instruction is useful, but it needs to be related directly to the Nikon D300 as much as possible.

I've tried to make *David Busch's Nikon D300 Guide to Digital SLR Photography* different from your other D300 learn-up options. The roadmap sections use larger, color pictures to show you where all the buttons and dials are, and the explanations of what they do are longer and more comprehensive. Instead of the checklists devoted to general topics like "architectural photography" or "landscape photography," you'll find tips and techniques for using all the features of your Nikon D300 to take *any kind of picture* you want.

Nor is this book a lame rewriting of the manual that came with the camera. Some folks spend five minutes with a book like this one, spot some information that also appears in the original manual, and decide "Rehash!" without really understanding the differences. Yes, you'll find information here that is also in the owner's manual, such as the parameters you can enter when changing your D300's operation in the various menus. Basic descriptions—before I dig in and start providing in-depth tips and information—may also be vaguely similar. There are only so many ways you can say, for example, "Hold the shutter release down halfway to lock in exposure and focus."

But not *everything* in the manual is included in this book. I don't include a table of error messages, for instance, because their appearance is fairly rare to begin with, and I'd expect you to go grab the manual to look one up if an error occurs. Nor do I provide advice on how to store your camera, or a complete list of memory card capacities for various file formats. I want you to *use* your D300, not store it, and you can easily figure out the capacity of any freshly-formatted memory card you own from the figure displayed on the top panel LCD. Thinking of buying a card with twice as many gigabytes as your current memory card? Multiply the figure you get with the old card by two; that will be close enough. Not *everything* should be included in a guidebook like this one.

David Busch's Nikon D300 Guide to Digital SLR Photography is aimed at both Nikon and dSLR veterans as well as newcomers to digital photography and digital SLRs. Both groups can be overwhelmed by the options the D300 offers, while underwhelmed by the explanations they receive in their user's manual. The manuals are great if you already know what you don't know, and you can find an answer somewhere in a booklet arranged by menu listings and written by a camera vendor employee who last threw together instructions on how to operate a point-and-shoot digital camera.

Once you've read this book and are ready to learn more, I hope you pick up one of my other guides to digital SLR photography. All but one are aimed at photographers who are less advanced than you are likely to be. However, if you've jumped right into the pool with the Nikon D300 as your first digital SLR, one of them may provide the kind of introductory material you need to get up to speed. Four of these dSLR guides are offered by Course Technology PTR (a part of Cengage Learning), and each approaches topics from a different perspective. They include:

David Busch's Quick Snap Guide to Digital SLR Lenses

A bit overwhelmed by the features and controls of digital SLR lenses, and not quite sure when to use each type? This book explains lenses, their use, and lens technology in easy-to-access two- and four-page spreads, each devoted to a different topic, such as depth-of-field, lens aberrations, or using zoom lenses. If you have a friend or significant other who is less versed in photography, but who wants to borrow and use your Nikon D300 from time to time, this book can save you a ton of explanation.

Quick Snap Guide to Digital SLR Photography

Consider this a prequel to the book you're holding in your hands. It, too, might make a good gift for a spouse or friend who may be using your D300, but who lacks even basic knowledge about digital photography, digital SLR photography, and Nikon photography. It serves as an introduction that summarizes the basic features of digital SLR cameras in general (not just the D300), and what settings to use and when, such as continuous autofocus/single autofocus, aperture/shutter priority, EV settings, and so forth. The guide also includes recipes for shooting the most common kinds of pictures, with step-by-step instructions for capturing effective sports photos, portraits, landscapes, and other types of images. (Here is where you will find those bullet-point checklists I've left out of *this* book.)

Mastering Digital SLR Photography, Second Edition

This book is an introduction to digital SLR photography, with nuts-and-bolts explanations of the technology, more in-depth coverage of settings, and whole chapters on the most common types of photography. While not specific to the Nikon D300, this book can show you how to get more from its capabilities.

Digital SLR Pro Secrets

This is my more advanced guide to dSLR photography with greater depth and detail about the topics you're most interested in. If you've already mastered the basics in *Mastering Digital SLR Photography*, this book will take you to the next level.

Who Are You?

When preparing a guidebook for a specific camera, it's always wise to consider exactly who will be reading the book. Indeed, thinking about the potential audience for *David Busch's Nikon D300 Guide to Digital SLR Photography* is what led me to take the approach and format I use for this book. I realized that the needs of readers like you had to be addressed both from a functional level (what you will use the D300 for) as well as from a skill level (how much experience you may have with digital photography, dSLRs, or Nikon cameras specifically).

From a functional level, you probably fall into one of these categories:

- Professional photographers who will be taking photos for events, publication, portrait, or product photography studio work, or to meet other client needs.

- Individuals who want to get better pictures, or perhaps transform their growing interest in photography into a full-fledged hobby or artistic outlet with a Nikon D300 and advanced techniques.

- Those who want to produce more professional-looking images for their personal or business website, and feel that the Nikon D300 will give them more control and capabilities.

- Small business owners with more advanced graphics capabilities who want to use the Nikon D300 to document or promote their business.

- Corporate workers who may or may not have photographic skills in their job descriptions, but who work regularly with graphics and need to learn how to use digital images taken with a Nikon D300 for reports, presentations, or other applications.

- Professional webmasters with strong skills in programming (including Java, JavaScript, HTML, Perl, etc.) but little background in photography, but who realize that the D300 can be used for sophisticated photography.

- Graphic artists and others who already may be adept in image editing with Photoshop or another program, and who may already be using a film SLR (Nikon or otherwise), but who need to learn more about digital photography and the special capabilities of the D300 dSLR.

Addressing your needs from a skills level can be a little trickier, because the D300 is such a great camera that a full spectrum of photographers will be buying it, from absolute beginners who have never owned a digital camera before up to professionals with years of shooting experience who will be using the Nikon D300 as a backup body, or even their main camera.

Before tackling this book, it would be helpful for you to understand the following:

- **What a digital SLR is:** It's a camera that generally shows an optical (not LCD) view of the picture that's being taken through the (interchangeable) lens that actually takes the photo, thanks to a mirror that reflects an image to a viewfinder, but flips up out of the way to allow the sensor to be exposed. Some dSLRs, like the D300, also have a *Live View* option that flips up the mirror to allow a real-time display on the LCD.

- **How digital photography differs from film:** The image is stored not on film (which I call the *first* write-once optical media), but on a memory card as pixels that can be transferred to your computer, and then edited, corrected, and printed without the need for chemical processing.

- **What the basic tools of correct exposure are:** Shutter speed determines the amount of time the sensor is exposed to incoming light; the f/stop or aperture is like a valve that governs the quantity of light that can flow through the lens; the sensor's sensitivity (ISO setting) controls how easily the sensor responds to light. All three factors can be varied individually and proportionately to produce a picture that is properly exposed (neither too light nor too dark).

If you have a good understanding of those points, you're ready to go. I'm not going to explain those fundamentals in a lot of detail in this book. After some introductory material that lays out a roadmap of the D300 and its controls and settings, we're going to move quite quickly into more advanced topics. It's tough to provide something for everybody, so here is my advice for each group at typical skill levels:

- **Digital photography newbies:** If you've used only point-and-shoot digital cameras, or have worked only with non-SLR film cameras, you're to be congratulated for selecting one of the very best digital SLRs available as your first advanced model. This book can help you understand the controls and features of your D300, and lead you down the path to better photography with your camera, but it doesn't spend a lot of time with the basic-basics, including what shutter speeds are, or how to compose a photo. You'll need to work extra hard to get up to speed. I don't want to seem like I am hawking my other books relentlessly, but you actually could benefit from other resources in addition to this guide, whether written by me or another author. Once you've absorbed the fundamentals, however, you'll find that the D300 will allow you to take your best photos ever.

- **Advanced point-and-shooters moving on up:** There are some quite sophisticated pocket-sized digital cameras available, including those with many user-definable options and settings, so it's possible you are already a knowledgeable photographer, even though you're new to the world of the digital SLR. You've recognized the limitations of the point-and-shoot camera: even the best of them have more noise at higher sensitivity (ISO) settings than cameras like the Nikon D300; the speediest still have an unacceptable delay between the time you press the shutter and the photo is actually taken; even a non-interchangeable super-zoom camera with 12X to 20X magnification often won't focus close enough, include an aperture suitable for low-light photography, or take in the really wide view you must have. Interchangeable lenses and other accessories available for the Nikon D300 are another one of the reasons you moved up. Because you're an avid photographer already, you should pick up the finer points of using the D300 from this book with no trouble.

- **Film SLR veterans new to the digital world:** You understand photography, you know about f/stops and shutter speeds, and thrive on interchangeable lenses. If you own a recent film SLR, it probably has lots of electronic features already, including autofocus and sophisticated exposure metering. Perhaps you've even been using a Nikon film SLR and understand many of the available accessories that work with both film and digital cameras. All you need is information on using digital-specific features, working with the D300 itself, and how to match—and exceed—the capabilities of your film camera with your new Nikon D300.

- **Experienced dSLR users upgrading to the D300:** Perhaps you started out with the Nikon D70 back in 2004, a D100 before that, or have been working extensively with a more recent model, like the Nikon D40/D40x. It's very likely that a large number of you used the Nikon D200 before the bug to advance to more megapixels and more advanced features bit you. You may have used a digital SLR from Canon or another vendor and are making the switch. You understand basic photography, and want to learn more. And, most of all, you want to transfer the skills you already have to the Nikon D300, as quickly and seamlessly as possible.

- **Pro photographers and other advanced shooters:** I expect my most discerning readers will be those who already have extensive experience with Nikon intermediate and pro-level cameras. An amazing number of D300 cameras have been purchased by those who feel it is superior, in some respects, to their previous "favorite" camera, the Nikon D2x or D2xs. Others (like myself) own the D3 and find that the D300 fills a specific niche incredibly well. And not only as a backup camera; because the D3 and D300 both produce 12-megapixel images, there are many who prefer the D3 for wide-angle and low-light photography, and the D300 with the MB-D10 battery grip for sports, because the DX crop factor "magnifies" the reach of telephoto lenses, and the grip ups the D300's frame rate to an impressive 8 fps when fitted with the EN-EL4a battery pack or AA batteries. (There's not a heck of a lot of difference between 8 fps and the D3's top full-resolution rate of 9 fps.) You pros and semi-pros, despite your depth of knowledge, should find this book useful for learning about the features the D300 has that your previous cameras lacked.

Who Am I?

After spending years as the world's most successful unknown author, I've become slightly less obscure in the past few years, thanks to a horde of camera guidebooks and other photographically-oriented tomes. You may have seen my photography articles in *Popular Photography & Imaging* magazine. I've also written about 2,000 articles for magazines like *Petersen's PhotoGraphic* (which is now defunct through no fault of my own), plus *The Rangefinder, Professional Photographer,* and dozens of other photographic publications. But, first, and foremost, I'm a photojournalist and made my living in the field until I began devoting most of my time to writing books. Although I love writing, I'm happiest when I'm out taking pictures, which is why I took 14 days late in 2007 for a solo visit to Spain—not as a tourist, because I've been to Spain no less than a dozen times in the past—but solely to take photographs of the people, landscapes, and monuments that I've grown to love.

Like all my digital photography books, this one was written by a Nikon devotee with an incurable photography bug. My first Nikon SLR was a venerable Nikon F back in the 1960s, and I've owned most of the newer digital models since then. (My current stable consists of a Nikon D3, D2x, D200, D60, D40, and D70—converted to full-time infrared use—in addition to my D300. I had to sell my D50 and D80 to make room for more lenses.)

Over the years, I've worked as a sports photographer for an Ohio newspaper and for an upstate New York college. I've operated my own commercial studio and photo lab, cranking out product shots on demand and then printing a few hundred glossy 8 x 10s on a tight deadline for a press kit. I've served as a photo-posing instructor for a modeling agency. People have actually paid me to shoot their weddings and immortalize them with portraits. I even prepared press kits and articles on photography as a PR consultant for a large Rochester, N.Y., company, which shall remain nameless. My trials and travails with imaging and computer technology have made their way into print in book form an alarming number of times, including a few dozen on scanners and photography.

Like you, I love photography for its own merits, and I view technology as just another tool to help me get the images I see in my mind's eye. But, also like you, I had to master this technology before I could apply it to my work. This book is the result of what I've learned, and I hope it will help you master your Nikon D300 digital SLR, too.

1

Setting Up Your Nikon D300

I'm going to divide my introduction to the Nikon D300 into three parts. The first part will cover what you absolutely *need* to know just to get started using the camera (you'll find that in this chapter). The second part offers a more comprehensive look at what you *should* know about the camera and its controls to use its features effectively (that'll be found in Chapter 2). Finally, you'll learn how to make key settings using the menu system, so you'll be able to fine-tune and tweak the D300 to operate exactly the way you want, in Chapters 3, 4, and 5.

If you've previously used the Nikon D200, or, perhaps a D2x/D2xs model, you may be able to skim through this chapter quickly, and move on to the four that follow. The next few pages are designed to get your camera fired up and ready for shooting as quickly as possible. Of course, I recognize that anyone who purchases an advanced camera like the D300 probably hasn't the inclination—or patience—to sit down with a book and slog through basic instructions before snapping off a few—or maybe a few hundred—photos using nothing more than intuition and a general familiarity with digital SLRs. I understand the urge, because my own response to buying a new camera is usually to take a few pictures of the guy in the camera store who sold me my latest treasure. I generally bring along a memory card and a suitable lens (if purchasing a body) when I sidle in to pick up the camera. Assuming there's enough of a residual charge in my new camera's battery to power up the device, I'm off and shooting as soon as the shop's door slaps my behind on the way out.

Now that you've got that initial creative burst out of your system, you'll want to take a more considered approach to operating the camera. After all, the Nikon D300 is not a point-and-shoot camera, although you can easily set it up in a semi-automated mode using Program exposure mode and a basic autofocus setting for easy capture of grab shots. There are no "scene mode" options with icons on a handy dial representing a person (for portraits), flower (close-ups), mountain scene (landscapes), or runner (sports activity). Instead, there are only the dials and buttons and settings that you might expect to find on a mid-level camera like this one. So I'm going to provide a basic pre-flight checklist that you need to complete before you really spread your wings and take off. You won't find a lot of detail in this chapter. Indeed, I'm going to tell you just what you absolutely *must* understand, accompanied by some interesting tidbits that will help you become acclimated to your D300. I'll go into more depth and even repeat some of what I explain here in later chapters, so you don't have to memorize everything you see. Just relax, follow a few easy steps, and then go out and begin taking your best shots—ever.

First Things First

The Nikon D300 comes in an impressive gold box filled with stuff, including connecting cords, booklets, a CD, and lots of paperwork. The most important components are the camera and lens (if you purchased your D300 with a lens), battery, battery charger, and, if you're the nervous type, the neck strap. You'll also need a Compact Flash memory card, as one is not included. If you purchased your D300 from a camera shop, as I did, the store personnel probably attached the neck strap for you, ran through some basic operational advice that you've already forgotten, tried to sell you another Compact Flash card, and then, after they'd given you all the help you could absorb, sent you on your way with a handshake.

Perhaps you purchased your D300 from one of those mass merchandisers that also sell washing machines and vacuum cleaners. In that case, you might have been sent on your way with only the handshake, or, maybe, not even that if you resisted the hard-sell efforts to sell you an extended warranty. You save a few bucks at the big box stores, but you don't get the personal service a professional photo retailer provides. It's your choice. There's a third alternative, of course. You might have purchased your camera from a mail order or Internet source, and your D300 arrived in a big brown (or purple/red or yellow/red) truck. Your only interaction when you took possession of your camera was to scrawl your signature on an electronic clipboard.

In all three cases, the first thing to do is to carefully unpack the camera and double-check the contents with the checklist on one end of the box, helpfully designated under the [**Supplied Accessories**] bracketed heading. While this level of setup detail may seem as superfluous as the instructions on a bottle of shampoo, checking the contents *first* is always a good idea. No matter who sells a camera, it's common to open boxes, use a particular camera for a demonstration, and then repack the box without replacing all the pieces and parts afterwards. Someone might actually have helpfully checked out your camera on your behalf—and then mispacked the box. It's better to know *now* that something is missing so you can seek redress immediately, rather than discover two months from now that the video cable you thought you'd never use (but now *must* have) was never in the box. I once purchased a brand-new Nikon dSLR kit that was supposed to include a second focusing screen; it wasn't in the box, but because I discovered the deficiency right away, the dealer ordered a replacement for me post haste.

At a minimum, the box should have the following:

■ **Nikon D300 digital camera.** It almost goes without saying that you should check out the camera immediately, making sure the back and top panel LCDs aren't scratched or cracked, the Compact Flash and battery doors open properly, and, when a charged battery is inserted and lens mounted, the camera powers up and reports for duty. Out-of-the-box defects like these are rare, but they can happen. It's probably more common that your dealer played with the camera or, perhaps, it was a customer return. That's why it's best to buy your D300 from a retailer you trust to supply a factory-fresh camera.

■ **Rechargeable Li-ion battery EN-EL3e.** You'll need to charge this 7.4V, 1500mAh (milliampere hour) battery before using, and then navigate immediately to the **Setup** menu's **Battery info** entry to make sure the battery accepted the juice and is showing a 100% charge. (You'll find more on accessing this menu item in Chapter 5.) You'll want a second EN-EL3e battery as a spare (trust me), so buy one as soon as possible. It's the same battery as the one used in the Nikon D200, and also works in cameras like the D100, D80, D70/D70s, and D50, so you may already own one. This battery has a gray casing, to distinguish it from the earlier, black-encased Nikon EN-EL3 and Nikon EN-EL3a batteries, which do *not* work in the D300. Both the D200 and D300 require the latest version's third contact to provide "smart" battery condition feedback.

■ **Quick charger MH-18a.** This charger is functionally identical to the earlier MH-18 unit, so, if you already have an MH18 or MH-18a charger, you might want to store your new one away for a rainy day.

■ **Video cable EG-D100.** Use this cable to connect your D300 to a standard definition (analog) television through the set's yellow RCA video jack when you want to view the camera's output on a larger screen. Although the D300 can be connected to a high definition television, you'll need to buy a high definition multimedia interface (HDMI) cable to do that. No HDMI cable is included with the camera.

■ **USB Cable UC-E4.** You can use this cable to transfer photos from the camera to your computer (I don't recommend that because direct transfer uses a lot of battery power), to upload and download settings between the camera and your computer (highly recommended), and to operate your camera remotely using Nikon Camera Control Pro software (not included in the box). This cable is a standard one that works with the majority of digital cameras—Nikon and otherwise—so if you already own one, you now have a spare.

■ **Neck strap.** Nikon provides you with a neck strap emblazoned with your camera model. It's not very adjustable, and, while useful for showing off to your friends exactly which nifty new camera you bought, the Nikon strap also can serve to alert observant unsavory types that you're sporting a higher-end model that's worthy of their attention. I never attach the Nikon strap to my cameras (although once I put a D3 strap on a Nikon D40 as a jest), and instead opt for a more serviceable strap from Op-Tech (**www.optechusa.com**) or Upstrap (**www.upstrap-pro.com**). A typical Op-Tech strap is shown in Figure 1.1 attached to my *other* dSLR, a D3.

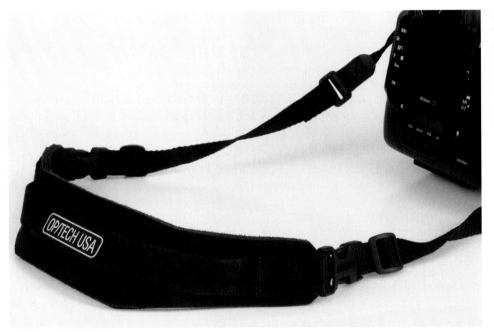

Figure 1.1
Third-party neck straps like this Op-Tech model, are often preferable to the Nikon-supplied strap.

■ **BF-1A body cap.** The body cap keeps dust from infiltrating your camera when a lens is not mounted. Always carry a body cap (and rear lens cap) in your camera bag for those times when you need to have the camera bare of optics for more than a minute or two. (That usually happens when repacking a bag efficiently for transport, or when you are carrying an extra body or two for backup.) The body cap/lens cap nest together for compact storage.

Note

If you happen to have one of the earlier BF-1 body caps for older film cameras, do not use it, as it may damage the lens mount.

■ **DK-21 eyecup.** This is the square rubber eyecup that comes installed on the D300. It slides on and off the viewfinder. If you prefer, you can also use round, screw-in eyepiece accessories, such as the DK-3 circular rubber eyecup or DG-2 eyepiece 2x magnifier by substituting the Nikon No. 2370 eyepiece adapter for the DK-21 eyecup.

■ **DK-5 Eyepiece cap.** This small piece can be clipped over the viewfinder window to prevent strong light sources from entering the viewing system when your eye is not pressed up against it, potentially affecting exposure measurement. That can be a special problem when the camera is mounted on a tripod, because additional illumination from the rear can make its way to the 1005-segment CCD that interprets light reaching the focusing screen. I pack this widget away to keep from losing it. As a practical matter, you'll never find it when you really need it, and covering the viewfinder with your hand (hover *near* the viewfinder window rather than touch it, to avoid shaking a tripod-mounted camera) works almost as well.

■ **LCD monitor cover BM-8.** The glass covering the D300's big 3-inch LCD is tough, but this plastic cover adds another layer of protection, and it can be replaced for a few dollars if scratched. If I were going to worry about shielding the LCD from damage, I'd use a less obtrusive acrylic cover from DaProducts (**www.daproducts.com**) at a cost of about $6. My big problem with Nikon's clip-on protector is that it easily fogs up when you breathe on it.

■ **User's manuals.** Even if you have this book, you'll probably want to check the user's guide that Nikon provides, if only to check the actual nomenclature for some obscure accessory, or to double-check an error code. Google "Nikon D300 manual PDF" to find a downloadable, non-printable version that you can store on your laptop, a CD-ROM, or other media in case you want to access this reference when the paper version isn't handy. If you have an old Compact Flash card that's too small to be usable on a modern dSLR (I still have some 128MB and 256MB cards), you can store the PDF on that. But an even better choice is to put the manual on a low-capacity USB "thumb" drive, which you can buy for less than $10. You'll then be able to access the reference anywhere you are, because you can always find someone with a computer that has a USB port and Adobe Acrobat Reader available. You might not be lucky enough to locate a computer with a Compact Flash reader.

■ **Quick guide.** This little booklet tucked away in the camera's paperwork offers a reasonable summary of the Nikon D300's basic commands and settings, and can be stowed in your camera bag more easily than a "field guide" or even this book.

■ **Software CD-ROM.** Here you'll find the Nikon Software Suite, which includes various drivers required by some operating systems; Nikon Transfer (to move your files from camera or memory card to your computer); Nikon ViewNX (a useful image management program); as well as various third-party utilities (some of which you may already have installed on your computer), such as DirectX9, QuickTime, and Kodak EasyShare software. I'll cover all the Nikon software offerings later in this book.

- **Warranty and registration card.** Don't lose these! You can register your Nikon D300 by mail or online (in the USA, the URL is **www.nikonusa.com/register**) and may need the information in this paperwork (plus the purchase receipt/invoice from your retailer) should you require Nikon service support.

- **Nikon Capture NX software CD-ROM or serial number card.** At the time I wrote this book, Capture NX, Nikon's NEF (Raw) conversion and image tweaking software, was being included free in all shipments of the D300 (and D3). Nikon says that it will provide up to 300,000 copies worldwide, but I suspect that outcries from later purchasers may prod the company into making Capture NX a free item with all its more advanced dSLRs. Some buyers received a CD with the utility, while other early purchasers got a card that had a registration number hidden behind a peel-off label (to ensure that only the camera buyer would be able to use the number). Card recipients can download the try-out version of Capture NX from their local Nikon website, and upgrade it to the full, registered version using the serial number provided. I don't know how long this essential software will be provided free (it's previously been available only as an extra-cost option), so if you receive Capture NX on a CD or with a serial number card, treasure it.

Don't bother rooting around in the box for anything beyond what I've listed previously. There are a few things Nikon classifies as optional accessories, even though you (and I) might consider some of them essential. Here's a list of what you *don't* get in the box, but might want to think about as an impending purchase. I'll list them roughly in the order of importance:

- **Compact Flash card.** First-time digital camera buyers are sometimes shocked that their new tool doesn't come with a memory card. Why should it? The manufacturer doesn't have the slightest idea of what capacity or speed card you prefer, so why should they pack one in the box and charge you for it? That's especially true for the Nikon D300, which is likely to be purchased by photographers who have quite definite ideas about their ideal memory card. Perhaps you want to use tiny 2GB cards—and lots of them. I've met many paranoid wedding photographers who like to work with a horde of smaller Compact Flash cards (and then watch over them *very* protectively), on the theory that they are reducing their chances of losing a significant chunk of the event or reception at one time (of course, that's why you hire a second shooter as backup). Others, especially sports photographers, instead prefer an 8GB or 16GB Compact Flash card with room to spare. If you are shooting fast action at high frame rates, or transfer lots of photos to your computer with a speedy Compact Flash card reader, you might opt for the speediest possible memory card. Buy one (or two, or three) of your own and have your flash memory ready when you unpack your D300.

■ **Extra EN-EL3e battery.** I mentioned the need for an extra battery earlier, and I'll mention it here, again. Even though you might get 1,000 or more shots from a single battery, it's easy to exceed that figure in a few hours of shooting sports at 5 to 8 fps. Batteries can unexpectedly fail, too, or simply lose their charge from sitting around unused for a week or two. Buy an extra (I own four, in total), keep it charged, and free your mind from worry.

■ **Camera Control Pro 2 software.** This is the utility you'll use to operate your camera remotely from your computer. Nikon charges extra for this software, but you'll find it invaluable if you're hiding near a tethered, tripod-mounted camera while shooting, say, close-ups of hummingbirds. There are lots of applications for remote shooting, and you'll need Camera Control Pro to operate your camera. Buy a suitably longer USB cable, too, unless you plan to use the Nikon WT-4a wireless transmitter (described below).

■ **Add-on speedlight.** One of the best uses for your Nikon D300's built-in electronic flash is as a remote trigger for an off-camera speedlight such as the Nikon SB-800 or SB-600. Your built in flash can function as the main light, diffused and used for fill, or dialed down in power so it has virtually no effect on the finished photo at all (other than triggering your remote flash units). But, you'll have to own one or two (or more) external flash units to gain that flexibility. If you do much flash photography at all, consider an add-on speedlight as an important accessory.

■ **Remote control cable MC-30.** You can plug this accessory electronic release into the 10-pin socket hidden behind the rubber cover on the front of the D300, and then fire off the camera without the need to touch the camera itself. In a pinch, you can use the D300's self-timer to minimize vibration when triggering the camera, or even take advantage of the mirror up (M-UP) and delayed release features to reduce camera shake. (These are all described later in this book.) But when you want to take a photo at the exact moment you desire (and not when the self-timer happens to trip), or need to eliminate all possibility of human-induced camera shake, you need this release cord.

> **Note**
>
> The Nikon MC-30 can be tricky to find in stock. I've had excellent luck using the Phottix Remote N1 and Phottix wireless remote at a fraction of the cost. I buy them from reliable Hong Kong dealer HKSupplies, which deals in the USA as eBay seller etefore-usacs. Check out **www.ebay.com** and **www.phottix.com**.

- **MC-21 extension cable.** This is a three meter extension cord for the 10-pin terminal connector, allowing the use of the MC-30 remote cable and other accessories at greater distances.

- **MC-36 remote shutter release.** This is a pricey ($130) 33-inch remote shutter release that plugs into the 10-pin terminal connector and allows timed long exposures and interval shooting (time-lapse photography) of up to 999 shots with up to 99 hours, 99 minutes, and 99 seconds between shots.

- **ML-3 remote control.** An even more expensive ($175) remote release for the D300, but this one operates wirelessly by infrared. I prefer the much cheaper Phottix wireless remote mentioned earlier, which uses radio control and has a much longer range (up to 320 feet instead of 26 feet).

- **AC Adapter EH-5a.** There are several typical situations where this AC adapter for your D300 can come in handy: when you're cleaning the sensor manually and want to totally eliminate the possibility that a lack of juice will cause the fragile shutter and mirror to spring to life during the process; when in the studio shooting product photos, portraits, class pictures, and so forth for hours on end; when using your D300 for remote shooting as well as time-lapse photography; for extensive review of images on your standard definition or high definition television; or for file transfer to your computer. These all use prodigious amounts of power, which can be provided by this AC adapter. (Beware of power outages and blackouts when cleaning your sensor, however!)

> **Note**
>
> The D300 uses the same AC adapter as the Nikon D40/D40x, Nikon D70/D70s, and D100. This is good news if you own one of those cameras, but a major *downgrade* if you own a Nikon D200, D2x/D2xs, D3 or other camera with an AC Adapter EH-6. Previously, owners of any of those cameras could get by with one AC adapter for all of them; now, particularly if you use a D3 with a D300 as a backup, you must own *two*.

- **Multi-power battery pack MB-D10.** Lots of photographers consider this battery pack/vertical grip to be an essential item (I'm going to cover it in detail later in this book), but you must buy it as an extra. (See Figure 1.2.) The price is reasonable at less than $250. Unfortunately, it is delivered "bare," with no extra power sources at all. You'll need to purchase AA batteries (alkalines or rechargeables) for the supplied AA battery tray, or have an extra EN-EL3e battery to use this accessory. (I *told* you that you'd need that extra battery.) If you want to gain the 8 fps continuous

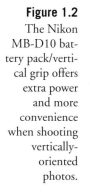

Figure 1.2
The Nikon MB-D10 battery pack/vertical grip offers extra power and more convenience when shooting vertically-oriented photos.

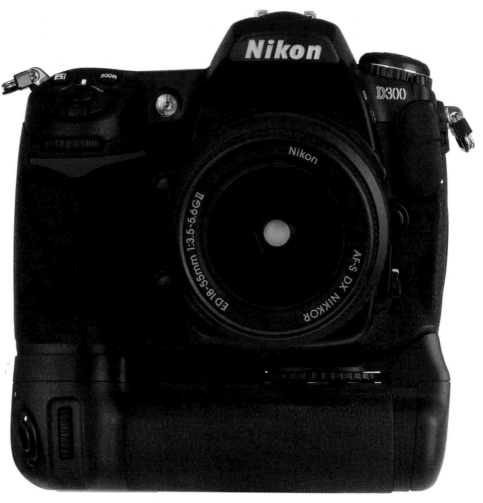

shooting rate, you'll also need to use AA batteries, or a Nikon EN-EL4a battery. It's the same one used with the D2x/D2xs and some other Nikon pro cameras but, to further add to the insults, the MD-D10 doesn't come with the clip-on end-piece/door that must be affixed to the end of the beefier battery. The "door" from the D2xs won't fit the D300 (although the one furnished as an option for the Nikon MB-40 battery pack for the Nikon F6 will). So, you'll need to spend about $35 additional for a tiny plastic gadget that Nikon calls the BL-3 Battery Chamber Cover. You also must have battery chargers for your AA batteries and EN-EL4a battery, as well as for your EN-EL3e battery.

- **MH-19 multiple battery charger.** If you own several EN-EL3e batteries, you can charge two at once using this charger.

- **DR-6 right angle viewer.** Fastens in place of the standard square rubber eyecup and provides a 90-degree view for framing and composing your image at right angles to the original viewfinder, useful for low-level (or high-level) shooting. (Or, maybe, shooting around corners!)

- **DK-21M magnifying eyepiece.** Provides a 1.17X magnification factor of the entire viewing area (unlike the 2X DG-2 eyepiece, which enlarges the center of the image), making it easier to check focus. You might have to move your eye around a little to see all the indicators outside the image frame, but this magnifier is still suitable for everyday use.

- **Wireless transmitter WT-4a.** This is the gadget for wireless remote control operation with Nikon Camera Control Pro 2 software. Wedding and event photographers can get a lot of use out of this accessory, and studio photographers can benefit from it, too. Not only can you back up all your photos to a laptop or desktop computer as they are taken, you or an assistant can be viewing, editing, and displaying them virtually simultaneously to clients, art directors, or anyone else.

- **GPS adapter cord MC-35.** Use this accessory to record location information such as latitude, longitude, altitude, and UTC (Coordinated Universal Time) at which a shot is taken. You don't need to be a National Geographic photographer to find this capability useful. The adapter cord plugs into the 10-pin connector beneath the rubber cover on the front of the D300, and then plugs into your compatible GPS unit.

- **SC-28 TTL flash cord.** Allows using Nikon speedlights off-camera, while retaining all the automated features.

- **SC-29 TTL flash cord.** Similar to the SC-28, this unit has its own AF-assist lamp, which can provide extra illumination for the D300's autofocus system in dim light (which, not coincidentally, is when you'll probably be using an electronic flash).

Initial Setup

Once you've unpacked and inspected your camera, the initial setup of your Nikon D300 is fast and easy. Basically, you just need to charge the battery, attach a lens, and insert a Compact Flash card. I'll address each of these steps separately, but if you already are confident you can manage these setup tasks without further instructions, feel free to skip this section entirely. While most buyers of a D300 tend to be experienced photographers, I realize that some readers are ambitious, if inexperienced, and should, at the minimum, skim the contents of the next section, because I'm going to list a few options that you might not be aware of.

Setting the Clock

It's likely that your Nikon D300's internal clock hasn't been set to your local time, so you may need to do that first. If so, the flashing CLOCK indicator on the top panel LCD will be the giveaway. You'll find complete instructions for setting the four options for the date/time (time zone, actual date and time, the date format, and whether you want the D300 to conform to Daylight Savings Time) in Chapter 5. However, if you think you can handle this step without instruction, press the Menu button, use the multi-selector (the thumb-friendly button to the immediate right of the back panel LCD) to scroll down to the Setup menu, press the multi-selector button to the right, and scroll down to World Time and press right again. The options will appear on the screen that appears next. Keep in mind that you'll need to reset your camera's internal clock from time to time, as it is not 100 percent accurate.

Battery Included

Your Nikon D300 is a sophisticated hunk of machinery and electronics, but it needs a charged battery to function, so rejuvenating the EN-EL3e lithium-ion battery pack furnished with the camera should be your first step. A fully charged power source should be good for approximately 1,000 shots, based on standard tests defined by the Camera & Imaging Products Association (CIPA) document DC-002. Nikon's own standards are quite a bit more optimistic (it predicts as many as 3,000 shots from a single charge). In the real world, of course, the life of the battery will depend on how much image review you do, how many shots you take with the built-in flash, and many other factors. You'll want to keep track of how many pictures *you* are able to take in your own typical circumstances, and use that figure as a guideline, instead.

A BATTERY AND A SPARE

I always recommend purchasing Nikon brand batteries (for about $50) over less-expensive third-party packs, even though the $30 substitute batteries may offer more capacity at a lower price (some top the 1,500 mAh offered by the Nikon battery). My reasoning is that it doesn't make sense to save $20 on a component for a $1,799 camera, especially since batteries have been known to fail in potentially harmful ways. You need only look as far as Nikon's own recall of its earlier EN-EL3 batteries, which forced the company to ship out thousands of free replacement cells. You're unlikely to get the same support from a third-party battery supplier that sells under a half-dozen or more different product labels and brands, and may not even have an easy way to get the word out that a recall has been issued.

If your pictures are important to you, always have at least one spare battery available, and make sure it is an authentic Nikon product.

All rechargeable batteries undergo some degree of self-discharge just sitting idle in the camera or in the original packaging. Lithium-ion power packs of this type typically lose a few percent of their charge every day, even when the camera isn't turned on. The small amount of juice used to provide the "shots remaining" figure on the top panel monochrome LCD when the D300 is turned off isn't the culprit; Li-ion cells lose their power through a chemical reaction that continues when the camera is switched off. So, it's very likely that the battery purchased with your camera is at least partially pooped out, so you'll want to revive it before going out for some serious shooting.

Charging the Battery

When the battery is inserted into the MH-18a charger properly (it's impossible to insert it incorrectly), a Charge light begins flashing, and remains flashing until the status lamp glows steadily indicating that charging is finished. (See Figure 1.3.) When the battery is charged, flip the lever on the bottom of the camera and slide the battery in, as shown in Figure 1.4. Check the **Setup** menu's **Battery info** entry as I recommended earlier to make sure the battery is fully charged. If not, try putting it in the charger again. One of three things may be the culprit: a.) the actual charging cycle sometimes takes longer

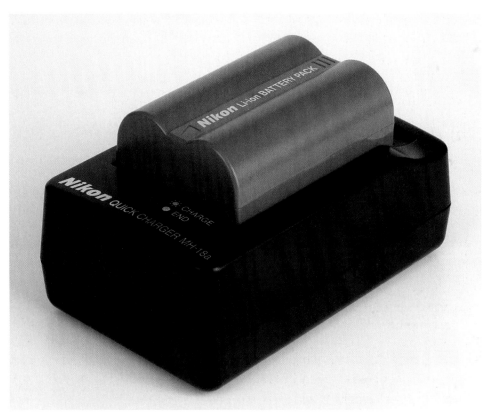

Figure 1.3
The flashing status light will illuminate while the battery is being charged.

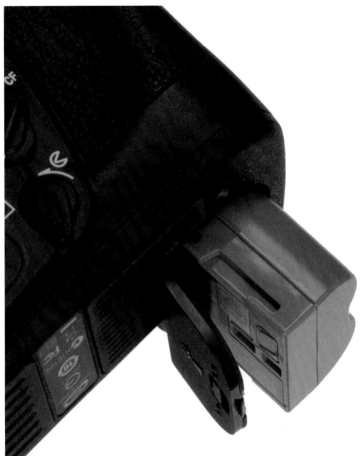

than you (or the charger) expected; b.) the battery is new and needs to be "seasoned" for a few charging cycles, after which it will accept a full charge and deliver more shots (buyers of the earlier Nikon D200 discovered that seasoning seemed to give them 10-20 percent more exposures with a new battery); c.) you've got a defective battery. The last is fairly rare, but before you start counting on getting a particular number of exposures from a battery, it's best to make sure it's fully charged, seasoned, and ready to deliver.

Nikon seems to have fixed a problem with the D200 model, which sometimes required an extra, positive click of the battery door to lock it properly. Sometimes, the door would seemingly flip open on its own, the battery would drop down unnoticed (but not fall out; an internal catch would prevent that), leaving the puzzled photographer with a dead camera until the escaping battery was noticed. The D300 battery door closes solidly and doesn't flip open until you intentionally nudge the catch.

Final Steps

Your Nikon D300 is almost ready to fire up and shoot. You'll need to select and mount a lens, adjust the viewfinder for your vision, and insert a Compact Flash card. Each of these steps is easy, and if you've used any Nikon before, you already know exactly what to do. I'm going to provide a little extra detail for those of you who are new to the Nikon or SLR worlds.

Mounting the Lens

As you'll see, my recommended lens mounting procedure emphasizes protecting your equipment from accidental damage and minimizing the intrusion of dust. If your D300 has no lens attached, select the lens you want to use and loosen (but do not remove) the rear lens cap. I generally place the lens I am planning to mount vertically in a slot in my camera bag, where it's protected from mishaps, but ready to pick up quickly. By loosening the rear lens cap, you'll be able to lift it off the back of the lens at the last instant, so the rear element of the lens is covered until then.

After that, remove the body cap by pressing the release button next to the lens mount, and rotating the cap towards the release button. You should always mount the body cap when there is no lens on the camera, because it helps keep dust out of the interior of the camera, where it can settle on the mirror, focusing screen, interior mirror box, and potentially find its way past the shutter onto the sensor. (While the D300's sensor cleaning mechanism works fine, the less dust it has to contend with, the better.) The body cap also protects the vulnerable mirror from damage caused by intruding objects (including your fingers, if you're not cautious).

Once the body cap has been removed, remove the rear lens cap from the lens, set it aside, and then mount the lens on the camera by matching the alignment indicator on the lens barrel with the white dot on the camera's lens mount. (See Figure 1.5.) Rotate the lens toward the shutter release until it seats securely. Some lenses are trickier to mount than others, particularly telephotos and telephoto zooms with swiveling collars that allow the lens to be fastened to a tripod. You might need to rotate the collar so the tripod foot doesn't bump into the front overhang of the D300's prism.

Set the focus mode switch on the lens to AF or M-AF (autofocus). If the lens hood is bayoneted on the lens in the reversed position (which makes the lens/hood combination more compact for transport), twist it off and remount with the "petals" (found on virtually all Nikon lens hoods) facing outward. (See Figure 1.6.) A lens hood protects the front of the lens from accidental bumps, and reduces flare caused by extraneous light arriving at the front element of the lens from outside the picture area.

Figure 1.5
Match the indicator on the lens with the white dot on the camera mount to properly align the lens with the bayonet mount.

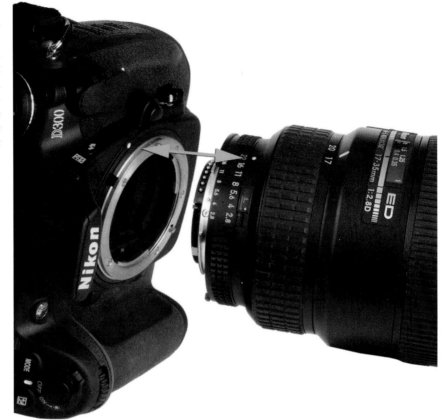

Figure 1.6
A lens hood protects the lens from extraneous light and accidental bumps.

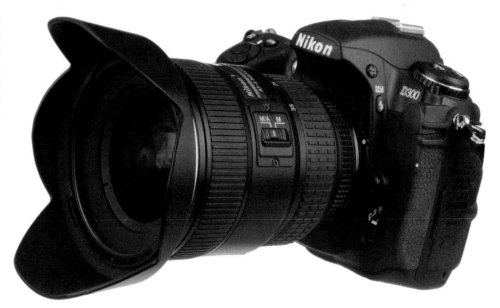

DEALING WITH ERRORS

After you've mounted your lens properly (or *think* you have), you might find various error codes appearing on the top panel LCD, viewfinder, and back panel color LCD. Here are the most common error codes, and what you should do next:

- **FE E.** This error code, with a smaller uppercase F followed by two Es indicates that you've mounted a lens that has an aperture ring, but haven't set the lens to its smallest f/stop (usually f/22 or f/32). Nikon autofocus lenses with an aperture ring have a lock level that allows you to set the minimum aperture and lock it there so that this problem doesn't occur. However, you may have unlocked the aperture ring when you needed to set the aperture manually with the lens mounted on an older camera that didn't allow setting the aperture electronically. Or, you might have mounted the lens on a non-autoaperture extension tube, bellows, or other accessory.

- **F.** This symbol, preceded by a leaning triangle symbol that I can't reproduce in text, indicates that there is no lens attached to the D300 (although you'd probably notice that), or that you have mounted an older, non-CPU lens (such as an AI lens as described in Chapter 8)—one that doesn't report to the camera its current aperture electronically. You can set the maximum aperture and focal length of up to nine such lenses using the Setup menu's Non-CPU lens data option, which I'll detail in Chapter 8.

- **E r r.** Some other error has taken place. Release the shutter, turn off the camera, remove the lens, and remount it. Try another lens. If the message persists, then there is a problem unrelated to your lens, and your D300 may need service.

Adjusting Diopter Correction

Those of us with less than perfect eyesight can often benefit from a little optical correction in the viewfinder. Your contact lenses or glasses may provide all the correction you need, but if you are a glasses wearer and want to use the D300 without your glasses, you can take advantage of the camera's built-in diopter adjustment, which can be varied from -2 to +1 correction. Press the shutter release halfway to illuminate the indicators in the viewfinder, then rotate the diopter adjustment wheel next to the viewfinder (see Figure 1.7) while looking through the viewfinder until the indicators appear sharp.

If more than one person uses your D300, and each requires a different diopter setting on the camera itself, you can save a little time by noting the number of clicks and direction (clockwise to increase the diopter power; counterclockwise to decrease the diopter value) required to change from one user to the other. Should the available correction be insufficient, Nikon offers nine different Diopter-Adjustment Viewfinder Correction lenses for the viewfinder window, ranging from -5 to +3, at a cost of $15-$20 each.

Figure 1.7
Viewfinder
diopter correc-
tion from -2 to
+1 can be
dialed in.

*Diopter
correction dial*

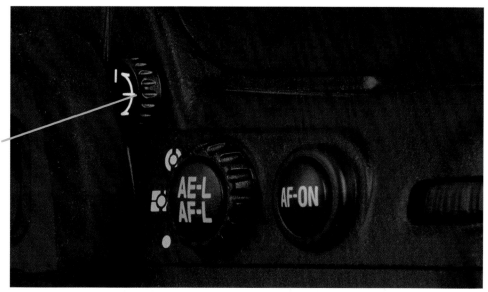

Inserting a Compact Flash Card

You've probably set up your D300 so you can't take photos without a Compact Flash card inserted. (There is a **No memory card** entry, Custom Setting Menu **CSM #f9** that enables/disables shutter release functions when a memory card is absent—learn about that in Chapter 4). So, your final step will be to insert a Compact Flash card. Rotate the "Pac-man" lever on the lower back right edge of the body counterclockwise to release the cover, and then open it. (You should only remove the memory card when the camera is switched off, or, at the very least, the yellow-green CF access light that indicates the camera is writing to the card is not illuminated.)

MORE ABOUT CSM OPTIONS IN CHAPTER 4

You'll find a complete list of Custom Settings Menu options and parameters in Chapter 4.

Insert the memory card with the label facing the back of the camera oriented so the edge with the double row of tiny holes goes into the slot first. Close the door, and, if necessary, format the card. When you want to remove the memory card later, press the gray button (shown at the bottom of Figure 1.8) to make the Compact Flash card pop out.

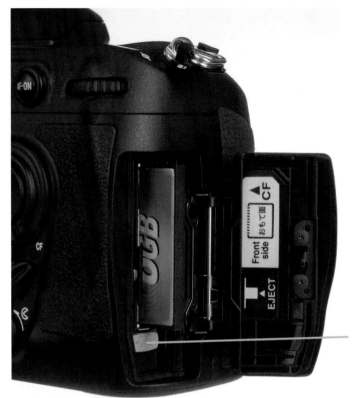

Figure 1.8
The Compact Flash card is inserted with the label facing the back of the camera.

Compact Flash card release button

Formatting a Memory Card

There are four ways to create a blank Compact Flash card for your D300, and two of them are wrong. Here are your options, both correct and incorrect:

- **Transfer (move) files to your computer.** When you transfer (rather than copy) all the image files to your computer from the Compact Flash card (either using a direct cable transfer or with a card reader, as described later in this chapter), the old image files are erased from the card, leaving the card blank. Theoretically. Unfortunately, this method does *not* remove files that you've labeled as Protected (by pressing the Protect button to the left of the LCD while viewing the image on the LCD), nor does it identify and lock out parts of your CF card that have become corrupted or unusable since the last time you formatted the card. Therefore, I recommend always formatting the card, rather than simply moving the image files, each time you want to make a blank card. The only exception is when you *want* to leave the protected/unerased images on the card for awhile longer, say, to share with friends, family, and colleagues.

- **(Don't) Format in your computer.** With the CF card inserted in a card reader or card slot in your computer, you can use Windows or Mac OS to reformat the memory card. Don't! The operating system won't necessarily install the correct file system. The only way to ensure that the card has been properly formatted for your camera is to perform the format in the camera itself. The only exception to this rule is when you have a seriously munged memory card that your camera refuses to format. Sometimes it is possible to revive such a corrupted card by allowing the operating system to reformat it first, then trying again in the camera.

- **Setup menu format.** To use one of the recommended methods to format a memory card, press the **Menu** button, use the up/down buttons of the multi-selector (that thumb-pad-sized control to the right of the LCD) to choose the **Setup** menu (which is represented by a wrench icon), navigate to the **Format memory card** entry with the right button of the multi-selector, and select **Yes** from the screen that appears. Press **OK** to begin the format process.

- **Two-button format.** The second recommended method requires no menus. Hold down the **Mode** button (on top of the camera, just southwest of the shutter release button) and the trash can button (on the upper-left corner of the back) simultaneously for about two seconds. (A **Format** label, color-coded red, appears next to each button.) The characters **For** and the exposures remaining displays will blink in the viewfinder and top panel LCD. Press the pair of buttons again, and the D300 will format your card. To cancel the format, press any other button.

Table 1.1 shows the typical number of shots you can expect using 12-bit color depth and an 8GB memory card (which I expect will be the favorite size card among D300 users during the life of this book). (Hold down the **Qual** button and rotate the main command dial to change the file/formats in column 1, and rotate the sub command dial to change the image sizes in columns 2, 3, and, 4.)

Table 1.1 TableTitle

	Large	Medium	Small
JPEG Fine	750	1,300	2,900
JPEG Normal	1,400	2,500	5,700
JPEG Basic	2,900	5,000	10,500
TIFF	215	378	846
RAW	400	N/A	N/A
RAW+JPEG Fine	261	307	352
RAW+JPEG Normal	315	346	374
RAW+JPEG Basic	351	371	385

HOW MANY SHOTS?

The D300 provides a fairly accurate estimate of the number of shots remaining on the top panel LCD at all times (even when the camera is turned off), as well as at the lower-right edge of the viewfinder display when the display is active. (Tap the shutter release button to activate it.)

It is only an estimate, because the actual number will vary, depending on the capacity of your memory card, the file format(s) you've selected, and the content of the image itself. (Some photos may contain large areas that can be more efficiently compressed to a smaller size.)

For example, an 8GB card can hold about 750 JPEG Fine shots in full resolution (Large) format; 1,400 shots using Normal JPEG compression; or 2,900 shots with Basic JPEG compression. When numbers exceed 1,000, the D300 displays a figure and decimal point, followed by a K superscript, so that 2,900 shots (or thereabouts) is represented by $[2.9]^K$ in the LCD and viewfinder. The D300 offers three different resolution settings that provide different numbers of exposures: Large (4288 × 2848; 12.2 megapixels), Medium (3216 × 2139; 6.8 megapixels), and Small (2144 × 1424; 3 megapixels). For example, JPEG Basic using the Small resolution setting yields 10.5K exposures on a single 8GB memory card!

Using RAW/NEF format (more on that later) reduces the number of shots. An 8GB card has enough room for 400 RAW photos in Nikon's NEF format, or 261 pictures if you're shooting RAW+JPEG Fine pairs. Table 1.1 shows some typical capacities for an 8GB memory card. You should know that the D300 has various compression options for JPEG and RAW files, as well as 12-bit and 14-bit dynamic range settings for the RAW format; we'll look into those options in more detail in Chapter 3.

TIFF, a very memory-hungry format that the D300 records to the memory card at a snail's pace (a minimum of several seconds per photo) eats up so much space that you can fit a mere 215 images on an 8GB card, with little discernable quality difference from RAW files (at the same time discarding the fine-tunability that you get from Nikon's NEF/RAW format).

Choosing a Release Mode

The shooting mode determines when (and how often) the D300 makes an exposure. If you're coming to the dSLR world from a point-and-shoot camera, you might have used a model that labels these options as Drive modes, dating back to the film era when cameras could be set for single-shot or "motor drive" (continuous) shooting modes. Your D300 has six release (shooting) modes: single shot, two continuous shooting options, Live View, self-timer, and mirror up. I'll explain all these modes in more detail and provide tips for using them in particular situations in Chapter 7. The shooting modes are:

- **Single frame.** In single shot mode, the D300 takes one picture each time you press the shutter release button down all the way. If you press the shutter and nothing happens (which is very frustrating!) you may be using a focus mode that requires sharp focus to be achieved before a picture can be taken. This is called focus priority, and is discussed in more detail under "Choosing a Focus Mode," later in this chapter.

- **Continuous low speed (C_L).** This "low speed" shooting mode can be set to produce bursts of 1 to 7 frames per second (the latter hardly qualifies as *low* speed). You can set the frame rate in the Custom Settings menu entry **CSM #d4.** Note that if you choose the 7 fps setting, the D300 will use that speed *only* if the MB-D10 battery pack is attached and is fitted with the beefier EN-EL4a battery; otherwise, the maximum frame rate is 6 fps. I use this setting when slicing a scene into tiny fragments of time isn't necessary or desirable (say, I'm bracketing in three shot bursts, or don't want a zillion versions of a scene that really isn't changing that fast).

- **Continuous high speed (C_H).** This mode fires off shots at up to 6 fps. The frame rate can slow down as your D300's memory buffer fills, which forces the camera to wait until some of the pictures you have already taken are written to the Compact Flash card, freeing up more space in the buffer. The frame rate may also decrease at shutter speeds slower than 1/250 second, or when operations like continuous-servo autofocus (described later in this chapter) force the D300 to work at a slightly slower interval. With the MB-D10 battery/grip attached with an EN-EL4a battery, frame rates of up to 8 fps can be achieved.

- **Live View.** This setting activates the D300's Live View modes, which allow previewing an image on the color LCD before the picture is taken. As you'll learn in Chapter 7, Live View can be a useful tool for macrophotography, for previewing an image when using the viewfinder is not convenient, and for other applications.

- **Self-Timer.** You can use the self-timer as a replacement for a remote release, to reduce the effects of camera/user shake when the D300 is mounted on a tripod or, say, set on a firm surface, or when you want to get in the picture yourself. Use Custom Settings menu choice **CSM #c3** to specify delays of 2, 5, 10, or 20 seconds. Any time you use the camera on a tripod (with the self-timer or otherwise) make sure there is no bright light shining on the viewfinder window; if so, cover it or locate that DK-5 eyepiece cap and block the window.

Note

If you plan to dash in front of the camera to join the scene, consider using manual focus so the D300 won't refocus on your fleeing form and produce unintended results. (Nikon really needs to offer an option to autofocus at the *end* of the self-timer cycle.)

■ **Mup (Mirror Up).** This mode delays the taking of the picture until after the mirror is flipped up out of the way (blanking the viewfinder), producing a short delay that also minimizes the effect of the mirror's movement on a picture taken using a long shutter speed. When shooting with telephoto lenses or during close-up photography, a "long" shutter speed can be anything from 1/125 seconds to several seconds. (Mirror movement has only an imperceptible effect on exposures longer than a second or two.) When Mup is activated, pressing the shutter release down all the way once lifts the mirror; pressing it a second time takes the picture and returns the mirror to its down position. To use Mup to take a picture after a delay, press the shutter just once. About 30 seconds after the mirror is raised, the camera will take the picture automatically, with no further action required on your part.

> **Note**
>
> The Mup facility is an offbeat way of producing a self-timer delay of 30 seconds, rather than the maximum 20 seconds that the D300's self-timer feature provides.

Selecting an Exposure Mode

The D300's selected exposure mode determines how the lens opening (aperture) and shutter speed are selected by the camera. Turn your camera on by flipping the power switch, located concentric with the shutter release button, clockwise to the ON position. Then, choose an exposure mode by holding down the **Mode** button (located just south-west of the shutter release on the top panel), and spinning the main command dial on the back of the camera until the mode you want to use appears from among M (Manual), A (Aperture Priority), S (Shutter Priority), or P (Programmed). (See Figure 1.9.) The D300 has no "scene" modes (Landscape, Portrait, Night, etc.) or fully Automatic mode, like you might find in one of the Nikon amateur dSLR or point-and-shoot camera models.

If you're very new to digital photography, you might want to set the camera to P (Program mode) and start snapping away. That mode will make all the appropriate settings for you for many shooting situations. If you have more photographic experience, you might want to opt for one of the semi-automatic modes. These, too, are described in more detail in Chapter 6. These modes all let you apply a little more creativity to your camera's settings.

■ **M (Manual).** Select when you want full control over the shutter speed and lens opening, either for creative effects or because you are using a studio flash or other flash unit not compatible with the D300's automatic flash metering.

Figure 1.9
Hold down the Mode button and rotate the main command dial to change shooting mode.

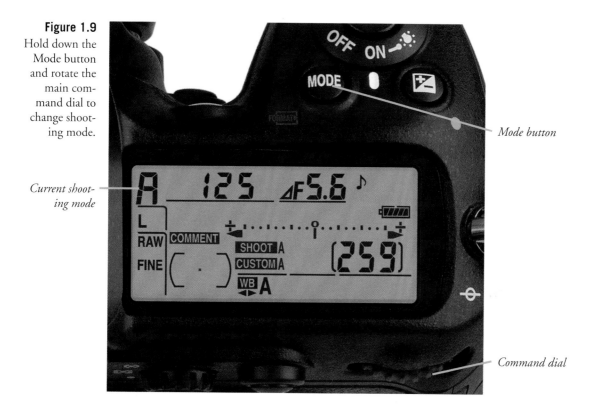

Mode button

Current shooting mode

Command dial

- **A (Aperture Priority).** Choose when you want to use a particular lens opening, especially to control sharpness or how much of your image is in focus. Specify the f/stop you want, and the D300 will select the appropriate shutter speed for you.

- **S (Shutter Priority).** This mode is useful when you want to use a particular shutter speed to stop action or produce creative blur effects. Choose your preferred shutter speed, and the D300 will select the appropriate f/stop for you.

- **P (Program).** This mode allows the D300 to select the basic exposure settings, but you can still override the camera's choices to fine-tune your image, while maintaining metered exposure.

Choosing a Metering Mode

The metering mode you select determines how the D300 calculates exposure. You might want to select a particular metering mode for your first shots, although the default Matrix metering is probably the best choice as you get to know your camera. I'll explain when and how to use each of the three metering modes later.

To change metering modes, rotate the metering button, located to the right of the viewfinder window, to select from among the choices shown in Figure 1.10:

- **Center-Weighted Averaging metering.** The D300 meters the entire scene, but gives the most emphasis to the central area of the frame, measuring about 8mm.

- **Matrix metering.** The standard metering mode; the D300 attempts to intelligently classify your image and choose the best exposure based on readings from a 1005-segment color CCD sensor that interprets light reaching the viewfinder using a database of hundreds of thousands of patterns.

- **Spot metering.** Exposure is calculated from a smaller 3mm central spot, about 2 percent of the image area.

You'll find a detailed description of each of these modes in Chapter 6.

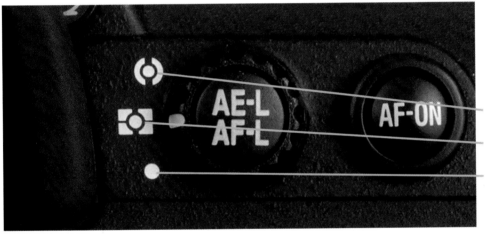

Figure 1.10
Metering modes are selected using this dial.

Center-Weighted

Matrix

Spot

Choosing a Focus Mode

You can easily switch between automatic and manual focus by moving the AF/MF or M-AF/MF switch on the lens mounted on your camera. When using autofocus, you have additional choices. You can select the autofocus mode (*when* the D300 measures and locks in focus) and autofocus pattern (*which* of the 51 available autofocus points or zones are used to interpret correct focus). The autofocus mode is chosen using a lever on the camera body, shown in Figure 1.11. Select from the following:

- **Continuous Servo Autofocus.** This mode, sometimes called *Continuous Autofocus*, or AF-C, sets focus when you partially depress the shutter button (or other auto-focus activation button), but continues to monitor the frame and refocuses if the camera or subject is moved. This is a useful mode for photographing sports and moving subjects. Focus or release priority can be specified for AF-C mode using **CSM #a1**.

Figure 1.11
Set Autofocus
mode.

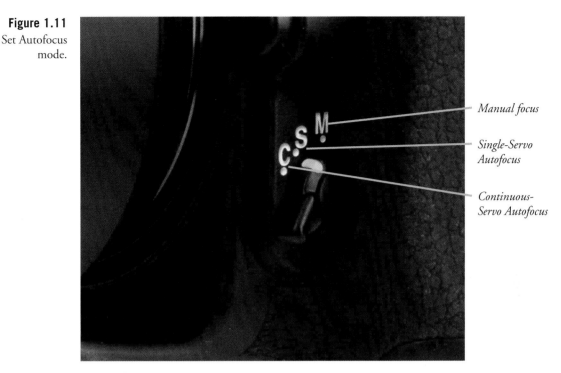

Manual focus

Single-Servo
Autofocus

Continuous-
Servo Autofocus

■ **Single Servo Autofocus.** This mode, sometimes called *Single Autofocus*, or AF-S, locks in a focus point when the shutter button is pressed down halfway (there are other autofocus activation button options, described in Chapter 4), and the focus confirmation light glows at bottom left in the viewfinder. The focus will remain locked until you release the button or take the picture. This mode is best when your subject is relatively motionless. As you'll learn in Chapter 4, you can set your Nikon D300 using the Custom Settings Menu (**CSM #a2**) so that the camera will not take a photo unless sharp focus is achieved (*focus priority*), or so that it will go ahead and snap a photo while still adjusting focus (*release priority*).

■ **Manual focus.** With the lever set to this position, you always focus manually using the focus ring on the lens. The focus confirmation indicator in the viewfinder operates reliably, as long as the lens mounted has a maximum aperture of at least f/5.6.

 Note

Note that the autofocus/manual focus switches on the lens and camera body must agree; if either is set to manual focus, then the D300 defaults to manual focus regardless of how the other switch is set.

The Nikon D300 uses up to 51 different focus points to calculate correct focus, using one or more points you can select yourself, or which the camera can choose. For your initial foray into shooting with the D300, you can set the camera for Single Area auto-focus (you choose the focus point using the multi-selector pad), Dynamic Area autofocus (you select the focus point, but the camera can override in Continuous Servo mode), or Auto Area autofocus (the camera always chooses the autofocus point) using the selection switch shown in Figure 1.12. I'll elaborate on this (slight) oversimplification of the various point selection options in Chapter 2.

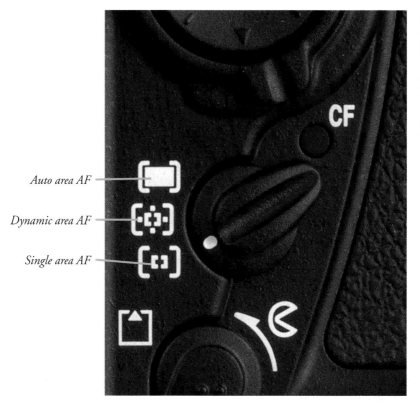

Auto area AF

Dynamic area AF

Single area AF

Figure 1.12
Choose (top to bottom) Automatic Area autofocus, Dynamic Area, or Single Area autofocus point selection.

Other Settings

There are a few other settings you can make if you're feeling ambitious, but don't feel ashamed if you postpone using these features until you've racked up a little more experience with your D300.

Adjusting White Balance and ISO

If you like, you can custom-tailor your white balance (color balance) and ISO sensitivity settings. To start out, it's best to set white balance (WB) to Auto, and ISO to ISO

200 for daylight photos, and ISO 400 for pictures in dimmer light. (Don't be afraid of ISO 1600 or even higher, however; the D300 does a *much* better job of producing low-noise photos at higher ISOs than its D200 predecessor.) You'll find complete recommendations for both these settings in Chapter 6. You can adjust either one now by pressing the WB (for white balance) or ISO buttons on the release mode dial (on the top left side of the camera) and rotating the main command dial until the setting you want appears on the status LCD on top of the camera. Both buttons are shown in Figure 1.13.

Figure 1.13
Press the WB or ISO buttons and rotate the main command dial to adjust white balance or sensitivity settings.

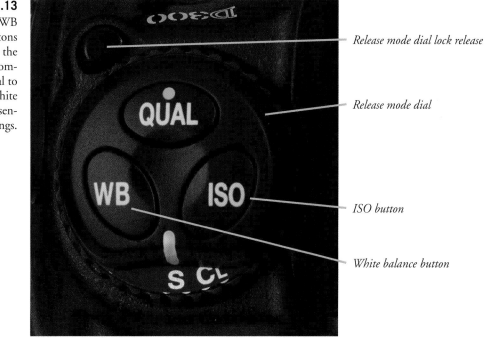

Release mode dial lock release

Release mode dial

ISO button

White balance button

MAKING SETTINGS UNDER LOW LIGHT

When working under low light levels, you might experience some difficulty seeing the white balance, ISO, or other settings on the top-panel monochrome LCD as you make them. You can always rotate the ON-OFF switch an additional push in the clockwise direction to illuminate the LCD backlight, but there is a better way. Instead, press the Info button (it's to the left of the color LCD, the second button from the top, marked with a "key" icon) to show the much larger and easier-to-read Shooting Information Display on the color LCD. Then press the WB or ISO button (or the button for whatever setting you're changing) and rotate the appropriate dial until the value you want appears on the Shooting Information Display. Indeed, you can press the Info button at any time to pop up this information screen, which is especially helpful when working with the camera on a tripod, or under dim illumination.

Using the Self-Timer

If you want to set a short delay before your picture is taken, you can use the self-timer. Press the lock release button to free the release mode dial wheel, and rotate it five detents clockwise until the self-timer icon appears next to the indicator line. Press the shutter release to lock focus and start the timer. The self-timer lamp on the front of the camera will blink and the beeper will sound (unless you've silenced it in the menus) until the final two seconds, when the lamp remains on and the beeper beeps more rapidly. The default delay is 10 seconds, but you can set it to 2, 5, 10, or 20 seconds using **Custom Settings** menu option **CSM #c3**, as described in Chapter 3. As I mentioned earlier, you can also use the **Mup** release mode to get a 30-second delay.

Reviewing the Images You've Taken

The Nikon D300 has a broad range of playback and image review options, and I'll cover them in more detail in Chapter 3. For now, you'll want to learn just the basics. Here is all you really need to know at this time, as shown in Figure 1.14:

- Press the Playback button (marked with a white right-pointing triangle) at the upper-left corner of the back of the camera to display the most recent image on the LCD.

- Press the multi-selector left or right to review additional images. Press right to advance to the next image, or left to go back to a previous image.

- Press the multi-selector button up or down to change among overlays of basic image information or detailed shooting information.

- Press the Zoom button repeatedly to zoom in on the image displayed; the Zoom Out button reduces the image. A thumbnail representation of the whole image appears in the lower-right corner with a yellow rectangle showing the relative level of zoom. At intermediate zoom positions, the yellow rectangle can be moved around within the frame using the multi-selector.

- Press the Playback button again, or just tap the shutter release button to exit playback view.

You'll find information on viewing thumbnail indexes of images, automated playback, and other options in Chapter 3.

Figure 1.14
Review your
images.

*Press Playback
to review images*

Change info

Reverse

Forward

Zoom out

Zoom in

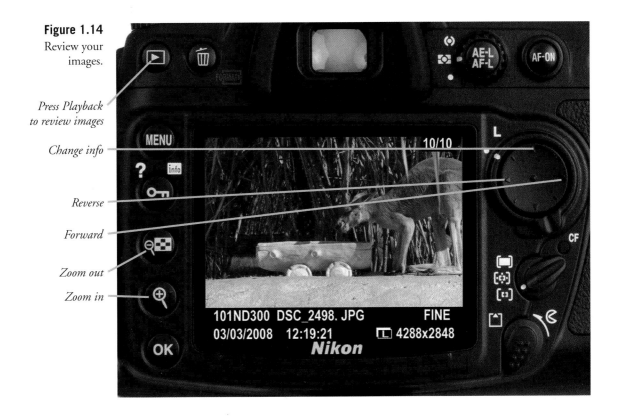

Using the Built-in Flash

Working with the D300's built-in flash (as well as external flash units like the Nikon SB-800) deserves a chapter of its own, and I'm providing one (see Chapter 9.). But the built-in flash is easy enough to work with that you can begin using it right away, either to provide the main lighting of a scene, or as supplementary illumination to fill in the shadows. For example, if you choose matrix or center-weighted metering (as described earlier), you can even use the flash in full daylight, as the D300 will even automatically balance the amount of light emitted from the flash so that it illuminates the shadows nicely, without overwhelming the highlights and producing a glaring "flash" look. (Think *Baywatch* when they're using too many reflectors on the lifeguards!)

The D300's flash has a power rating of 17/56 (meters/feet) at ISO 200, using the GN (guide number) system that dates back to the film era and before electronic flash units had any sort of automatic features. I'll explain guide numbers (which can be a little confusing) in more detail in Chapter 10, but in plain terms, the flash's rating means that the unit is powerful enough to allow proper illumination of a subject that's 10 feet away at f/5.6 at the *lowest* ISO (sensitivity) setting of your camera. Boost the ISO (or use a wider f/stop) and you can shoot subjects that are located at a great distance. For example, at ISO 800, the D300's flash is good enough for a subject at 20 feet using f/5.6 or, alternatively, you can expose that scene at the original 10 feet distance at f/11. Ordinarily, the D300 takes care of all these calculations for you. If you need a bigger blast of light, you can add an external flash, like the Nikon SB-800, which lets you reach out to 32-45 feet at ISO 200 and f/5.6 (or even farther at larger f/stops).

To use the built-in flash, just press the flash pop-up button (shown in Figure 1.15). (Unlike some of Nikon's entry-level cameras, the D300's flash never pops up automatically; when you're finished using it, you need to push it back down, too.) When the flash is fully charged, a lightning bolt symbol will flash at the right side of the viewfinder display. When using P (Program), A (Aperture Priority) exposure modes,

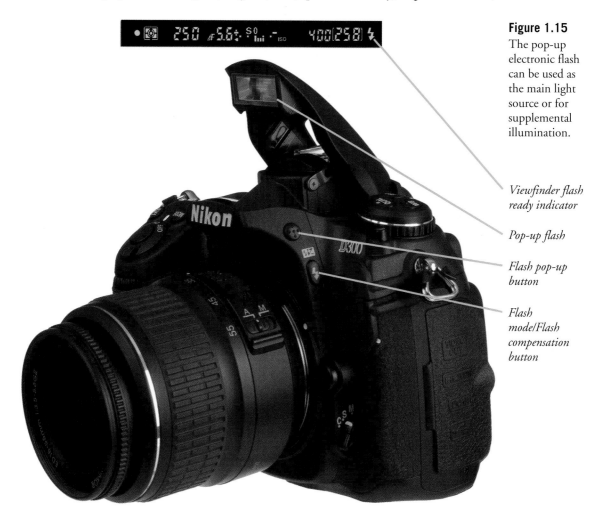

Figure 1.15
The pop-up electronic flash can be used as the main light source or for supplemental illumination.

Viewfinder flash ready indicator

Pop-up flash

Flash pop-up button

Flash mode/Flash compensation button

the D300 will select a shutter speed for you automatically from the range 1/250 to 1/60 seconds (with a couple exceptions described in Chapter 10). In S (Shutter Priority) and M (Manual) modes, you select the shutter speed from 1/250 to 30 seconds (again, with a couple exceptions that I won't get into here). When using the built-in flash, if you select a shutter speed higher than 1/250 second (which prevents the camera from synchronizing with the shutter; see Chapter 10), the D300 will set 1/250 second for you automatically.

You can preview the effect of your flash visually by pressing the depth-of-field button, which activates a brief, continuous series of bursts (which look to the eye like a single, long flash of light)—unless you've disabled this "modeling light" using Custom Settings Menu entry **CSM #e4.**

You'll also learn in Chapter 10 how to change the flash synching mode (and why you might want to do so), as well as how to increase/reduce the effects of the flash on your scene using *flash compensation* adjustments.

Transferring Photos to Your Computer

The final step in your picture-taking session will be to transfer the photos you've taken to your computer for printing, further review, or image editing. Your D300 allows you to print directly to PictBridge-compatible printers and to create print orders right in the camera, plus you can select which images to transfer to your computer. I'll outline those options in Chapter 3.

I always recommend using a card reader attached to your computer to transfer files, because that process is generally a lot faster and doesn't drain the D300's battery. However, you can also use a cable for direct transfer, which may be your only option when you have the cable and a computer, but no card reader (perhaps you're using the computer of a friend or colleague, or at an Internet café).

To transfer images from the camera to a Mac or PC computer using the USB cable:

1. Turn the camera off.

2. Pry back the rubber cover that protects the D300's USB port, and plug the USB cable furnished with the camera into the USB port. (See Figure 1.16.)

3. Connect the other end of the USB cable to a USB port on your computer.

4. Turn the camera on. The operating system itself, or installed software such as Nikon Transfer or Adobe Photoshop Elements Transfer usually detects the camera and offers to copy or move the pictures. Or, the camera appears on your desktop as a mass storage device, enabling you to drag and drop the files to your computer.

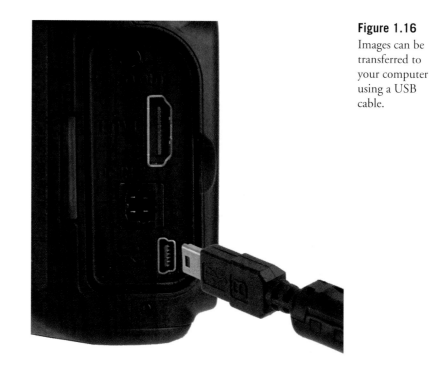

Figure 1.16
Images can be transferred to your computer using a USB cable.

To transfer images from a Compact Flash card to the computer using a card reader, as shown in Figure 1.17:

1. Turn the camera off.

2. Rotate the "Pac Man" lever on the back of the camera to release the Compact Flash card door on the side, and press the gray button, which ejects the card.

3. Insert the Compact Flash card into your memory card reader. Your installed software detects the files on the card and offers to transfer them. The card can also appear as a mass storage device on your desktop, which you can open and then drag and drop the files to your computer.

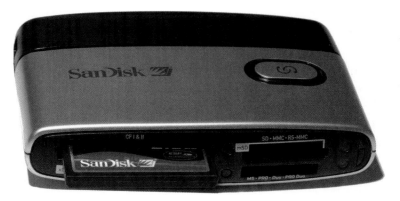

Figure 1.17
A card reader is the fastest way to transfer photos.

2

Nikon D300 Roadmap

Most of the Nikon D300's key functions and settings that are changed frequently can be accessed directly using the array of dials, buttons, and knobs that populate the camera's surface. With so many dedicated controls available, you'll find that the bulk of your shooting won't be slowed down by a visit to the vast thicket of text options called Menu-land. That's a distinct paradigm shift from early point-and-shoot cameras, which had only four or five buttons, and relied on menus to control virtually every setting you might want to make. With the D300, you can press specific buttons dedicated to image quality, white balance, ISO sensitivity, shooting mode, exposure compensation, and playback options, and then spin a command dial or make adjustments using the multi-selector.

While it might take some time to learn the position and function of each of these controls, once you've mastered them, the D300 camera is remarkably easy to use. That's because dedicated buttons with only one or two functions each are much faster to access than the alternative—a maze of menus that must be navigated every time you want to use a feature. The advantage of menu systems—dating back to early computer user interfaces of the 1980s—is that they are easy to *learn*. The ironic disadvantage of menus is that they are clumsy to *use*.

Imagine that you are familiar with digital SLRs in general, but know virtually nothing about the Nikon D300. You've decided that you want to format the memory card. A-ha! There's a big 'ole MENU button on the left side of the camera. Press it, and you'll see a series of different menu icons, which, when you scroll through them, have titles like Playback Menu, Shooting Menu, Custom Setting Menu, and Setup Menu. You might guess that the Setup Menu is the likely repository for a Format command, but even if you guess wrong, it takes only a minute or two to check out the other menus and discover the Format command tucked away within the Setup Menu. A couple more button presses, and you've successfully formatted your memory card.

You didn't really need instructions—the menu system itself led you to the right command. If you don't format another card for weeks and weeks, you can come back to the menus and discover how to perform the task all over again. The main cost to you was the time required to negotiate through all the menus to carry out the function; while menus are easy to learn, the multiple steps they call for (10 or more button presses may be required) can be cumbersome to use. Direct access buttons are the exact opposite: you have to teach yourself how to use them, and then remember what you've learned over time, but once learned, buttons are much faster to use.

For example, simple direct button presses can also format your memory card, as I pointed out in the last chapter. Recall how easy it is to just hold down the Mode button and the trash can button simultaneously for about two seconds. When the characters **For** and the exposures remaining displays blink in the viewfinder and top panel LCD, press the pair of buttons again, and the D300 formats your card. To cancel the format, press any other button. The sequence may be tricky to learn or remember (although red **Format** labels appear next to the pair of buttons), but it's much faster to use than threading through a series of menu options.

If you want to operate your D300 efficiently, you'll need to learn the location, function, and application of all these controls. What you really need is a street-level roadmap that shows where everything is, and how it's used. But what Nikon gives you in the user's manual is akin to a world globe with an overall view and many cross-references to the pages that will tell you what you really need to know. Check out the **Getting to Know the Camera** pages in Nikon's manual, which offers four tiny black-and-white line drawings of the camera body that show front, back, two sides, and the top and bottom of the D300. There are more than 60 callouts pointing to various buttons and dials. If you can find the control you want in this cramped layout, you'll still need to flip back and forth among multiple pages (individual buttons can have several different cross-references!) to locate the information.

Most other third-party books follow this format, featuring black-and-white photos or line drawings of front, back, and top views, and many labels. I originated the up-close-and-personal full-color, street-level roadmap (rather than a satellite view) that I use in this book and my previous camera guidebooks. I provide you with many different views and lots of explanation accompanying each zone of the camera, so that by the time you finish this chapter, you'll have a basic understanding of every control and what it does. I'm not going to delve into menu functions here—you'll find a discussion of your setup, shooting, and playback menu options in Chapter 3. Everything here is devoted to the button pusher and dial twirler in you.

You'll also find this "roadmap" chapter a good guide to the rest of the book, as well. I'll try to provide as much detail here about the use of the main controls as I can, but some topics (such as autofocus and exposure) are too complex to address in depth right away. So, I'll point you to the relevant chapters that discuss things like setup options, exposure, use of electronic flash, and working with lenses with the occasional cross-reference.

Nikon D300: A Physical Comparison

For a camera tough enough and fully-featured enough to withstand the rigors of professional photography, the Nikon D300 is remarkably compact, even when compared to Nikon's entry-level cameras, like the venerable Nikon D80, shown at right in Figure 2.1. The dimensions and weight of the D300 are almost identical to that of its predecessor, the Nikon D200, and the newer D300 is virtually the same thickness as the D80, about half an inch wider and four-tenths of an inch taller (See Table 2.1). Its magnesium body, however, weighs in at 133% of the heft of the polycarbonate-shelled D80. The D300's reasonable size makes it popular with professionals looking to cut down the bulk of their traveling kit, too. Lacking the built-in vertical grip of the D3 and D2xs, the D300 is a full 1.4-1.7 inches shorter than its pro siblings are and about a half an inch less wide. The two-pound D300 puts a lot less strain on your neckstrap (and neck) than the (roughly) three-pound D3, too.

Table 2.1 Dimensions of Typical Nikon Pro, Mid-Level, and Amateur Cameras				
Camera	Width	Height	Thickness	
D3	6.3	6.2	3.5	46 oz
D2xs	6.2	5.9	3.4	42 oz
D300	5.8	4.5	2.9	32 oz
D80	5.2	4.1	3	24 oz

The control layout of the D300 is most similar to that of the D200, but shares a family resemblance to the button and dial distribution of the pro cameras, too. For the benefit of those upgrading to the D300, or using it as a replacement or in conjunction with one of the pro cameras, I'll provide some notes on control placement differences in the sections that follow.

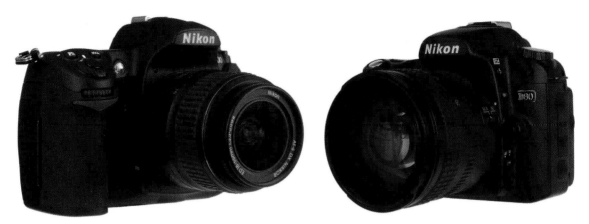

Figure 2.1

Nikon D300: Full Frontal

This is the face seen by your victims as you snap away. For the photographer, though, the front is the surface your fingers curl around as you hold the camera, and there are really only a few buttons to press, all within easy reach of the fingers of your left and right hands. There are additional controls on the lens itself. You'll need to look at several different views to see everything.

Figure 2.2 shows a front view of the Nikon D300. The main components you need to know about are as follows:

- **Shutter button.** Angled on top of the handgrip is the shutter release button, which has multiple functions. Press this button down halfway to lock exposure and focus, unless you've redefined the functions of this control, plus the AF-ON, and AE/AF Lock buttons on the back panel of the camera using the Custom Settings menu (**CSM #f3**, explained in Chapter 4). Press it down all the way to actually take a photo or sequence of photos if you've changed the mode dial to either of the continuous shooting modes, C_L or C_H (continuous shooting low speed and continuous shooting high speed). Tapping the shutter button when the D300's exposure meters have turned themselves off reactivates them, and a tap can be used to remove the display of a menu or image from the rear color LCD.

- **Sub-command dial.** This dial is used to change shooting settings. When settings are available in pairs (such as shutter speed/aperture), this dial will be used to make one type of setting, such as aperture, while the main command dial (on the back of the camera) will be used to make the other, such as aperture setting. Using the Custom Settings menu adjustments in **CSM #f7**, you can reverse the default rotational direction, swap the functions of the sub-command and main command dials, control how the sub-command dial is used to set aperture, and tell the D300 that you want to use the main command dial to scroll through menus and images. All these options are discussed in more detail in Chapter 4.

■ **Red-Eye reduction/self-timer lamp.** This LED provides a blip of light shortly before a flash exposure to cause the subjects' pupils to close down, reducing the effect of red-eye reflections off their retinas. When using the self-timer, this lamp also flashes to mark the countdown until the photo is taken. Also AF assist.

■ **Handgrip.** This provides a comfortable handhold, and also contains the D300's battery. Unlike the D200 model, it's not necessary to remove the battery of the D300 to mount the accessory battery/vertical grip.

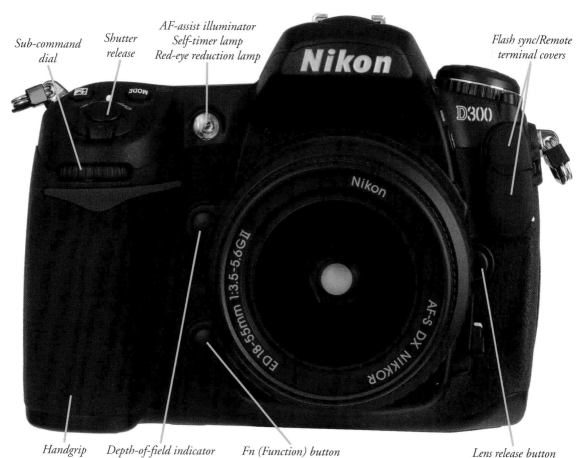

Sub-command dial

Shutter release

AF-assist illuminator
Self-timer lamp
Red-eye reduction lamp

Flash sync/Remote terminal covers

Handgrip   Depth-of-field indicator   Fn (Function) button

Lens release button

Figure 2.2

■ **Fn (Function button).** This conveniently located button can be programmed to perform any one of 13 different functions, ranging from metering modes (matrix, center-weighted, spot) to flash off or bracketing bursts. The Fn button can be given a different function for when you press it or press it while spinning a command dial. I'll explain how to define a function using Custom Setting menu entry **CSM #f4** in Chapter 4.

■ **Depth-of-Field button.** By default, this button closes down the lens aperture to the opening that will be used to take the picture, as set by the D300's light meters or by you (when in Manual or Aperture Priority modes). The DOF button can be redefined using the same 13 functions offered for the Fn button, with both solo button presses and presses while spinning a command dial, so two different functions can be assigned. I'll explain how to define a function using Custom Setting menu entry **CSM #f5** in Chapter 4.

■ **Lens release button.** Press this button to unlock the lens, then rotate it towards the shutter release button to dismount your optics.

■ **Flash sync connector.** This connector hides beneath a rubber cover, along with the 10-pin remote terminal. You can see the two connectors uncovered in Figure 2.3. Connect a standard PC/X-contact cable or other accessory to this connector. If you are connecting a non-dedicated flash unit to your Nikon D300 (say, a studio strobe or some other non-automatic non-Nikon flash), it would plug in here.

■ **10-pin remote terminal.** This connector is used for a variety of accessories, including cable release cords, remote releases of other types (including radio/IR receivers), GPS links, and so forth.

LOSE THE RUBBER COVER

I don't like the rubber cover over the flash sync and 10-pin remote connectors. I use studio flash and remote devices so often that the cover ends up dangling at the side of the camera 90 percent of the time. If you're in the same boat, help is on the way. The rubber cover fastens to the D300 around the neck strap lug, so you can carefully remove it (it's easier when no neckstrap is attached) and store the cover away for re-installation when you sell your D300. If you'd rather not leave your connectors "naked" (or just want to protect them when shooting in rain and other harsh conditions), the plastic PC connector and 10-pin terminal covers provided for earlier Nikon pro cameras screw into the connectors just fine. They can be purchased for a few dollars each from **www.bocaphoto.com**, which offers many other inexpensive Nikon replacement parts. I buy a bunch of them at a time, because the tiny connectors are easy to lose, but I find the inconvenience of screwing one of these connectors on and off from time to time, or replacing a lost one is much less of a hassle than dealing with that floppy rubber cover installed at the factory.

Figure 2.3

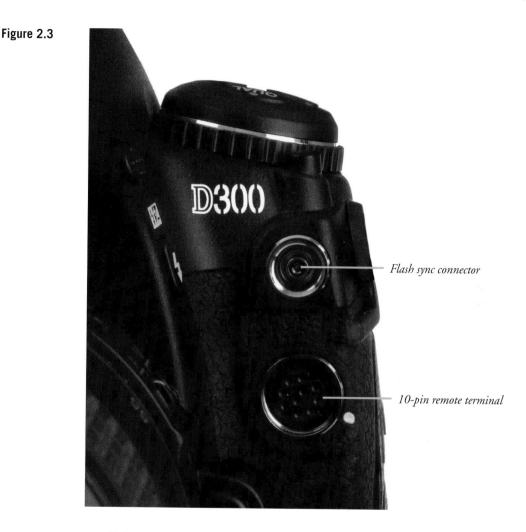

Flash sync connector

10-pin remote terminal

You'll find more controls on the other side of the D300, shown in Figure 2.4. In the illustration, you can see the mode dial on top, and the rubber cover on the side that protects the camera's USB, TV, HDMI, and DC power ports. The main points of interest shown include:

■ **Lens autofocus/manual switch.** You can change from Autofocus mode to Manual using this switch, or the switch on the camera body (which has additional options).

■ **Lens release button.** This is another view of the button used to unlock the lens so it can be removed from the camera body.

■ **Neckstrap lug.** It comes with a split-ring attached that can be used to fasten a neckstrap to the D300.

■ **Port cover.** This rubber cover protects the video, HDMI, DC power, and USB port connectors when not in use.

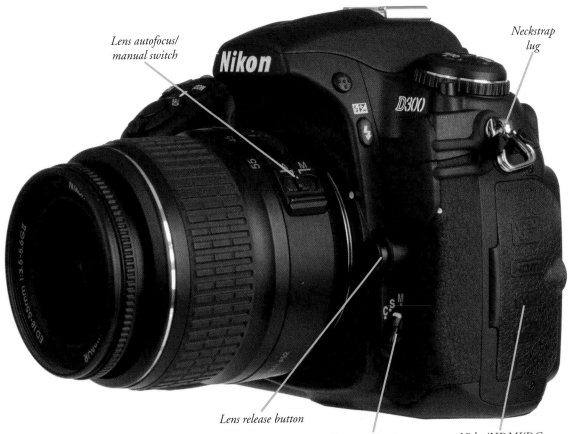

*Lens autofocus/
manual switch*

*Neckstrap
lug*

Lens release button

Focus mode selector

*Video/HDMI/DC
power/USB port cover*

Figure 2.4

- **Focus mode selector.** Use this switch to change from Continuous-Servo Autofocus (AF-C) to Single-Servo Autofocus (AF-S) or Manual focus (M). I'll explain the focusing modes in more detail in Chapter 6, but you should remember that the modes selected with this switch and the Autofocus/Manual focus switch on the lens must agree. If you've chosen A (or M/A, which allows for manual fine-tuning of autofocus) on the lens, then the camera body switch must be set to either AF-C or AF-S. If either the lens or body switch (or both) are set to M, then the lens must be focused manually.

Controls for using the D300's built-in electronic flash (also called a strobe or speed-light) are shown in Figure 2.5. These components include:

- **Pop-up flash.** The flash elevates from the top of the camera, theoretically reducing the chances of red-eye reflections, because the higher light source is less likely to reflect back from your subjects' eyes into the camera lens. In practice, the red-eye effect is still possible (and likely), and can be further minimized with the D300's red-eye reduction lamp (which flashes before the exposure, causing the subjects' pupils to contract, and the after-shot red-eye elimination offered in the Retouch menu. (Your image editor may also have anti-red-eye tools.) Of course, the best strategy is to use an external speedlight that mounts on the accessory shoe on top of the camera (and thus is even higher) or a flash that is off-camera entirely.

- **Flash pop-up button.** This button releases the built-in flash so it can flip up and start the charging process. If you decide you do not want to use the flash, you can turn it off by pressing the flash head back down.

- **Flash mode/flash compensation button.** This button is held down while spinning the main command dial (to choose flash mode) or sub-command dial (to add or subtract exposure using flash compensation). I'll explain how to use the various flash modes (red-eye reduction, front/rear curtain sync, and slow sync) in Chapter 10, along with some tips for adjusting flash exposure.

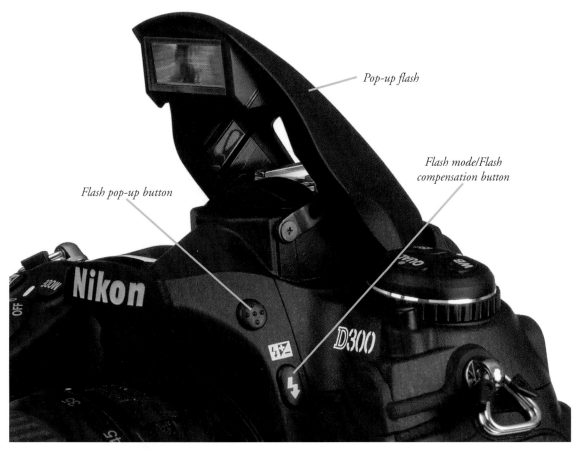

Figure 2.5

The main feature on the side of the Nikon D300 is a rubber cover that protects the four connector ports underneath from dust and moisture. The four connectors, shown in Figure 2.6, with the rubber cover removed, are as follows:

- **Video port.** You can link this connector with a television to view your photos on a large screen.

- **HDMI port.** You need to buy an accessory cable to connect your D300 to an HDTV, as one to fit this port is not provided with the camera. If you have a high-resolution television, it's worth the expenditure to be able to view your camera's output in all its glory.

- **DC power port.** Connect the Nikon EH5/EH5a AC adapters to provide DC power to your D300 for long periods when shooting in the studio, displaying slide shows, or doing interval/remote photography.

- **USB port.** Plug in the USB cable furnished with your Nikon D300 and connect the other end to a USB port in your computer to transfer photos, to upload Picture Control settings, or to upload/download other settings between your camera and computer.

Figure 2.6

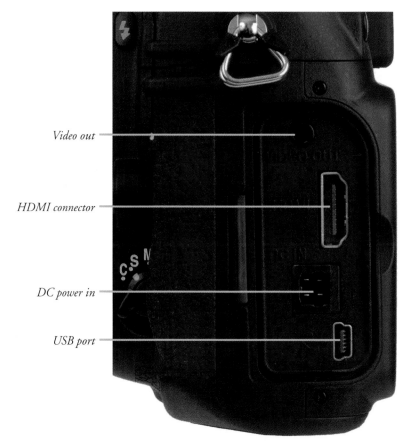

Video out

HDMI connector

DC power in

USB port

DIFFERENCES IN LAYOUT BETWEEN D300, D200, D2xs, and D3

If you're already familiar with one of Nikon's other popular advanced cameras, you'll find that the D300 is remarkably similar, and easy to adjust to. Of the features and controls described so far, the shutter release, sub-command dial, Fn (function) button, depth-of-field preview, lens release button, and focus mode switch are in the same locations and have the same functions in all four cameras. However, the focus mode switch on the D200 and D300 seem to be labeled differently than their counterpart on the D2xs and D3 (even though they actually operate identically). The *switch* is just oriented differently on the D200/D300. When you look at the D3/D2xs from the front, the top setting is C (Continuous-Servo Autofocus), with S (Single-Servo Autofocus) in the middle, and M (Manual focus) on the bottom. The D200/D300 rotates the switch and label about 90 degrees, so the C is lowest, the S remains in the middle, and the M is at the highest position. But functionally they are the same: the most counter-clockwise position on all four cameras is C, and the most clockwise position is M. As you rotate the focus mode switch from counter-clockwise to clockwise, the order of the modes is identical.

While all four cameras place the 10-pin terminal on the front, the flash sync connector (or PC/X connector) is located on the side of the D200; the D300, D2xs, and D3 put this connector on the front. Other differences are minor: the D300 has a flash pop-up button that's larger and rounder compared to that of the D200 (the D2xs and D3, which have no built-in flash, lack the button completely), and the D300 has a slightly smaller lens release button than any of its siblings.

The Nikon D300's Business End

The back panel of the Nikon D300 (see Figure 2.7) bristles with more than a dozen different controls, buttons, and knobs. That might seem like a lot of controls to learn, but you'll find, as I noted earlier, that it's a lot easier to press a dedicated button and spin a dial than to jump to a menu every time you want to change a setting.

You can see the controls clustered along the top edge of the back panel in Figure 2.8. The key buttons and components and their functions are as follows:

■ **Playback button.** Press this button to review images you've taken, using the controls and options I'll explain in the next section. To remove the displayed image, press the Playback button again, or simply tap the shutter release button.

■ **Trash/Format #1.** Press to erase the image shown on the LCD. A display will pop up on the LCD asking you to press the Trash button once more to delete the photo, or press the Playback button to cancel. Hold down this button and the Mode button on the top right surface of the camera (both are marked with red Format labels). **For** will appear in the monochrome status LCD. Press the buttons again to begin formatting your memory card.

■ **Viewfinder eyepiece.** You can frame your composition by peering into the viewfinder. It's surrounded by a soft rubber frame that seals out extraneous light when pressing your eye tightly up to the viewfinder, and it also protects your eyeglass lenses (if worn) from scratching. It can be removed and replaced by the DK-5 eyepiece cap when you use the camera on a tripod, to ensure that light coming

Figure 2.7

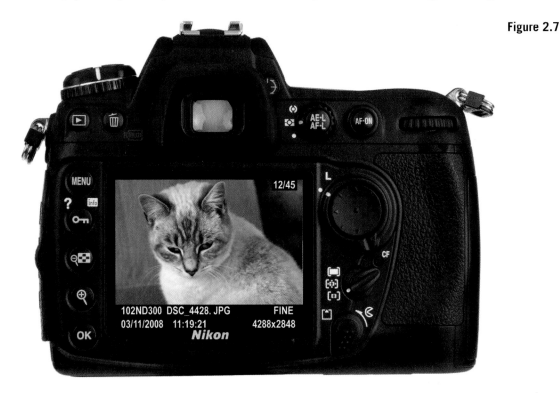

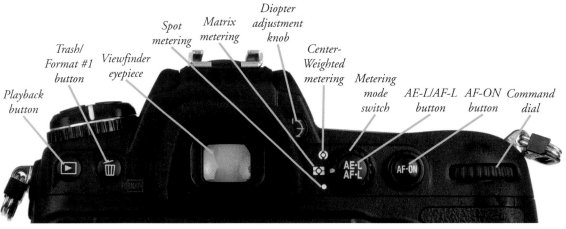

Figure 2.8

from the back of the camera doesn't venture inside and possibly affect the exposure reading. Shielding the viewfinder with your hand may be more convenient (unless you're using the self-timer to get in the photo yourself).

- **Diopter adjustment knob.** Rotate this knob to adjust the diopter correction for your eyesight, as described in Chapter 1.

- **AF-ON.** Press this button to activate the autofocus system without needing to partially depress the shutter release. This control, used with other buttons, allows you to lock exposure and focus separately: Lock exposure by pressing the shutter release halfway, or by pressing the AE Lock (AE-L) button; autofocus by pressing the shutter release halfway, or by pressing the AF-ON button. There are lots of cool ways you can use the AF-ON button, and I'll explain them in detail in Chapter 6.

- **AE-L/AF-L (auto exposure/autofocus) lock.** This button can be programmed by you to provide a variety of autoexposure/autofocus locking functions, which I'll explain in Chapter 4. By default, it locks the exposure or focus that the camera sets when you partially depress the shutter button. The exposure lock indication (AE-L icon) appears in the viewfinder. If you want to recalculate exposure or autofocus with the shutter button still partially depressed, press the button again. The exposure/autofocus will be unlocked when you release the shutter button or take the picture. To retain the exposure/autofocus lock for subsequent photos, keep the button pressed while shooting.

- **Metering mode switch.** This rotating switch, which is concentric with the AE-L/AF-L button, chooses from among Center-Weighted (top), Matrix (middle), or Spot metering. If you'd like to switch back and forth between one metering mode and another rapidly, set your default mode, such as Matrix Metering, with this switch, then program the Fn or depth-of-field preview button to provide your alternate mode (say, Spot Metering) with a simple press.

- **Command dial.** This is the main command dial of the D300, used to set or adjust most functions, such as shutter speed, bracketing sequence, white balance, ISO, and so forth, either alone or when another button is depressed simultaneously. It is often used in conjunction with the sub-command dial on the front of the camera when pairs of settings can be made, such as image formats (main command dial: image format; sub-command dial: resolution); exposure (main: shutter speed; sub: aperture); flash (main: flash mode; sub: flash compensation); or white balance (main: WB preset; sub: fine-tune WB). You can swap functions of the main and sub-command dials, reverse the rotation direction, choose whether the aperture ring on the lens or the sub-command dial will be used to set the f/stop, and activate the main command dials to navigate menus and images. You'll learn about these Custom Setting menu options (**CSM #f7**) in Chapter 4.

You'll be using the five buttons to the left of the LCD (shown in Figure 2.9) quite frequently, so learn their functions now.

■ **Menu button.** Summons/exits the menu displayed on the rear LCD of the D300. When you're working with submenus, this button also serves to exit a submenu and return to the main menu.

■ **Info/Help/Protect button.** Press this button to activate the Shooting Information Display (shown in Figure 2.10). Press again to remove the information display (or simply tap the shutter release button). The display will also clear after the period you've set for LCD display (the default value is 20 seconds). The information display can be set to alternate between modes that are best viewed under bright daylight, as well as in dimmer illumination. When viewing most menu items on the LCD, pressing this button produces a concise Help screen with tips on how to make the relevant setting. This triple-duty button also can be used to protect an image

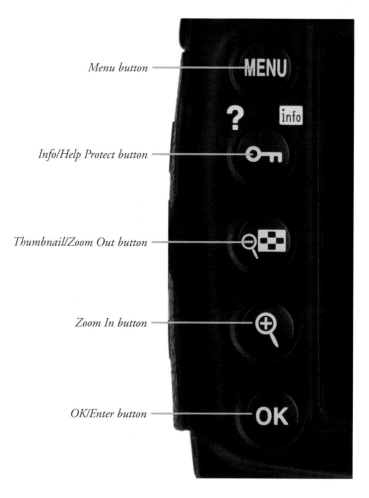

Figure 2.9

Menu button

Info/Help Protect button

Thumbnail/Zoom Out button

Zoom In button

OK/Enter button

from accidental erasure when reviewing a picture on the LCD. Press once to protect the image, a second time to unprotect it. A key symbol appears when the image is displayed to show that it is protected. (This feature safeguards an image from erasure when deleting or transferring pictures only; when you format a card, protected images are removed along with all the others.)

■ **Thumbnail/Zoom Out button.** Use this button to change from full-screen view to six or nine thumbnails, or to zoom out. I'll explain zooming and other playback options in the next section.

■ **Zoom In button.** Press to zoom in on an image.

■ **OK/Enter button.** Use this button to confirm a selection. When working with menus, press the Menu button instead to back out without making a selection.

Figure 2.10

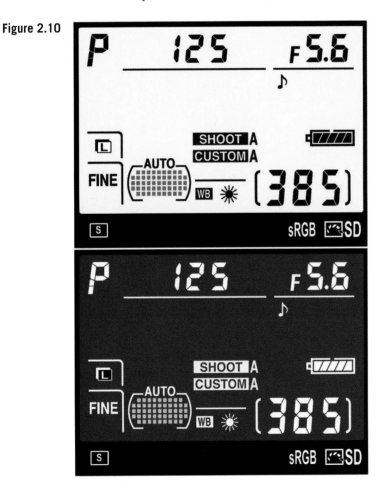

More buttons reside on the right side of the back panel, as shown in Figure 2.11. The key controls and their functions are as follows:

- **Multi-selector.** This joypad-like button can be shifted up, down, side to side, and diagonally for a total of eight directions, or pressed. It can be used for several functions, including AF point selection, scrolling around a magnified image, trimming a photo, or setting white balance correction. Within menus, pressing the up/down arrows moves the on-screen cursor up or down; pressing towards the right selects the highlighted item and displays its options; pressing left cancels and returns to the previous menu.

- **AF-Area Mode selector.** Use this rotating switch to choose among auto-area autofocus (the camera selects the focus point); dynamic-area AF (you select the focus point from a selectable number of available zones); and single-point AF (you

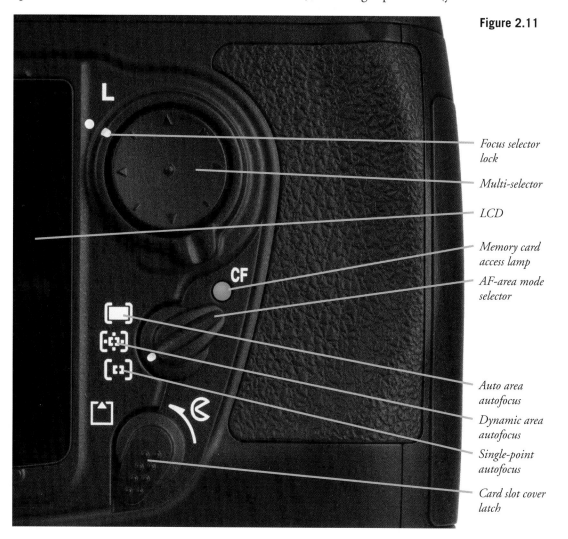

Figure 2.11

Focus selector lock

Multi-selector

LCD

Memory card access lamp

AF-area mode selector

Auto area autofocus

Dynamic area autofocus

Single-point autofocus

Card slot cover latch

choose a single focus point only). These three modes have several options and may behave differently in Single-Servo AF and Continuous-Servo AF, as I'll explain in Chapter 6.

- **Point Selection/Zoom In button.** In Shooting mode, this button activates autofocus point selection. (See Chapter 6 for information on setting autofocus/exposure point selection.) In Playback mode, this button zooms in on the image that's displayed, or the highlighted thumbnail index image.

- **Focus selector lock.** Rotate this switch to the L position to disable changing the focus point with the multi-selector.

- **Access lamp.** When lit or blinking, this lamp indicates that the Compact Flash card is being accessed.

- **LCD.** View your images and navigate through the menus on this screen.

DIFFERENCES BETWEEN D300, D200, D2xs, and D3

The back panels of the four most popular advanced Nikon dSLRs have some similarities in control layout so that adapting to the D300 is easy for most of us. The main command dial, AF-ON, AE-L/AF-L, and Trash buttons are located in roughly the same positions on the D300/D200, D2xs, and D3. So are the multi-selector, focus selector lock, and AF area mode selector.

However, with both the D2xs and D3, the exposure mode dial is located on the side of the prism, just forward of the diopter correction knob, and the Playback button (positioned as a fifth button on the left side of the LCD on the D200) has been moved on the D300 next to the Trash button, to better conform with the layout of the D3 and D2x. There are too many differences in the placement and function of the buttons to the left of the LCD to list, and, of course, the D3 and D2xs have an additional monochrome LCD and button located beneath the LCD for direct access to ISO, Quality, and White Balance, as well as an adjacent Microphone button for recording comments.

Playing Back Images

Reviewing images is a joy on the Nikon D300's big three-inch LCD. The display is big and bright, and there is abundant detail on that 920,000-dot, VGA-resolution screen. What is *not* joyful is that Nikon has "improved" the ergonomics of viewing those images, changing the control sequence from the previous Nikon D200 and D2xs models (which, happily, shared most playback controls), and, worse, making the D300's playback operation different from that of the new D3 as well. So, if you're used to reviewing images on a D200 or D2xs, be prepared to unlearn some old habits, and if you use several of

Nikon's more advanced cameras, remember that the D300 is (at present), the odd bird among them. The changes are especially disconcerting when it comes to zooming in and out, and moving the zoomed area around within the image.

Basic Image Review

Here are the basics involved in reviewing images on the LCD screen (or on a television/HDTV screen you have connected with a cable). You'll find more details about some of these functions later in this chapter, or, for more complex capabilities, in the chapters that I point you to. This section just lists the must-know information.

- **Start review.** To begin review, press the Playback button at the upper-left corner of the back of the D300. The most-recently viewed image will appear on the LCD.

- **Playback folder.** Image review generally shows you the images in the currently selected folder on your Compact Flash card. A given card can contain several folders (a new one is created anytime you exceed 999 images in the current folder). You can use the Playback folder menu option in the Playback menu (as I'll explain in Chapter 3) to select a specific folder, or direct the D300 to display images from all the folders on the memory card.

- **View thumbnail images.** To change the view from a single image to four or nine thumbnails, follow the instructions in the "Viewing Thumbnails" section that follows.

- **Zoom in and out.** To zoom in or out, press the Zoom/Thumbnail key, following the instructions in the "Zooming the Nikon D300 Playback Display" in the next section. (It also shows you how to move the zoomed area around using the multi-selector keypad.)

- **Move back and forth.** To advance to the next image, press the right edge of the multi-selector pad; to go back to a previous shot, press the left edge. When you reach the beginning/end of the photos in your folder, the display "wraps around" to the end/beginning of the available shots.

- **See different types of data.** To change the type of information about the displayed image that is shown, press the up and down portions of the multi-selector pad. To learn what data is available, read the "Using Shooting Data" section later in this chapter.

Note

You can swap the functions of the up/down and right/left keys during playback using Custom Setting menu entry **CSM #f3**, as described in Chapter 3.

- **Remove images.** To delete an image that's currently on the screen, press the Trash button once, then press it again to confirm the deletion. To select and delete a group of images, use the Delete option in the Playback menu to specify particular photos to remove, as described in more detail in Chapter 3.

- **Cancel playback.** To cancel image review, press the Playback button again, or simply tap the shutter release button.

CENTER FUNCTIONS

The center button of the multi-selector can be programmed to perform one of four different functions during playback, as I'll describe in Chapter 3. Those functions are thumbnails on/off (the default); view histograms; zoom on/off; and choose the memory card folder used for image review.

Zooming the Nikon D300 Playback Display

The old way of zooming (with the D200 and D2x/D2xs) is shown at left in Figure 2.12. The zoom sequence with those cameras goes like this:

1. When an image is displayed, press the Enter/OK button to "activate" the zoom feature. The shooting information data vanishes and the image fills the D200/D2xs screen.

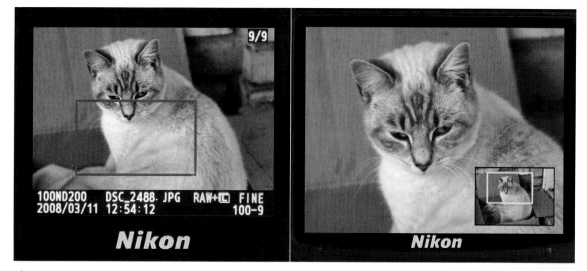

Figure 2.12 The Nikon D200's zooming system used the entire screen as a navigation window (left); the D300 incorporates a small thumbnail image with a yellow box showing the current zoom area (right).

2. Hold down the Thumbnail button, and a red box with blue corners appears, like the one at left in Figure 2.12.

3. Spin the main command dial to change the size of the zoom box. When you release the Thumbnail button, the screen zooms in on the selected area. At that point, spinning the main command dial advances to the next image (at the same zoom level) or to the previous image.

4. Press the Thumbnail button and spin the main command dial again to zoom in or out.

5. Use the multi-selector buttons to move the zoomed area around within the image.

6. Press the Enter/OK button again to cancel zooming and go back to the full image view with informational data shown.

The *new* way of zooming with the Nikon D300 isn't necessarily better or worse. It's just different. You'll need to follow these steps instead.

1. When an image is displayed (use the Playback button to start), press the Zoom In button to fill the screen with a slightly magnified version of the image.

2. A navigation window appears in the lower-right corner of the LCD showing the entire image. Keep pressing to continue zooming in to the maximum of 27X enlargement (with a full resolution large image).

3. A yellow box in the navigation window shows the zoomed area within the full image. The entire navigation window vanishes from the screen after a few seconds, leaving you with a full-screen view of the zoomed portion of the image.

4. Use the main command dial to move to the same zoomed area of the next/previous image.

5. Use the Zoom Out/Thumbnail button to zoom back out of the image.

6. Use the multi-selector buttons to move the zoomed area around within the image. The navigation window will reappear for reference when zooming or scrolling around within the display.

7. To exit zoom in/zoom out display, keep pressing the Zoom Out button until the full screen/full image/information display appears again.

This new scheme isn't a bad one, although it's easy to press the Zoom In button too enthusiastically and zoom in too far, and the old blue-cornered red box used with the D200 seemed to make it easier to select the precise area you wanted to study. The big problem for those who have more than one advanced Nikon dSLR is that it's different from the system used with the D3, as well as the earlier cameras. There is no Zoom Out button on the D3. Simply press the single Zoom/Thumbnail button and spin the main command dial to the right to zoom in and to the left to zoom out. A yellow box shows the zoomed area, and when you release the Zoom button, the screen fills with the area you've chosen. That's even easier than the system used with the D200 and D2x/D2xs.

Of course, if you're not planning to use the D300 side-by-side with any of the other three most recent advanced Nikon dSLRs, all you need to do is learn the new system and forget about the alternate sequences.

Viewing Thumbnails

The Nikon D300 provides other options for reviewing images in addition to zooming in and out. You can switch between single image view and either four or nine reduced-size thumbnail images on a single LCD screen.

Pages of thumbnail images offer a quick way to scroll through a large number of pictures quickly to find the one you want to examine in more detail. The D300 lets you switch quickly from single- to four- to nine-image views, with a scroll bar displayed at the right side of the screen to show you the relative position of the displayed thumbnails within the full collection of images in the active folder on your memory card. Figure 2.13 offers a comparison between the two levels of thumbnail views. The Zoom In and Zoom Out/Thumbnail buttons are used, which is another change from the D200 and D2x/D2xs, which used only the Zoom Out/Thumbnail button to change the number of thumbnails on the screen at once.

- **Add thumbnails.** To increase the number of thumbnails on the screen, press the Zoom Out button once or twice. The D300 will switch from single image to four thumbnails to nine thumbnails. Additional presses do nothing (the display doesn't cycle back to single image again).

- **Reduce thumbnails.** To decrease the number of thumbnails on the screen, press the Zoom In button to change from nine thumbnails to four thumbnails, or from four to single-image display. Continuing to press the Zoom In button once you've returned to single-image display starts the zoom process described in the previous section.

- **Toggle between thumbnails and full image.** When viewing thumbnails, you can quickly toggle between thumbnail view and full image display by pressing the center of the multi-selector (unless you've redefined it for some other function, using Custom Setting menu **CSM #f1,** as described in Chapter 4). Pressing it again returns to the previously chosen thumbnail view.

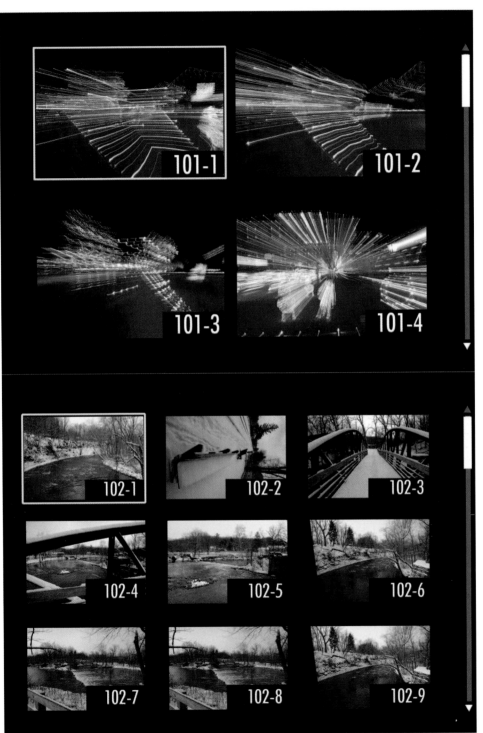

Figure 2.13
Switch between four thumb-nails (top) and nine thumb-nails (bottom) by pressing the Zoom Out and Zoom In buttons.

- **Move zoomed area.** Use the multi-selector to move the yellow highlight box around among the thumbnails.

- **Protect and delete images.** When viewing thumbnails or a single page image, press the Protect button to preserve the image against accidental deletion (a key icon is overlaid over the full-page image) or the Trash button (twice) to erase it.

- **Exit image review.** Tap the shutter release button or press the Playback button to exit image review. You don't have to worry about missing a shot because you were reviewing images; a half-press of shutter release automatically brings back the D300's exposure meters, the autofocus system, and (unless you've redefined your controls or are using manual focus) cancels image review.

Working with Shooting Data

When reviewing an image on the screen, your D300 can supplement the image itself with a variety of shooting data, ranging from basic information presented at the bottom of the LCD display, to three text overlays that detail virtually every shooting option you've selected. There is also a display for GPS data if you're using a GPS device, and two views of histograms. There's actually a third histogram view that can be summoned when you reprogram the center button of the multi-selector. I'll explain how to do that (Custom Setting menu **CSM #f1** for the impatient) and how to work with histograms in the discussion on achieving optimum exposure in Chapter 6. However, this is a good place to provide an overview of the kind of information you can view when playing back your photos.

You can change the types of information displayed using the Display Mode entry in the Playback menu. There you will find checkboxes you can mark for both basic photo information (overexposed highlights and the focus point used when the image was captured) and detailed photo information (which includes an RGB histogram and various data screens). I'll show you how to activate these info options in Chapter 3, and provide more detailed reasons why you might want to see this data when you review your pictures. This section will simply show you the type of information available. Most of the data is self-explanatory, so the labels in the accompanying figures should tell you most of what you need to know. To change to any of these views while an image is on the screen in Playback mode, press the multi-selector up/down buttons (unless you've swapped the up/down functions with the left/right functions in the Custom Settings menu).

- **File information screen.** The basic full image review display is officially called the File Information screen, and looks like Figure 2.14. When Highlights display is active (after being chosen in the Display Mode entry of the Playback menu), any overexposed areas will be indicated by a flashing black border. As I am unable to make the printed page flash, you'll have to check out this effect for yourself.

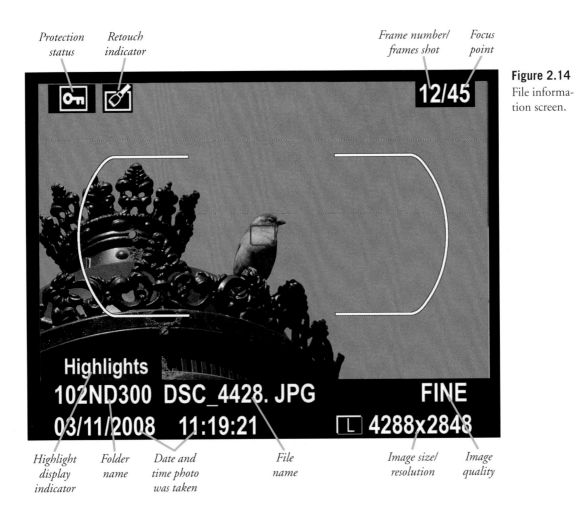

Protection status

Retouch indicator

Frame number/ frames shot

Focus point

Highlight display indicator

Folder name

Date and time photo was taken

File name

Image size/ resolution

Image quality

Figure 2.14
File information screen.

- **Overview data.** This screen, shown in Figure 2.15, provides a smaller image of your photo, but more information, including a luminance (brightness) histogram, metering mode used, lens focal length, exposure compensation, flash compensation, and lots of other data that's self-explanatory. The only puzzler in this dense screen is likely to be the image authentication indicator, used with a special authentication kit by law enforcement and judicial agencies to insure that a digital image presented as evidence has not been modified. It also can show up on the File information screen, but I left it out of the illustration, because 99.9 percent of the readers of this book will not be using that feature.

- **Shooting Data 1.** This is the first in a series of three screens that collectively provide everything else you might want to know about a picture you've taken. I'm not providing any labels in Figure 2.16, because the information in the first seven lines in the screen should be obvious (although new photographers may still need to learn what some of them, such as *exposure compensation,* mean).

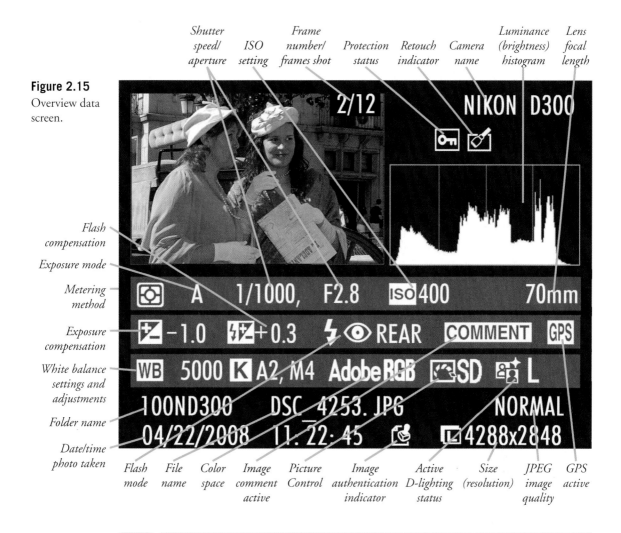

Figure 2.15
Overview data screen.

Shutter speed/ aperture *ISO setting* *Frame number/ frames shot* *Protection status* *Retouch indicator* *Camera name* *Luminance (brightness) histogram* *Lens focal length*

Flash compensation
Exposure mode
Metering method
Exposure compensation
White balance settings and adjustments
Folder name
Date/time photo taken

Flash mode *File name* *Color space* *Image comment active* *Picture Control* *Image authentication indicator* *Active D-lighting status* *Size (resolution)* *JPEG image quality* *GPS active*

> **Note**
>
> The ISO setting appears in red when the ISO Auto option, which allows the D300 to adjust the ISO for you, has been selected. (More info in Chapter 6.) The exception to the self-explanation rule might be **Exp. Tuning**, which refers to the blanket adjustment you can make to fine tune optimal exposure using Custom Setting menu **CSM #b6**, as I'll explain in Chapter 4. The cluster of settings at the bottom of the screen deal with flash settings in Commander mode, which comes into play when the D300 is used to control one or more external flash units. (That's a topic for Chapter 9.)

- **Shooting Data 2.** This screen shows white balance data and adjustments, the color space you've selected, and lists any Picture Control tweaks you've entered. (See Figure 2.17.)

- **Shooting Data 3.** The final screen shows any noise reduction you've specified, Active D-Lighting status, and any Retouch menu changes you may have made. Although none of them apply to the background image shown in Figure 2.18, I've added a few entries to show the kind of changes that can be made. You'll learn more about the Retouch menu in Chapter 5, which also will tell you how to create an image comment, like the one shown in the figure.

- **RGB Histogram.** Another optional screen is the RGB histogram, which you can see in Figure 2.19. As I mentioned earlier, if you've reprogrammed the center button of the multi-selector, pressing it can produce a large luminance (brightness) histogram like the one shown in Figure 2.20. I'm going to leave the discussion of histograms for Chapter 6.

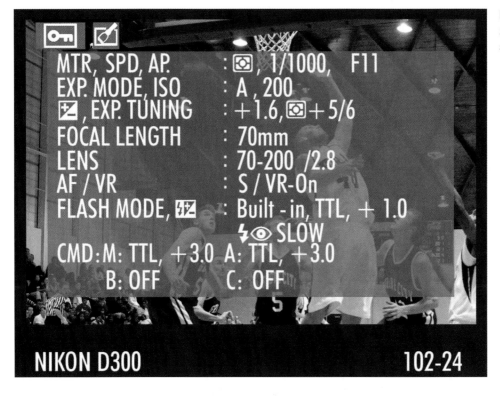

Figure 2.16
Shooting data screen 1.

Figure 2.17
Shooting data
screen 2.

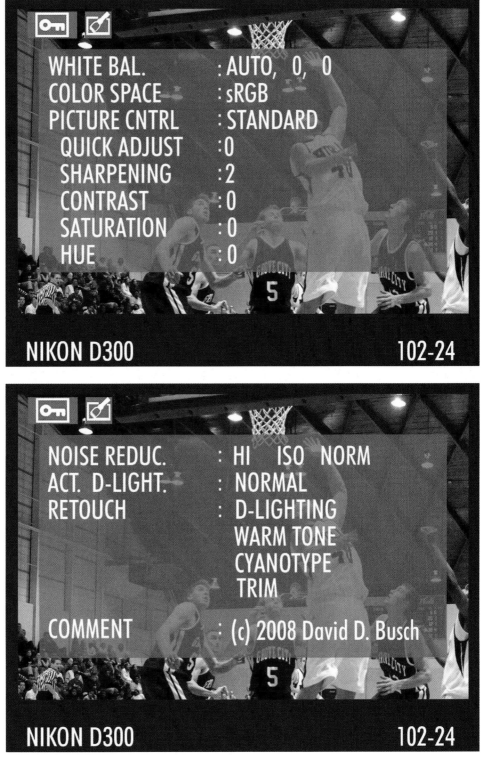

Figure 2.18
Shooting data
screen 3.

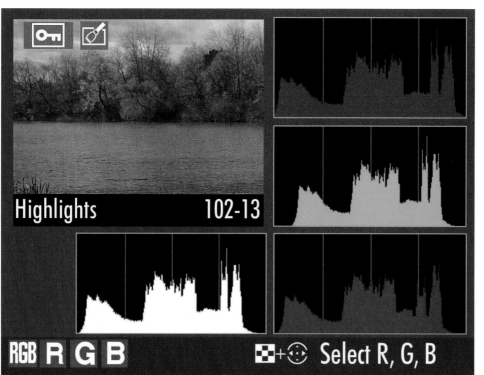

Figure 2.19
RGB histogram
screen.

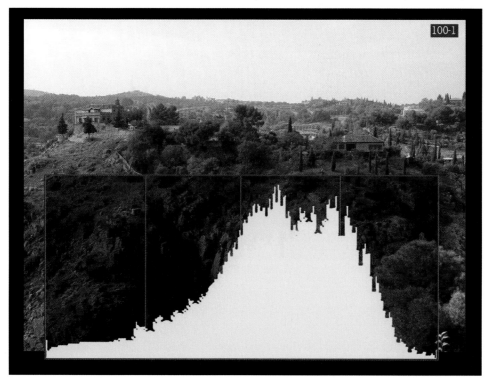

Figure 2.20
Luminance
(brightness)
histogram
screen.

Going Topside

The top surface of the Nikon D300 (see Figure 2.21) has its own set of frequently accessed controls. I'm going to divide them into two parts: those to the left side of the camera, and those on the right side. The left side controls offer some settings that you may change frequently, perhaps even during a shooting session (white balance and ISO sensitivity), and one that you'll probably change once at the beginning: image quality (when you choose whether to shoot RAW, JPEG [and which compression level you want], or a combination of the two). Also on the left side of the camera is the release mode dial itself, which you'll use to flip among Single Shot, Continuous Shooting, Self-Timer, Live View, and other modes. Figure 2.22 shows this side of the D300's top panel up close.

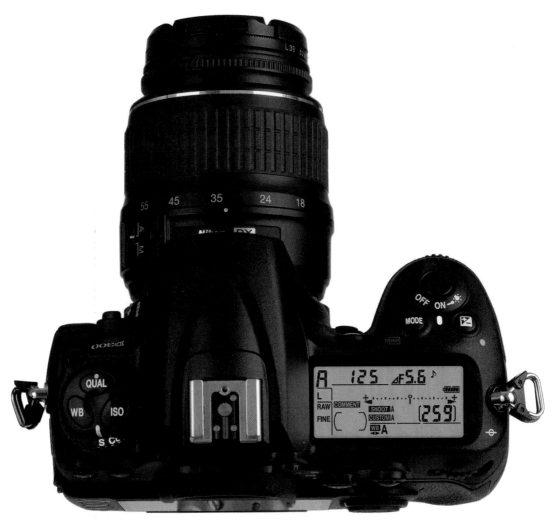

Figure 2.21

■ **Mode dial lock release.** Before you can choose any of the release mode dial's settings, you must hold down this button to free the dial so it can rotate.

■ **Release mode dial.** Your choices include S (Single Shot), C_L (Continuous Low Speed), C_H (Continuous High Speed), Live View (to preview your shots on the LCD *before* you take them), Self-Timer, and M_{UP} (Mirror Up). I'll have more information on using these modes in Chapter 6.

■ **QUAL button.** Hold down this button and rotate the main command dial to choose from among three JPEG options (Fine, Norm, and Basic), RAW (only), RAW+ one of the three JPEG quality levels, plus TIFF, which is a loss-free file format that provides high quality files, but, like JPEG, doesn't offer the option of changing the camera settings in your image editor (as RAW does). Hold down the QUAL button while rotating the sub-command dial to change resolution among L (4288 × 2848 pixels), M (3216 × 2136 pixels), and S (2144 × 1424 pixels) sizes.

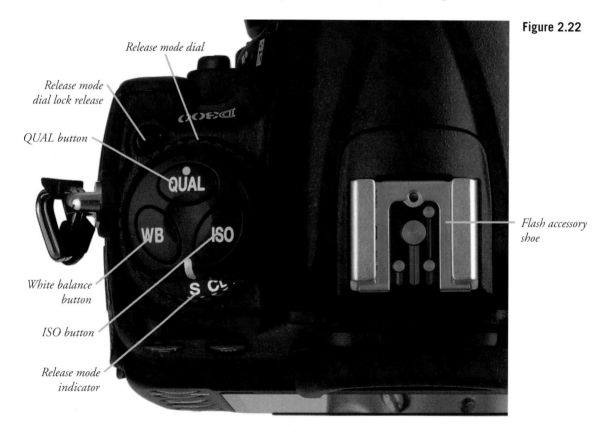

Figure 2.22

Release mode dial

Release mode
dial lock release

QUAL button

Flash accessory
shoe

White balance
button

ISO button

Release mode
indicator

- **WB button.** Hold down this button and rotate the main command dial to choose one of the predefined white balance settings available (such as Auto, Daylight, Fluorescent, or Tungsten). When any predefined setting is chosen, other than PRESET or K (choose your own color temperature), you can fine-tune the white balance by holding down the WB button and rotating the sub-command dial to the right to increase the amount of blue or to the left to increase the amount of amber (indicators will appear on the monochrome LCD status panel showing b1…b6 and A1…A6). You can also use the White Balance adjustments in the Shooting menu. If white balance and color temperatures are a mystery to you now, I'll cover them thoroughly in Chapter 6.

- **ISO button.** Press this button while spinning the main command dial to set an ISO sensitivity from ISO 200 to ISO 3200. Higher settings, up to H1 (ISO 6400 equivalent) and lower settings (LO1 is the equivalent of ISO 100) are also available. You can also use the ISO Sensitivity entry in the Shooting menu. You'll learn more about ISO, and the option of having the D300 set it for you automatically based on parameters you enter, in Chapter 6.

- **Flash hot shoe.** Slide an electronic flash into this mount when you need a more powerful speedlight. A dedicated flash unit, like the Nikon SB-800, can use the multiple contact points shown to communicate exposure, zoom setting, white balance information, and other data between the flash and the camera. There's more on using electronic flash in Chapter 10.

On the right side of the camera is another batch of controls and a display panel, as shown in Figure 2.23:

- **Power switch.** Rotate this switch clockwise to turn on the Nikon D300 (and virtually all other Nikon dSLRs). Continue past the ON position to illuminate the monochrome LCD control panel's backlight for a few seconds. If you'd rather have the backlight remain on for the length of time the exposure meters are active, you can specify this using the Custom Menu settings **CSM #d8** (set to On). For this setting to be useful, you'll need to set the automatic meter-off delay to something other than the default six seconds. If you're carefree about battery usage, you can specify meter-off delays of four seconds to 10 minutes using **CSM #c2**, as described in Chapter 4.

- **Shutter release button.** Partially depress this button to lock in exposure and focus (unless you've redefined the focus activation button, as outlined in Chapter 4). Press all the way to take the picture. Tapping the shutter release when the camera has turned off the auto exposure and autofocus mechanisms reactivates both. When a review image is displayed on the back-panel color LCD, tapping this button removes the image from the display and reactivates the auto exposure and autofocus mechanisms.

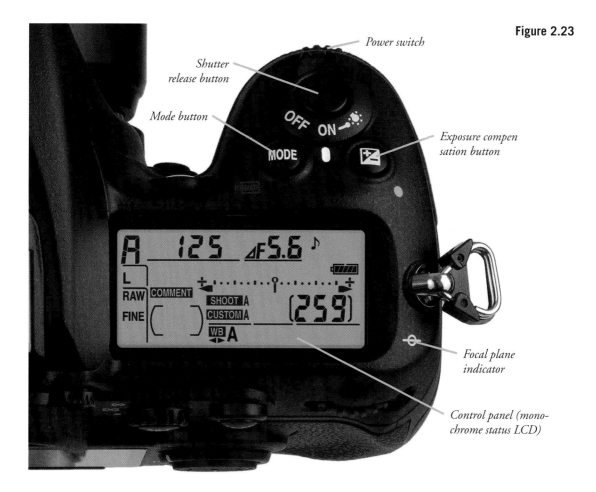

Figure 2.23

Power switch

Shutter
release button

Mode button

Exposure compen
sation button

Focal plane
indicator

Control panel (mono-
chrome status LCD)

- **Exposure compensation button/Reset #1.** Hold down this button and spin the main command dial to add or subtract exposure when using Program, Aperture Priority, or Shutter Priority modes. (In Manual mode, the exposure remains the same, but the "ideal" exposure shown in the electronic analog display [more on that in the next section] is modified to reflect the extra/reduced exposure you're calling for.) The exposure compensation amount is shown on the monochrome status panel as plus or minus values. This button is also used in conjunction with the QUAL button to provide a quick two-button reset of the camera to (most of) its factory default settings (any reassignment of the AE-L/AF-L button you made using Custom Setting menu **CSM #f6** is unaffected). Hold down the two buttons, each marked with a green dot, for about two seconds to affect the reset.

■ **Focal plane indicator.** This indicator shows the *plane* of the sensor, for use in applications where exact measurement of the distance from the focal plane to the subject are necessary. (These are mostly scientific/close-up applications.)

■ **Control panel.** I find Nikon's term for the top monochrome status panel confusing, so that's the term I use most of the time. This useful indicator shows the status of many settings. Unfortunately, because it's on top of the camera, you may not be able to *see* those settings when the camera is elevated (especially on a tripod). In that case, use the Shooting Information Display, described earlier in this chapter, which can show much of the same information on the back panel color LCD when you press the Info button.

■ **Mode button.** Hold down this button and rotate the main command dial to choose between Program, Aperture Priority, Shutter Priority, and Manual exposure modes. Your choice will be displayed on the monochrome status panel and in the viewfinder, both described in the next sections.

LCD Control Panel Readouts

The top panel of the Nikon D300 (see Figure 2.24) contains a monochrome LCD readout (the "control panel") that displays status information about most of the shooting settings. All of the information segments available are shown in Figures 2.25a and b. I've color-coded the display to make it easier to differentiate them; the information does *not* appear in color on the actual D300. Many of the information items are mutually exclusive (that is, in the White Balance area at lower right, only one of the possible settings illustrated will appear).

Figure 2.24

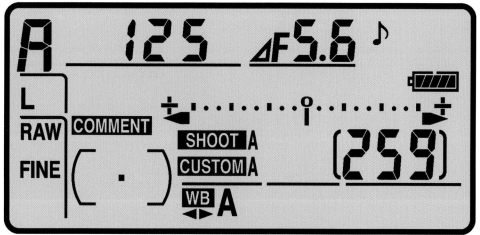

Figure 2.25a

Shutter speed/Exposure compensation value/Flash compensation value ISO sensitivity/White balance fine-tuning/Color temperature/White balance preset number/Number of shots in WB bracket sequence/Number of intervals for interval timer photos/Focal length of non-CPU lens

Exposure mode

Aperture/Exposure and flash bracketing increment/White balance bracketing increment/Number of shots per interval/Maximum aperture of non-CPU lens/PC connection mod

Flash mode

Battery status

MB-D10 battery indicator

Thousands of exposures

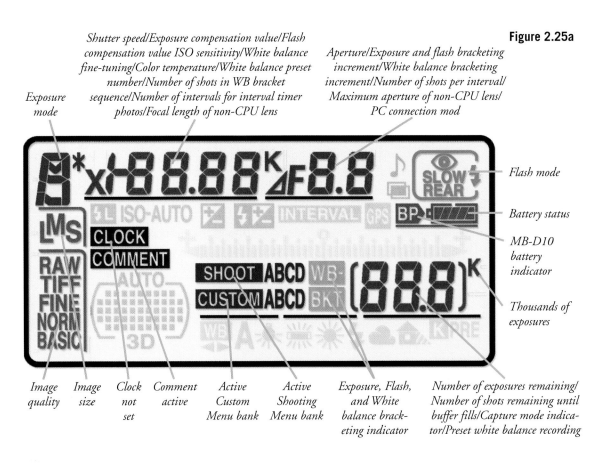

Image quality

Image size

Clock not set

Comment active

Active Custom Menu bank

Active Shooting Menu bank

Exposure, Flash, and White balance bracketing indicator

Number of exposures remaining/ Number of shots remaining until buffer fills/Capture mode indicator/Preset white balance recording

Figure 2.25b

Auto-area autofocus indicator

Flash value lock

ISO indicator

Exposure compensation active

Flash compensation active

Interval time indicator

GPS active

Beep on

Multiple exposures

Electronic analog display/ Exposure compensation/ Exposure and flash bracketing progress/ WB bracketing progress/ PC connection indicator

White balance setting

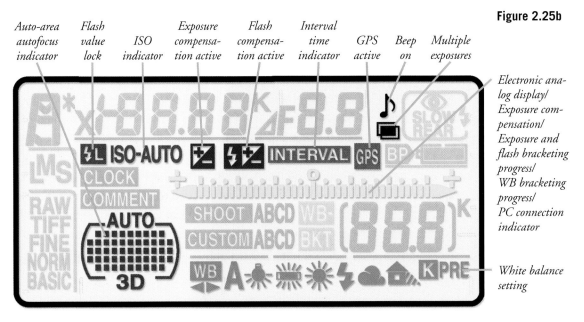

Some of the items on the status LCD also appear in the viewfinder, such as the shutter speed and aperture (pictured at top in pink in the figure), and the exposure level (in yellow at the middle). This is a thicket of information, but I'll spell out what the categories of data include:

- **Exposure mode (blue).** This indicator tells you whether the D300 is set for Program, Aperture Priority, Shutter Priority, or Manual exposure modes. An asterisk appears next to the P when you have used Flexible Program mode, which allows you to depart from the camera's programmed exposure setting to set a different combination of shutter speed/aperture that produces the same exposure. You'll find more about this feature in Chapter 6.

- **Image Size (dark orange).** Shows whether the D300 is shooting Large (4288 × 2848 pixels), Medium (3216 × 2136 pixels), or Small (2144 × 1424 pixels) sizes.

- **Image Quality (dark orange).** Shows current image quality, including TIFF, JPEG, RAW, and RAW+JPEG.

- **Autofocus-area indicator (dark red).** Displays the autofocus area status, with the active focus zone shown from among the 51 available points.

- **Clock not set (dark blue).** This indicator is displayed when your clock needs to be reset. You'll see it when your camera is activated for the first time, any time that the internal clock battery runs down (say, when you've removed the main battery for a few days), and when your internal clock battery wears out and will no longer hold a charge.

- **Comment active (dark blue).** Shows when you've entered a comment in the Setup menu, and have made it active (so the comment will be embedded in each image you shoot).

- **Flash value lock (brown).** This appears when you've locked in a particular flash value setting.

- **ISO indicator (brown).** Displayed when you've set the D300 to adjust ISO for you automatically.

- **Electronic analog display/additional functions (yellow).** This is a continuous scale that shows that correct exposure is achieved when the indicator is in the center, and how many stops off exposure is when the indicator veers to the right (underexposure) or left (overexposure). This scale is also used to display other information, such as exposure compensation and bracketing progress.

- **Active Shooting Menu bank (purple).** Indicates which Shooting Menu bank of settings is active: A, B, C, or D. You'll learn more about banks in Chapter 3.

- **Active Custom Menu bank (purple).** Shows which Custom Menu bank is active: A, B, C, or D. (See Chapter 4 for more.)

- **Exposure compensation active (dark gray).** Appears when you've dialed in exposure compensation. Monitor this indicator, as it's easy to forget that you've told the Nikon D300 to use more or less exposure than what its (reasonably intelligent) metering system would otherwise select.

- **Flash compensation active (dark gray).** Reminds you that you've tweaked the D300's electronic flash exposure system with more or less exposure requested.

- **White balance setting (light blue).** One of the white balance settings will appear here, depending on the selection you've made.

- **Exposure/Flash/White balance bracketing indicator (tan).** Shows that exposure, flash, or white balance bracketing is underway.

- **Number of exposures/additional functions (red).** This indicator shows the number of exposures remaining on your memory card, as well as other functions, such as the number of shots remaining until your memory buffer fills.

- **Battery status (gray).** Five segments show the approximate battery power remaining. A better indicator is the Battery Info entry in the Setup menu.

- **MB-D10 battery indicator (gray).** Appears when the D300 is being powered by the MB-D10 battery grip.

- **GPS active (pink).** If you have a GPS device attached and working, you'll know it when this indicator shows up.

- **Interval timer active (pink).** When using the D300's interval timer facility (as described in Chapter 5), this indicator appears.

- **Electronic flash mode (green).** The current mode for the D300's built-in electronic flash unit is shown here.

- **Multiple exposures (black).** If you're shooting multiple exposures (selected under Multiple Exposures in the Shooting menu) this indicator will be shown. You can dial in a specific number of exposures when you set the sequence up, as I'll describe in Chapter 3.

- **Beep indicator (black).** Indicates that a helpful beep will sound when using the self-timer or when the D300 successfully focuses when in Single-Servo Autofocus mode (AF-S) (as long as Release priority hasn't been specified in CSM #a2). You can specify a loud or soft beep, or none at all in **CSM #d1**.

- **Aperture/additional functions (magenta).** The selected f/stop appears here, along with a lot of other alternate information, as shown in the label in the figure.

- **Shutter speed/additional functions (magenta).** Here you'll find the shutter speed, ISO setting, color temperature, and other useful data.

Lens Components

The typical lens, like the one shown in Figure 2.26, has several common features:

■ **Filter thread.** Most lenses have a thread on the front for attaching filters and other add-ons. Some also use this thread for attaching a lens hood (you screw on the filter first, and then attach the hood to the screw thread on the front of the filter). Some lenses, such as the AF-S Nikkor 14-24mm f/2.8G ED lens introduced at the same time as the D300, have no front filter thread, either because their front elements are too curved to allow mounting a filter and/or because the front element is so large that huge filters would be prohibitively expensive. Some of these front-filter-hostile lenses allow using smaller filters that drop into a slot at the back of the lens.

Figure 2.26

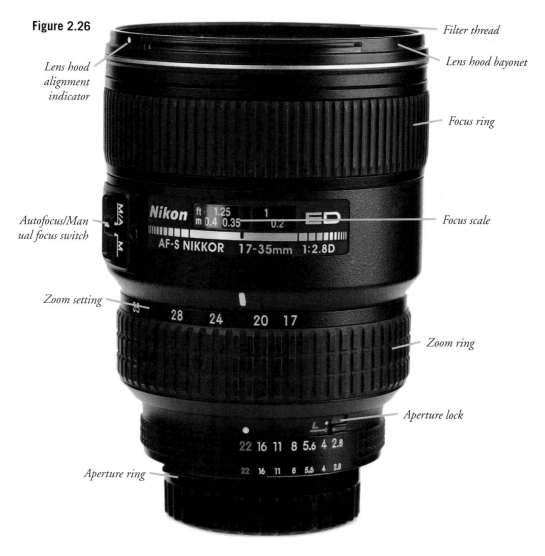

Lens hood alignment indicator

Autofocus/Manual focus switch

Zoom setting

Aperture ring

Filter thread

Lens hood bayonet

Focus ring

Focus scale

Zoom ring

Aperture lock

- **Lens hood bayonet.** This is used to mount the lens hood for lenses that don't use screw-mount hoods (the majority). Such lenses generally will have a dot on the edge showing how to align the lens hood with the bayonet mount.

- **Focus ring.** This is the ring you turn when you manually focus the lens, or fine-tune autofocus adjustment.

- **Focus scale.** This is a readout that rotates in unison with the lens' focus mechanism to show the distance at which the lens has been focused. It's a useful indicator for double-checking autofocus, roughly evaluating depth-of-field, and for setting manual focus guesstimates. Chapter 8 deals with the mysteries of lenses and their controls in more detail.

- **Zoom setting.** These markings on the lens show the current focal length selected.

- **Zoom ring.** Turn this ring to change the zoom setting.

- **Autofocus/Manual switch.** Allows you to change from automatic focus to manual focus.

- **Aperture ring.** Some lenses have a ring that allows you to set a specific f/stop manually, rather than use the camera's internal electronic aperture control. An aperture ring is useful when a lens is mounted on a non-automatic extension ring, bellows, or other accessory that doesn't couple electronically with the camera. Aperture rings also allow using a lens on an older camera that lacks electronic control.

- **Aperture lock.** If you want your D300 (or other Nikon dSLR) to control the aperture electronically, you must set the lens to its smallest aperture (usually f/22 or f/32) and lock it with this control.

- **Focus limit switch.** Some lenses have this switch (shown in Figure 2.27), which limits the focus range of the lens, thus potentially reducing focus seeking when shooting distant subjects. The limiter stops the lens from trying to focus at closer distances (in this case, closer than 2.5 meters).

- **Vibration reduction switch.** Lenses with Nikon's Vibration Reduction (VR) feature include a switch for turning the stabilization feature on and off, and for changing from normal vibration reduction to a more aggressive "active" VR mode useful for, say, shooting from moving vehicles. More on VR and other lens topics in Chapter 6.

The back end of a lens intended for use on a Nikon camera has other components that you seldom see (except when you swap lenses), shown in Figure 2.28, but still should know about:

- **Lens bayonet mount.** This is the mounting mechanism that attaches to a matching mount on the camera. Although the lens bayonet is usually metal, some lenses use a rugged plastic for this key component.

Vibration reduction
On/Off switch

Focus limit
switch

Normal/Active VR
mode switch

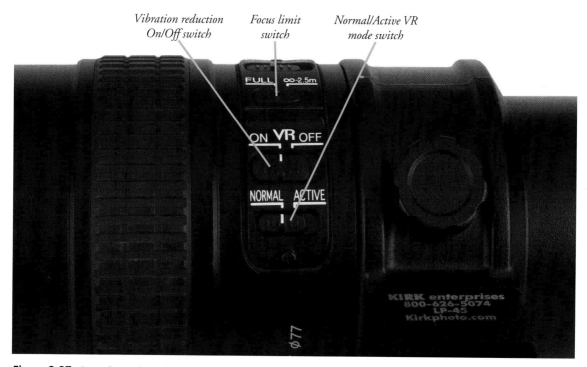

Figure 2.27 Some lenses have focus limit switches and controls for vibration reduction (VR) features.

- **Automatic diaphragm lever.** This lever is moved by a matching lever in the camera to adjust the f/stop from wide open (which makes for the brightest view) to the *taking aperture*, which is the f/stop that will be used to take the picture. The actual taking aperture is determined by the camera's metering system (or by you when the D300 is in Manual mode), and is communicated to the lens through the electronic contacts described next. (An exception is when the aperture ring on the lens itself is unlocked and used to specify the f/stop.) However, the spring-loaded physical levers are what actually push the aperture to the selected f/stop—even with advanced cameras like the D300 or D3. The aperture lever is also activated when you press the depth-of-field button.

- **Electronic contacts.** These metal contacts pass information to matching contacts in the camera body allowing a firm electrical connection so that exposure, distance, and other information can be exchanged between the camera and lens.

- **Lens type signal notch.** This is a machined groove in the lens mount, designed to tell older (non-dSLR) cameras that the aperture stops were linear. Today, this information would be conveyed electronically, except that all current lenses already have linear f/stops.

Figure 2.28

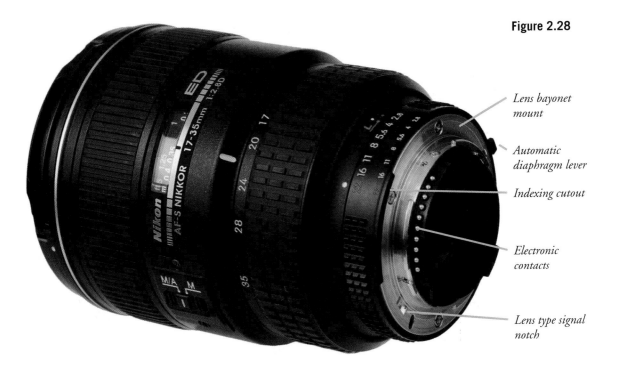

Lens bayonet
mount

Automatic
diaphragm lever

Indexing cutout

Electronic
contacts

Lens type signal
notch

- **Indexing cutout.** The base of any Nikon lens made after 1977 that has an aperture ring includes a cutout notch that mates with a ring around the lens mount of Nikon's advanced cameras (D200, D300, D2x/D2xs/D3, and some older pro models). It tells the camera what the maximum aperture is and what f/stop has been set. For a D300 owner, this means that older manual focus lenses (including pre-1977 lenses that have been converted to this system) can be used for automatic metering with the Aperture Priority exposure mode, and for manual metering in Manual exposure mode.

- **Autofocus drive screw slot.** (Not shown in the figure.) As you'll learn in Chapter 8, older autofocus lenses (given the AF designation in Nikon nomenclature) lack an internal autofocus motor. Focus is set using a screw drive built into the camera body of every Nikon autofocus camera (film or digital) except (at the time I write this) the Nikon D40 and D40x. Lenses given the AF-S designation lack this connection, because autofocus is achieved internally using a tiny motor.

Looking Inside the Viewfinder

Much of the important shooting status information is shown inside the viewfinder of the Nikon D300. As with the status LCD up on top, not all of this information will be shown at any one time. Figure 2.29 shows what you can expect to see. These readouts include:

■ **Alignment grid.** This optional grid (it can be turned on and off in the Custom Setting menu option **CSM #d2**) can be useful when aligning horizontal or vertical shapes as you compose your image.

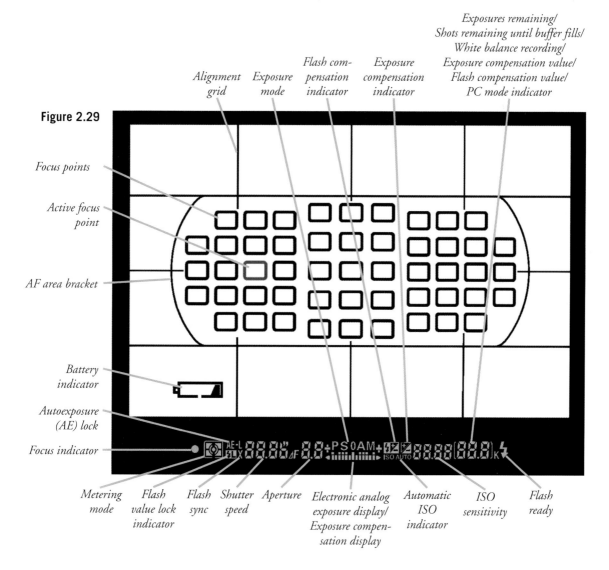

Figure 2.29

- **Focus points.** Can display the 51 areas used by the D300 to focus. The camera can select the appropriate focus zone for you, or you can manually select one or all of the zones.

- **Active focus point.** The currently selected focus point can be highlighted with red illumination, depending on focus mode.

- **AF area bracket.** Shows the area covered by the autofocus sensors. Nikon D300 owners are fortunate that Nikon chose the same AF point display system for this camera as for the full-frame D3 model. As a result, in the "cropped" viewfinder of the D300, the autofocus points fill up more of the viewfinder (and sensor) area. The same 51 points are distributed over a proportionately smaller area of the D3's sensor, concentrating covering into a less-expansive area in the middle of the screen/sensor.

- **Battery indicator.** Appears when the D300's battery becomes depleted.

- **Focus indicator.** This green dot stops blinking when the subject covered by the active autofocus zone is in sharp focus, whether focus was achieved by the AF system, or by you using manual focusing.

- **Metering mode.** Shows whether you've selected Matrix, Center-Weighted, or Spot metering.

- **Auto exposure lock.** Shows that exposure has been locked.

- **Flash value lock indicator.** A reminder that flash exposure has been locked.

- **Flash sync.** Shows that the shutter speed has been locked at the 250X (1/250 second) setting (located, not between 1/125 and 1/500 second, but as the speed past bulb or 30 seconds).

- **Shutter speed.** Displays the current shutter speed selected by the camera, or by you in Manual exposure mode.

- **Aperture.** Shows the current aperture chosen by the D300's autoexposure system, or specified by you when using Manual exposure mode.

- **Exposure mode.** Shows whether you've selected Program, Shutter Priority, Aperture Priority, or Manual exposure modes.

- **Automatic ISO indicator.** Is shown as a reminder that the D300 has been set to adjust ISO sensitivity automatically.

- **Electronic analog exposure display.** This scale shows the current exposure level, with the bottom indicator centered when the exposure is correct as metered. The indicator may also move to the left or right to indicate over- or underexposure (respectively). The scale is also used to show the amount of exposure compensation dialed in.

- **Flash compensation indicator.** Appears when flash EV changes have been made.

- **Exposure compensation indicator.** This is shown when exposure compensation (EV) changes have been made. It's easy to forget you've dialed in a little more or less exposure, and then shoot a whole series of pictures of a different scene that doesn't require such compensation. Beware!

- **Flash ready indicator.** This icon appears when the flash is fully charged.

- **ISO Sensitivity.** This useful indicator shows the current ISO setting value. Those who have accidentally taken dozens of shots under bright sunlight at ISO 1600 because they forgot to change the setting back after some indoor shooting will treasure this addition.

- **Exposures remaining/maximum burst available.** Normally displays the number of exposures remaining on your memory card, but while shooting it changes to show a number that indicates the number of frames that can be taken in continuous shooting mode using the current settings. This indicator also shows other information, such as exposure/flash compensation values, and whether the D300 is connected to a PC through a USB cable.

Underneath Your Nikon D300

There's not a lot going on with the bottom panel of your Nikon D300. You'll find the battery compartment access door, and a tripod socket, which secures the camera to a tripod. The socket accepts other accessories, such as quick release plates that allow rapid attaching and detaching the D300 from a matching platform affixed to your tripod. The socket is also used to secure the optional MB-D10 battery grip, which provides more juice to run your camera to take more exposures with a single charge. It also adds a vertically oriented shutter release, main command dial, sub-command dial, an AF-ON button, and miniature joystick-like version of the multi-selector, all arranged for easier vertical shooting. There's a terminal connector under a rubber cover to provide a connection between the D300 and accessories that fasten to the underside. To mount the grip, remove the rubber contact cover (it can be stored in a recess provided in the MB-D10 grip), then tighten the grip's tripod socket screw to lock the grip onto the bottom of your D300. Figure 2.30 shows the underside view of the camera. I'll explain more about the MB-D10 grip/battery pack in Chapter 7.

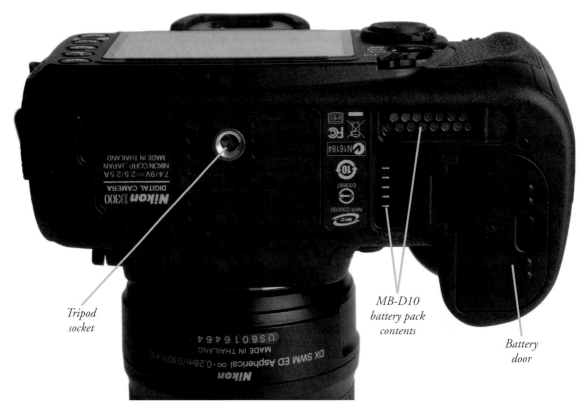

Tripod
socket

MB-D10
battery pack
contents

Battery
door

Figure 2.30

3

Setup: Playback and Shooting Menus

The Nikon D300 is undoubtedly one of the most customizable, tweakable, fine-tunable cameras Nikon has ever offered. In fact, this versatility has made the D300 popular among professional photographers as well as advanced amateurs. If your camera doesn't behave in exactly the way you'd like, chances are you can make a small change in the Playback, Shooting, Custom Settings, and Setup menus that will tailor the D300 to your needs. In fact, if you don't like the *menus* you can create your own using the clever My Menu system.

This chapter will help you sort out the settings for the Playback and Shooting menus, which determine how the D300 displays images on review, and how it uses many of its shooting features to take a photo. The following chapters will focus on the Custom Settings menu (Chapter 4), and Setup, Retouch, and My Menu options (Chapter 5).

As I've mentioned before, this book isn't intended to replace the manual you received with your D300, nor have I any interest in rehashing its contents. You'll still find the original manual useful as a standby reference that lists every possible option in exhaustive (if mind-numbing) detail—without really telling you how to use those options to take better pictures. There is, however, some unavoidable duplication between the Nikon manual and the next three chapters, because I'm going to explain all the key menu choices and the options you may have in using them. You should find, though, that I will give you the information you need in a much more helpful format, with plenty of detail on why you should make some settings that are particularly cryptic.

I'm not going to waste a lot of space on some of the more obvious menu choices in these chapters. For example, you can probably figure out that the Beep option in Custom Setting menu **CSM #d1** deals with the solid-state beeper in your camera that sounds off during various activities (such as the self-timer countdown). You can certainly decipher the import of the two options available for the Beep entry (On and Off). In this chapter, I'll devote no more than a sentence or two to the blatantly obvious settings and concentrate on the more confusing aspects of D300 setup, such as automatic exposure bracketing. I'll start with an overview of using the D300's menus themselves.

Anatomy of the Nikon D300's Menus

If you used any Nikon digital SLR before you purchased your Nikon D300, you're probably already familiar with the basic menu system. The menus consist of a series of screens with entries, as shown in Figure 3.1. Navigating among the various menus is easy and follows a consistent set of rules:

- Press the Menu button to display the main menu screens.

- Use the multi-selector's left/right/up/down buttons to navigate among the menu entries to highlight your choice. Moving the highlighting to the left column lets you scroll up and down among the six top-level menus. From the top in Figure 3.1, they are Playback, Shooting, Custom Settings, Setup, Retouch, and My Menu, with Help access represented by a question mark at the bottom of the column.

- A highlighted top-level menu's icon will change from black and white to yellow, white, and black. Use the multi-selector's right button to move into the column containing that menu's choices, and the up/down buttons to scroll among the entries. If more than one screen full of choices is available, a scroll bar appears at the far right of the screen, with a position slider showing the relative position of the currently highlighted entry.

- To work with a highlighted menu entry, press the OK button at lower left on the back of the D300 or, more conveniently, just press the right button on the multi-selector. Any additional screens of choices will appear. You can move among them using the same multi-selector movements.

- You can confirm a selection by pressing the OK button or, frequently, by pressing the right button on the multi-selector once again. Some functions require scrolling to a Done menu choice, or include an instruction to Set a choice using some other button.

- Pressing the multi-selector left button usually backs you out of the current screen, and pressing the Menu button again usually does the same thing. You can exit the menu system at any time by tapping the shutter release button.

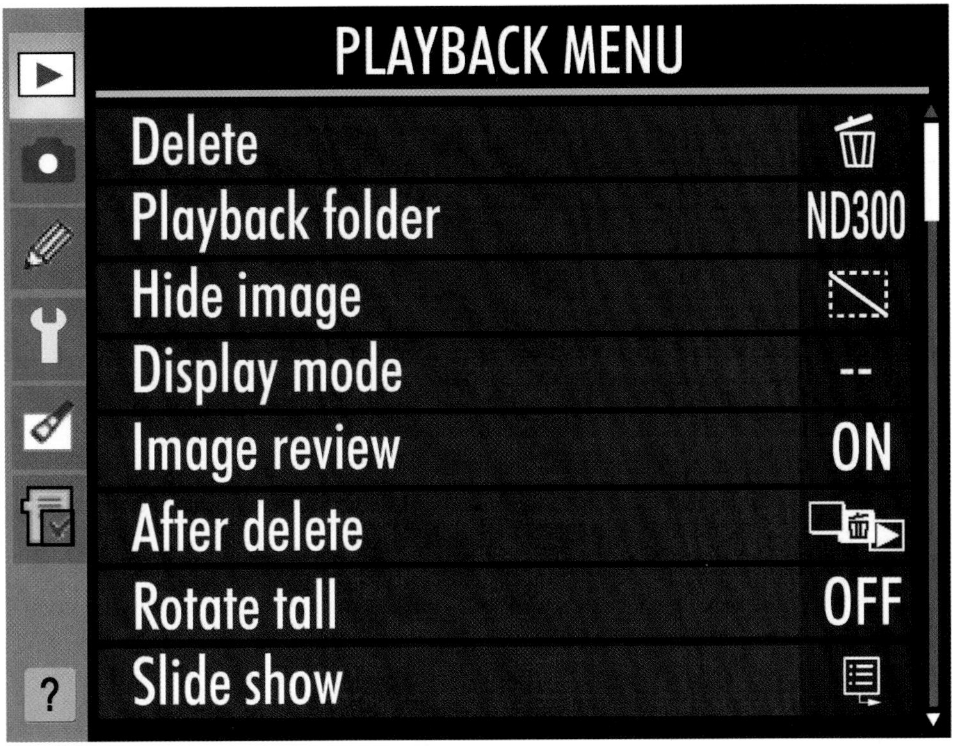

Figure 3.1
The multi-selector's navigational buttons are used to move among the various menu entries.

- The Nikon D300 "remembers" the top-level menu and specific menu entry you were using (but not any submenus) the last time the menu system was accessed, so pressing the Menu button brings you back to where you left off. So, if you were working with an entry in the Custom Setting menu's Metering/exposure section, then decided to take a photo, the next time you press the Menu button the Custom Setting menu and the Metering/exposure entry will be highlighted, but not the specific submenu (b1 through b6) that you might have selected.

The top-level menus are color coded, and a bar in that color is displayed underneath the menu title when one of those menus is highlighted. The colors are: Playback menu (blue); Shooting menu (green); Custom Setting menu (red); Setup menu (orange); Retouch menu (purple); and My Menu (gray). The Custom Setting menu has six submenus that are themselves color-coded to help you keep track of where you are located in the menu system. You'll learn about the Custom Setting, Setup, Retouch, and My Menu options in Chapters 4 and 5.

Playback Menu Options

The blue-coded Playback menu has nine entries where you select options related to the display, review, transfer, and printing of the photos you've taken. The choices you'll find include:

- Delete
- Playback folder
- Hide image
- Display mode
- Image review
- After delete
- Rotate tall
- Slide show
- Print set (DPOF)

Delete

Choose this menu entry and you'll be given two choices: Selected and All. If you choose Selected, you'll see an image selection screen like the one shown in Figure 3.2. Then, follow these instructions:

1. Use the multi-selector cursor keys to scroll among the available images.

2. When you highlight an image you think you might like to delete, press the Zoom/Thumbnail button to temporarily enlarge that image so you can evaluate it further. When you release the button, the selection screen returns.

3. To mark an image for deletion, press the multi-selector center button (*not* the Trash button). A trash can icon will appear overlaid on that image's thumbnail. To unmark an image, press the multi-selector center button again.

4. When you've finished marking images to delete, press **OK**. A final screen will appear asking you to confirm the removal of the image(s). Choose **Yes** to delete the image(s) or **No** to cancel deletion, and then press OK. If you selected Yes, then you'll return to the Playback menu; if you chose No, you'll be taken back to the selection screen to mark/unmark images.

5. To back out of the selection screen, press the Menu button.

Figure 3.2
Select images
to delete.

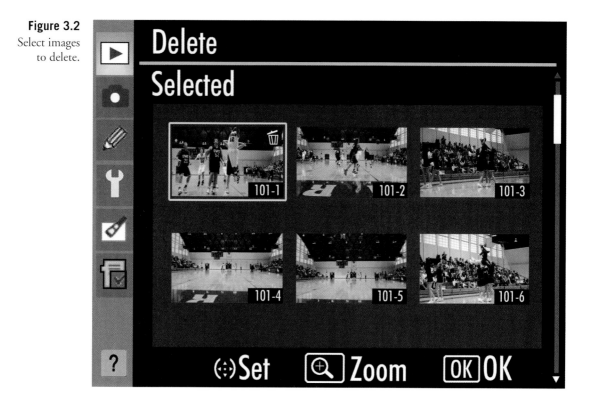

Using this menu to delete images will have no effect on images that have been marked as protected with the Protect key. Keep in mind that deleting images in this way is slower than just wiping out the whole card with the Format command, so using Format is generally much faster than choosing Delete: All, and it is also is a safer way of returning your memory card to a fresh, blank, state.

Playback Folder

Your Nikon D300 will create folders on your memory card to store the images that it creates. It assigns the first folder a number, like ND300, and when that folder fills with 999 images, the camera automatically creates a new folder numbered one higher, such as ND301. If you use the same memory card in another camera, that camera will also create its own folder (say, ND200 for a Nikon D200). Thus you can end up with several folders on the same memory card, until you eventually reformat the card and folder creation starts anew.

This menu item allows you to choose which folders are accessed when displaying images using the D300's Playback facility. Your choices are as follows:

- **ND300.** The camera will use only the folders on your memory card created by the D300 and ignore those created by other cameras. Images in all the D300's folders will be displayed. This is the default setting.

- **All.** All folders containing images that the D300 can read will be accessed, regardless of which camera created them. You might want to use this setting if you swap memory cards among several cameras and want to be able to review all the photos (especially when considering reformatting the memory card). You will be able to view images even if they were created by a non-Nikon camera if those images conform to the Design Rule for Camera File system (DCF) specifications.

- **Current.** The D300 will display only images in the current folder. For example, if you have been shooting heavily at an event and have already accumulated more than 999 shots in one folder and the D300 has created a new folder for the overflow, you'd use this setting to view only the most recent photos, which reside in the current folder. You can change the current folder to any other folder on your memory card using the Active Folder option in the Shooting menu, described later in this chapter.

Hide Image

Use this menu option to protect *and* hide images. When you choose Hide Image, you'll be given a choice to select/set images (using a selection screen almost identical to the one used to delete images, as shown in Figure 3.2) or the option of deselecting all hidden images.

Unlike the Protect option, which just marks images to keep them from accidental deletion, this selection also hides them from view using the regular Playback functions. Pictures that have been hidden can only be viewed from the selection screen. I use this facility in two different ways:

- Sometimes I have a memory card filled with images and I want to show some of the images, perhaps as a slideshow, or sometimes just by handing the camera to someone and asking them to browse through the photos. I can hide the non-relevant images so only the relevant pictures appear.

- Hiding images is a good way to make your real stinkers invisible if you haven't quite made up your mind to delete them.

Remember that if you "unhide" an image you are also removing the Protect attribute. If you want the photo to be visible, but still protected, press the Protect button (it has a key icon as a label) while viewing the image on the LCD. The key icon will be superimposed on the image, showing you that it is now protected from accidental erasure.

Reformatting the card removes the Hidden and Protected attributes, of course—because it removes those images as well!

Display Mode

You'll recall from Chapter 2 that a great deal of information, available on multiple screens, can be displayed when reviewing images. This menu item helps you reduce/increase the clutter by specifying which information and screens will be available. To activate or deactivate an info option, scroll to that option and press the right multi-selector button to add a check mark to the box next to that item. Press the right button to unmark an item that has previously been checked. Important: when you're finished, you must scroll up to **Done** and press **OK** or the right multi-selector button to confirm your choices. Exiting the Display mode menu any other way will cause any changes you may have made to be ignored. Your info options include:

- **Highlights.** When enabled, overexposed highlight areas in your image will blink with a black border during picture review. That's your cue to consider using exposure compensation to reduce exposure, unless a minus-EV setting will cause loss of shadow detail that you want to preserve. You can read more about correcting exposure in Chapter 6.

- **Focus point.** Activate this option to display the active focus point(s) with red highlighting, as shown in Figure 3.3.

- **RGB histogram.** Displays both luminance (brightness) and RGB histograms on a screen that can be displayed using the up/down multi-selector buttons, as shown in Figure 2.19 in Chapter 2. If you're viewing this histogram with the Highlights display enabled, you can change the Highlights focus from the luminance histogram to any of the three RGB channels by holding down the Thumbnail button and pressing the multi-selector right button until the channel you want is selected. I'll explain the use of this feature in more detail in Chapter 6.

- **Data.** Activates the three pages of shooting data shown in Figures 2.16, 2.17, and 2.18 in Chapter 2.

Image Review

There are certain shooting situations in which it's useful to have the picture you've just shot pop up on the LCD automatically for review. Perhaps you're fine-tuning exposure or autofocus and want to be able to see whether your most recent image is acceptable. Or maybe, you're the nervous type and just want confirmation that you actually took a picture. Instant review has saved my bacon a few times; for example, when I was shooting with studio flash in Manual mode and didn't notice that the shutter speed had been set to a (non-syncing) 1/320 second by mistake.

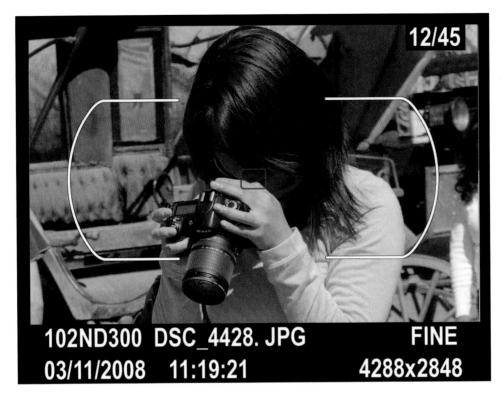

Figure 3.3
Use the Display mode menu entry to activate data display, like the focus point shown in this reviewed image.

A lot of the time, however, it's a better idea to *not* automatically review your shots in order to conserve battery power (the LCD is one of the major juice drains in the camera) or to speed up or simplify operations. For example, if you've just fired off a burst of eight shots at 6 fps during a football game, do you *really* need to have each and every frame display as the D300 clears its buffer and stores the photos on your memory card? This menu operation allows you to choose which mode to use:

- **On.** Image review is automatic after every shot is taken.

- **Off.** Images are displayed only when you press the Playback button. Nikon, in its wisdom, has made this the default setting.

After Delete

When you've deleted an image, you probably will want to do one of three things: have the D300 display the next picture (in the order shot); show the *previous* picture; or show either the next *or* previous picture, depending on which way you were scrolling during picture review. Your D300 lets you select which action to take:

- **Show next.** It's likely that you'll want to look at the picture taken after the one you just deleted, so Nikon makes this the default action.

- **Show previous.** I use this setting a lot when shooting sports with a continuous shooting setting. After the sequence is taken, I press the Playback button to see the last picture in the series and sometimes discover that the whole sequence missed the boat. I sometimes go ahead and press the Trash button twice to delete the offending image, then continue moving backwards to delete the five or six or eleven other pictures in the wasted sequence. You'll often find yourself with time on your hands at football games, and the urge to delete some stinker series to save your time reviewing back at the computer, while freeing up a little space on your card

- **Continue as before.** This setting actually makes a lot of sense: if you were scrolling backwards or forwards and deleting photos as you go, you might want to continue in the same direction weeding out bad shots. Use this setting to set your Nikon 300 to behave that way.

Rotate Tall

When you rotate the D300 to photograph vertical subjects in portrait, rather than landscape orientation, you probably don't want to view them tilted onto their sides later on. The D300 is way ahead of you. It has a directional sensor built in that can detect whether the camera was rotated when the photo was taken. You can apply this information in two different ways—to automatically rotate images when they are displayed on the camera monitor, or to automatically rotate images in your image editing application.

Rotation works only if you've set **Auto image rotation** to **On** in the Setup menu (I'll show you how to do that later in this chapter). Once you've done that, the D300 will embed information about orientation in the image file, and your image editor (such as Adobe Photoshop or Photoshop Elements) will rotate the images for you as the files are loaded.

This menu choice deals with a different use for that rotation information: whether the image should be rotated when displayed on the camera monitor. You might or might not want to do that. When Rotate Tall is activated, the Nikon D300 rotates pictures taken in vertical orientation on the LCD screen so you don't have to turn the camera to view them comfortably. However, this orientation also means that the longest dimension of the image is shown using the shortest dimension of the LCD, so the picture is reduced in size.

So, turn this feature **On** (as well as Auto image rotation in the Setup menu), if you'd rather not turn your camera to view vertical shots in their natural orientation, and don't mind the smaller image. Turn the feature **Off** if, as I do, you'd rather see a larger image and are willing to rotate the camera to do so.

Slide Show

The D300's Slide Show feature is a convenient way to review images in the current play-back folder one after another, without the need to manually switch between them. To activate, just choose **Start** from this entry in the Playback menu. If you like, you can choose **Frame interval** before commencing the show in order to select an interval of either 2, 3, 5, or 10 seconds between "slides."

During playback, you can press the **OK** button to pause the "slide show" (in case you want to examine an image more closely), or the up/down buttons to change the amount of information displayed on the screen with each image. For example, you might want to review a set of images and their histograms to judge the exposure of the group of pic-tures. You can press the left/right buttons to move back to a previous frame or jump ahead to the next one. Press the Menu button to exit the slide show and return to the menu, or the Playback button to exit the menu system totally. As always, while review-ing images you can tap the shutter release button if you want to remove everything from the screen and return to shooting mode.

At the end of the slide show, or when you've paused it, you'll be offered the choice of restarting the sequence, changing the frame interval, or exiting the slide show feature completely.

Print Set (DPOF)

The Nikon D300 supports the DPOF (Digital Print Order Format) that is now almost universally used by digital cameras to specify which images on your memory card should be printed, and the number of prints desired of each image. This information is recorded on the memory card and can be interpreted by a compatible printer when the camera is linked to the printer using the USB cable, or when the memory card is inserted into a card reader slot on the printer itself. Photo labs are also equipped to read this data and make prints when you supply your memory card to them.

When you choose this menu item, you're presented with a set of screens that looks very much like the Delete photos screens described earlier, only you're selecting pictures for printing rather than deleting them. The button sequences are slightly different, however:

1. Use the multi-selector cursor keys to scroll among the available images.

2. When you highlight an image you might want to print, press the Playback Zoom/Thumbnail button to temporarily enlarge that image so you can evaluate it further. When you release the button, the selection screen returns.

3. To mark an image for printing, press the Protect/Info button and hold it down while pressing the multi-selector up and down buttons to choose the number of prints you want, up to 99 per image. A printer icon and the number specified will appear overlaid on that image's thumbnail. (See Figure 3.4.)

Figure 3.4
Select images
for printing.

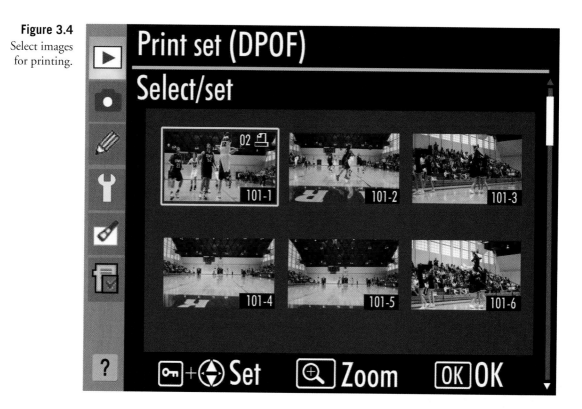

4. To unmark an image for printing, highlight and hold down the Protect/Info button while pressing the down button until the number of prints reaches zero. The printer icon will vanish.

5. When you've finished marking images to print, press **OK**.

6. A final screen will appear in which you can request a data imprint (shutter speed and aperture) or imprint date (the date the photos were taken). Use the up/down buttons to select one or both of these options, if desired, and press the left/right buttons to mark or unmark the check boxes. When a box is marked, the imprint information for that option will be included on *all* prints in the print order.

7. Scroll up to **Done** when finished, and press **OK** or the right cursor button.

Shooting Menu Options

The various direct setting buttons and dials on the D300, for image quality, autofocus mode, white balance, release mode, ISO sensitivity, metering mode, and flash, along with exposure compensation (EV) adjustments, are likely to be the most common settings changes you make, with changes during a particular session fairly common. You'll find some of these duplicated in the Shooting menu (see Figure 3.5), along with options that you access second-most frequently when you're using your Nikon D300, such as

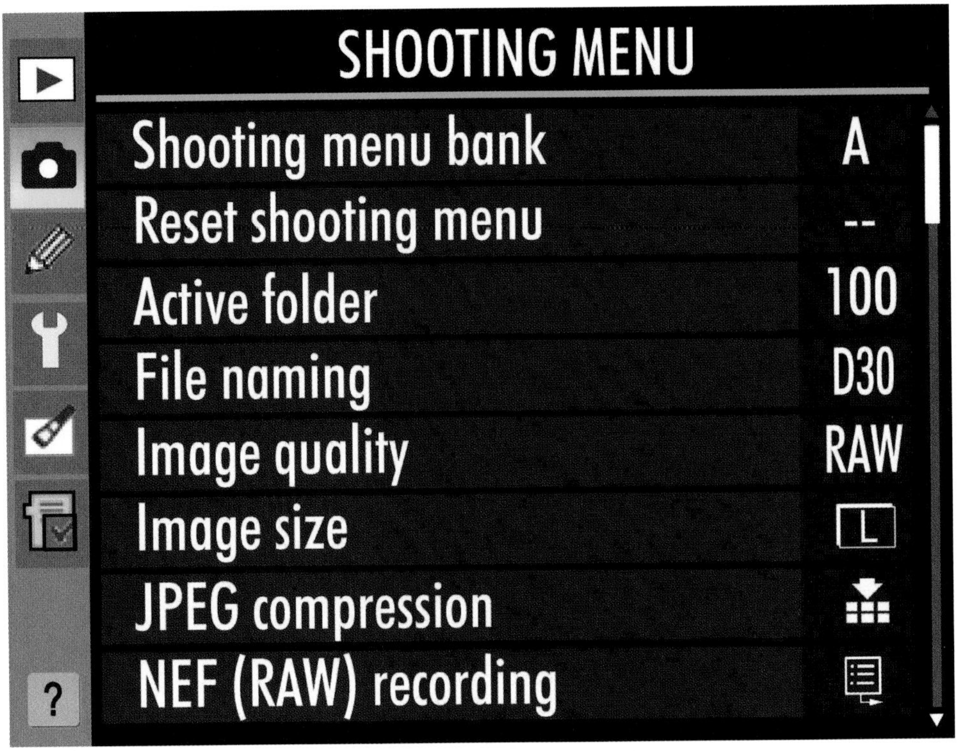

Figure 3.5
Common shooting settings can be changed in this menu.

specifying noise reduction for long exposures or high ISO settings. You might make such adjustments as you begin a shooting session, or when you move from one type of subject to another. Nikon makes accessing these changes very easy.

This section explains the options of the Shooting menu and how to use them. The options you'll find in these red-coded menus include:

- Shooting menu bank
- Reset shooting menu
- Active folder
- File naming
- Image quality
- Image size
- JPEG compression
- NEF (RAW) recording
- White balance
- Set Picture Control

- Manage Picture Control
- Color space
- Active D-Lighting
- Long exp. NR
- High ISO NR
- ISO sensitivity settings
- Live view
- Multiple exposure
- Interval timer shooting

Shooting Menu Bank

The Nikon D300's Shooting Menu Banks are four groups named, initially, A, B, C, and D that store specific collections of Shooting menu settings that you can recall at any time by switching to the bank containing the preferences you want to use. These banks are one of the primary reasons why the D300 is more versatile than Nikon's entry-level dSLRs, which lack the ability to change shooting specifications *en masse* using a simple menu command. The Shooting Menu Banks A, B, C, and D should not be confused with the four similarly named Custom Setting Menu Banks A, B, C, and D, which provide similar, but *separate* storage of your CSM settings. You can use your Shooting Menu Banks and Custom Setting Menu Banks in any combination.

The D300 uses Bank A by default. To switch to another bank:

- Press **Menu** and select the Shooting menu.
- Scroll to Shooting Menu Bank and press the multi-selector right button.
- Scroll to the bank you want to use with the multi-selector up/down buttons, and either press OK or press the multi-selector right button to confirm your choice.
- The Shooting menu appears again. Press the Menu button to back out of the menu, or simply tap the shutter release.

Any changes you make to one menu bank do not affect the other banks, so you can set one up with the settings you like to use in particular situations. For example, you could use Bank A for sports, Bank B for landscapes, Bank C for portraits, and Bank D for general shooting. Or, if you're a specialist, one bank could be dedicated to indoor sports (with high ISO settings and tungsten or fluorescent light balance) and another for outdoor sports (normal ISO and daylight white balance), with both specifying JPEG FINE capture only, because RAW or RAW+JPEG can slow down continuous shooting.

You could even tailor a D300's operation using parameters other than typical shooting sessions. For example, a wedding photography studio that shares a pool of Nikon D300 cameras among several photographers could have one bank named Peter, another named Paul, and a third dedicated to shooter Mary. The currently selected bank is indicated in the monochrome LCD status panel, and in the Shooting Information Display.

Customized names of up to 20 characters each can be used to replace the generic A, B, C, and D designations. You can use the standard Nikon text entry screen to enter the name you want to use. Now is a good time to master text entry, because you can use it to enter comments, rename folders, and perform other functions.

- Press **Menu** and select the Shooting menu.

- Scroll to Shooting Menu Bank and press the multi-selector right button.

- Scroll down to Rename and press the multi-selector right button to confirm your choice.

- Scroll down to the bank you want to rename, and press the multi-selector right button to confirm.

- Use the multi-selector navigational buttons to scroll around within the array of alphanumerics, as shown in Figure 3.6. Then, enter your text:

  - Press the multi-selector's center button to insert the highlighted character. The cursor will move one place to the right to accept the next character.

  - Hold down the Thumbnail/Zoom Out button and use the left/right buttons to move the cursor within the line of characters.

  - To remove a character you've already input, move the cursor to highlight that character, and then press the Trash button.

  - When you're finished entering text, press the OK button to confirm your entry, then press the left button twice to return to the Shooting menu, or just tap the shutter release to exit the menu system entirely.

As you work with menu banks, keep in mind that while changes you make to a particular bank don't affect the other banks, they are "sticky" within that bank once you've made them. That is, if you've set up a "sports" menu bank to use a high ISO sensitivity setting, and then during a session change the value to ISO 200, that's what you'll get the next time you access that menu bank (unless you remember to change it back to your preferred value at the end of the session).

Figure 3.6
Use the D300's
text entry
screen to name
your menu
banks.

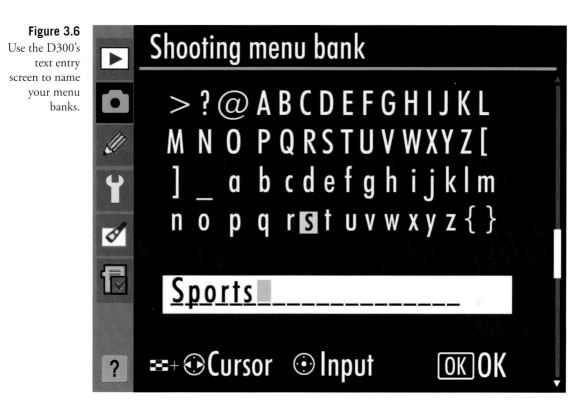

Reset Shooting Menu

Don't feel bad over being confused about what this menu item does. The Nikon D300 has, in effect, *three* different kinds of resets. This is one of them.

- **Shooting menu reset.** Use this option to reset the values of the currently selected shooting menu bank *except for image quality, image size, white balance, and ISO sensitivity* to their default values. When you select this menu item, your choices are **Yes** and **No**. Note that the defaults are restored *only* for the menu bank that is active, and not any of the other three shooting menu banks, except for multiple exposure and interval timer shooting settings, which are reset for all four banks. A reset has no effect on the four settings noted above.

- **Custom menu settings reset.** This option, which I'll describe in Chapter 4, is used to reset any of the four Custom Settings menu banks. It has no effect on camera settings or shooting menu banks.

- **Two-button reset.** The Nikon D300's two-button reset (holding down the Exposure Value and QUAL buttons simultaneously for more than two seconds) will *not* reset your shooting menu banks or Custom Settings menu banks. This particular reset is for focus point, exposure mode, flexible program, exposure/flash compensation, autoexposure hold, bracketing, flash mode, flash value lock, and multiple exposure settings.

Table 3.1 shows the default values that are set using Reset shooting menu option. If you don't know what some of these settings are, I'll explain them later in this section.

Table 3.1 Default Shooting Menu values			
Function	**Value**	**Function**	**Value**
File Naming	*DSC*	Active D-Lighting	*Off*
Image Quality	*JPEG Normal*	Long exp. NR	*Off*
Image Size	*Large*	High ISO NR	*Normal*
JPEG Compression	*Size priority*	ISO sensitivity	
NEF (RAW Recording)		Sensitivity	*200*
Type	*Lossless compressed*	Auto control	*Off*
Bit Depth	*12-bit*	Live View	
White Balance	*Auto*	Live View mode	*Hand held*
Fine tuning	*Off*	Release Mode	*Single frame*
Color temperature	*5,000K*	Multiple exposure	*Reset*
Set Picture Control	*Standard*	Interval timer shooting	*Reset*
Color Space	*sRGB*	Color gamut	*sRGB*

Active Folder

If you want to store images in a folder other than the one created and selected by the Nikon D300, you can switch among available folders on your Compact Flash card, or create your own folder. Remember that any folders you create will be deleted when you reformat your memory card.

To change the currently active folder:

■ Choose Active folder in the Shooting menu.

■ Scroll down to Select folder and press the multi-selector right button.

■ From among the available folders shown, scroll to the one that you want to become active for image storage and playback. (Handy when displaying slide shows.)

■ Press the OK button to confirm your choice, or press the multi-selector right button to return to the Shooting menu.

Why create your own folders? Perhaps you're traveling and have a high-capacity memory card and want to store the images for each day (or for each city that you visit) in a separate folder. Maybe you'd like to separate those wedding photos you snapped at the ceremony from those taken at the reception. As I mentioned earlier, the Nikon D300 automatically creates a folder on a newly-formatted memory card with a name like 100ND300, and when it fills with 999 images, it will automatically create a new folder with a number incremented by one (such as 101ND300). To create your own folder:

- Choose Active folder in the Shooting menu.

- Scroll down to New folder number and press the multi-selector right button.

- A three-number value, such as **101**, appears. Use the left/right multi-selector buttons to change from one column to the next to modify the hundreds, tens, or single digits from 100 up to 999. Use the up/down multi-selector buttons to increment or decrement the values in the currently selected column.

- Press **OK** when finished to create and activate the new folder.

File Naming

The D300, like other cameras in the Nikon product line, automatically applies a name like _DSC0001.jpg or DSC_0001.nef to your image files as they are created. You can use this menu option to change the names applied to your photos—but only within certain strict limitations. In practice, you can change only three of the eight characters, the *DSC* portion of the file name. The other five are mandated either by the Design Rule for Camera File System (DCF) specification that all digital camera makers adhere to or to industry conventions.

DCF limits file names created by conforming digital cameras to a maximum of eight characters, plus a three-character extension (such as .jpg, .tif, .nef) that represents the file format of the image. The eight-plus-three (usually called 8.3) length limitation dates back to an evil and frustrating computer operating system that we older photographers would like to forget (its initials are D.O.S), but which, unhappily, lives on as the wraith of a file naming convention.

Of the eight available characters, four are used to represent, in a general sense, the type of camera used to create the image. By convention, one of those characters is an underline, placed in the first position (as in _DSCxxxx.xxx) when the image uses the Adobe RGB color space (more on color spaces later), and in the fourth position (as in DSC_xxxx.xxx) for sRGB and RAW (NEF) files. That leaves just three characters for the manufacturer (and you) to use. Nikon, Sony, and some other vendors use DSC (which may or may not stand for Digital Still Camera, depending on who you ask), while Canon prefers IMG. The remaining four characters are used for numbers from 0000 to 9999, which is why your D300 "rolls over" to DSC_0000 again when the 9999 number limitation is reached.

When you select File Naming in the Shooting menu, you'll be shown the current settings for both sRGB (and RAW) and Adobe RGB. Press the right multi-selector button, and you'll be taken to the (mostly) standard Nikon text entry screen (go back to Figure 3.6 if you've forgotten what it looks like) and allowed to change the DSC value to something else. In this version of the text entry screen, however, only the numbers from 0 to 9 and characters A-Z are available; the filename cannot contain other characters. As always, press the OK button to confirm your new setting.

Because the default DSC characters don't tell you much, don't hesitate to change them to something else. I own, or used to own, a whole collection of Nikon digital cameras, so I've used D40_, D50_, D70_, and D80_ as my templates over the years. My D2X and D200 received D2X_ and D20_ assignments to help me differentiate between pictures taken with each camera. When the D3 and D300 cameras were introduced, I used D3X_ and D30_, even though the D3 has no "X" in its model name.

If you don't need to differentiate between different camera models, you can change the three characters to anything else that suits your purposes, including your initials (DDB_ or JFK_ for example) or even customize for particular shooting sessions (EUR_, GER_, FRA_, and JAP_ when taking vacation trips). You can also use the file name flexibility to partially overcome the 9999 numbering limitation. You could, for example, use the template D31_ to represent the first 10,000 pictures you take with your D300, and then D32_ for the next 10,000, and D33_ for the 10,000 after that.

That's assuming that you don't rename your image files in your computer. In a way, file naming verges on a moot consideration, because, they apply *only* to the images as they exist in your camera. After (or during) transfer to your computer you can change the names to anything you want, completely disregarding the 8.3 limitations (although it's a good idea to retain the default extensions). If you shot an image file named DSC_4832.jpg in your camera, you could change it to Paris_EiffelTower_32.jpg later on. Indeed, virtually all photo transfer programs, including Nikon Transfer and Photoshop Elements Transfer, allow you to specify a template and rename your photos as they are moved or copied to your computer from your camera or memory card.

I usually don't go to that bother (I generally don't use transfer software; I just drag and drop images from my memory card to folders I have set up), but renaming can be useful for those willing to take the time to do it.

Image Quality

As I noted in Chapter 2, you can choose the image quality settings used by the D300 to store its files. The quickest way to do that is to hold down the QUAL button on the top-left side of the camera and spin the main command dial until the quality setting you want is shown in the topside monochrome status LCD. You can also use this menu option to make the quality settings using the bigger, brighter three-inch color LCD.

You might want to do that when the D300 is mounted on a tripod and the top panel LCD is above eyelevel, or you simply might prefer the color LCD's display, which can be easier to read. You have two choices to make:

■ **JPEG compression.** To reduce the size of your image files and allow more photos to be stored on a given Compact Flash card, the D300 uses JPEG compression to squeeze the images down to a smaller size. This compacting reduces the image quality a little, so you're offered your choice of Fine (a 1:4 reduction), Normal (1:8 reduction), and Basic (1:16) compression. You can see an exaggerated version of the effects of JPEG compression in Figure 3.7. There is a further tweak you can make, specifying whether JPEG compression should be optimized for the smallest possible image size at a given compression level, or whether you'd prefer to sacrifice some compression for optimal quality. You won't find those options in this menu entry; instead, use the JPEG Compression menu item, described later in this section.

Figure 3.7
At low levels of JPEG compression the image looks sharp even when you enlarge it enough to see the actual pixels (top); when using extreme JPEG compression (bottom) an image obviously loses quality.

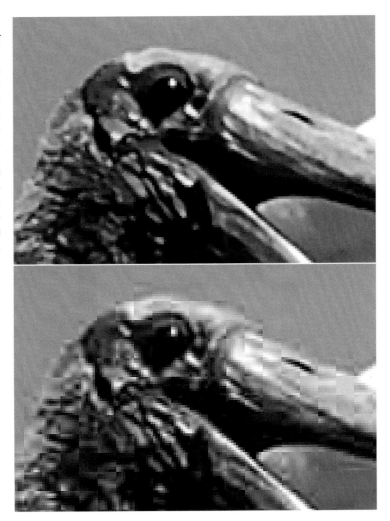

- **JPEG, RAW, or both.** You can elect to store only JPEG versions of the images you shoot, or you can save your photos as RAW files, which consume more than twice as much space on your memory card. Or, you can store both at once as you shoot. Many photographers elect to save *both* JPEG and a RAW, so they'll have a JPEG version that might be usable as-is, as well as the original "digital negative" RAW file in case they want to do some processing of the image later. You'll end up with two different versions of the same file: one with a .jpg extension, and one with the .nef extension that signifies a Nikon RAW file.

Tip

The D300 always saves a full resolution 4288 × 2848 pixel RAW image even if you choose a smaller image size (resolution) for the JPEG version (such as Medium (M) or Small (S)).

To choose the combination you want, access the Shooting menu, scroll to **Image quality**, and select it. A screen similar to the one shown in Figure 3.8 will appear. Scroll to highlight the setting you want, and either press **OK** or push the multi-selector right button to confirm your selection.

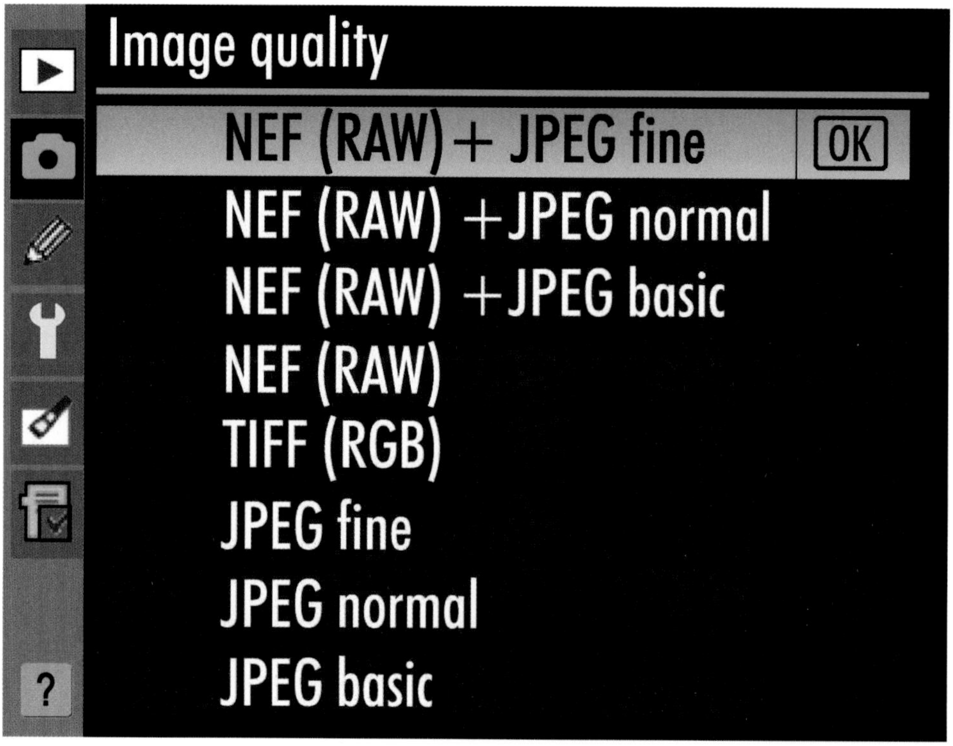

Image quality

- NEF (RAW) + JPEG fine [OK]
- NEF (RAW) +JPEG normal
- NEF (RAW) +JPEG basic
- NEF (RAW)
- TIFF (RGB)
- JPEG fine
- JPEG normal
- JPEG basic

Figure 3.8
You can choose RAW, JPEG, RAW+JPEG, or TIFF formats here.

In practice, you'll probably use the JPEG Fine, RAW+JPEG Fine selections most often. Why so many choices, then? There are some limited advantages to using the JPEG Normal and JPEG Basic settings, either at full resolution (Large) or when using the Medium and Small resolution settings. Settings that are less than max allow stretching the capacity of your Compact Flash card so you can shoehorn quite a few more pictures onto a single memory card. That can come in useful when on vacation and you're running out of storage, or when you're shooting non-critical work that doesn't require 12 megapixels of resolution (such as photos taken for real estate listings, web page display, photo ID cards, or similar applications). Some photographers like to record RAW+JPEG Normal so they'll have a moderate quality JPEG file for review only and no intention of using for editing purposes, while retaining access to the original RAW file for serious editing.

For most work, using lower resolution and extra compression is false economy. You never know when you might actually need that extra bit of picture detail. Your best bet is to have enough memory cards to handle all the shooting you want to do until you have the chance to transfer your photos to your computer or a personal storage device.

However, reduced image quality can sometimes be beneficial if you're shooting sequences of photos rapidly, as the D300 is able to hold more of them in its internal memory buffer before transferring to the Compact Flash card. Still, for most sports and other applications, you'd probably rather have better, sharper pictures than longer periods of continuous shooting. Do you really need 20 or 30 shots of a pass reception in a football game, or a dozen or two slightly different versions of your local basketball star driving in for a lay-up?

JPEG vs. RAW

You'll sometimes be told that RAW files are the "unprocessed" image information your camera produces, before it's been modified. That's nonsense. RAW files are no more unprocessed than your camera film is after it's been through the chemicals to produce a negative or transparency. A lot can happen in the developer that can affect the quality of a film image—positively and negatively—and, similarly, your digital image undergoes a significant amount of processing before it is saved as a RAW file. Nikon even applies a name (EXPEED) to the digital image processing (DIP) chip used to perform this magic.

A RAW file is more similar to a film camera's processed negative. It contains all the information, captured in 12-bit or 14-bit channels per color (and stored in a 16-bit space), with no sharpening, no application of any special filters or other settings you might have specified when you took the picture. Those settings are *stored* with the RAW file so they can be applied when the image is converted to a form compatible with your favorite image editor. However, using RAW conversion software such as Adobe Camera Raw or

Nikon Capture NX, you can override those settings and apply settings of your own. You can select essentially the same changes there that you might have specified in your camera's picture-taking options.

RAW exists because sometimes we want to have access to all the information captured by the camera, before the camera's internal logic has processed it and converted the image to a standard file format. RAW doesn't save as much space as JPEG. What it does do is preserve all the information captured by your camera after it's been converted from analog to digital form.

So, why don't we always use RAW? Some photographers avoid using Nikon's RAW NEF files on the misguided conviction that they don't want to spend time in post-processing, forgetting that, if the camera settings you would have used for JPEG are correct, each RAW image's default attributes will use those settings and the RAW image will not need much manipulation. Post-processing in such cases is *optional*, and overwhelmingly helpful when an image needs to be fine-tuned.

Although some photographers do save *only* in RAW format, it's more common (and frequently more convenient) to use RAW plus one of the JPEG options, or, if you're confident about your settings, just shoot JPEG and eschew RAW altogether. In some situations, working with a RAW file can slow you down a little. RAW images take longer to store on the Compact Flash card, and must be converted from RAW to a format your image editor can handle, whether you elect to go with the default settings in force when the picture was taken, or make minor adjustments to the settings you specified in the camera.

As a result, those who depend on speedy access to images or who shoot large numbers of photos at once may prefer JPEG over RAW. Wedding photographers, for example, might expose several thousand photos during a bridal affair and offer hundreds to clients as electronic proofs for inclusion in an album. Wedding shooters take the time to make sure that their in-camera settings are correct, minimizing the need to post-process photos after the event. Given that their JPEGs are so good, there is little need to get bogged down shooting RAW.

Sports photographers also eschew RAW files. I visited a local Division III college one sunny September afternoon (armed with my Nikon D200, because the D300 had not been released yet). I covered the first half of a football game, trotted down a hill to shoot a women's soccer match later that afternoon, and ended up in the adjacent field house shooting a volleyball invitational tournament an hour later. I managed to shoot 1,920 photos, most of them at a 5 fps clip, in about four hours. I certainly didn't have any plans to do post-processing on very many of those shots, and firing the D200 at its maximum frame rate didn't allow RAW shooting, so carefully exposed and precisely focused JPEG images were my file format of choice that day.

JPEG was invented as a more compact file format that can store most of the information in a digital image, but in a much smaller size. JPEG predates most digital SLRs and was initially used to squeeze down files for transmission over slow dial-up connections. Even if you were using an early dSLR with 1.3 megapixel files for news photography, you didn't want to send them back to the office over a modem at 1,200 bps.

But, as I noted, JPEG provides smaller files by compressing the information in a way that loses some image data. JPEG remains a viable alternative because it offers several different quality levels. At the highest quality Fine level, you might not be able to tell the difference between the original RAW file and the JPEG version, even though a lossless compressed, 14-bit RAW file (I'll explain the bit-business later in this chapter) occupies, by Nikon's estimate, 16.7MB on your memory card, while the Fine JPEG takes up only 5.8MB of space. You've squeezed the image by more than 70 percent without losing much visual information at all. If you don't mind losing some quality, you can use more aggressive Normal compression with JPEG to cut the size in half again, to 2.9MB.

In my case, I shoot virtually everything at RAW+JPEG Fine. Most of the time, I'm not concerned about filling up my memory cards, as I usually have a minimum of three to five 8GB Compact Flash cards with me. If I know I may fill up all those cards, I have a tiny battery-operated personal storage device that can copy an 8GB card in about 15 minutes. As I mentioned earlier, when shooting sports I'll shift to JPEG FINE (with no RAW file) to squeeze a little extra speed out of my camera's continuous shooting mode, and to reduce the need to wade through eight-photo bursts taken in RAW format. On the other hand, on my last trip to Europe, I took only RAW (instead of my customary RAW+JPEG Fine) photos to fit more images onto my 60GB personal storage device, shown in Figure 3.9, as I planned on doing at least some post-processing on many of the images for a travel book I was working on.

You may notice that I am not going into the TIFF option in any detail. To oversimplify things, for most of us, TIFF provides the worst of both worlds: it has heftier storage space requirements than the "worst" case RAW file (25.3 megabytes for NEF, uncompressed, 14-bit files, and 36.5 MB for full-resolution TIFF) and the same relatively limited image editing flexibility as JPEG files. Those who absolutely require TIFF files don't mind waiting up to four or five seconds for a single image to be stored to the Compact Flash card, and who have prodigious skills at getting their in-camera settings correct the first time, will want to use TIFF. The main reason to use TIFF is because of its ability to include an embedded ICC color profile. The format itself doesn't provide much in the way of perceptible quality improvement, and if the image requires extensive editing, it may actually limit the quality of the photo.

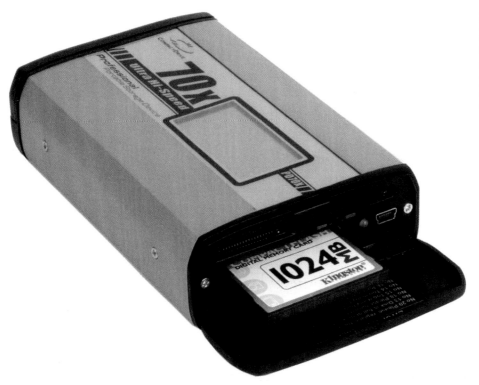

Figure 3.9
If storage space is a concern, consider a portable storage device like this one.

HIDDEN JPEGS

You may not be aware that your RAW file contains an embedded JPEG file, hidden inside in the JPEG Basic format. It's used to provide thumbnail previews of JPEG files, which is why you may notice an interesting phenomenon when loading a RAW image into a program like Nikon Capture NX or Adobe Lightroom. When the software first starts interpreting the RAW image, it may immediately display this hidden JPEG view which has, as you might expect, all the settings applied that you dialed into the camera. Then, as it finishes loading the RAW file, the application (Lightroom in particular) uses its own intelligence to fine-tune the image and display what it thinks is a decent version of the image, replacing the embedded JPEG. That's why you may see complaints that Lightroom or another program is behaving oddly: the initial embedded JPEG may look better than the final version, so it looks as if the application is degrading the image quality as the file loads. Of course, in all cases, once the RAW file is available, you can make your own changes to optimize it to your taste.

There is a second use for these hidden JPEG files. If you shoot RAW without creating JPEG files and later decide you want a JPEG version, there are dozens of utility programs that will extract the embedded JPEG and save it as a separate file. (Google "JPEG extractor" to locate a freeware program that will perform this step for your Mac, PC, or other computer.)

Image Size

The next menu command in the Shooting menu lets you select the resolution, or number of pixels captured as you shoot with your Nikon D300. Your choices range from Large (L—4288 × 2848 pixels, 12.2 megapixels), Medium (M—3216 × 2136 pixels, 6.9 megapixels), and Small (S—2144 × 1424 pixels, 3.1 megapixels). You can select image sizes by holding down the QUAL button on the top-left panel of the D300, while spinning the sub-command dial until the resolution you want appears on the monochrome LCD status screen. Or, you can use this menu to perform the task (usually because you find the color LCD easier to view under the particular circumstances). There are no additional options available from the Image size menu screen.

JPEG Compression

This menu entry is a simple one, offering you the choice of specifying either **Size priority** (variable compression) or **Optimal quality** (minimal compression) when the D300 creates JPEG files. I'll explain image compression in more detail in the next section.

- **Size priority.** When this option is selected, the D300 will create files that are fairly uniformly sized at about 5.8MB for a JPEG Fine image. Because some photos have content that is more easily compressible (for example, plain areas of sky can be squeezed down more than areas filled with detail), to maintain the standard file size the camera must apply more compression to some images, and less to others. As a result, there may be a barely noticable loss of detail in the more heavily compressed images. The uniform file size also means that the D300's buffer will hold the maximum number of shots during continuous shooting, allowing you to shoot longer sequences without the need to pause and wait for some images to be written to the Compact Flash card.

- **Optimal quality.** Choose this option if you want to maintain the best image quality possible at a particular JPEG setting (Fine, Normal, or Basic) and don't care if the file size varies. Because the D300 will use only the minimum amount of compression required at each JPEG setting, file size will vary depending on scene content, and your buffer may hold fewer images during continuous shooting.

NEF (RAW) Recording

You can choose the type (amount) of compression applied to NEF (RAW) files as they are stored on your Compact Flash card, and whether the images are stored using 12-bit or 14-bit depth. The default values for type (Lossless compressed) and color depth (12-bit) work best for most situations, but there are times when you might want to use one of the other choices.

Compression is a mathematical technique for reducing the size of a collection of information (such as an image; but other types of data or even programs can be compressed, too) in order to reduce the storage requirements and/or time required to transmit or transfer the information. Some compression algorithms arrange strings of bits that are most frequently used into a table, so that a binary number like, say, 1001011011100111 (16 digits long) doesn't have to be stored as two eight-bit bytes every time it appears in the image file. Instead, a smaller number that points to that position in the table can be used. The more times the pointer is used rather than the full number, the more space is saved in the file. Such a compression scheme can be used to reproduce exactly the original string of numbers, and so is called *lossless* compression.

Other types of compression are more aggressive and actually discard some of the information deemed to be redundant from a visual standpoint, so that, theoretically, you won't *notice* that details are missing, and the file can be made even more compact. The Nikon D300's RAW storage routines can use this kind of size reduction, which is called *lossy* compression, to reduce file size by up to about half with very little effect on image quality. JPEG compression can be even more enthusiastic, resulting in images that are 15X smaller (or more) and which display noticeable loss of image quality.

Under Type in the NEF (RAW) recording menu, you can select from:

- **Lossless compressed.** This is the default setting, not available with the earlier Nikon D200, that uses what you might think of as reversible algorithms that discard no image information, so that the image can be compressed from 20-40 percent for a significantly smaller file size. Typically, you'll get up to 400 RAW images on a single 8GB Compact Flash card at this setting. The squeezed file can always be restored to its original size precisely, with no effect on image quality.

- **Compressed.** Use this setting if you want to store more images on your Compact Flash card and are willing to accept a tiny potential loss in image quality (I've never been able to detect any effect at all). The D300 can achieve from 40-55 percent compression with this option, giving you 550 or more RAW exposures on an 8GB Compact Flash card. It uses a two-step process, first grouping some very similar tonal values in the mid-tone and lighter areas of the image together, and then storing each group as a single value, followed by a lossless compression scheme that is applied to the dark tones, further reducing the file size. The process does a good job of preserving tones in shadow areas of an image, with only small losses in the midtone and lighter areas. The differences may show up only if you perform certain types of extensive post-processing on an image, such as image sharpening or some tonal corrections. This setting and Uncompressed were the sole options available with the Nikon D200.

■ **Uncompressed.** At this setting, RAW images are not compressed at all, giving you 350-400 RAW images on an 8GB Compact Flash card, and also increasing the time needed to transfer these slightly larger files to your memory card. You might want to use this option to ensure the optimum image quality for your RAW shots. But, in truth, I've *really* never been able to tell the difference between uncompressed and lossless compressed photos—except for the slightly increased time (perhaps 5–10 percent) needed to save uncompressed images to the memory card.

The Bit Depth setting is another option that looks good on paper but, in the real world, is less useful than you might think. For most applications, the default value that produces 12-bit image files is probably your best choice.

As you may know, bit depth is a way of measuring the amount of color data that an image file can contain. What we call "24-bit color" actually consists of three channels of information—red, green, and blue—with one eight-bit byte assigned to each channel, so a 24-bit image contains three 8-bit channels (each with 256 different shades of red, green, or blue). A 24-bit color image can contain up to 16.8 million different colors (256 × 256 × 256; you do the math). Because each of the red, green, and blue channels always is stored using the same number of bits, it's become the custom to refer only to the channel bit depth to describe the amount of color information that can be collected.

So, when we're talking about 12-bit color, what we really mean are three 12-bit RGB channels, each capable of recording colors from 000000000000 to 111111111111 hues in a particular channel (in binary), or 4096 colors per channel (decimal) and a total of 68,719,476,736 (68.7 billion) different hues. By comparison, 14-bit color offers 16,384 colors per channel and a total of 4,398,046,511,104 (4.4 trillion) colors.

The advantage of having such a humongous number of colors for an image that will, in the end, be boiled down to 16.8 million hues in Photoshop or another image editor is that, to simplify things a little, there is a better chance that the mere millions of colors you end up with have a better chance of being the *right* colors to accurately represent the image. For example, if there are subtle differences in the colors of a certain range of tones that represent only, say, 10 percent of a channel's colors, there would be only 26 colors to choose from in an 8-bit channel, but 410 colors in a 12-bit channel, and a whopping 1638 colors in a 14-bit channel. The larger number of colors improves the odds of ending up with accurate hues.

It's not quite that simple, of course, because bit depth also improves the chances of having the right number of colors to choose from after the inevitable loss of some information due to noise and other factors. But in the real world, the difference between 26 colors and 410 colors is significant (which is why digital cameras always capture at least 12 bits per channel), and the difference between 12-bits and 14-bits (410 and 1638 colors, respectively in our example) is less significant. Because there is a penalty in terms of file size and the amount of time needed to process the image as it is recorded to your

Compact Flash, 14-bits-per-channel is usually not your best option. Your two choices look like this:

- **12-bit.** This is the default bit depth for the Nikon D300. Images are recorded at 12-bits per channel in the RAW file, and end up with 12 bits of information per channel that is translated during conversion for your image editor either into 12 bits within a 16-bits-per-channel space or interpreted down to 8 bits per channel.

- **14-bit.** At this setting, the D300 grabs 16,384 colors per channel instead of 4096, ending up as 14 bits in a 16 channel space or reduced to 256 colors by the RAW conversion software that translates the image for your image editor. You'll find that such 14 bit files end up almost one-third larger than 12-bit files, and that your camera's continuous shooting rate falls to 2.5 frames per second (which alone is a good argument for not using the 14-bit setting any time you may need to shoot bursts of images).

White Balance

This menu entry, the first on the second "page" of shooting menu entries (see Figure 3.10) allows you to choose one of the white balance values from among Auto, incandescent, seven varieties of fluorescent illumination, direct sunlight, flash, cloudy, shade, a specific color temperature of your choice, or a preset value taken from an existing photograph, or a measurement you make. Some of the settings you make here can be duplicated using the WB button on the camera's top-left panel and main and sub-command dials, but the menus offer even more choices, as you'll see. Your white balance settings can have a significant impact on the color rendition of your images, as you can see in Figure 3.11.

In this section I'm going to describe only the menu commands at your disposal for setting white balance. To learn more about the theory behind why and when you should make white balance adjustments, check out the more complete description in Chapter 6.

BIG CHANGES

There have been some significant changes in the way white balance is set on the Nikon D300 (and its contemporary, the Nikon D3) compared to the D200 (and even the D2xs), so if you've used earlier cameras you'll want to read this section carefully. Previous mid- and pro-level cameras in the Nikon line offered similar pre-defined white balance settings, which you could fine-tune by pressing the multi-selector right button and then adjusting plus/minus three "levels," which are actually values corresponding to 10 *mireds* or (*micro reciprocal degrees*; more on that measurement in Chapter 6). With earlier cameras, pressing the up button dialed in a slightly cooler color temperature while the down button dialed in a warmer color temperature. No more. The D300/D3 gives you a *lot* more flexibility than that, as you'll learn from reading on.

Figure 3.10
The second "page" of the Shooting menu looks like this.

SHOOTING MENU

White balance	☀
Set Picture Control	VI
Manage Picture Control	--
Color space	Adobe
Active D-Lighting	OFF
Long exp. NR	OFF
High ISO NR	NORM
ISO sensitivity settings	

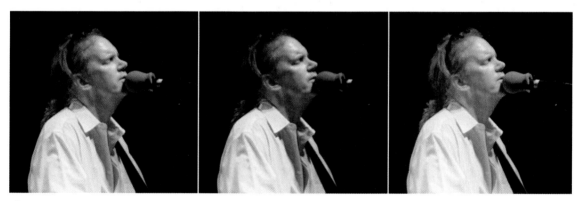

Figure 3.11 Adjusting color temperature can provide different results of the same subject at settings of 3,400K (left), 5,000K (middle), and 2,800K (right).

When you select the White Balance entry on the Shooting menu, you'll see an array of choices like those shown in Figure 3.12. (One additional choice, **PRE Preset Manual** is not visible until you scroll down to it.) If you choose Fluorescent, you'll be taken to another screen that presents seven different types of lamps, from sodium-vapor through warm-white fluorescent down to high temperature mercury-vapor. If you know the exact type of non-incandescent lighting being used, you can select it, or settle on a likely compromise.

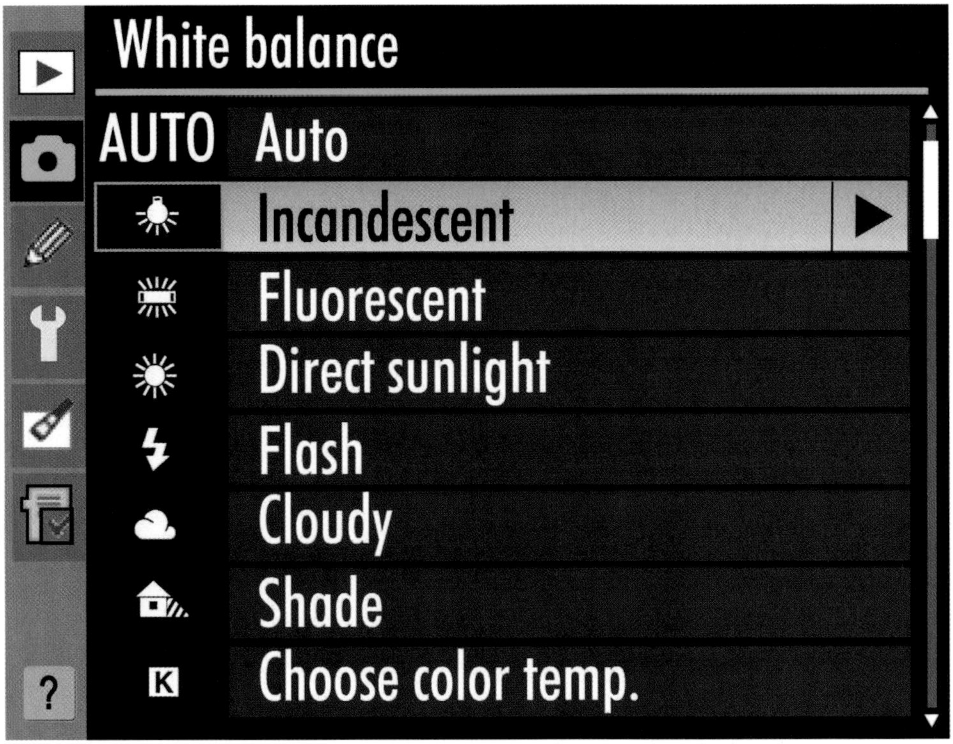

Figure 3.12
The White Balance menu has predefined values, plus the option of setting color temperature and presets you measure yourself.

The **Choose color temp.** selection allows you to select from an array of color temperatures in degrees Kelvin (more on this in Chapter 6) from 2,500K to 10,000K, and then further fine-tune the color bias using the fine-tuning feature described below. Select **Preset Manual** to record or recall custom white balance settings suitable for environments with unusual lighting or mixed lighting, as described later in this section.

For all other settings (Auto, incandescent, direct sunlight, flash, cloudy, or shade), highlight the white balance option you want, then press the multi-selector right button (or press OK) to view the fine-tuning screen shown in Figure 3.13 (and which uses the incandescent setting as an example). The screen shows a grid with two axes, a blue/amber axis extending left/right, and a green/magenta axis extending up and down the grid. By default, the grid's cursor is positioned in the middle, and a readout to the right of the

Figure 3.13
Specific white balance settings can be fine-tuned by changing their bias in the amber/blue, magenta/green directions—or along both axes simultaneously.

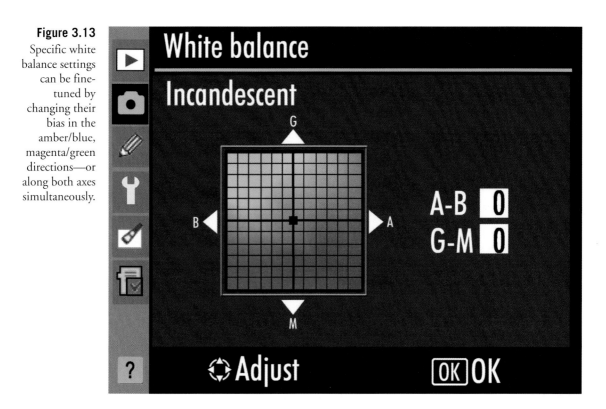

grid shows the cursor's coordinates on the A-B axis (yes, I know the display has the end points reversed) and G-M axis at 0,0.

You can use the multi-selector's up/down and right/left buttons to move the cursor to any coordinate in the grid, thereby biasing the white balance in the direction(s) you choose. The amber-blue axis makes the image warmer or colder (but not actually yellow or blue). Similarly, the green/magenta axis preserves all the colors in the original image, but gives them a tinge biased toward green or magenta. Each increment equals about five mired units, but you should know that mired values aren't linear; five mireds at 2,500K produces a much stronger effect than five mireds at 6,000K. If you really want to fine-tune your color balance, you're better off experimenting and evaluating the results of a particular change.

When you've fine-tuned white balance, either using the Shooting menu options or the WB button, left/right triangles appear in the white balance section of the monochrome LCD at lower right to remind you that this tweaking has taken place.

Using Preset Manual White Balance

If automatic white balance or one of the predefined settings available aren't suitable, you can set a custom white balance using the Preset Manual menu option. You can apply the white balance from a scene, either by shooting a new picture on the spot and using the resulting white balance (**Direct measurement**), or using an image you have already shot (**Copy from existing photograph**). To perform direct measurement from your current scene using a reference object (preferably a neutral gray or white object), follow these steps:

1. Place the neutral reference under the lighting you want to measure.

2. Hold down the WB button on the top-left panel of the camera and rotate the main command dial until you see PRE displayed in the monochrome LCD.

3. Release the WB button for a moment, then press and hold it again until the PRE icon on the monochrome LCD begins a flashing cycle of about six seconds.

4. While the PRE icon is flashing, take a picture of the reference object. The white balance will be stored in a preset menu slot numbered d-0, as shown in Figure 3.14. No photo is actually taken, so the preset slot appears to be blank.

5. If the camera successfully measured white balance, **Good** will flash on the monochrome LCD for about six seconds, and **Gd** will appear in the bottom line of the viewfinder. Otherwise, you'll see no **Gd** on the LCD and viewfinder. White balance measurement can fail when the reference object is too brightly or poorly illuminated. In that case, repeat steps 2-5 until the measurement is successful.

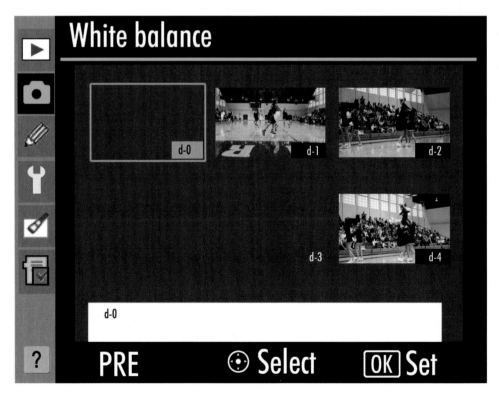

Figure 3.14
When you capture a scene's white balance, it will be stored in slot d-0.

The preset value you've captured will remain in slot d-0 until you replace that white balance with a new captured value. It can be summoned at any time (press the WB button on the top left of the camera and dial it in by rotating the sub-command dial until d-0 is displayed on the monochrome LCD). If you want to preserve the captured white balance, it can be copied to one of four additional slots, numbered d-1 to d-4. You can also use those four slots to store white balance information from a picture you've already taken, using the **Copy from existing photograph** option, as described next:

1. Choose **Preset Manual** from the White Balance menu.

2. A screen of thumbnails appears, showing the additional four "slots" numbered d-1 to d4, which you can use to store information from slot d-0, or from images that contain the white balance information you want to apply. Use the multi-selector buttons to highlight one of the four thumbnail slots, and press the multi-selector center button.

3. The next screen that appears (see Figure 3.15) has four options: **Set**, **Edit Comment**, **Select image**, and **Copy d-0**.

   ■ Choose **Set** to fine-tune the amber/blue/magenta/green white balance of an image already stored in d-0 or one of the four user slots.

   ■ Choose **Edit Comment** to add or change the comment applied to d-0 to d-4. The comment can be used as a label to better identify the white balance information in the slot, with terms like Gymnasium Daytime or Rumpus Room. (The standard D300 Edit Comment screen, as in Figure 3.6, appears.)

   ■ Choose **Select Image** to view the D300's standard image selection screen (see Figure 3.4 again) and highlight and choose the existing image slot you want to use. Press the multi-selector center button to confirm your choice and copy the white balance of the selected image to the slot you selected in Step 2.

   ■ Choose **Copy d-0** to copy the white balance setting currently stored in slot d-0 to the slot you selected in Step 2. Use this to preserve a captured white balance setting, freeing d-0 for a new capture.

4. Press **OK** to confirm your white balance setting.

A WHITE BALANCE LIBRARY

Consider dedicating a low-capacity Compact Flash card to stow a selection of images taken under a variety of lighting conditions. If you want to "recycle" one of the color temperatures you've stored, insert the card and load one of those images into your choice of preset slots d-1 to d-4, as described above.

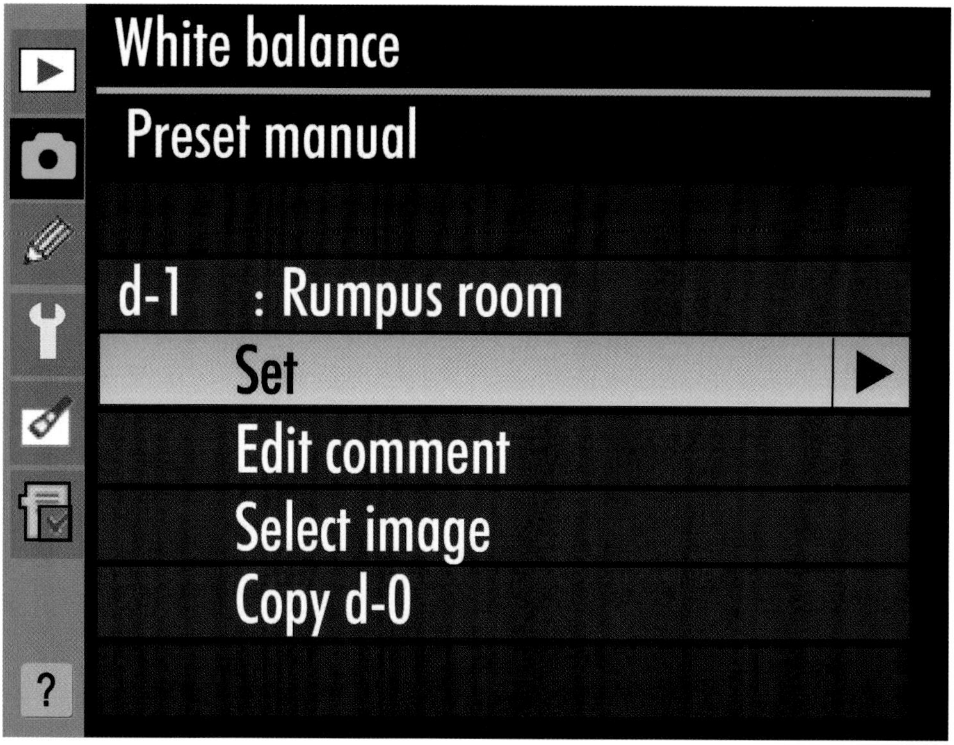

Figure 3.15
The Preset Manual screen lets you fine-tune preset white balance settings, label them with a comment, select an image to use as a white balance reference, and copy captured settings.

Set Picture Control

Nikon's Picture Control styles are a major improvement over the Optimize Image feature found in the D200 and other cameras from Nikon when it comes to choosing your own sharpness, contrast, color saturation, and hue settings applied to your images. If you have used a camera with the Optimize Image option, you'll recall that it offered five fixed settings to choose from (Normal, Softer, Vivid, More Vivid, Portrait), plus Black-and-White, and a single Custom entry that allowed you to specify sharpening, tone compensation (contrast), color mode, saturation, and hue. Yes, that's right—you got *one* Custom Settings slot, and although you could create your own custom settings on your computer and upload them to the camera, the five predefined settings and single set of custom parameters was quite a limitation.

Happily, the Nikon D300 sweeps those limitations aside with the Picture Control styles. There are only four pre-defined styles offered, which Nikon calls Original Picture Controls: Standard, Neutral, Vivid, and Monochrome. However, you can *edit* the settings of any of those styles so they better suit your taste. But that's only the beginning, the D300 also offers *nine* (count 'em) user-definable Picture Control styles, which you can edit to your heart's content, assign descriptive names, and deploy at the press of a few buttons. Even better, you can *copy* these styles to a memory card, edit them on your computer, and reload them into your camera at any time. So, effectively, you can have a lot more than nine custom Picture Control styles available: the nine in your camera, as well as a virtually unlimited library of user-defined styles that you have stored on memory cards.

Moreover, Nikon insists that these styles have been standardized to the extent that if you re-use a style created for one camera (say, your D300) and load it into a different compatible camera (such as a Nikon D3), you'll get substantially the same rendition. In a way, Picture Control styles are a bit like using a particular film. Do you want the look of Kodak Ektachrome or Fujifilm Velvia? Load the appropriate style created by you—or anyone else. Picture Control styles are important enough and cool enough that I am going to devote a large chunk of Chapter 6 to discussing them. In this chapter, I'm going to provide *only* the barebones information you need to set and edit Picture Control styles. If you need to know more immediately, it's OK to skip ahead to Chapter 6.

Using and managing Picture Control styles is accomplished using two different menu entries, **Set Picture Control**, which allows you to choose an existing style and to edit the predefined styles that Nikon provides, and **Manage Picture Control**, discussed in the next section, which gives you the capability of creating and editing user-defined styles.

Choosing a Picture Control Style

To choose from one of the predefined styles (Standard, Neutral, Vivid, or Monochrome) or select a user-defined style (numbered C-1 to C-9), follow these steps:

1. Choose **Set Picture Control** from the Shooting menu. The screen shown in Figure 3.16 appears. Note that Picture Controls that have been modified from their standard settings have an asterisk next to their name.

2. Scroll down to the Picture Control you'd like to use.

3. Press **OK** to activate the highlighted style. (Although you can usually select a menu item by pressing the multi-selector right button, in this case, that button activates editing instead.)

4. Press the Menu button or tap the shutter release to exit the menu system.

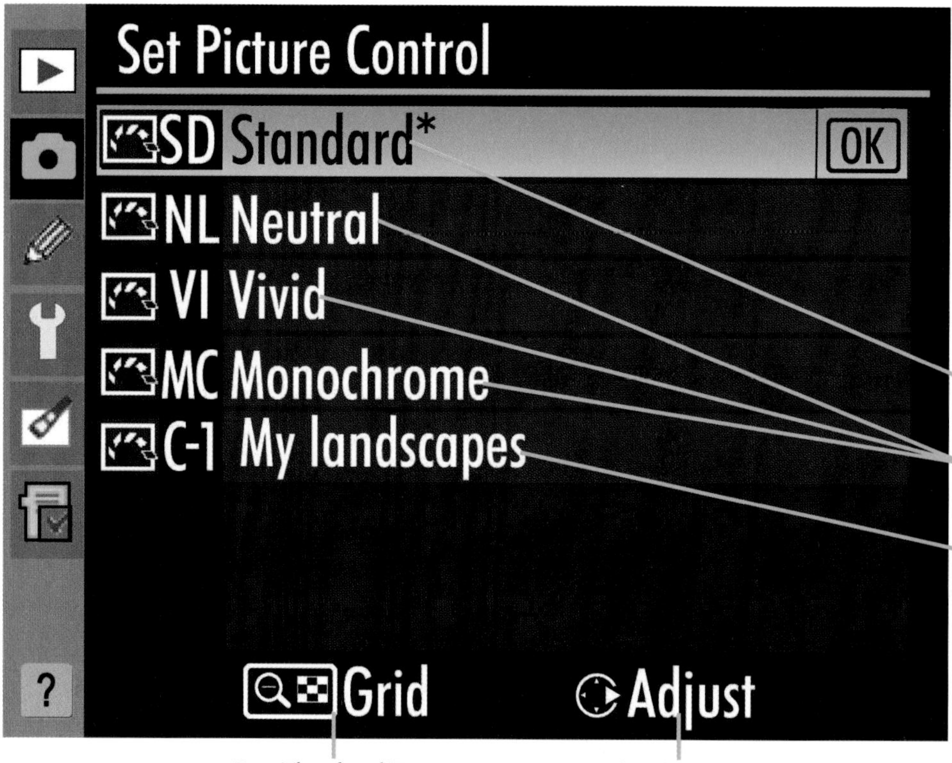

Set Picture Control

☑SD Standard*   [OK]

☑NL Neutral

☑VI Vivid

☑MC Monochrome

☑C-1 My landscapes

🔍⊞Grid   ⟳Adjust

Press Thumbnail/Zoom   Press multi-selector right button
Out to view grid   to adjust highlighted style

Figure 3.16
You can choose from the four predefined Picture Controls, or select a user-defined style, such as *C-1 My landscapes* shown here.

Indicates custom setting

Original Picture Controls

User-defined Picture Control

Editing a Picture Control Style

You can change the parameters of any of Nikon's predefined Picture Controls, or any of the nine user-defined styles you create. You are given the choice of using the quick adjust/fine-tune facility to modify a Picture Control with a few sliders, or to view the relationship of your Picture Controls on a grid. To make quick adjustments to any Picture Control except the Monochrome style, follow these steps:

1. Choose **Set Picture Control** from the Shooting menu.

2. Scroll down to the Picture Control you'd like to edit.

3. Press the multi-selector right button to produce the adjustment screen shown in Figure 3.17.

4. Use the Quick Adjust slider to exaggerate the attributes of the Standard or Vivid styles (Quick Adjustments are not available with other styles).

5. Scroll down to the Sharpening, Contrast, Brightness, Saturation, and Hue sliders with the multi-selector up/down buttons, then use the left/right buttons to decrease

or increase the effects. A line will appear under the original setting in the slider whenever you've made a change from the defaults.

6. Instead of making changes with the slider's scale, you can move the cursor to the far left and choose A (for auto) instead when working with the Sharpening, Contrast, and Saturation sliders. The D300 will adjust these parameters automatically, depending on the type of scene it detects.

7. Press the Trash button to reset the values to their defaults.

8. Press the Thumbnail/Zoom Out button to view an adjustment grid (discussed next).

9. Press OK when you're finished making adjustments.

Editing the Monochrome style is similar, except that the parameters differ slightly. Sharpening, Contrast, and Brightness are available, but, instead of Saturation and Hue, you can choose a filter effect (Yellow, Orange, Red, Green, or none) and a toning effect (black and white, plus seven levels of Sepia, Cyanotype, Red, Yellow, Green, Blue Green, Blue, Purple Blue, and Red Purple). (Keep in mind that once you've taken a JPEG photo using a Monochrome style, you can't convert the image back to full color.)

Figure 3.17
Sliders can be used to make quick adjustments to your Picture Control styles.

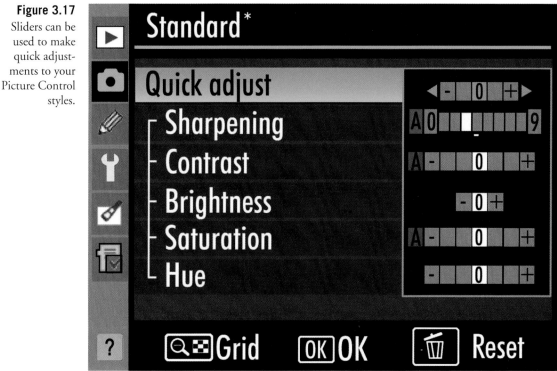

FILTERS VS. TONING

Although some of the color choices seem to overlap, you'll get very different looks when choosing between Filter Effects and Toning. Filter Effects add no color to the mono-chrome image. Instead, they reproduce the look of black-and-white film that has been shot through a color filter. That is, Yellow will make the sky darker and the clouds will stand out more, while Orange makes the sky even darker and sunsets more full of detail. The Red filter produces the darkest sky of all and darkens green objects, such as leaves. Human skin may appear lighter than normal. The Green filter has the opposite effect on leaves, making them appear lighter in tone. Figure 3.18 shows the same scene shot with no filter, then Yellow, Green, and Red filters.

The Sepia, Blue, Green, and other toning effects, on the other hand, all add a color cast to your monochrome image. Use these when you want an old-time look or a special effect, without bothering to recolor your shots in an image editor.

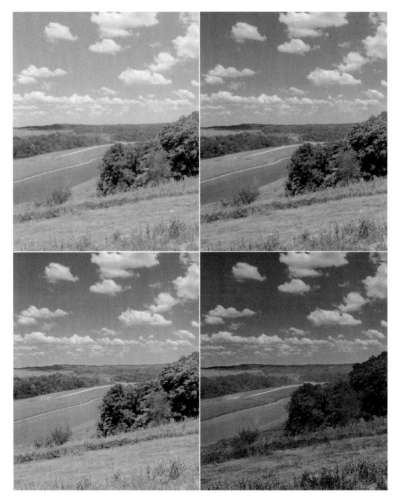

Figure 3.18
No filter
(upper left);
yellow filter
(upper right);
green filter
(lower left),
and red filter
(lower right).

When you press the Thumbnail/Zoom Out button, a grid display, like the one shown in Figure 3.19, appears, showing the relative contrast and saturation of each of the pre-defined Picture Controls. If you've created your own custom Picture Controls, they will appear on this grid, too, represented by the numbers 1-9. Because the values for auto-contrast and autosaturation may vary, the icons for any Picture Control that uses the Auto feature will be shown on the grid in green, with lines extending up and down from the icon to tip you off that the position within the coordinates may vary from the one shown.

You'll find more on Picture Controls in Chapter 6.

Figure 3.19
This grid shows the relationship of the Picture Controls being used.

Amount of contrast

Picture Control using Auto contrast or saturation

User-defined Picture Control

Amount of saturation

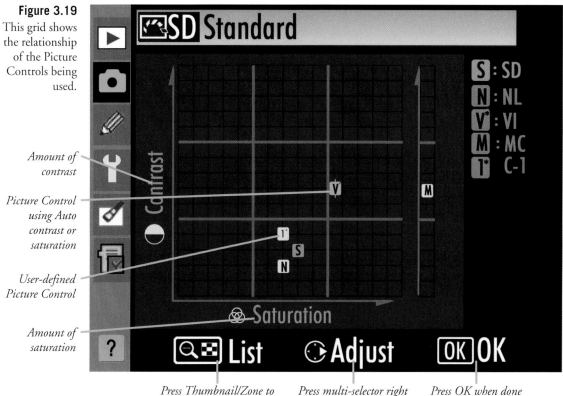

Press Thumbnail/Zone to return to Picture Control list

Press multi-selector right button to adjust style

Press OK when done

Manage Picture Control

The Manage Picture Control menu entry can be used to create new styles, edit existing styles, rename or delete them, and store/retrieve them from the Compact Flash card. Here are the basic functions of this menu item, which can be found on the Shooting menu directly below the Set Picture Control entry:

- **Make a copy.** Choose **Save/edit**, select from the list of available Picture Controls, and press **OK** to store that style in one of the user-defined slots C-1 to C-9, as shown in Figure 3.20.

- **Save an edited copy.** Choose **Save/edit**, select from the list of available Picture Controls, and then press the multi-selector right button to edit the style, as described in the previous section. Press **OK** when finished editing, and then save the modified style in one of the user-defined slots C-1 to C-9.

- **Rename a style.** Choose **Rename**, select from the list of user-defined Picture Controls (you cannot rename the default styles), and then enter the text used as the new label for the style, using the standard D300 text entry screen shown earlier in Figure 3.6. You may use up to 19 characters for the name.

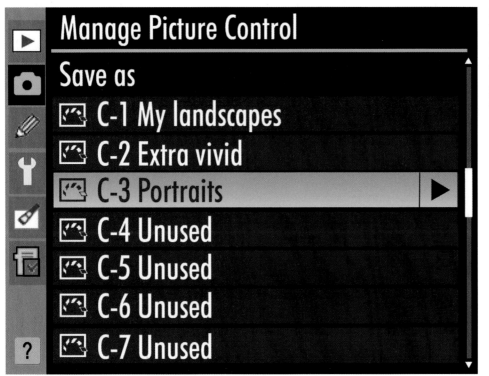

Figure 3.20
Picture Controls that you define can be stored in your D300's settings.

- **Remove a style.** Select **Delete**, choose from the list of user-defined Picture Controls (you can't remove one of the default styles), press the multi-selector right button, then highlight **Yes** in the screen that follows and press **OK** to remove that Picture Control.

- **Store/retrieve style on card.** Choose **Load/save**, then select **Copy to camera** to locate a Picture Control on your Compact Flash card and copy it to the D300; **Delete from Card** to select a Picture Control on your memory card and remove it; or **Copy to card** to duplicate a style currently in your camera onto the Compact Flash card. This last option allows you to create and save Picture Controls in excess of the nine that can be loaded into the camera at one time. Once you've copied a style to your memory card, you can modify the version in the camera, give it a new name, and, in effect, create a whole new Picture Control.

Color Space

The Color Space entry is the first one on the third "page" of the Shooting menu, as shown in Figure 3.21. You can select one of two color gamuts (the range of colors available to represent an image) using this menu entry. You might prefer sRGB, which is the default for the Nikon D300 and most other cameras, as it is well suited for the range of

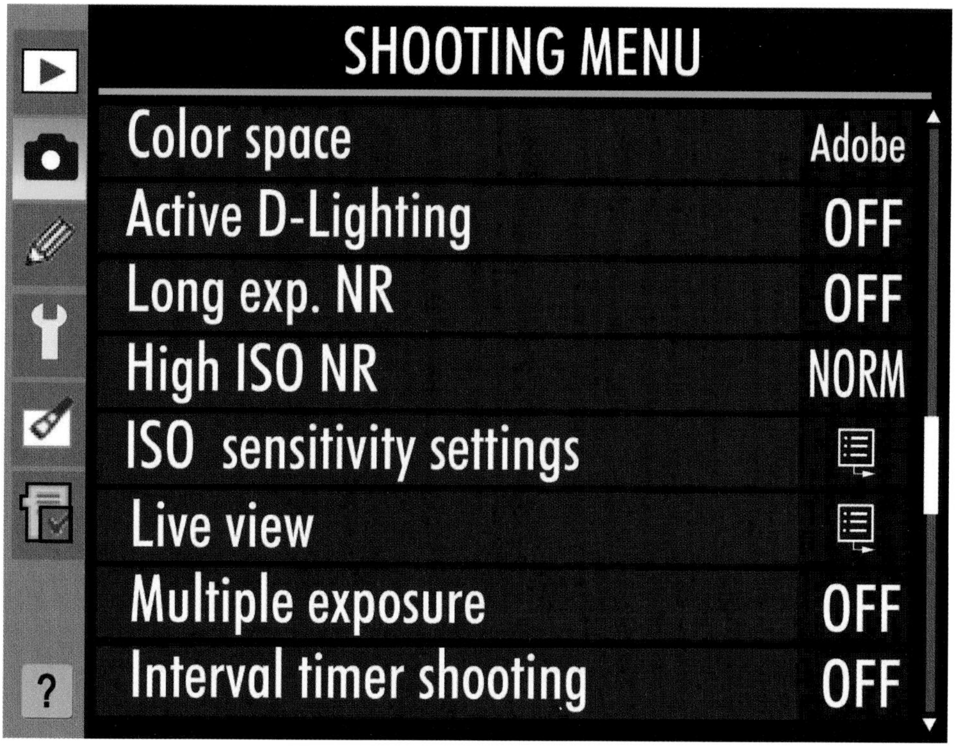

Figure 3.21
If you scroll through the Shooting menu, Color Space eventually appears at the top of the listing.

SHOOTING MENU

Color space	Adobe
Active D-Lighting	OFF
Long exp. NR	OFF
High ISO NR	NORM
ISO sensitivity settings	
Live view	
Multiple exposure	OFF
Interval timer shooting	OFF

colors that can be displayed on a computer screen and viewed over the Internet. The sRGB setting is recommended for images that will be output locally on the user's own printer, as this color space matches that of the typical inkjet printer fairly closely. If you plan to take your image file to a retailer's kiosk for printing, sRGB is your best choice, because those automated output devices are calibrated for the sRGB color space.

Adobe RGB is an expanded color space useful for commercial and professional printing, and it can reproduce a wider range of colors. It can also come in useful if an image is going to be extensively retouched, especially within an advanced image editor, like Adobe Photoshop, which has sophisticated color management capabilities that can be tailored to specific color spaces. As an advanced user, you don't need to automatically "upgrade" your D300 to Adobe RGB, because images tend to look less saturated on your monitor and it is likely significantly different from what you will get if you output the photo to your personal inkjet. (You can *profile* your monitor for the Adobe RGB color space to improve your on-screen rendition.) Strictly speaking, both sRGB and Adobe RGB can reproduce the exact same absolute *number* of colors (16.8 million when reduced to 8-bits per channel from the original 12-bit or 14-bit capture). Adobe RGB spreads those colors over a larger space.

Think of a box of crayons (the jumbo 16.8 million crayon variety). Some of the basic crayons from the original sRGB set have been removed and replaced with new hues not contained in the original box. Your "new" box contains colors that can't be reproduced by your computer monitor, but which work just fine with a commercial printing press. For example, Adobe RGB has more "crayons" available in the cyan-green portion of the box, compared to sRGB, which is unlikely to be an advantage unless your image's final destination is a conversion to the cyan, magenta, yellow, and black colors used in the inks of a printing press.

BEST OF BOTH WORLDS

If you plan to use RAW+JPEG for most of your photos, go ahead and set sRGB as your color space. You'll end up with JPEGs suitable for output on your own printer, but you can still extract an Adobe RGB version from the RAW file at any time. It's like shooting two different color spaces at once—sRGB and Adobe RGB—and getting the best of both worlds.

Active D-Lighting

D-lighting is a feature that improves the rendition of detail in highlights and shadows when you're photographing high contrast scenes. It's been available as an internal retouching option in Nikon's lower-end cameras (by that I mean the CoolPix point-and-shoot line) for some time, and has gradually worked its way up through the company's dSLR products, in late 2007 becoming available in the Nikon D300 (and D3). You'll find the feature in the Retouch menu, which I'll describe later in the chapter.

A new wrinkle, however, is the *active D-lighting* capability introduced with Nikon's new higher-end models, which, unlike the Retouch menu post-processing feature, applies its tonal improvements *while you are actually taking the photo.* That's good news and bad news. It means that, if you're taking photos in a contrasty environment, active D-lighting can automatically improve the apparent dynamic range of your image as you shoot, without additional effort on your part. However, you'll need to disable the feature once you leave the high contrast lighting behind, and the process does take some time. You wouldn't want to use active D-lighting for continuous shooting of sports subjects, for example. There are many situations in which the selective application of D-lighting using the Retouch menu is a better choice.

For best results, use your D300's matrix metering mode, so the active D-lighting feature can work with a full range of exposure information from multiple points in the image. Active D-lighting works its magic by subtly *underexposing* your image so that details in the highlights (which would normally be overexposed and become featureless white pixels) are not lost. At the same time, it adjusts the values of pixels located in mid-tone and shadow areas so they don't become too dark because of the underexposure. Highlight tones will be preserved, while shadows will eventually be allowed to go dark more readily. Bright beach or snow scenes, especially those with few shadows (think high noon, when the shadows are smaller) can benefit from using active D-lighting.

You have four choices: Off, High, Normal, and Low. You may need to experiment with the feature a little to discover how much D-lighting you can apply to a high contrast image before the shadows start to darken objectionably. Note that when this feature is activated, brightness and contrast Picture Control settings cannot be changed. Figure 3.22 shows some examples of active D-light applied. By the time the sample images shown have been half-toned and rendered to the printed page, the differences may be fairly subtle. Look at the amount of detail in the overhanging rock in the upper-right area of each version.

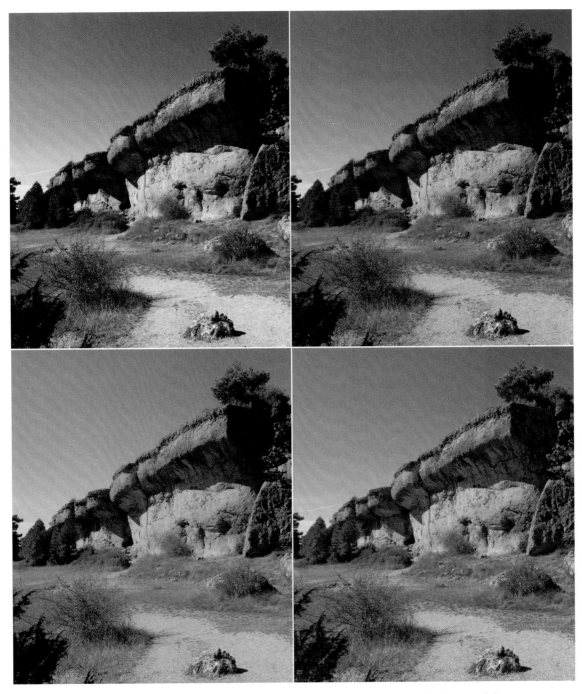

Figure 3.22 No D-lighting (upper left); low (upper right); normal (lower left); and high (lower right).

Long Exp. NR

Visual noise is that awful graininess caused by long exposures and high ISO settings, and which shows up as multicolored specks in images. This setting helps you manage the kind of noise caused by lengthy exposure times. In some ways, noise is like the excessive grain found in some high-speed photographic films. However, while photographic grain is sometimes used as a special effect, it's rarely desirable in a digital photograph. There are easier ways to add texture to your photos.

Some noise is created is when you're using shutter speeds longer than eight seconds to create a longer exposure. Extended exposure times allow more photons to reach the sensor, but increase the likelihood that some photosites will react randomly even though not struck by a particle of light. Moreover, as the sensor remains switched on for the longer exposure, it heats, and this heat can be mistakenly recorded as if it were a barrage of photons. This menu setting can be used to activate the D300's long exposure noise-canceling operation performed by the EXPEED digital signal processor.

- **Off.** This default setting disables long exposure noise reduction. Use it when you want the maximum amount of detail present in your photograph, even though higher noise levels will result. This setting also eliminates the extra time needed to take a picture caused by the noise reduction process. If you plan to use only lower ISO settings (thereby reducing the noise caused by ISO amplification), the noise levels produced by longer exposures may be acceptable. For example, you might be shooting a waterfall at ISO 100 (L 1.0) with the camera mounted on a tripod, using a neutral density filter and a long exposure to cause the water to blur. (Try exposures of 2 to 16 seconds, depending on the intensity of the light and how much blur you want.) (See Figure 3.23.) To maximize detail in the non-moving portions of your photos for the exposures that are eight seconds or longer, you can switch off long exposure noise reduction.

- **On.** When exposures are eight seconds or longer, the Nikon D300 takes a second, blank exposure to compare that to the first image. (While the second image is taken, the warning **Job nr** appears on the monochrome LCD panel and in the viewfinder.) Noise (pixels that are bright in a frame that *should* be completely black) in the "dark frame" image is subtracted from your original picture, and only the noise-corrected image is saved to your memory card. Because the noise-reduction process effectively doubles the time required to take a picture, you won't want to use this setting when you're rushed. Some noise can be removed later on, using tools like Bibble Pro or the noise reduction features built into Nikon Capture NX.

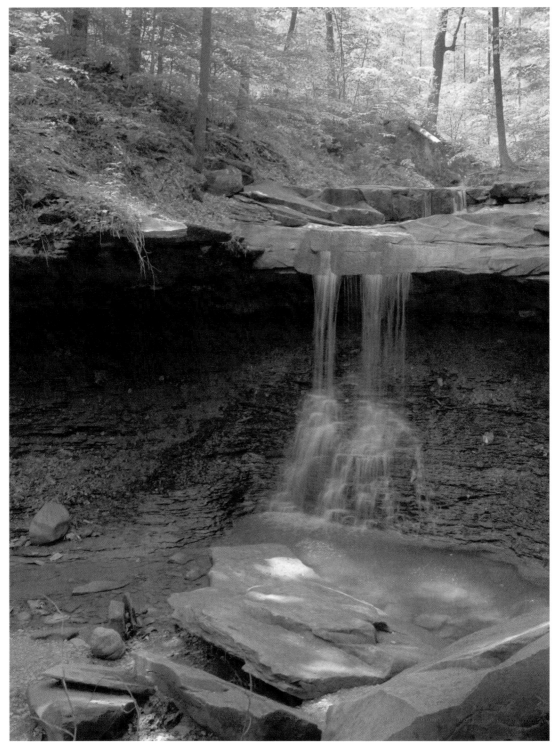

Figure 3.23 A long exposure with the camera mounted on a tripod produces this traditional waterfall photo.

High ISO NR

Noise can also be caused by higher ISO sensitivity settings, and the Nikon D300, which offers settings up to ISO 3200 (and thence up to the equivalent of ISO 6400 with the H 1.0 setting) has a loftier ISO ceiling than most cameras. Indeed, the D300 uses a reduced-noise CMOS sensor (instead of the CCD sensor found in the Nikon D200) and gives you results that are at least one or two stops better than its immediate predecessor. That is, you can expect the Nikon D300 to produce results at ISO 3200 that you might have expected from the D300 at ISO 800 to ISO 1600. Even so, high ISO noise reduction, which can be set with this menu option, may be a good option in many cases. You can choose Off when you want to preserve detail at the cost of some noise graininess, and the D300 will apply high ISO NR only at the "boosted" settings of HI 0.3, HI 0.6, and HI 1.0. Or, you can select Low, Normal, and High noise reduction, which is applied when ISO sensitivity has been set to ISO 800 or higher.

The effects of high ISO noise are something like listening to a CD in your car, and then rolling down all the windows. You're adding sonic noise to the audio signal, and while increasing the CD player's volume may help a bit, you're still contending with an unfavorable signal to noise ratio that probably mutes tones (especially higher treble notes) that you really want to hear.

The same thing happens when the analog image signal is amplified: You're increasing the image information in the signal, but boosting the background fuzziness at the same time. Tune in a very faint or distant AM radio station on your car stereo. Then turn up the volume. After a certain point, turning up the volume further no longer helps you hear better. There's a similar point of diminishing returns for digital sensor ISO increases and signal amplification as well.

As the captured information is amplified to produce higher ISO sensitivities, some random noise in the signal is amplified along with the photon information. Increasing the ISO setting of your camera raises the threshold of sensitivity so that fewer and fewer photons are needed to register as an exposed pixel. Yet, that also increases the chances of one of those phantom photons being counted among the real-life light particles, too.

Fortunately, the Nikon D300's CMOS sensor and its EXPEED digital processing chip are optimized to produce the low noise levels, so ratings as high as ISO 1600 to ISO 3200 can be used routinely (although there will be some noise, of course), and even ISO 6400 can generate good results. Some kinds of subjects may not require this kind of noise cancellation, particularly with images that have a texture of their own that tends to hide or mask the noise. Figure 3.24 is an example of this type of shot. It was taken in the waning light just before dusk, and though there is a fair amount of noise in the brickwork of the building, even at this extreme enlargement the multicolored speckles are not objectionable. (The entire frame is shown in the inset.)

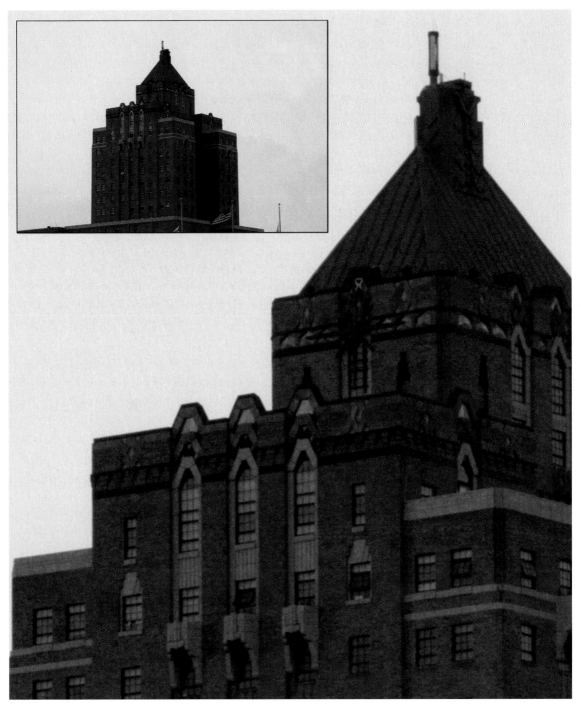

Figure 3.24 This enlargement shows that noise levels can be acceptable even at ISO 3200.

ISO Sensitivity Settings

This menu entry has two parts, **ISO sensitivity** and **ISO sensitivity auto control.** The former is simply a screen that allows you to specify the ISO setting, just as you would by spinning the main command dial while holding down the ISO button on the top-left panel of the D300. The available settings range from LO 1 (ISO 100 equivalent) through ISO 3200 to HI 1 (ISO 6400 equivalent). The available settings are determined by the size of the increment you've specified in Custom Setting menu **CSM #b1**: 1/3, 1/2, or 1 step values. For example, if you had chosen 1 step increments, then LO 1.0, 200, 400, 800, 1600, 3200, and HI 1 would be available. (I'll explain the use of increments later in this chapter.) Use the ISO sensitivity menu when you find it more convenient to set ISO using the three-inch color LCD.

The ISO sensitivity auto control menu entry lets you specify how and when the D300 will adjust the ISO value for you automatically under certain conditions. This capability can be potentially useful, although experienced photographers tend to shy away from any feature that allows the camera to change basic settings like ISO that have been carefully selected. Fortunately, you can set some boundaries so the D300 will use this adjustment in a fairly intelligent way.

When Auto ISO is activated, the camera can bump up the ISO sensitivity, if necessary, whenever an optimal exposure cannot be achieved at the current ISO setting. Of course, it can be disconcerting to think you're shooting at ISO 400 and then see a grainier ISO 1600 shot during LCD review. While the D300 provides a flashing **ISO-Auto** alert in the viewfinder and top panel status LCD, the warning is easy to miss. Here are the important considerations to keep in mind when using the options available for this feature:

- **Off.** Set ISO sensitivity auto control to off, and the ISO setting will not budge from whatever value you have specified. Use this setting when you don't want any ISO surprises, or when ISO increases are not needed to counter slow shutter speeds. For example, if the D300 is mounted on a tripod, you can safely use slower shutter speeds at a relatively low ISO setting, so there is no need for a speed bump. On the other hand, if you're hand-holding the camera and the D300 set for Program (P) or Aperture Priority (A) mode wants to use a shutter speed slower than, say, 1/30 second, it's probably a good idea to increase the ISO to avoid the effects of camera shake. If you're using a longer lens, a shutter speed of 1/125 second or higher might be the point where an ISO bump would be a good idea. In that case, you can turn the ISO sensitivity auto control on, or remember to boost the ISO setting yourself.

- **Maximum sensitivity.** Use this parameter to indicate the highest ISO setting you're comfortable having the D300 set on its own. You can choose from ISO 400, 800, 1600, 3200, and HI 1 (ISO 6400 equivalent) as the max ISO setting the camera will use. (Note that the increments are fixed at those listed, regardless of how **CSM #b1** is set.) Use a low number if you'd rather not take any photos at a high ISO without manually setting that value yourself. Dial in a higher ISO number if getting the photo at any sensitivity setting is more important than worrying about noise.

■ **Minimum shutter speed.** This setting allows you to tell the D300 how slow the shutter speed must be before the ISO boost kicks in, within the range 1 second to 1/250 second. The default value is 1/30 second, because for most shooters in most situations, any shutter speed longer than 1/30 is to be avoided, unless you're using a tripod, monopod, or looking for a special effect. If you have steady hands, or the camera is partially braced against movement (say, you're using that monopod), a slower shutter speed, down to 1 full second, can be specified. Similarly, if you're working with a telephoto lens and find even a relatively brief shutter speed "dangerous," you can set a minimum shutter speed threshold of 1/250 second. When the shutter speed is faster than the minimum you enter, auto ISO will not take effect.

Live View

Live View is the surprising new feature that new users of the D300 often rave about, but may not understand fully. So, I'll cover Live View more completely in Chapter 7. This brief section simply outlines the two options you can set for Live View in the Shooting menu. Live View is activated by rotating the release mode dial to **Lv** and pressing the shutter release button to flip up the mirror and display the preview on the color LCD.

This menu entry allows you to specify which of two Live View modes are used, as well as whether you want to take pictures using single-shot, continuous low speed, or continuous high speed release modes.

■ **Live View mode.** Choose from **Hand-held** (the default value) or **Tripod** modes. The chief difference between the two is that Hand-held mode is useful for shooting moving subjects and for framing images at angles that might not be convenient to compose with the camera mounted on a tripod. Tripod mode is better for non-moving subjects and allows zooming your view in for easier and more precise manual or automatic focus. Hand-held mode uses phase-detection autofocus, using focus information provided from the same sensor used to focus the D300 when Live View is not active. As you'll learn in Chapter 7, the mirror temporarily flips down when the shutter release or AF-ON button is pressed and the camera focuses (automatically in AF-S or AF-C modes, or manually in M mode), returning to Live View when either button is released. Tripod mode focuses with contrast-detect autofocus, a slower method that evaluates the contrast of the image reaching the sensor and adjusts autofocus until the highest contrast image is achieved. You can select the focus point yourself using the multi-selector, and then autofocus by pressing the AF-ON button (but *not* by pressing the shutter release halfway) or manually focus.

■ **Release mode.** Obviously, if the release mode dial is set to Lv, there is no way to use the dial to specify single shot or either of the two continuous shooting modes. This menu entry is the workaround. You can select S (single shot), C$_L$ (continuous low speed), or C$_H$ (continuous high speed) modes here.

Multiple Exposure

This option lets you combine two exposures into one image without the need for an image editor like Photoshop and can be an entertaining way to return to those thrilling days of yesteryear, when complex photos were created in the camera itself. In truth, prior to the digital age, multiple exposures were a cool, groovy, far-out, hep/hip, phat, sick, fabulous way of producing composite images. Today, it's more common to take the lazy way out, snap two or more pictures, and then assemble them in an image editor like Photoshop.

However, if you're willing to spend the time planning a multiple exposure (or are open to some happy accidents), there is a lot to recommend the multiple exposure capability that Nikon has bestowed on the D300. For one thing, the camera is able to combine two or more images using the RAW data from the sensor, producing photos that are blended together more smoothly than is likely for anyone who's not a Photoshop guru. To take your own multiple exposures, just follow these steps (although it's probably a good idea to do a little planning and maybe even some sketching on paper first):

1. Choose **Multiple exposure** from the Shooting menu.

2. Select **Number of shots**, choose a value from 2 to 10 with the multi-selector up/down buttons, and press **OK**.

3. Choose **Auto gain** and specify either **On** (the default) or **Off.** When On is selected, the D300 will divide the total exposure of the image by the number of shots specified; for example, applying 1/4 of the exposure time to each shot in a four-image series. Choose Off, and the full exposure is applied to each picture. You'd want to use Off when using a dark background that would allow successive exposures to add details, and On to avoid the risk of overlapping images washing each other out.

4. Press **OK** to set the gain.

5. Move the cursor up to **Done** and press **OK.** The multiple exposure icon appears in the monochrome LCD status panel.

6. Take the photo by pressing the shutter release button multiple times until all the exposures in the series have been taken. (In continuous shooting mode, the entire series will be shot in a single burst.) The blinking multiple exposure icon vanishes when the series is finished.

Keep in mind if you wait longer than 30 seconds between any two photos in the series, the sequence will terminate and combine the images taken so far. If you want a longer elapsed time between exposures, go to the Playback menu and make sure **On** has been specified for **Image Review**, and then extend the monitor display time using **CSM #c4** to an appropriate maximum interval. The Multiple Exposure feature will then use the monitor-off delay as its maximum interval between shots.

Figure 3.25 shows an odd double exposure created by flipping the camera upside down between the first shot (of the chessboard) and the second shot (of the vase), with both pictured against a black background. Auto gain was turned off in this case.

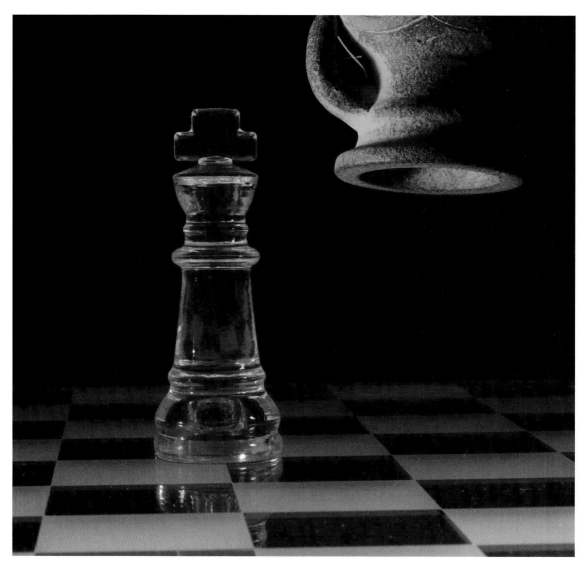

Figure 3.25 The D300's Multiple Exposure capability allows combining images without an image editor.

Interval Timer Shooting

The Nikon D300's built-in time-lapse photography feature allows you to take pictures for up to 999 intervals in bursts of as many as nine shots, with a delay of up to 23 hours and 59 minutes between shots/bursts, and an initial start-up time of as long as 23 hours and 59 minutes from the time you activate the feature. That means that if you want to photograph a rosebud opening and would like to photograph the flower once every two minutes over the next 16 hours, you can do that easily. If you like, you can delay the first photo taken by a couple hours so you don't have to stand there by the D300 waiting for the right moment.

Or, you might want to photograph a particular scene every hour for 24 hours to capture, say, a landscape from sunrise to sunset to the following day's sunrise again. The D300 can do that, too, and, in fact, offers most of the features of the expensive ($130) Nikon MC-36 Multi-Function Remote control. Nikon has done us all a huge favor by including this functionality essentially for free! I will offer two practical tips right now, in case you want to run out and try interval timer shooting immediately: *use a tripod, and for best results over longer time periods, plan on connecting your D300 to an external power source!*

The Interval Timer Shooting screen (see Figure 3.26) is confusingly designed, in my opinion. It's needlessly complex; the display changes in a quirky way depending on what information you're entering, and some portions of the screen aren't accessible until you've performed a prerequisite function. I would have set up this menu with nothing more than five entries, each with their own screen of options: On/Off, start time, interval delay, total number of shots to expose, and the number of shots in the burst per interval (if more than one image per interval is desired).

To set up interval timer shooting, just follow these steps.

Before you start:

1. The D300 uses its internal World Time clock to activate, so make sure the time has been set accurately in the Setup menu before you begin.

2. If you want to shoot bursts of images each time an interval elapses, set the release mode dial to C_L (low speed continuous; pictures will be taken at the rate specified in **CSM #d4**) or C_H (high speed continuous; pictures will be taken at a rate of up to 6 fps). If you prefer to take one picture per interval, set the release mode dial to **S**. However, you can still specify multiple shots per interval when using S; the D300 will use the frame rate specified in **CSM #d4** just as if you had set the release mode to C_L.

3. If you'd like to bracket exposures during interval shooting, set up bracketing prior to beginning. (You'll learn how to bracket in Chapter 6.)

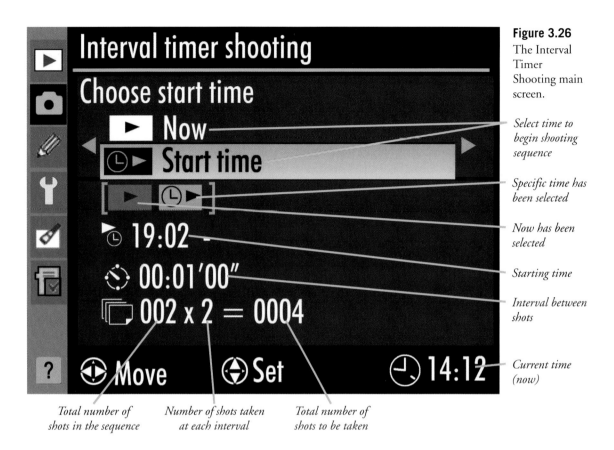

Figure 3.26
The Interval
Timer
Shooting main
screen.

Select time to
begin shooting
sequence

Specific time has
been selected

Now has been
selected

Starting time

Interval between
shots

Current time
(now)

Total number of
shots in the sequence

Number of shots taken
at each interval

Total number of
shots to be taken

4. Mount the camera on a tripod or other secure support.

5. Fully charge the battery. You might want to mount the MB-D10 battery grip if you have one, or connect the D300 to the Nikon AC Adapter EH-5a or EH-5 if you plan to shoot long sequences. Although the camera more or less goes to sleep between intervals, some power is drawn, and long sequences with bursts of shots can drain power even when you're not using the interval timer feature.

6. Make sure the camera is protected from the elements, accidents, and theft, and that the viewfinder is covered (using the DK-5 eyepiece cap if necessary) if you need to keep strong ambient light from entering the viewfinder and affecting exposure.

When you're ready to go, set up the D300 for interval shooting:

1. Choose Interval timer shooting from the Shooting menu.

2. Specify a starting time. You must do this before the D300 will let you set other parameters. Highlight either **Now** or **Start time** and press the multi-selector right button. If you choose **Now**, the interval shooting will begin approximately three seconds after you've finished setting the parameters beginning with Step 5. If you select **Start** time, you'll be able to enter a specific time, as described in Steps 3 and 4.

3. When the **Start time** sub-screen appears, use the multi-selector left/right buttons to highlight the hours or minutes, and the up/down buttons to increase or decrease the hours/minutes entry. The 24-hour clock is used, so you can specify a time from 00:00 (midnight) to 23:59 (one minute to midnight). When both hours and minutes have been set, press the multi-selector right button to move the highlighting to the Interval section of the sub-screen.

4. Set the interval between exposures. You can use the left/right buttons to move among hours, minutes, and seconds, and use the up/down buttons to choose an interval from one second to 24 hours. Press the right button when finished to move down to the number of intervals/shots per interval sub-screen.

Tip

The interval cannot be shorter than the shutter speed; for example, you can not set one second as the interval if the images will be taken at two seconds or longer.

5. Set number of intervals and shots per interval. Use the left/right buttons to highlight the number of intervals, the number of shots taken after each interval has elapsed, and the total number of shots to be exposed overall. You can highlight each number column separately, so that to enter, say, 250 intervals you can set the 100s, 10s, and 1s columns individually (rather than press the up button 250 times!). You can select up to 999 intervals, and 9 shots per interval for a maximum of 8991 exposures with one interval shooting cycle.

6. When all the parameters have been entered, press the multi-selector right button once more, and the Start subscreen appears, with the choices On or Off. Choose either one and press OK. If you activate interval shooting, a message is displayed on the monitor one minute before each series of shots begins.

PAUSE OR CANCEL INTERVAL SHOOTING

Press the Menu button between intervals (but not when images are still being recorded to the Compact Flash card), choose the Interval timer shooting menu entry, and select Pause. Interval shooting can also be paused by turning the camera on or off, or by rotating the release mode dial to Live View, self-timer, or mirror-up positions. To resume the Interval timer shooting menu again, press the multi-selector left button, and choose Restart. You may also select Off to stop the shooting entirely.

4

Setup: The Custom Setting Menu

Unlike the Shooting menu options, which you are likely to modify frequently as your picture-taking environment changes, Custom Settings are slightly more stable sets of preferences that let you tailor the behavior of your camera in a variety of different ways for longer-term use.

Some options are minor tweaks useful for specific shooting situations. You can turn off the autofocus assist lamp, the back panel LCD's shooting information display, and the D300's built-in beeper when you are shooting an acoustic music concert, when you'd rather not disrupt the environment. Others make the camera more convenient to use. Perhaps you'd like to assign a frequently used feature to the Func button, or turn on the viewfinder grid display to make it easier to align vertical or horizontal shapes.

Best of all are the settings that actually *improve* the way the D300 operates. **CSM #b6**, for example, provides a way to fine-tune the exposures your camera calculates for each of the metering modes: Matrix, Center-Weighted, and Spot. If you find that one or the other consistently over- or under-exposes more than you like, it's easy to dial in a permanent correction. Should you feel that the D300 is taking a few pictures that are out-of-focus, you can tell it not to fire until optimum focus is achieved.

This chapter concentrates on explaining all the options of the Custom Setting menu and, most importantly, when and why you might want to use each setting.

Custom Settings Menu Layout

There are 48 different Custom Settings, three more than were available in the D200, arranged in six different categories, as shown in Figure 4.1: autofocus, metering/exposure, timers/AE lock, shooting/display, bracketing/flash, and controls. Some of those may seem to be an odd match. What does bracketing have to do with flash? Oh, wait! You can *bracket* flash (as well as non-flash) exposures. The category system does have an advantage. Once you've learned what settings are available within each category, you can select the Custom Settings menu, scroll down to the specific category you want, and enter the CSM system at that point, skipping the other entries.

However, once you get past the main CSM screen, the entries are one long scrolling list, so if you've guessed wrong about where you want to start, you can enter the list at any point and then scroll up or down until you find the entry you want. The CSM menu items are all color- and letter-coded: **a** (red) for autofocus functions; **b** (orange) for metering/exposure; **c** (green) for timers and AE/lock features; **d** (light blue) for shooting/display functions; **e** (dark blue) for bracketing/flash; and **f** (purple) for adjustments to the D300's controls.

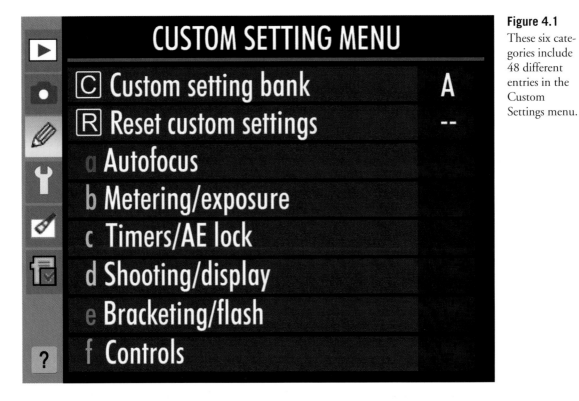

Figure 4.1

These six categories include 48 different entries in the Custom Settings menu.

For simplicity, in this book I have been consistently referring to the Custom Settings menu entries by their letter/names, so that you always know that when I mention **CSM #a8**, I am describing the eighth entry in the autofocus menu, **AF point selection**. That terminology makes it easy to jump quickly to the specific entry.

You can select a CSM function as you do any menu entry, by pressing the multi-selector right button, and navigating through the screen that appears with the up/down (and sometimes left/right) buttons. Confirming an option is usually done by pressing the OK button, pushing the multi-selector right button, or sometimes by choosing **Done** when a series of related options have been chosen.

At the top level, you'll see these entries:

- Custom setting bank
- Reset custom settings
- a. Autofocus
- b. Metering/exposure
- c. Timers/AE lock
- d. Shooting/display
- e. Bracketing/flash
- f. Controls

Custom Setting Bank

The Custom Setting menu has four banks, counterparts to the A, B, C, and D banks in the Shooting menu, that store specific collections of CSM settings. As with the Shooting menu banks, you can recall any of the four at any time. As I mentioned in Chapter 3, the Custom Setting Banks A, B, C, and D should not be confused with the four similarly named Shooting Menu Banks A, B, C, and D, which provide storage of separate sets of options. You can use your Shooting Menu Banks and Custom Setting Menu Banks in any combination.

The D300 uses Bank A by default. To switch to another bank:

- Press **Menu** and select the Custom Setting menu.
- Scroll to Custom Setting Bank and press the multi-selector right button.
- Scroll to the bank you want to use with the multi-selector up/down buttons, and either press **OK** or press the multi-selector right button to confirm your choice.
- The Custom Setting menu appears again. Press the Menu button to back out of the menu, or simply tap the shutter release.

If you've changed a bank from its default values, the active bank's letter will be shown in the monochrome LCD status panel and the Shooting Information Display. As with Shooting Menu Banks, any changes you make to one menu bank do not affect the other banks, so you can set one up with the settings you like to use in particular situations, and assign each of them customized names of up to 20 characters to replace the generic A, B, C, and D designations. As with the Shooting Menu Banks, use the standard Nikon text entry screen to enter the name you want to use.

- Press **Menu** and select the Custom Settings menu.

- Scroll to the Custom Setting Menu Bank entry and press the multi-selector right button.

- Scroll down to Rename and press the multi-selector right button to confirm your choice.

- Scroll down to the bank you want to rename, and press the multi-selector right button to activate the text entry screen.

- Use the multi-selector navigational buttons to scroll around within the array of alphanumerics, as described in Chapter 3. Press the multi-selector's center button to insert the highlighted character; hold down the Thumbnail/Zoom Out button and use the left/right buttons to move the cursor within the line of characters; remove a character by highlighting the character and pressing the Trash button. Press OK when finished, then press the left button twice to return to the Custom Settings menu, or just tap the shutter release to exit the menu system entirely.

Reset Custom Settings

You can restore the settings of the Custom Settings banks to their default values by choosing this menu entry and selecting **Yes** or **No**. Only the currently active bank is reset; the other three are untouched. In Chapter 9, I'll provide a list of recommended Custom Settings Menu Bank settings for typical photo environments. Tables 4.1–4.6 show the default values as the Nikon D300 comes from the factory, and after a reset. If you don't know what some of these settings are, I'll explain them later in this chapter. Be careful when changing any of your carefully tailored customized settings back to the defaults.

Table 4.1 Default Custom Setting Bank Values: Autofocus

Function	Option	Default
a1	AF-C priority selection	Release
a2	AF-S priority selection	Focus
a3	Dynamic AF area	9 points
a4	Focus tracking with lock-on	Normal
a5	AF activation	Shutter/AF-ON
a6	AF point illumination	Auto
a7	Focus point wrap-around	No wrap
a8	AF point selection	51 points
a9	Built-in AF-assist illuminator	On
a10	AF-ON for MB-D10	AF-ON

Table 4.2 Default Custom Setting Bank Values: Metering/Exposure

Function	Option	Default
b1	ISO sensitivity step value	1/3 step
b2	EV steps for exposure cntrl.	1/3 step
b3	Exp comp/fine	1/3/step
b4	Easy exposure compensation	Off
b5	Center-weighted area	8mm
b6	Fine-tune optimal exposure	
	Matrix metering	0
	Center-weighted metering	0
	Spot metering	0

Table 4.3 Default Custom Setting Bank Values: Timers/AE Lock

Function	Option	Default
c1	Shutter release button AE-L	Off
c2	Auto meter-off delay	6 seconds
c3	Self-timer delay	10 seconds
c4	Monitor off delay	20 seconds

Table 4.4 Default Custom Setting Bank Values: Shooting/Display

Function	Option	Default
d1	Beep	High
d2	Viewfinder grid display	Off
d3	Viewfinder warning display	On
d4	CL mode shooting speed	3 fps
d5	Max. continuous release	100
d6	File number sequence	On
d7	Shooting info display	Auto
d8	LCD illumination	Off
d9	Exposure delay mode	Off
d10	MB-D10 battery type	LR6 (AA alkaline)
d11	Battery order	Use MB-D10 batteries first

Table 4.5 Default Custom Setting Bank Values: Bracketing/Flash

Function	Option	Default
e1	Flash sync speed	1/250 second
e2	Flash shutter speed	1/60 second
e3	Flash control for built-in flash	TTL
e4	Modeling flash	On
e5	Auto bracketing set	AE & Flash
e6	Auto bracketing (Mode M)	Flash/speed
e7	Bracketing order	MTR>under>over

Table 4.6 Default Custom Setting Bank Values: Controls

Function	Option	Default
f1	Multi-selector button	
	Shooting mode	Select center focus point
	Playback mode	Thumbnail on/off
f2	Multi-selector	Do nothing

Table 4.6 Default Custom Setting Bank Values: Controls (continued)

Function	Option	Default
f3	Photo info/playback	Info (up/down)/Playback (left/right)
f4	Assign FUNC. Button	
	FUNC. button press	None
	FUNC. button+ command dials	Autobracketing
f5	Assign preview button	
	Preview button press	Preview
	Preview+command dials	None
f6	Assign AE-L/AF-L button	
	AE-L/AF-L button press	AE/AF lock
	AE-L/AF-L+command dials	None
f7	Customize command dials	
	Reverse rotation	None
	Change main/sub	Off
	Aperture setting	Sub command dial
	Menus and playback	No
f8	Release button to use dial	No
f9	No memory card?	Enable release
f10	Reverse indicators	+ / -

a. Autofocus

The red-coded Autofocus options (see Figure 4.2) deal with some of the potentially most vexing settings available with the Nikon D300. After all, incorrect focus is one of the most damaging picture-killers of all the attributes in an image. You may be able to compensate for bad exposure, partially fix errant color balance, and perhaps even incorporate motion blur into an image as a creative element. But if focus is wrong, the photograph doesn't look right, and no amount of "I meant to do that!" pleas are likely to work. The D300's autofocus options enable you to choose how and when focus is applied (using the AF-S or AF-C focus mode you selected on the camera body), the controls used to activate the feature, and the way focus points are selected from the available 51 zones.

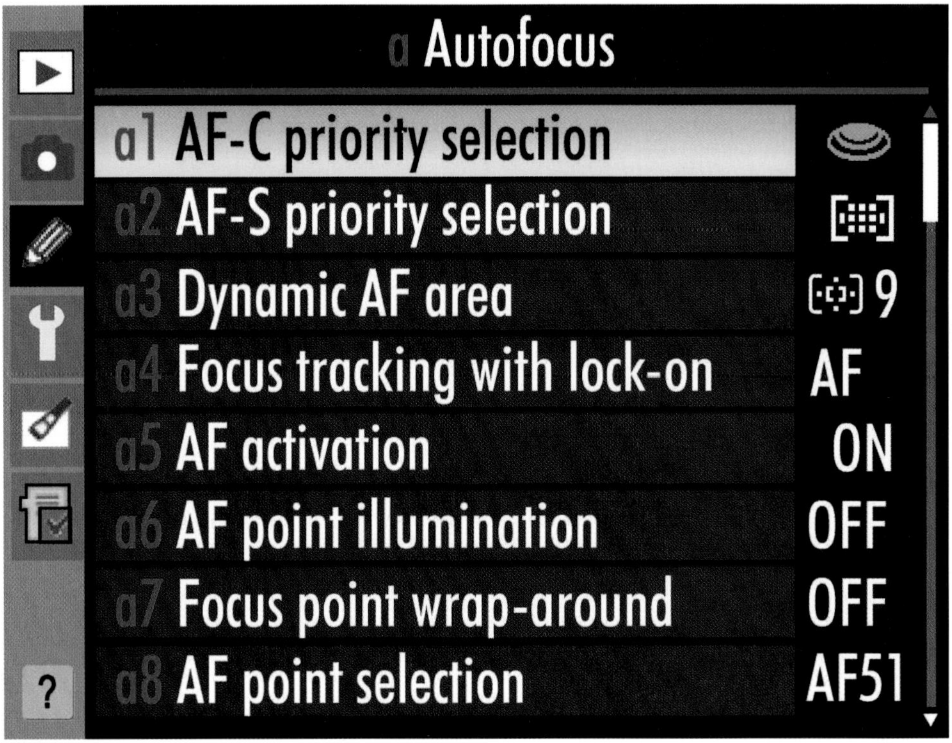

a Autofocus

a1 **AF-C priority selection**	⬭
a2 AF-S priority selection	[⬚]
a3 Dynamic AF area	[·:·] 9
a4 Focus tracking with lock-on	AF
a5 AF activation	ON
a6 AF point illumination	OFF
a7 Focus point wrap-around	OFF
a8 AF point selection	AF51

Figure 4.2
The first eight entries in the autofocus options menu.

a1 AF-C Priority Selection

As you'll learn in Chapter 6, the Nikon D300 has two primary autofocus modes, Continuous-Servo Autofocus (AF-C) and Single-Servo Autofocus (AF-S). This menu entry allows you to specify what takes precedence when you press the shutter release all the way down to take a picture: focus (called *focus priority*) or the release button (called *release priority*). You can choose from:

- **Release.** When this option is selected (the default), the shutter is activated when the release button is pushed down all the way, even if sharp focus has not yet been achieved. Because AF-C focuses and refocuses constantly when autofocus is active, you may find that an image is not quite in sharpest focus. Use this option when taking a picture is more important than absolute best focus, such as fast action or photojournalism applications. (You don't want to miss that record-setting home run, or the protestor's pie smashing into the Governor's face.) This option was called **FPS Rate** in the Nikon D200 but is functionally identical. Using this setting doesn't mean that your image won't be sharply focused; it just means that you'll get a picture even if autofocusing isn't quite complete. If you've been poised with the shutter release pressed halfway, the D300 probably has been tracking the focus of your image.

- **Release + focus.** The shutter is released when the button is pressed, but the frame rate is reduced slightly to give the D300 more time to autofocus when AF-C mode is used. (In non-Live View modes, the D300 is able to autofocus *only* between shots when the mirror is down and the autofocus sensors can read the incoming light.) The Nikon D200 called this setting **FPS Rate+AF.** You would not want to use this setting if the highest possible continuous shooting rates are important to you.

- **Focus.** The shutter is not activated until sharp focus is achieved. This is best for subjects that are not moving rapidly. AF-C will continue to track your subjects' movement, but the D300 won't take a picture until focus is locked in. You might miss a few shots, but you will have fewer out-of-focus images.

a2 AF-S Priority Selection

This is the counterpart setting for Single-Servo Autofocus mode. Note that the order of your two choices is reversed, compared to the Nikon D200; the Release choice is now on top, and Focus (the default) is on the bottom:

- **Release.** The shutter is activated when the button is depressed all the way, even if sharp focus is not quite achieved. Keep in mind that, unlike AF-C, the D300 focuses only *once* when AF-S mode is used. So, if you've partially depressed the shutter release, paused, and then pressed the button down all the way, it's possible that the subject has moved and Release Priority will yield more out-of-focus shots than Release Priority with AF-C. This setting is most viable if you're using a fast lens with a speedy internal focus motor (designated AF-S, which is *not* the same as the AF-S focus mode).

- **Focus.** This default prevents the D300 from taking a picture until focus is achieved and the in-focus indicator in the viewfinder glows a steady green. If you're using Single-Servo Autofocus mode, this is probably the best setting. Moving subjects really call for AF-C mode in most cases.

a3 Dynamic AF Area

The D300 has three focus area selection modes: automatic area, dynamic area, and single area. These three have some significant differences from the dynamic area/closest subject, group dynamic, dynamic area, and single area modes found in the D200 (which is why I'll devote some space to describing AF area selection in Chapter 6).

In the D300's dynamic area mode, you choose the initial autofocus point using the multi-selector's up/down and left/right buttons. The camera will initially focus on the specified focus point, but in Continuous-Servo Autofocus (AF-C) mode will refocus if the subject moves outside that point. This setting lets you determine how the camera diverts its attention from your specified active focus point to choose a new point when the subject leaves the primary focus zone. Your choices (shown in Figure 4.3) include:

- **9 points.** Should the subject leave the selected focus point, the camera will refocus using information from eight surrounding focus points. This mode is best when your subjects are moving in a predictable way, or you have time to re-compose the image. The D300 responds by using only a limited number of points outside the initial zone, but acting very quickly within that range of points.

- **21 points.** Should the subject leave the selected focus point, the D300 will refocus based on information from 20 surrounding focus points. This mode is best for subjects that are moving erratically. Autofocus may take slightly longer because more points are considered.

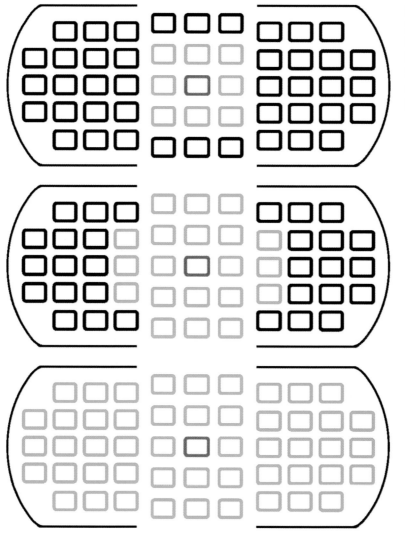

Figure 4.3
You can select from 9 (top), 21 (middle), or 51 (bottom) active focus points.

- **51 points.** Should the subject leave your selected focus point's coverage area, the camera will refocus based on information from all 50 surrounding focus points. This setting is best with subjects that are moving very quickly and/or not cooperative enough to be captured by your selected focus point. Nikon uses the example of birds and other hard-to-track subjects as suitable fodder for this mode.

- **51 points (3D-tracking).** Should the subject leave your selected focus zone, the D300 uses distance information to calculate the path of the subject and select a new focus point. Nikon recommends using this setting to focus subjects that move erratically from side to side (a halfback running towards you with the ball tucked under one arm comes to mind), because the camera can use the distance information to differentiate the original subject from objects that are closer or farther away.

a4 Focus Tracking with Lock-on

Sometimes new subjects interject themselves in the frame temporarily. Perhaps you're shooting an architectural photo from across the street and a car passes in front of the camera. Or, at a football game, a referee dashes past just as a receiver is about to make a catch. This setting lets you specify how quickly the D300 reacts to these transient interruptions that would cause relatively large changes in focus before refocusing on the "new" subject matter. You can specify a long delay, so that the interloper is ignored, a shorter delay, or turn lock-on off completely so that the D300 immediately refocuses when a new subject moves into the frame. Your options are:

- **Long.** The longest delay causes the D300 to ignore the intervening subject matter for a significant period of time. Use this setting when shooting subjects, such as sports, in which focus interruptions are likely to be frequent and significant.

- **Normal.** This default setting provides an intermediate delay before the camera refocuses on the new subject. It's usually the best choice when shooting sports in either of the continuous shooting modes, as the long delay can throw off autofocus accuracy at higher fps settings.

- **Short.** Choose this setting to tell the D300 to wait only a moment before refocusing. Very high frame rates (such as the 8 fps possible with the MB-D10 battery pack/grip attached) may work better when you allow refocusing to take place rapidly, without a lock-on delay.

- **Off.** Turn off focus lock-on if you want the D300 to refocus immediately. This may be the best choice for general subjects, because it allows the camera to smoothly follow-focus on a moving subject with no delay.

a5 AF Activation

This setting lets you change which controls are used to activate autofocus, either the shutter release button *and* the AF-ON button or the AF-ON button only. Most of us learned to use a half-press of the shutter release button to activate autofocus at the same time the exposure is calculated, but if you're willing to retrain yourself to use the AF-ON button, there are some nifty things you can do. For example, the AF-ON button can be used to lock focus in separately from exposure and taking the picture, and to produce the effect called *trap focus* in which you pre-focus at a certain point, press the shutter release, and the D300 doesn't take a picture until your subject (say, a horse crossing the finish line) moves into the pre-focused position. I'll describe trap focus in more detail in Chapter 7, but you can learn the basic use of this CSM setting now.

- **Shutter/AF-ON.** With this default setting, you can use either the shutter release button or the AF-ON button to initiate focus. For example, you could press the AF-ON button to start the autofocus operation as you initially frame the image, then press the shutter release when you're ready to take the picture to meter the scene. Or, without changing anything, you could press the shutter release button to perform autofocus and metering at the same time.

- **AF-ON only.** This setting decouples metering from autofocus activation. You must press AF-ON to start autofocus, and you must press the shutter release to start metering. So, you can activate and re-activate autofocus at any time. For example, suppose you're photographing a field goal attempt in a football game. Press AF-ON to lock in focus on the player who will be holding the ball for the kicker. When the play begins, focus will remain locked on the holder, even if defenders suddenly burst into the frame. As the kicker goes into motion, press the shutter release button to meter the scene and take the picture, confident that the focus you've set will not change. (In fast-moving situations, this is obviously more precise than manually focusing.) As a bonus, you don't have to worry about autofocus lag; the D300 will snap the picture virtually instantly. AF-ON can also be used in sneaky ways with the AE-L/AF-L button, and I'll cover those in Chapter 7.

> **Tip**
>
> The MB-D10 battery/grip has an AF-ON button for use in a vertical orientation, but does *not* have an AE-L/AF-L button (unless you reprogram the AF-ON button using **CSM #a10** described later in this section).

a6 AF Point Illumination

It's usually helpful to have the active focus point highlighted in red in the viewfinder, although the flashing indicator does use a minuscule amount of power. This setting lets you specify when/if this highlighting happens. Your choices include:

- **Auto.** With this default setting, the D300 will illuminate the selected focus point if it determines that highlighting is needed to sufficiently contrast the focus zone from the background.

- **On.** The selected focus point is always highlighted.

- **Off.** The selected focus point is never highlighted in red.

a7 Focus Point Wrap-Around

This setting is purely a personal preference parameter. When you press the multi-selector left/right and up/down buttons to choose a focus point, the D300 can be told to stop when the selection reaches the edge of the 51-point array—or, it can continue, wrapping around to the opposite edge, like Pac-Man leaving the playing area on one side or top/bottom to re-emerge on the other. (I hope I'm not revealing my age, here.) Your choices are simple; decide which behavior you prefer (and once again, Nikon has flopped the position of the settings from the Nikon D200 rendition):

- **Wrap.** Pressing the left/right or up/down buttons when you've reached the edge of the focus point display wraps the selection to the opposite side, still moving in the same direction.

- **No Wrap.** The focus point selection stops at the edge of the focus zone array.

a8 Focus Point Selection

You can choose the number of focus points available when you manually select a zone using the multi-selector up/down and left/right buttons. Your choices, shown in Figure 4.4, are as follows:

- **51 points.** This is the default. All 51 focus points can be selected.

- **11 points.** A more widely-spaced array of points is available. This can be the best choice for faster focus point selection when taking pictures of relatively large, evenly illuminated subject matter such that choosing precise focus zones is not particularly beneficial. I often use the 11-point option when photographing basketball games.

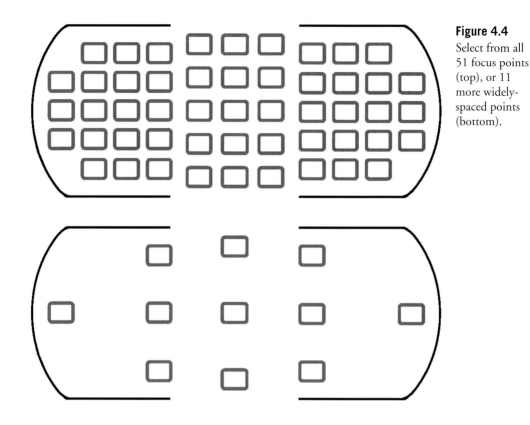

Figure 4.4
Select from all
51 focus points
(top), or 11
more widely-
spaced points
(bottom).

a9 Built-in AF-Assist Illuminator

Use this setting to control the AF-assist lamp built into the Nikon D300, or the more powerful AF-assist lamp built into Nikon electronic flash units (like the Nikon SB-800) and the Nikon SC-29 coiled remote flash cord (for firing the flash when not mounted on the camera).

- **On.** This default value will cause the AF-assist illuminator lamp to fire when lighting is poor, but only if Single-Servo Autofocus (AF-S) is active, or you have selected the center focus point manually and either single-point or dynamic-area autofocus (rather than auto-area autofocus) has been chosen.

- **Off.** Use this to disable the AF-assist illuminator. You'd find that useful when the lamp might be distracting or discourteous (say, at a religious ceremony or acoustic music concert), or your subject is located closer than one foot, eight inches or farther than about 10 feet.

a10 AF-ON for MB-D10

You can use the AF-ON button included in the MB-D10 battery pack/grip for its intended purpose when firing the camera in vertical orientation, or you can redefine the button to a related function, depending on your working preferences. This setting changes *only* the behavior of the AF-ON button on the MB-D10; the AF-ON button on the D300 camera body may be set up to do something different (which can be *very* confusing).

Your choices, which are slightly different from the comparable options available with the D200, let you define the AF-ON button for three different functions: normal AF-ON behavior; AE-L/AF-L exposure lock/focus lock functions; and whatever action you've defined for the FUNC. button. The equivalent CSM setting for the D200 had an additional function for the MB-D200 battery/grip, setting the focus area (by pressing the AF-ON button while rotating the sub-command dial). The D300 doesn't need that option, because it incorporates a mini multi-selector button into its design. Your choices are as follows:

- **AF-ON.** This default setting defines the AF-ON button as an AF-ON button, natch. Autofocus is initiated when the button is pressed.

- **AE/AF lock.** With this setting, both focus and exposure are locked when the AF-ON button is held down.

- **AE lock only.** Exposure is locked while this button is held down.

- **AE lock (Reset on release).** Exposure locks when the button is held down, and remains locked even when the button is released. You can cancel the AE lock by pressing the button a second time, by taking a picture, or allowing the exposure meters to turn off at the end of their normal meter-off delay.

- **AE lock (Hold).** This Exposure locks when the AF-ON button is pressed, and remains locked at that exposure until the button is pressed again, or the meters turn off.

- **AF lock only.** This setting locks autofocus as long as the button is pressed.

- **Same as FUNC. button.** Choosing this setting tells the D300 to perform whatever function has been defined for the FUNC. button in **CSM #f4** (described later in this chapter).

b. Metering/Exposure

The orange-coded Metering/Exposure Custom Settings (see Figure 4.5) let you define six different parameters that affect exposure metering in the Nikon D300.

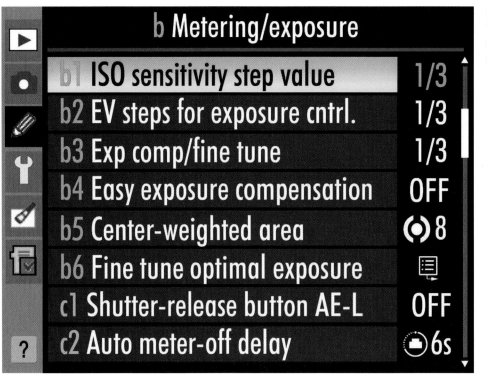

Figure 4.5
There are six metering/exposure options.

b1 ISO Sensitivity Step Value

This setting determines the size of the "jumps" it should use when making ISO adjustments—either one-third or one full stop. At the one-third stop setting, typical ISO values would be 200, 250, 320, 400, 500, 640, 800, 1000, 1250, 1600, and so forth. Choose 1/2 stop settings, and your choices would be 200, 280, 400, 560, 800, 1100, and 1600 over the same range. For really large increments, set the full-stop option, and choose 200, 400, 800, and 1600, and so forth. The larger increment can help you leap from one ISO setting to one that's much larger with one click in environments where you don't care to fine-tune sensitivity. As you've surmised, your choices include **1/3 step** (the default); **1/2 step**; and **1 step**.

b2 EV Steps for Exposure Cntrl.

This setting tells the Nikon D300 the size of the "jumps" it should use when making exposure adjustments—either one-third, one-half, or one full stop. The increment you specify here applies to f/stops, shutter speeds, EV changes, and autoexposure bracketing. As with ISO sensitivity step value, you can select from **1/3 step** (the default); **1/2 step**; and **1 step** increments.

Choose the 1/3 stop setting when you want the finest increments between shutter speeds and/or f/stops. For example, the D300 will use shutter speeds such as 1/60, 1/80, 1/100, 1/125, and 1/160 second, and f/stops such as f/5.6, f/6.3, f/7.1, and f/8, giving you (and the autoexposure system) maximum flexibility.

With 1/2 stop increments, you will have larger and more noticeable changes between settings. The D300 will apply shutter speeds such as 1/60th, 1/125th, 1/250th, and 1/500th second, and f/stops including f/5.6, f/6.7, f/8, f/9.5, and f/11. These coarser adjustments are useful when you want more dramatic changes between different exposures.

b3 Exp Comp/Fine-Tune

This third "increment" setting functions identically to the other two but applies to exposure compensation and flash exposure compensation adjustments you make by holding down the relevant EV adjustment buttons on the camera. (The exposure compensation button is on the top panel, just south-east of the shutter release button, as described in Chapter 2.) The flash compensation button can be found on the left side of the pentaprism, just below the flash-pop-up button. Both add or subtract from the exposure when held down while the main command dial is rotated. This setting tells the Nikon D300 the size of the "jumps" it should use when making these exposure adjustments. As with ISO sensitivity and exposure control step values, you can select from **1/3 step** (the default); **1/2 step**; and **1 step** increments.

b4 Easy Exposure Compensation

This setting potentially simplifies dialing in EV (exposure value compensation) adjustments by specifying whether the exposure compensation button must be pressed while adding or extracting EV compensation. Because of the possibility of confusion or error, I tend to leave this setting turned off. Your choices are as follows:

- **On (Auto reset).** This setting allows you to add or subtract exposure by rotating the sub-command dial when in Program (P) or Shutter Priority (S) exposure modes, or by rotating the main command dial when using Aperture Priority (A) mode. Rotating either dial has no effect in Manual (M) exposure mode. (If you've reversed the behavior of the command dials using **CSM #f7**, the "opposite" command dial must be used to make the changes.) Any adjustments you've made are canceled when the camera is shut off, or the meter-off time expires and the D300's exposure meters go back to sleep. That's a useful mode, because most of us have made an EV adjustment and then forgotten about it, only to expose a whole series of improperly exposed photos. You can still have "sticky" EV settings when Easy Exposure Compensation is turned on: just hold down the exposure compensation button when you make your changes.

- **On.** This setting brings the Easy Compensation Mode into conformance with the D300's behavior when the exposure compensation button is pressed: in either case, any EV modifications you make will remain until you countermand them. As I have mentioned several times, forgetting to "turn off" EV changes after you've moved on to a different shooting environment is a primary cause of over and underexposure among those of us who are forgetful or who ignore the D300's flashing EV warnings.

- **Off.** With this default setting, you must always press the exposure compensation button while rotating the main command dial to add or subtract exposure. Use this choice when you don't want any EV changes unless you deliberately make them by pressing the button.

b5 Center-Weighted Area

This setting changes the size of the center-weighted exposure spot when the D300 is used with a non-CPU (generally older AI and AI-S and earlier lenses that haven't been updated with a "computer" chip). Your choices include **6mm**, **8mm**, **10mm**, **13mm**, or **full-frame average** (which turns the metering mode from a center-weighted system to an old-fashioned averaging system). If you're using a non-CPU lens, the center-weighted area is fixed at 8mm, and the camera ignores whatever choice you may have entered here. Because, unlike the D200, the D300 does not show the default 8mm area in the viewfinder, you don't have any visual indication of what area is being emphasized by the metering system. Personally, I don't think that's much of a problem, so go ahead and choose whatever center-weighted area works best for you.

b6 Fine-Tune Optimal Exposure

This setting is a powerful adjustment that allows you to dial in a specific amount of exposure compensation that will be applied, invisibly, to every photo you take using each of the three metering modes. No more can you complain, "My D300 always underexposes by 1/3 stop!" If that is actually the case, and the phenomenon is consistent, you can use this Custom Menu adjustment to compensate.

Exposure compensation is usually a better idea (does your camera *really* underexpose that consistently?), but this setting does allow you to "recalibrate" your D300 yourself. You can fine-tune exposure separately in each of the four A, B, C, D Custom Settings banks, and your dialed in modifications will survive a two-button reset. However, you have no indication that fine-tuning has been made, so you'll need to remember what you've done. After all, you someday might discover that your camera is consistently *over*exposing images by 1/3 stop, not realizing that your **CSM #b6** adjustment is the culprit.

In practice, it's rare that the Nikon D300 will *consistently* provide the wrong exposure in any of the three metering modes, especially matrix metering, which can alter exposure dramatically based on the D300's internal database of typical scenes. This feature may be most useful for spot metering, if you always take a reading off the same type of subject, such as a human face or 18 percent gray card. Should you find that the gray card readings, for example, always differ from what you would prefer, go ahead and fine-tune optimal exposure for spot metering, and use that to read your gray cards. To use this feature:

1. Choose **b6 Fine-tune optimal exposure** from the Custom Setting menu.

2. In the screen that appears, choose **Yes** after carefully reading the warning that Nikon insists on showing you each and every time this option is activated.

3. Choose **Matrix metering**, **Center-Weighted**, or **Spot metering** in the screen that follows by highlighting your choice and pressing the multi-selector right button.

4. Press the up/down buttons to dial in the exposure compensation you want to apply. You can specify compensation in increments of 1/6 stop, half as large a change as conventional exposure compensation. This is truly *fine-tuning*.

5. Press **OK** when finished. You can repeat the action to fine-tune the other two exposure modes if you wish.

c. Timers/AE Lock

This category (see Figure 4.6) is a mixed bag of settings, covering both entries that adjust delay times (**c2** through **c4**) and how the shutter release and AE-L buttons interact (**c1**). I think the latter setting, changed slightly for the D300, should have been placed in the purple f-coded Controls section, especially since Nikon moved the assignment of AE-L/AF-L Button setting (which used to reside here with the Nikon D200) to that location. They moved one of the settings, but not the other. Go figure.

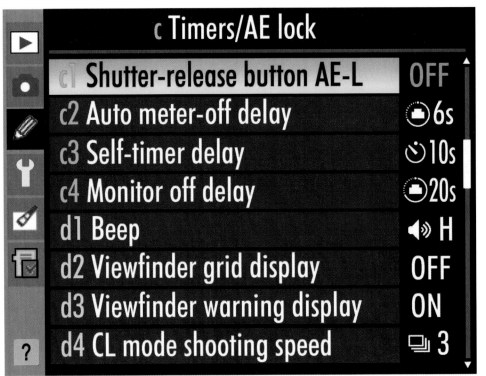

Figure 4.6
The Timers/AE
Lock settings.

c1 Shutter Release Button AE-L

This is another of Nikon's easily-confusing options for controlling how and when autofocus and exposure are activated and locked. The intent is to allow you to separate autofocus and autoexposure activation and locking. Because the options are scattered in various places in the Custom Setting menu, I'll sort out the interaction for you in Chapter 6. Meanwhile, all you need to know is:

- **Off.** Exposure is locked *only* when the AE-L/AF-L button is pressed. This is the default, as it was on the Nikon D200.

- **On.** Exposure locks when either the shutter release button is depressed halfway or the AE-L/AF-L button is held down. In the Nikon D200, this option was called **+Release.**

c2 Auto Meter-Off Delay

Use this setting to determine how long the D300's exposure meter continues to operate after the last operation, such as autofocusing, focus point selection, and so forth, was performed. The default value is 6 seconds, but you can also select 4, 8, 16, and 30 seconds, as well as 1, 5, 10, and 30 minutes, or No limit, which keeps the meter active until the camera is switched off. Nikon D200 owners will recall that the earlier camera offered only 4, 6, 8, and 16 second delays, plus No Limit.

To save power, you should select an intermediate value, such as 8, 16, or 30 seconds if the default 6 seconds is not long enough. When the Nikon EH5a or EH-5 AC adapter is connected to the D300, the exposure meter will remain on indefinitely, just as if you'd specified No limit. Absent an external power source, any setting longer than 8 seconds will definitely eat up power.

Even so, sports shooters and some others prefer a longer delay, because they are able to keep their camera always "at the ready" with no delay to interfere with taking an action shot that unexpectedly presents itself. Extra battery consumption is just part of the price paid. For example, when I am shooting football, a meter-off delay of 16 seconds is plenty, because the players lining up for the snap is my signal to get ready to shoot. But for basketball or soccer, I typically set the meter-off delay for No Limit, because action is virtually continuous. I typically use the MB-D10 battery pack/grip at these events, so my D300 has plenty of power, and I carry two sets of spares. I rarely shoot much more than 1000-1200 shots at any sports event, so that's sufficient juice even with meter-off delay set for No Limit.

Of course, if the meters have shut off, if the power switch remains in the On position, you can bring the camera back to life by tapping the shutter button.

c3 Self-Timer Delay

This setting lets you choose the length of the self-timer shutter release delay. The default value is 10 seconds. You can also choose 2, 5, or 20 seconds. These are unchanged from the D200. If I have the camera mounted on a tripod or other support and am too lazy to attach the MC-30 cable release (I have three, one for each camera bag, so I *always* have one available), I can set a two-second delay that is sufficient to let the camera stop vibrating after I've pressed the shutter release. I use a longer delay time if I am racing to get into the picture myself and am not sure I can make it in 10 seconds.

> **Tip**
>
> If you want a longer delay and are *really* lazy, just turn the D300's release mode dial to the **M-Up** position. No menu changes required! When you press the shutter release all the way down, the mirror will raise (reducing vibration so you can take a picture immediately), but if you do nothing else, the picture will be taken anyway 30 seconds later. (To take a picture immediately after the mirror is raised, press the shutter release a second time.) Return the release mode dial to the single shot or continuous shooting modes to cancel this temporary self-timer option.

c4 Monitor Off Delay

You can adjust the amount of time the monitor remains on when no other operations are being performed. As with the meter-off delay, if the EH-5a or EH-5 AC adapter is attached, the monitor will remain on for the maximum amount, about 10 minutes. On battery power, the default value is 20 seconds, but you can also select 10 seconds, plus 1, 5, or the full 10 minutes. Choosing a brief duration can help preserve battery power. However, the D300 will always override the review display when the shutter button is partially or fully depressed, so you'll never miss a shot because a previous image was on the screen.

SAVING POWER WITH THE Nikon D300

There are six settings and several techniques you can use to help you stretch the longevity of your D300's battery. To get the most from each charge, consider these steps:

- **Playback Menu.** Image Review: Turn off image review after each shot. You can still review your images by pressing the Playback button.

- **Auto meter-off-delay.** Set to 4 seconds if you can tolerate such a brief active time.

- **Monitor off Delay.** Set for the minimum, 10 seconds. That big 3-inch LCD uses a lot of juice, so reducing the amount of time it is used when you don't turn it off manually (either for automatic review or for playing back your images) can boost the effectiveness of your battery.

- **Reduce LCD illumination.** Set CSM #d8 to Off, so the monochrome LCD status panel will be backlit only when you manually use the switch around the shutter release.

- **Reduce LCD brightness.** In the Setup menu, select the lowest of the seven brightness settings that work for you under most conditions. If you're willing to shade the LCD with your hand, you can often get away with lower brightness settings outdoors, which will further increase the useful life of your battery.

- **Turn off modeling flash.** Set CSM #e4 to Off.

- **Reduce internal flash use.** No flash at all or fill flash use less power than a full blast.

- **Cancel VR.** Turn off vibration reduction if your lens has that feature and you feel you don't need it.

- **Use a card reader.** When transferring pictures from your D300 to your computer, use a card reader instead of the USB cable. Linking your camera to your computer and transferring images using the cable takes longer and uses a lot more power.

d. Shooting/Display

This menu section (see Figure 4.7) offers a variety of mostly unrelated shooting and display options not found elsewhere, but which are not frequently changed, making them suitable for a Custom Settings entry.

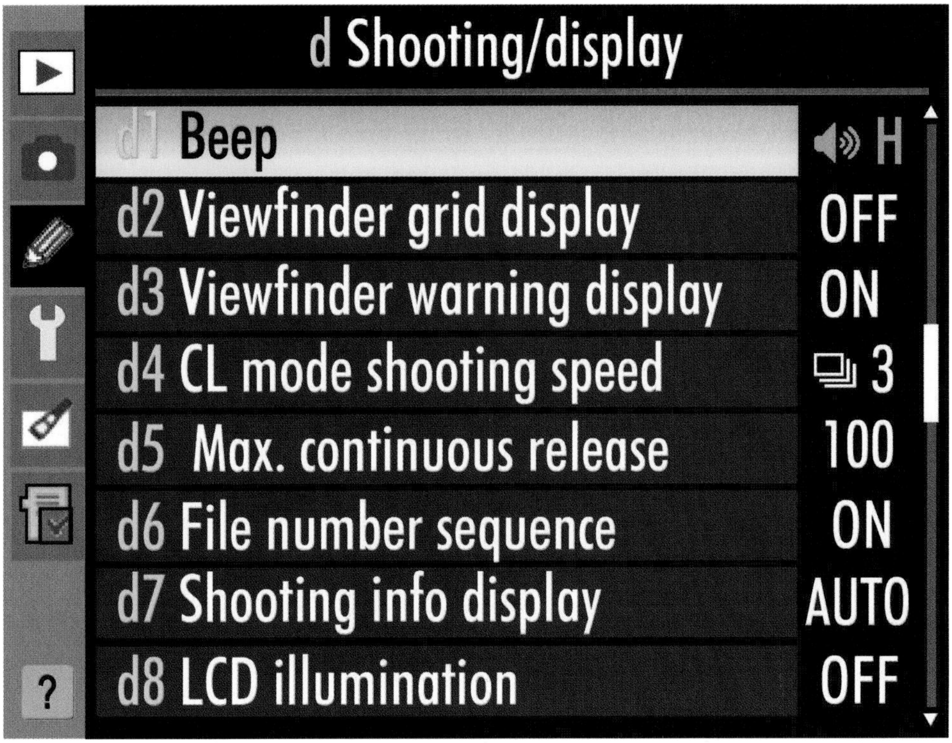

Figure 4.7
A mixed bag of entries is found in the shooting/display submenu.

d1 Beep

The Nikon D300's internal beeper provides a (usually) superfluous chirp to signify various functions, such as the countdown of your camera's self-timer or autofocus confirmation in AF-S mode (unless you've selected Release Priority in **CSM #a2.** You can (and probably should) switch it off if you want to avoid the beep because it's annoying, impolite, or distracting (at a concert or museum), or undesired for any other reason. It's one of the few ways to make the D300 a bit quieter. (I've actually had new dSLR owners ask me how to turn off the "shutter sound" the camera makes; such an option was available in the point-and-shoot camera they'd used previously.) Select **d1: Beep** from the menu, and select one of the following:

- **High.** This default value produces a high-pitched beep, and a quarter-note icon appears in the monochrome LCD status panel and the Shooting Information Display.

■ **Low.** A low-pitched beep is emitted, and the quarter-note icon appears in the status panel and Shooting Information Display.

■ **Off.** Turns the beeper off completely.

d2 Viewfinder Grid Display

The D300 can display a grid of lines overlaid on the viewfinder (see Figure 4.8), offering some help when you want to align vertical or horizontal lines. Note that the intersections of these lines do *not* follow the Rule of Thirds convention, and so are less useful for composition, assuming you want to follow the Rule of Thirds guideline in the first place. If you happen to subscribe to the Rule of Quarters, you're all set. Note that for critical applications, it's possible that your D300's viewfinder isn't absolutely accurate. I sometimes have to rotate images slightly in Photoshop because the grid is not perfectly aligned. Your options for this grid display are **On** and **Off** (the default).

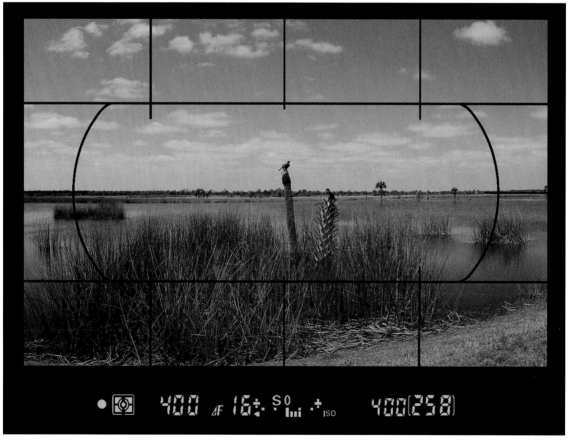

Figure 4.8 The D300's optional grid display can help with composing and aligning images in the viewfinder.

d3 Viewfinder Warning Display

The D300 has a low-battery warning that can be overlaid in the viewfinder, unlike the D200, which had low-battery, black-and-white mode warning, and a "no card loaded" advisory. Your options are **On** (the default) and **Off**. When I was using my D200 I found the **B/W** and **No Card** warnings obtrusive and turned this warning off. Because the D300 displays only the more-useful low-battery warning, I recommend leaving this feature turned on.

d4 CL Mode Shooting Speed

While the frames per second shooting rate at the high speed continuous shooting mode (C_H) is fixed at 6 fps (8 if the MB-D10 battery/grip is attached and loaded with either AA batteries or an EN-EL4/4a pack), you can adjust the speed for the low speed mode (C_L). You can select 1 to **7** fps rates (although the 7 fps choice will be activated only when the MB-D10 grip is mounted with the appropriate battery pack). Choose a firing speed suitable for the kind of shooting environment you're in:

- **Normal continuous shooting.** I set my D300 to the 1 fps rate most of the time, so that I can take multiple shots quickly without needing to press the shutter release repeatedly. A one-second rate isn't so fast that I end up taking a bunch of shots that I don't want, but it is fast enough that I can shoot a series.

- **Bracketing.** When I'm using bracketing, I generally have the D300 set to shoot a bracketed set of three pictures: normal, over, and under exposure. With the camera set to 3 fps (the default), I can press the shutter once and take all three bracketed shots, with basically the same framing, within about one second.

- **Slower action sequences.** The 6 fps and faster rates available for sports photography often produce an embarrassing plethora of pictures that are a pain to wade through after the event is over. For some types of action, such as long distance running, golf, swimming, or routine baseball plays, a rate of 3 to 5 fps might be sufficient. You can make this more reasonable speed available by defining it here.

d5 Max. Continuous Release

Use this setting to limit the number of consecutive shots that can be taken in one burst when using continuous shooting modes. Your choices are any value between **1** and **100**. Choosing a particular setting does not mean that the D300 will actually *take* that many shots if you hold down the shutter button long enough. As your buffer fills, continuous shooting will slow down and eventually pause while the D300 dumps pictures to the Compact Flash card.

However, there are many image quality and size settings that will allow the D300 to shoot more or less forever when equipped with a very fast memory card. For example, at the JPEG Normal setting, you can theoretically shoot 90 full-resolution images consecutively, and even using JPEG Fine you may be able to fire off more than 40 pictures in one burst. If you'd rather not accumulate that many images of one action and don't trust yourself to let up on the shutter release (it would take about 13 seconds to shoot 100 pictures at 8 fps), you can limit thc maximum burst here.

d6 File Number Sequence

The Nikon D300 will automatically apply a file number to each picture you take, using consecutive numbering for all your photos over a long period of time, spanning many different memory cards, starting over from scratch when you insert a new card, or when you manually reset the numbers. Numbers are applied from 0001 to 9999, at which time the D300 "rolls over" to 0001 again.

The camera keeps track of the last number used in its internal memory and, if File Number Sequence is turned **On**, will apply a number that's one higher, or a number that's one higher than the largest number in the current folder on the memory card inserted in the camera. You can also start over each time a new folder has been created on the memory card, or reset the current counter back to 0001 at any time. Here's how it works:

- **On.** At this default setting, the D300 will use the number stored in its internal memory any time a new folder is created, a new memory card inserted, or an existing memory card formatted. If the card is not blank and contains images, then the next number will be one greater than the highest number on the card *or* in internal memory (whichever is higher). Here are some examples.

  - You've taken 1,235 shots with the camera, and you insert a blank/reformatted memory card. The next number assigned will be 1,236, based on the value stored in internal memory.

  - You've taken 1,235 shots with the camera, and you insert an old memory card you previously used with the D300, but which has a picture numbered 0728. The next picture will be numbered 1,236.

  - You've taken more than 9,999 shots with the camera and the counter has rolled over to 0001 again, and your new total is 1,235 shots. You insert an old memory card with a picture from before the rollover that's numbered 8,281. The next picture will be numbered 8,282, and that value will be stored in the camera's menu as the "high" shot number (and will be applied when you next insert a blank card). This misnumbering makes it a good idea to always reformat your memory cards before taking a photo, if at all possible.

- **Off.** If you're using a blank/reformatted memory card, or a new folder is created, the next photo taken will be numbered 0001. File number sequences will be reset every time you use or format a card, or a new folder is created (which happens when an existing folder on the card contains 999 shots).

- **Reset.** The D300 assigns a file number that's one larger than the largest file number in the current folder, unless the folder is empty, in which case numbering is reset to 0001. At this setting, new or reformatted memory cards will always have 0001 as the first file number.

HOW MANY SHOTS, REALLY?

The file numbers produced by the D300 don't provide information about the actual number of times the camera's shutter has been tripped—called actuations. For that data, you'll need a third-party software solution, such as the free Opanda iExif (**www.opanda.com**) for Windows (see Figure 4.9) or the non-free ($34.95) GraphicConverter for Macintosh (**www.lemkesoft.com**). These utilities can be used to extract the true number of actuations from the Exif information embedded in a JPEG file.

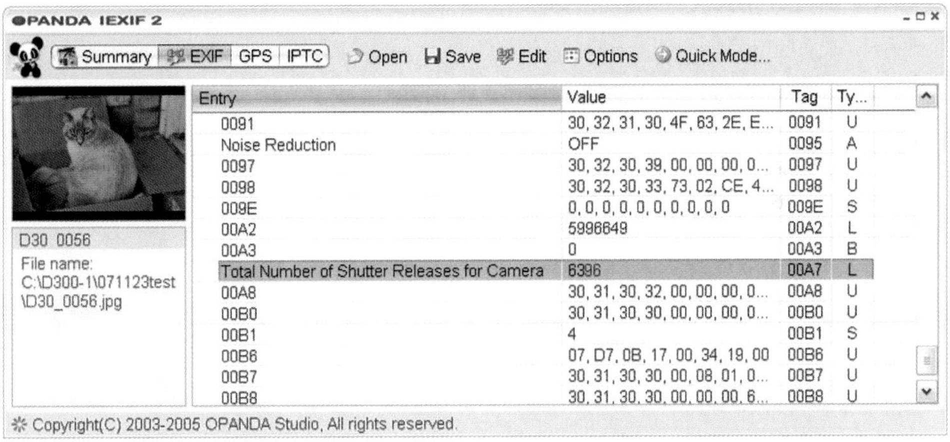

Figure 4.9
Opanda iExif shows the exact number of pictures that have been taken with your camera.

d7 Shooting Info Display

The Shooting Info Display that appears when you press the Info button can be set to change automatically from dark lettering on a light background to light lettering on a dark background (as seen previously in Figure 2.10 in Chapter 2), or you can select one or the other to be used all the time. The color LCD monitor will automatically change its brightness to provide the best contrast for the selected text display.

Your choices are:

- **Auto.** If the scene as viewed through the lens indicates a bright environment, the Shooting Info Display will appear as black letters on a white background, producing an improved view in full daylight. If the scene appears dark, the display will have lighter letters on a dark background. Note that it's easy to "fool" the camera. Until you take the lens cap off, you'll see the dark background display regardless of your shooting environment. If you're standing in a darkened location, but point the camera at a bright scene, the D300 will show you the "daylight" display.

- **Manual.** Select this option and you can choose B (Dark on light) or W (Light on dark).

d8 LCD Illumination

When set to **Off** (the default), the monochrome LCD status panel (and the status LCDs on any attached compatible Nikon speedlight, such as the Nikon SB-800) will illuminate for as long as the exposure meters are active, but only when the switch around the shutter release is pressed towards the maximum clockwise direction, just past the On indicator. Choose **On**, and the panel will be illuminated any time the exposure meters are active (and thus using more power), without the need to press the switch.

d9 Exposure Delay Mode

This is a marginally useful feature you can use to force the Nikon D300 to snap a picture about one second after you've pressed the shutter release button all the way. It's useful when you are using shutter speeds of about 1/8 to 1/60 second hand-held and want to minimize the effects of the vibration that results when you depress the shutter button. It can also be used when the camera is mounted on a tripod, although the self-timer function, set to a two-second delay, is more useful in that scenario. When switched **On**, the camera will pause while you steady your steely grip on the camera, taking the picture about one second later. When turned **Off,** the picture is taken when the shutter release is pressed, as normal. One interesting side-effect of this mode is that it separates the normally invisible preflash produced by the D300's internal flash (or any external flash that's connected) with the delay, so, if you're shooting living subjects (human or animal) they may be startled by the initial flash and close their eyes just before the main flash fires 1000 milliseconds later.

d10 MB-D10 Battery Type

This option is needed to communicate to the D300 what type of AA batteries are being used in the MB-D10 battery pack/grip, because the different varieties of AA batteries provide slightly different voltages, and change voltages at different rates as they are used up. The setting you select here has no effect when you're using an EN-EL3e or EN-EL4/EN-EL4a battery. Your choices include:

- **LR6 (AA alkaline).** For ordinary alkaline batteries

- **HR6 (AA NiMH).** For Nickel-Metal Hydride batteries

- **FR6 (AA lithium).** For non-rechargeable lithium batteries

- **ZR6 (AA NiMn).** For Nickel-Manganese batteries

Because of their limited capacity, you'll want to use conventional AA alkaline batteries or nickel-manganese batteries only as a last resort, and then only when the weather is warmer than 68 degrees Fahrenheit, because the chemical reactions that provide power decline at lower temperatures. Alkalines retain their power longer when not used, so they may be a reasonable choice if you rarely use your MB-D10 and want to keep it ready to go. But I expect few readers will have this useful accessory sitting on a shelf gathering dust.

d11 Battery Order

When using the MB-D10 battery pack/grip, the batteries in the pack and in your D300 are used consecutively. That is, one of them powers the camera until it is exhausted, and then the D300 switches to the other. You can choose the order in which this switch-off takes place.

The default setting is **MB-D10 Use MB-D10 batteries first.** You can also specify **D300 Use camera battery first**. If you were using AA batteries or an EN-EL4/EN-EL4a pack in the MB-D10 to achieve a higher shooting frame rate, you'd want to use the grip's batteries initially (and replace them as required to retain the higher fps). If you were using AA alkaline batteries in the MB-D10 as an emergency reserve, you'd probably want to use the D300's internal battery first, so the alkalines wouldn't be prematurely exhausted and could live to shoot as backup another day.

e. Bracketing/Flash

There are lots of useful settings in this sub-menu (see Figure 4.10) that deal with bracketing and electronic flash (hence the cleverly concocted name). I'll provide a thorough description of using bracketing in Chapter 6, and a complete run-down of flash options in Chapter 8. Here, I'll offer an introduction to the settings at your disposal.

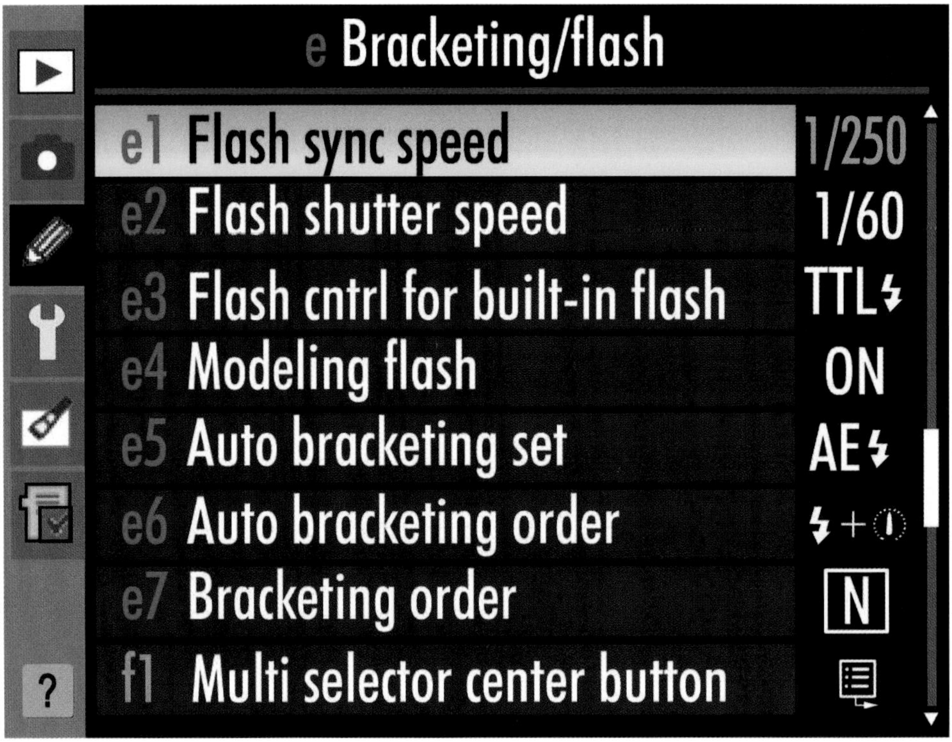

Figure 4.10
Bracketing and flash options are available in this menu.

e1 Flash Sync Speed

As you may already know (or will learn in Chapter 8), the focal plane shutter in the Nikon D300 must be fully open when the flash fires; otherwise, you'll image one edge or the other of the vertically traveling shutter curtain in your photo. Ordinarily, the fastest shutter speed during which the shutter is completely open for an instant is 1/250 second. However, there are exceptions when you can use faster shutter speeds with certain flash units (such as the Nikon SB-800, SB-600, and SB-R200) for automatic FP (focal plane) synchronization. There are also situations in which you might want to set flash sync speed to *less* than 1/250 second, say, because you *want* ambient light to produce secondary ghost images in your frame. (I'll address all these sync issues in Chapter 8.) You can choose the following settings:

- **1/320 s (Auto FP).** This setting can allow use of flash with any shutter speed from 1/320 second to 1/8,000 second, with certain external flash units, *but not with the D300's built-in flash.* If you're using the Nikon SB-800, SB-600, or SB-R200 external flash unit shutter speeds from 1/320-1/8,000 second can be used; synchronization is produced by firing the unit continuously over a longer time period in short repeating bursts, so the effective power of the flash is reduced (meaning that the *distance range* of the flash is curtailed). You'll need to shoot subjects that are closer to the camera. When using Program or Aperture Priority mode (which both automatically select a shutter speed), high-speed sync will kick in whenever the actual shutter speed is faster than 1/320 second. Other flash units, including the D300's *built-in* flash allow the D300 to sync with flash at speeds of up to 1/320 second.

- **1/250 s (Auto FP).** This setting allows using the named external flash units with high-speed synchronization at 1/250 second or faster, and activates auto FP sync when the camera selects a shutter speed of 1/250 second or faster in Program and Aperture Priority modes. Other flash units, including the D300's built-in flash, will be used at speeds no faster than 1/250 second.

- **1/250 s.** At this default setting, only shutter speeds up to 1/250 second can be used with flash, both internal and external. Note: To lock in shutter speed at 1/250 second, choose the **x 250** setting located after the **30 s** and **bulb** speeds.

- **1/200 s-1/60 s.** You can specify a shutter speed from 1/200 second to 1/60 second to be used as the synchronization speed for internal and external flash units.

e2 Flash Shutter Speed

This setting determines the *slowest* shutter speed that is available for electronic flash synchronization when you're not using a "slow sync" mode (described in Chapter 9). As you may know, when you're using flash, the flash itself provides virtually all of the illumination that makes the main exposure, and the shutter speed determines how much, if any, of the ambient light contributes to that second, non-flash exposure. Indeed, if the camera or subject is moving, you can end up with two distinct exposures in the same frame: the sharply defined flash exposure, and a second, blurry "ghost" picture created by the ambient light.

If you *don't* want that second exposure, you should use the highest shutter speed that will synchronize with your flash. This setting prevents Program or Aperture Priority modes (which both select the shutter speed for you) from inadvertently selecting a "too slow" shutter speed. You can select a value from **30 s** to **1/60 s**, and the D300 will avoid using speeds slower than the one you specify with electronic flash (unless you've selected **slow sync**, **slow rear-curtain sync**, or **red-eye reduction with slow sync**, as described in Chapter 9). The "slow sync" modes do permit the ambient light to contribute to the exposure (say, to allow the background to register in night shots, or to use the ghost image as a special effect). For brighter backgrounds, you'll need to put the camera on a tripod or other support to avoid the blurry ghosts that can occur from camera shake, even if the subject is stationary.

If you are able to hold the D300 steady, a value of **1/30 s** is a good compromise; if you have shaky hands, use **1/60 s** or higher. Those with extraordinarily solid grips can try the **1/15 s** setting. Remember that this setting only determines the slowest shutter speed that will be used, not the default shutter speed.

e3 Flash Cntrl for Built-in Flash

The Nikon D300's built-in flash has four modes, which I'll describe in a lot more detail in Chapter 9. Your four options are as follows:

- **TTL.** When the built-in flash is triggered, the D300 first fires a pre-flash and measures the light reflected back and through the lens to calculate the proper exposure when the full flash is emitted a fraction of a second later.

- **Manual.** You can set the level of the built-in flash from full power to 1/128 power.

- **Repeating flash.** The flash fires multiple bursts, producing a stroboscopic lighting effect. As I'll describe in Chapter 9, when you choose repeating flash you'll be asked to select Output (flash power level), Times (the number of times the flash is fired at the output level you specify), and Frequency (how often the flash fires per second). Note that these factors are interdependent. For example, if you tell the flash to fire at 1/8 output power, you can select from 2 to 5 flashes, at a rate of 1 to 50 flashes per second. That's because the flash has only enough power for a maximum of 5 flashes at the 1/8 output setting. At 1/128 power, there's enough juice for 2 to 35 individual flashes, at a rate of no more than 50 flashes per second.

- **Commander mode.** If you never use external flash, you can safely ignore this setting. If you do, you'll want to set up the D300 for your most frequently used options, to avoid having to fiddle with the camera if you decide to pull your SB-800 out of your bag for some impromptu multi-flash shooting. In Commander mode, the built-in flash emits preflashes that can be used to wirelessly control one or more remote external flash units.

> ### Tip
>
> If the Nikon SB-400 flash unit is attached and turned on, this menu choice is not available, because the SB-400 unit, unlike the D300's built-in flash and some other external flash units, cannot function in Commander mode. You'll be able to set flash compensation and flash mode for the built-in flash as well as individual "groups" of flashes (Groups A and B) and the triggering channels. As you'll see, using electronic flash with the Nikon D300 is worth a book of its own, but I'll do my best to explain the vagaries in Chapter 9.

e4 Modeling Flash

The Nikon D300, and certain compatible external flash units (like the SB-600 and SB-800) have the capability of simulating a modeling lamp, which gives you the limited capability of previewing how your flash illumination is going to look in the finished photo. The modeling flash is not a perfect substitute for a real incandescent or fluorescent modeling lamp, but it does help you see how your subject is illuminated, and spot any potential problems with shadows.

When this feature is activated, pressing the depth-of-field button on the D300 briefly triggers the modeling flash for your preview. Selecting **Off** disables the feature. You'll generally want to leave it **On**, except when you anticipate using the depth-of-field preview button for depth-of-field purposes (imagine that) and do *not* want the modeling flash to fire when the flash unit is charged and ready. Some external flash units, such as the SB-800, have their own modeling flash buttons. Although the SB-600 does not have this button, it works fine with the D300's modeling flash feature.

e5 Auto Bracketing Set

The Nikon D300 can automatically take several pictures using slightly different settings within a range that you specify, and apply the changes to automatic exposure, electronic flash, or white balance. This setting allows you to specify whether bracketing is used for both automatic exposure *and* flash (**AE & flash**), automatic exposure only (**AE**), flash bracketing only (**Flash only**), or white balance color bracketing alone (**WB bracketing**). No autoexposure or flash bracketing will be performed when white balance bracketing is activated. Because you can specify white balance manually when importing a RAW file, WB bracketing is not available when Quality has been set to **NEF (RAW)** or **NEF (RAW)+JPEG**. The results you get with flash bracketing can vary quite a bit, depending on the amount of ambient illumination and flash mode you've chosen, but exposure bracketing is fairly consistent. I tend to leave this option set to AE most of the time. White balance bracketing is useful when you're not quite sure of the color balance of your illumination.

e6 Auto Bracketing Mode (Mode M)

If you're using Manual exposure mode to set the shutter speed and f/stop yourself, you can still take advantage of exposure bracketing. The Nikon D300 will take the basic settings you specified and adjust the exposure to provide over, under, and as-set variations. This setting determines whether shutter speed, aperture, or both are used to create the bracketing exposures. Remember, *you* set the basic exposure using shutter speed and aperture, and the D300 brackets around those values. If your flash is used and has been activated for bracketing using CSM #e5, the flash will be factored in, as well. The menu entries can be tricky to understand, so I'm going to spell them out:

- **Flash/Speed.** With this default value, the D300 will vary the shutter speed to produce bracketed exposures and, if flash bracketing is available, will vary flash output as well. Use this option to keep your aperture set at the f/stop you select, say, to provide a certain desired amount (or lack) of depth-of-field. This setting works best when bracketing a moderate number of shots—say, 2 to 5 exposures—because the shutter speed changes among the bracketed set won't be dramatic.

- **Flash/Speed/Aperture.** This option tells the D300 to vary both shutter speed and aperture from your manual settings, and to vary flash output if flash bracketing is available. This setting is useful when creating a large bracket set, up to nine different exposures, because you'll rarely want to vary shutter speed or aperture alone over such a large range of shots. The Flash/Speed/Aperture option spreads the variation over a combination of shutter speeds and apertures.

- **Flash/Aperture.** The D300 will use the aperture to bracket your photos taken by ambient light, and if flash bracketing is available, will use flash output as well. This option is best if you're shooting sports with manual exposures and want to lock in a specific shutter speed. As with Flash/Speed, this setting works best when the number of exposures in your bracket set is limited to 2 to 5 exposures; otherwise, the f/stop selected can vary wildly.

e7 Bracketing Order

Use this setting to define the sequence in which bracketing is carried out. Your choices are the default: **MTR>Under>Over** (metered exposure, followed by the version receiving less exposure, and finishing with the picture receiving the most exposure); and **Under>MTR>Over**, which orders the exposures from least exposed to most exposed (for both ambient and flash exposures). The same order is applied to white balance bracketing, too, but the values are **Normal>More Yellow>More Blue** and **More Yellow>Normal>More Blue**. (Nikon actually calls "yellow" by the term "amber," but I've found "yellow" easier to understand.) You'll find lots more about bracketing in Chapter 6.

f. Controls

You can modify the way various control buttons and dials perform by using the options in this sub-menu, shown in Figure 4.11.

Figure 4.11
Modify the behavior of the D300's controls with these menu options.

f Controls

f1 Multiselector center button	
f2 Multi selector	OFF
f3 Photo info/playback	OFF
f4 Assign FUNC. button	
f5 Assign preview button	
f6 Assign AE-L/AF-L button	
f7 Customize command dials	
f8 Release button to use dial	OFF

f1 Multi-Selector Center Button

There are two groups of options available here, one for use when the camera is in Shooting mode, and another when you're reviewing images in Playback mode. So the multi-selector center button can have two different functions. In Shooting mode:

- **Select center focus point.** This default setting lets you quickly select the center focus point in the viewfinder simply by pressing the multi-selector center button.

- **Highlight active focus point.** This setting is useful when the active focus point is not illuminated in the viewfinder, and you want to determine what it is. Just press the multi-selector center button, and presto, there it is.

- **Not used.** Nothing happens when the multi-selector center button is pressed. If you find yourself sloppily pressing the center button in the heat of the moment while shooting, use this setting to deactivate it and avoid unwanted actions.

In Playback mode:

- **Thumbnail on/off.** This default setting alternates between full-frame and thumbnail playback.

- **View histograms.** When selected, a larger histogram is displayed while the multi-selector center button is pressed.

- **Zoom on/off.** Use the multi-selector center button to toggle between full-frame or thumbnail playback (whichever is active) and playback zoom. You can choose Low magnification, Medium Magnification, and High magnification.

- **Choose folder.** Use this setting to switch quickly among folders in use during Playback mode. When the multi-selector center button is pressed, a list of folders will be shown (unless only one folder exists or Current has been selected as the Playback folder in the Playback menu—as described in Chapter 3). If other folders are available, you can select one and press **OK.**

f2 Multi-Selector

By default, pressing the left/right or up/down buttons on the multi-selector when the exposure meters are off does nothing. If you would rather have the meters activated instead, switch from the **Do Nothing** default to **Reset meter-off delay.** The meters will spring to life when one of the directional buttons is pressed, and remain active until the delay you've set previously in **CSM #c2** has elapsed.

f3 Photo Info/Playback

During playback, pressing the multi-selector up/down buttons on the Nikon D300 (as well as on the MB-D10 battery pack) changes the type of photo information displayed, while pressing the left/right buttons moves forward and back among the available images. This action was reversed in some earlier Nikon dSLRs, and some prefer that the up/down buttons scroll among images and the left/right buttons change the information display. You can use this setting to specify either mode of operation.

f4 Assign FUNC. Button

You can define the action that the FUNC. button performs when pressed alone, or when pressed while the command dials are rotated. There are no less than 13 different actions you can define for the button alone (including **None**), and five for the button+a command dial. For the button alone you can choose from:

- **Preview.** Depth-of-field preview. Perhaps you'd like to use the DOF preview button for something else, and substitute the lower of the two buttons for DOF preview. Unfortunately, you cannot use this function if you've also selected a function for the **Fn button+command dials**. If you do use this function, then any Fn button+command dials function will be canceled and set to **None**. Conversely, if you go ahead and set a function for **Fn button+command dials**, this setting will be deactivated and set to **None**. They are what we like to call "mutually exclusive."

- **FV Lock.** Press the **Fn** button to lock the value of the built-in or external flash, and press again to unlock it. As with Preview, you cannot use this function if you've also selected a function for the **Fn button+command dials**. If you do set this function, then any Fn button+command dials function will be canceled and set to None. Should you go ahead and set a function for **Fn button+command dials**, this setting will be deactivated and the Fn button function set to **None.**

- **AE/AF lock.** Lock both focus and exposure while the **Fn** button is pressed. Use this setting or one of the next four when you want to have a specific mode of operation normally available from the AE-L/AF-L button, but would prefer to trigger the behavior with the Fn button pressed instead.

- **AE lock only.** Lock only the exposure while the **Fn** button is pressed.

- **AE lock (Reset on release).** Lock exposure while the **Fn** button is pressed, and it remains locked until the Fn button is pressed a second time, or a picture is taken, or the exposure meter-off delay expires. This is another of the four settings mutually exclusive with using a **Fn button+command dial** setting.

- **AE lock (Hold).** Exposure is locked when the **Fn** button is pressed, and remains locked until the button is pressed again, or the exposure meter-off delay expires. This the fourth of the settings mutually exclusive with using a **Fn button+command dial** setting.

- **AF lock only.** Focus is locked in while the **Fn** button is held down.

- **Flash off.** The built-in flash (if elevated) and any external flash attached and powered up will not fire while the **Fn** button is held down. Handy if you want to temporarily disable the flash, say, to take a picture or two by available light, and then return to normal flash operation.

- **Bracketing burst.** If the **Fn** button is pressed while exposure or flash bracketing have been activated in single frame mode, all the shots (from 2 to 9 exposures) will be taken, one after another, each time the shutter release is pressed. If high speed or low speed continuous shooting modes (C_H or C_L) are active (or if white balance bracketing is active), the D300 will repeat the bracketing bursts for as long as the shutter release button is pressed down.

- **Matrix metering.** Switch from the current metering mode to Matrix metering while the **Fn** button is held down.

- **Center-weighted metering.** Switch from the current metering mode to Center-Weighted metering while the **Fn** button is held down.

- **Spot metering.** Switch from the current metering mode to Spot metering while the **Fn** button is held down. This is my favorite setting, because I like to switch from Matrix to Spot metering from time to time.

- **None.** This is the default setting, so if you want the **Fn** button to actually have an Fn, you'll need to choose one of the other options.

To define the FUNC. button + command dials options, choose one of the following. Note that setting any of these while **Preview**, **FV Lock**, or **AE Lock (Reset on release)**, or **AE Lock (Hold)** are active will reset the Fn button (alone) to **None**:

- **1 step spd/aperture.** If you sometimes prefer coarser exposure settings of 1 whole step (instead of the 1/3 or 1/2 step increments that are normally set), use this option. When holding down the Fn button and rotating a command dial, shutter speed and aperture changes are made in whole step increments instead.

- **Choose non-CPU lens number.** If you swap out older non-CPU manual lenses frequently, this option provides a quicker way of telling the D300 which lens number (1 to 9) to use. I often mount an old manual focus 85mm f/1.8 lens or 55mm f/3.5 Micro Nikkor on my D300, and can use this facility to switch back and forth between the lens settings I've manually entered for these lenses. (Chapter 5 will show you how to do that in the Setup menu.)

- **Auto bracketing.** This default value is used to choose the number of shots in an auto bracketing program while the **Fn** button is depressed and the main command dial is rotated. Rotate the sub-command dial instead while holding down the **Fn** button to select the bracketing increment. (As I've threatened, there is more on bracketing in Chapter 6.) This feature substitutes for the **BKT** button found on the Nikon D200 in the position where the Playback button now resides on the D300.

- **Dynamic AF area.** Switch among the number of focus points active in dynamic-area AF mode when using Continuous-Servo Autofocus, from **9**, **21**, and **51** points.

- **None.** No action is performed when the Fn button is held down while the command dials are rotated.

USING BOTH FN PLUS FN+COMMAND DIALS

The settings that preclude the use of the **Fn button+command dials** combinations can be confusing. To make things simpler, you can define the **Fn** button to use **AE/AF lock, AE lock only, AF-lock only, Flash off, Bracketing burst, Matrix, Center-Weighted,** or **Spot metering** options with any of the Fn button+command dial options. If you define the Fn button to provide **Preview, FV lock, AE lock (Reset on release),** or **AE Lock (Hold)** functions, you cannot use *any* of the **Fn button+command dial** options at all. If you elect to use any **Fn button+command dial** settings, then the four antagonistic **Fn** button functions are disabled. It's as simple (or complicated) as that.

f5 Assign Preview Button

The Depth-of-Field button can also be defined as you wish, with the same options and limitations as for the **Fn** button, but the default action for the DOF button is **Preview**, and there is no default function for the **Preview button+command** dials. This definability is a departure from the Nikon D200, which allowed only the Fn button to be defined.

f6 Assign AE-L/AF-L Button

As if the Nikon D300 didn't have enough buttons that are user-definable, you can change the behavior of the AE-L/AF-L button, too, both when it is used alone and when held down while command dials are rotated. The D200 never had it this good!

The default value for the AE-L/AF-L button is AE/AF lock, and there is no default action for AE-L/AF-L button+command dials. To recap your options:

- **Preview.** Depth-of-field preview.

- **FV Lock.** Press the **AE-L/AF-L** button to lock the value of the built-in or external flash, and press again to unlock it.

- **AE/AF lock.** Lock both focus and exposure while the **AE-L/AF-L** button is pressed.

- **AE lock only.** Lock only the exposure while the **AE-L/AF-L** button is pressed.

- **AE lock (Reset on release).** Lock exposure while the **AE-L/AF-L** button is pressed, and remain locked until the **AE-L/AF-L** button is pressed a second time, or a picture is taken, or the exposure meter-off delay expires.

- **AE lock (Hold).** Exposure is locked when the **AE-L/AF-L** button is pressed, and remains locked until the button is pressed again, or the exposure meter-off delay expires.

- **AF lock only.** Focus is locked in while the **AE-L/AF-L** button is held down.

- **AF-ON.** The AE-L/AF-L button is used to initiate autofocus. (This option is not available for the FUNC. button or depth-of-field preview button.)

- **Flash off.** The built-in flash (if elevated) and any external flash attached and powered up will not fire while the **AE-L/AF-L** button is held down.

- **Bracketing burst.** If the **AE-L/AF-L** button is pressed while exposure or flash bracketing have been activated in single frame mode, all the shots (from 2 to 9 exposures) will be taken, one after another, each time the shutter release is pressed. If high speed or low speed continuous shooting modes (C_H or C_L) are active (or if white balance bracketing is active), the D300 will repeat the bracketing bursts for as long as the shutter release button is pressed down.

- **Matrix metering.** Switch from the current metering mode to Matrix metering while the **AE-L/AF-L** button is held down.

- **Center-Weighted metering.** Switch from the current metering mode to Center-Weighted metering while the **AE-L/AF-L** button is held down.

- **Spot metering.** Switch from the current metering mode to Spot metering while the **AE-L/AF-L** button is held down. This is my favorite setting, because I like to switch from Matrix to Spot metering from time to time.

- **None.** Nothing happens when the **AE-L/AF-L** button is pressed.

To define the **AE-L/AF-L button+command dials** options, choose one of the following. Note that setting any of these while **Preview, FV Lock,** or **AE Lock (Reset on release)** or **AE Lock (Hold)** are active will reset the **AE-L/AF-L button** (alone) to **AE-L/AF-L:**

- **Choose non-CPU lens number.** If you swap out older non-CPU manual lenses frequently, this option provides a quicker way of telling the D300 which lens number (1 to 9) to use. I often mount an old manual focus 85mm f/1.8 lens or 55mm f/3.5 Micro Nikkor on my D300, and can use this facility to switch back and forth between the lens settings I've manually entered for these lenses. (Chapter 5 will show you how to do that in the Setup menu.)

- **Auto bracketing.** This setting is used to choose the number of shots in an auto bracketing program while the **AE-L/AF-L button** is depressed and the main command dial is rotated. Rotate the sub-command dial instead while holding down the **AE-L/AF-L button** to select the bracketing increment.

- **Dynamic AF area.** Switch among the number of focus points active in dynamic-area AF mode when using Continuous-Servo Autofocus, from **9, 21,** and **51** points.

- **None.** With this default active, no action is performed when the **AE-L/AF-L button** is held down while the command dials are rotated.

f7 Customize Command Dials

You can use the options in this menu entry to change the behavior of the command dials. Use the available tweaks to change the behavior of the dials to better suit your preferences, or if you're coming to the Nikon world from another vendor's product that uses a different operational scheme. Keep in mind that redefining basic controls in this way can prove confusing if someone other than yourself uses your camera, or if you find yourself working with other Nikon cameras that have retained the normal command dial behavior. Your options include:

- **Reverse rotation.** Rotating the main command dial (on both the camera and MB-D10 battery pack) counter-clockwise causes shutter speeds to become shorter in Manual and Shutter Priority modes; rotating the sub-command dial counter-clockwise selects larger f/stops. If you want to reverse the directional orientation of the dials (so you'll need to rotate the main command dial clockwise to specify shorter shutter speeds, etc.), set this option to **Yes**. Set to **No** to return to the original D300 scheme of things.

■ **Change main/sub.** Select **On** to exchange the functions of the main and sub-command dials. When activated, the main dial will set the aperture in Manual and Aperture Priority modes, and the sub-command dial will adjust the shutter speed in Manual and Shutter Priority modes. All other normal functions are swapped, as well. Select **Off** to return to the Nikon D300's default arrangement.

■ **Aperture setting.** Ordinarily, autofocus lenses having an aperture ring are locked at their smallest aperture when mounted on the Nikon D300 (and other Nikon models) and f/stops are set using the sub-command dial (unless you've used the **Change main/sub** option above). The default setting of **sub-command dial** retains this behavior. If you'd rather unlock the aperture ring on the lens and use that instead, choose **Aperture ring**. Type G lenses, which lack an aperture ring, will still be adjusted using the sub-command dial, regardless of how this setting is made. Non-CPU lenses, which lack an electronic connection to the camera, are always set using the aperture ring.

f8 Release Button to Use Dial

Normally, any button used in conjunction with a command dial must be held down while the command dial or sub-command dial is rotated. Choose **Yes** for this option if you want to be able to press the button and release it, and then rotate the command dial. You can continue to make adjustments until the button is pressed again, or you press the Mode, Exposure Compensation, Flash, ISO, QUAL, or WB buttons, or the shutter release button is pressed halfway. Exposure meter time-out also turns off setting mode, unless the D300 is connected to an AC adapter. Chose **No** to return to the D300's default behavior, which requires that the button be held down while the adjustment is made.

f9 No Memory Card?

This entry gives you the ability to snap off "pictures" without a Compact Flash card installed—or to lock the camera shutter release if that is the case. It is sometimes called Play mode, because you can experiment with your camera's features or even hand your D300 to a friend to let them fool around, without any danger of pictures actually being taken.

Back in our film days, we'd sometimes finish a roll, rewind the film back into its cassette surreptitiously, and then hand the camera to a child to take a few pictures—without actually wasting any film. It's hard to waste digital film, but "shoot without card" mode is still appreciated by some, especially camera vendors who want to be able to demo a camera at a store or trade show, but don't want to have to equip each and every demonstrator model with a Compact Flash card. Choose **Enable release** to activate "play" mode or **Release locked** to disable it.

The pictures you actually "take" are displayed on the LCD with the legend "Demo" superimposed on the screen, and they are, of course, not saved. Note that if you are using the optional Camera Control Pro 2 software to record photos from a USB-tethered D300 directly to a computer, no memory card is required to unlock the shutter even if **Release locked** has been selected.

f10 Reverse Indicators

Refugees from the Canon world or other dSLR product lines are sometimes put off that Nikon cameras place the plus exposure values on the left side of the analog exposure display in the control panel, viewfinder, and Shooting Information Display, with the negative values on the right. This default setting (**+0-**) can be swapped for the opposite orientation (**-0+**) to change the display to the other orientation. My take is that if you've fled to Nikonland, you might as well get used to it. I suppose this setting is useful for a dedicated Canon shooter who sometimes uses a Nikon dSLR.

5

Setup: The Setup Menu, Retouch Menu, and My Menu

We're not done covering the Nikon D300's Setup options yet. There are three more menus to deal with. These include the Setup menu (which deals with adjustments that are outside the actual shooting experience, such as formatting a memory card, adjusting the time, or checking your battery); the Retouch menu (which enables you to fine-tune the appearance of images by trimming, adding filter effects, or removing red-eye); and the My Menu system, which can help you set up a customized menu that contains only the entries you want.

Setup Menu Options

There is a long list of 20 entries in the orange-coded Setup menu (see Figure 5.1), in which you can make additional adjustments on how your camera *behaves* before or during your shooting session, as differentiated from the Shooting menu, which adjusts how the pictures are actually taken. Your choices include:

- Format memory card
- LCD brightness
- Clean image sensor
- Lock mirror up for cleaning
- Video mode

- HDMI
- World time
- Language
- Image comment
- Auto image rotation
- USB
- Dust off ref photo
- Battery info
- Wireless transmitter
- Image authentication
- Save/load settings
- GPS
- Non-CPU lens data
- AF fine tune
- Firmware version

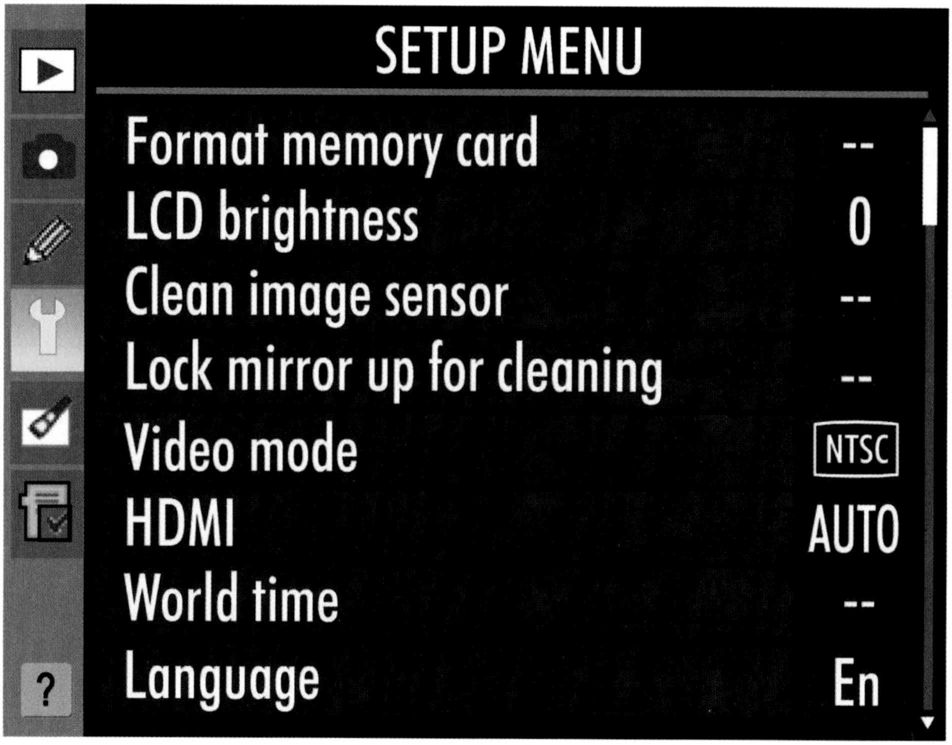

SETUP MENU	
Format memory card	--
LCD brightness	0
Clean image sensor	--
Lock mirror up for cleaning	--
Video mode	NTSC
HDMI	AUTO
World time	--
Language	En

Figure 5.1
The Setup menu allows you to adjust how the D300 behaves.

Format Memory Card

I recommend using this menu entry to reformat your memory card after each shoot. While you can move files from the memory card to your computer, leaving behind a blank card, or delete files using the Playback menu's Delete feature, both of those options can leave behind stray files (such as those that have been marked as Protected). Format removes those files completely and beyond retrieval (unless you use a special utility program as described in Chapter 10) and establishes a spanking new fresh file system on the card, with all the file allocation table (FAT) pointers (which tell the camera and your computer's operating system where all the images reside) efficiently pointing where they are supposed to on a blank card.

If you're an efficiency nut, you can reformat a memory card without a visit to the Setup menu by holding down the Mode and Trash buttons (both marked with red Format labels) for about two seconds, and then waiting until the **For** indicator has finished flashing on the monochrome LCD status panel. Personally, I prefer to use this menu entry instead. I'm not in *that* big of a hurry, and I like the comfort of formatting the hard way because the D300 makes it explicitly clear what you're doing and even asks for confirmation before destroying all the data on your card. I get distracted, and fear I might format a card when I had intended to perform a two-button reset, or some other function. Consistently use the menu, and it's more difficult to go wrong.

To format a memory card, choose this entry from the Setup menu, highlight **Yes** on the screen that appears, and press **OK**.

LCD Brightness

Choose this menu option and a grayscale strip appears on the LCD, as shown in Figure 5.2. Use the multi-selector up/down keys to adjust the brightness to a comfortable viewing level. Under the lighting conditions that exist when you make this adjustment, you should be able to see all 10 swatches from black to white. If the two end swatches blend together, the brightness has been set too low. If the two whitest swatches on the right end of the strip blend together, the brightness is too high. Brighter settings use more battery power, but can allow you to view an image on the LCD outdoors in bright sunlight. When you have the brightness you want, press **OK** to lock it in and return to the menu.

Clean Image Sensor

This entry gives you some control over the Nikon D300's automatic sensor cleaning feature, which removes dust through a vibration cycle that shakes the sensor until dust, presumably, falls off and is captured by a sticky surface at the bottom of the sensor area. If you happen to take a picture and notice an artifact in an area that contains little detail (such as the sky or a blank wall), you can access this menu choice, place the camera with its base downward, and choose **Clean now**. A message Cleaning sensor now appears, and the dust you noticed has probably been shaken off.

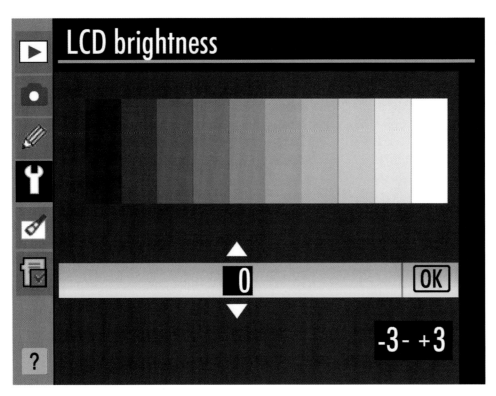

Figure 5.2
Adjust the LCD brightness so that all the grayscale strips are visible.

You can also tell the D300 when you'd like it to perform automatic cleaning without specific instructions from you. Select from:

■ **ON.** Clean at startup. This allows you to start off a particular shooting session with a clean sensor.

■ **OFF.** Clean at shutdown. This removes any dust that may have accumulated since the camera has been turned on, say, from dust infiltration while changing lenses. Note that this choice does not turn off automatic cleaning; it simply moves the operation to the camera power-down sequence.

■ **ON/OFF.** Clean at both startup and shutdown. Use this setting if you're paranoid about dust and don't mind the extra battery power consumed each time the camera is turned on or off. If you only turn off the D300 when you're finished shooting, the power penalty is not large, but if you're the sort who turns off the camera every time you pause in shooting, the extra power consumed by the dust removal may exceed any savings you get from leaving the camera off.

■ **Cleaning Off.** No automatic dust removal will be performed. Use this to preserve battery power, or if you prefer to use automatic dust removal only when you explicitly want to apply it.

Lock Mirror Up for Cleaning

You can also clean the sensor manually. Use this menu entry to raise the mirror and open the shutter so you'll have access to the sensor for cleaning with a blower, brush, or swab, as described in Chapter 11. You don't want power to fail while you're poking around inside the camera, so this option is available only when sufficient battery power (at least 60 percent) is available. Using a fully charged battery or connecting the D300 to an EH-5/EH5a AC adapter is an even better idea.

Video Mode

This setting controls the output of the Nikon D300 to a conventional video system though the video cable when you're displaying images on a monitor or connected to a VCR through the external device's yellow video input jack. You can select either **NTSC**, used in the United States, Canada, Mexico, many Central, South American, and Caribbean countries, much of Asia, and other countries; or **PAL**, which is used in the UK, much of Europe, Africa, India, China, and parts of the Middle East.

HDMI

The Nikon D300 has a High-Definition Multimedia Interface (HDMI) video connection, so you can play back your camera's images on HDTV or HD monitors using a type A cable, which Nikon does not provide to you, but which is readily available from third parties. Before you link up you'll want to choose the HDMI format to be used, from 480p (640 × 480 progressive scan); 576p (720 × 576 progressive scan); 720p (1280 × 720 progressive scan), or 1080i (1920 × 1080 interlaced scan).

World Time

Use this menu entry to adjust the D300's internal clock. Your options include:

- **Time zone.** A small map will pop up on the setting screen and you can choose your local time zone. I sometimes forget to change the time zone when I travel (especially when going to Europe), so my pictures are all time-stamped incorrectly. I like to use the time stamp to recall exactly when a photo was taken, so keeping this setting correct is important.

- **Date and time.** Use this setting to enter the exact year, month, day, hour, minute, and second.

- **Date format.** Choose from **Y/M/D** (year/month/day), **M/D/Y** (month/day/year), or **D/M/Y** (day/month/year) formats.

- **Daylight saving time.** Use this to turn daylight saving time **On** or **Off**. Because the date on which DST begins has been changed from time to time, if you turn this feature on you may need to monitor your camera to make sure DST has been implemented correctly.

Language

Choose from 15 languages for menu display, choosing from German, English, Spanish, Finnish, French, Italian, Dutch, Polish, Portuguese, Russian, Swedish, Traditional Chinese, Simplified Chinese, Japanese, or Korean.

Image Comment

The Image Comment, the first entry on the second "page" of Setup menu entries (see Figure 5.3), is your opportunity to add a copyright notice, personal information about yourself (including contact info), or even a description of where the image was taken (e.g., Seville Photos 2008), although text entry with the Nikon D300 is a bit too clumsy for doing a lot of individual annotation of your photos. (But you still might want to change the comment each time, say, you change cities during your travels.) The embedded comments can be read by many software programs, including Nikon ViewNX or Capture NX.

The standard text entry screen described in Chapter 2 can be used to enter your comment, with up to 36 characters available. For the copyright symbol, embed a lowercase

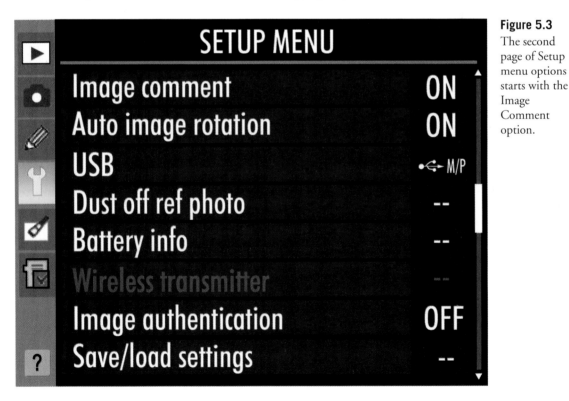

Figure 5.3
The second page of Setup menu options starts with the Image Comment option.

"c" within opening and closing parentheses: **(c)**. You can input the comment, turn attachment of the comment On or Off using the **Attach Comment** entry, and select **Done** when you're finished working with comments. If you find typing with a cursor too tedious, you can enter your comment in Nikon Capture NX and upload it to the camera through a USB cable.

Auto Image Rotation

Turning this setting **On** tells the Nikon D300 to include camera orientation information in the image file. The orientation can be read by many software applications, including Adobe Photoshop, Nikon ViewNX, and Capture NX, as well as the Rotate Tall setting in the Playback menu. Turn this feature **Off,** and none of the software applications or Playback's Rotate Tall will be able to determine the correct orientation for the image. Nikon notes that only the first image's orientation is used when shooting continuous bursts; subsequent photos will be assigned the same orientation, even if you rotate the camera during the sequence (which is something I have been known to do myself when shooting sports like basketball).

USB

This is where you specify whether the Nikon D300's USB connect will be defined as **MSC** (Mass Storage Class) or **MTP/PTP** (Media Transfer Protocol/Picture Transfer Protocol). The Mass Storage setting causes the D300 to appear to your computer to be just another mass storage device like a thumb drive or hard disk drive. It was required before the newest operating systems, such as Windows Vista, Windows XP, and Mac OS X gained the ability to communicate and actually control the camera through MTP/PTP.

Use the default MTP/PTP setting when connecting the D300 to a PictBridge-compatible printer, the optional WT-4 wireless transmitter, or when using Camera Control Pro 2 to control the camera from a computer. When using Nikon Transfer, you'll want to set the USB port to MSC if working with the Windows 2000 Professional, Windows Millennium Edition, or Windows 98 Second Edition operating systems. With Windows Vista or Windows XP, MTP/PTP is preferable with Nikon Transfer, but MSC will also work.

Dust Off Ref Photo

This menu choice lets you "take a picture" of any dust or other particles that may be adhering to your sensor. The D300 will then append information about the location of this dust to your photos, so that the Image Dust Off option in Capture NX can be used to mask the dust in the NEF image.

To use this feature, select **Dust off ref photo,** choose either **Start** or **Clean sensor and then start**, and then press **OK**. If directed to do so, the camera will first perform a self-cleaning operation by applying ultrasonic vibration to the low-pass filter that resides on top of the sensor. Then, a screen will appear asking you to take a photo of a bright featureless white object 10 cm from the lens. Nikon recommends using a lens with a focal length of at least 50mm. Point the D300 at a solid white card and press the shutter release. An image with the extension .NDF will be created, and can be used by Nikon Capture NX as a reference photo if the "dust off" picture is placed in the same folder as an image to be processed for dust removal.

Battery Info

This screen, which leads off the third page of Setup menu entries (see Figure 5.4), is purely informational; there are no settings to be made. When invoked, you can see the following information:

- **Bat. Meter.** The current battery level, shown as a percentage from 100 to 0 percent.

- **Pic. Meter.** This shows the number of actuations with the current battery since it was last recharged. This number can be larger than the number of photos taken, because other functions, such as white balance presetting, can cause the shutter to be tripped. This display is not shown when the MB-D10 battery pack is attached and loaded with AA batteries.

- **Calibration.** This entry is normally not shown. It appears only when the camera is powered by the MB-D10 battery pack with an EN-EL4/EN-EL4a battery installed. It shows when the battery should be recalibrated so the camera is able to detect battery power level more accurately.

- **Charging life.** Eventually, a battery will no longer accept a charge as well as it did when it is new, and must be replaced. This indicator shows when a battery is considered new (**0**); has begun to degrade slightly (**1,2,3**); or has reached the end of its charging life and is ready for replacement (**4**). Batteries charged at temperatures lower than 41 degrees F may display an impaired charging life temporarily, but return to their true "health" when recharged above 68 degrees F. This display is not shown when the MB-D10 battery pack is attached and loaded with AA batteries.

Wireless Transmitter

This menu entry is used to modify settings for connecting to a wireless network using the optional WT-4 a wireless transmitter. Consult the manual furnished with your transmitter for instructions on configuring the device and your computer's WiFi network.

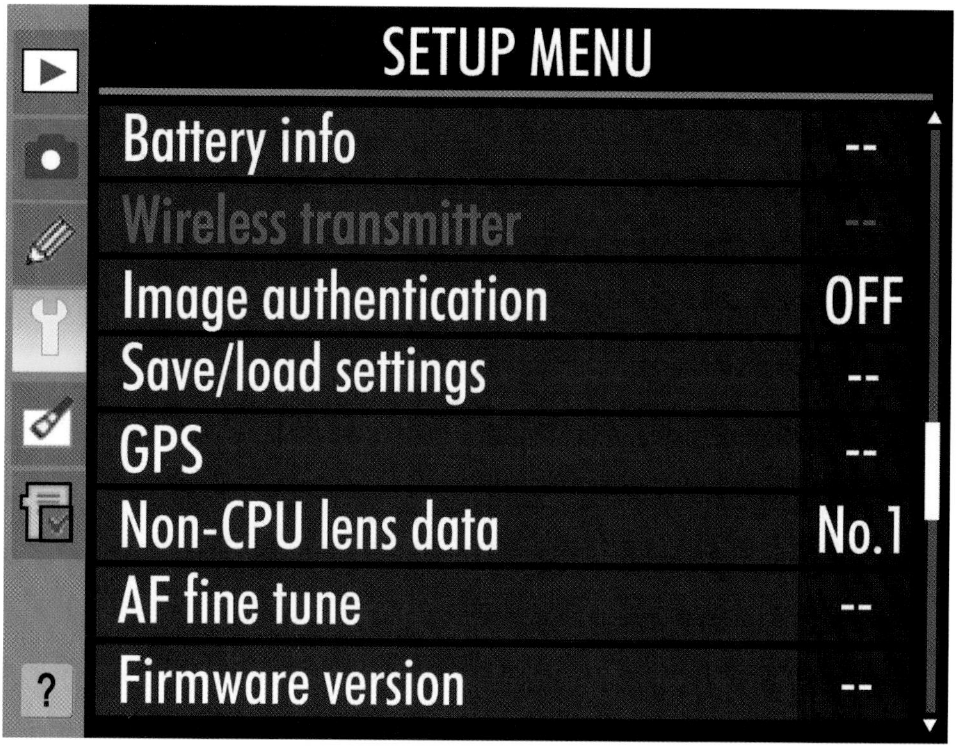

Figure 5.4
The final Setup menu entries include the Battery info option.

SETUP MENU

Battery info	--
Wireless transmitter	--
Image authentication	OFF
Save/load settings	--
GPS	--
Non-CPU lens data	No.1
AF fine tune	--
Firmware version	--

Image Authentication

The Nikon D300 has a special feature that allows determining whether a specific JPEG, TIFF, or NEF (RAW) image has been modified using Nikon's optional Image Authentication software. To embed the encrypted information in an image, turn this feature **On.** If you don't want image authentication information embedded, set this feature to the default value, **Off.**

Image authentication is used by law enforcement and government agencies, the media, insurance companies, and for other business applications where it is important to determine whether an image has been edited or modified since it was taken. Even the software is protected from modification, using both a product key and USB device that must be plugged into the computer before the software will run.

Save/Load Settings

You can store many camera settings to your memory card in a file named NCSETUP1, and then reload them later using this menu item. This is a good way to archive your favorite camera settings for the Playback menu, all four Shooting menu banks, the Setup menu settings, and all My Menu items. You can restore your settings if you've messed them up, or save multiple sets of settings to multiple memory cards. (You can save only one group of settings at a time to a card; the default name NCSETUP1 cannot be changed.) Note that storing/restoration is an all-or-nothing proposition. When you select **Save settings**, all your current settings are stored on the memory card; choose **Load settings**, and the camera's current settings are replaced with the values stored on the memory card.

GPS

This menu item is used with optional Garmin GPS units, and allows you to specify meter-off delays, position recording, heading, coordinated Universal Time (UTC) data, and other options.

Non-CPU Lens Data

You can specify lens focal length data and maximum aperture for up to nine older manual focus, non-CPU chipped lenses. When both values are entered, the D300 can use color matrix metering to calculate exposure in Aperture Priority and Manual exposure modes. The data also enables automatic power zoom when using the Nikon SB-800 and SB-600 speedlights; as well as improved flash exposures and balanced iTTL fill-flash. In addition, the current aperture can be listed in the monochrome LCD status panel and camera viewfinder, as well as embedded in the photo playback display.

If you're a veteran of the Nikon D200, this feature is a dramatic improvement of its implementation in that camera (or even with older "pro" cameras like the Nikon D2xs). Previously, the Non-CPU lens data entry screen was in the Shooting menu, and it was possible to enter information about *only one* lens. That's a fatal error for those of us who have a large collection of manual focus lenses that work just fine on modern Nikon digital cameras. Of course, you could enter a different lens's information in each of the Shooting menu banks A, B, C, and D, but you had to switch banks when you mounted a lens. I happen to use a manual focus 16mm f/3.5 Nikkor fisheye, a 55mm f/3.5 Micro-Nikkor, and an 85mm f/1.8 Nikkor several times a week, with other older lenses seeing occasional use. What was I supposed to do?

Switching to the Nikon D300 proved to be a smart move for me, because it allows defining up to nine different lenses, and I can choose any of them with a quick trip to this menu entry (or to the equivalent menu item in My Menu, described later in this chapter). Nikon wisely moved the feature from the Shooting menu to the Setup menu, so your lens definitions aren't locked into a single menu bank. You can use any defined lens in any Shooting menu or Custom Setting bank.

To enter this information, follow these steps using the screen shown in Figure 5.5:

1. Choose **Non-CPU lens data** from the Setup menu.

2. Highlight **Lens number** and press the multi-selector left/right buttons to choose a number between 1 and 9.

Figure 5.5
You can enter focal length and maximum aperture of up to nine manual focus lenses.

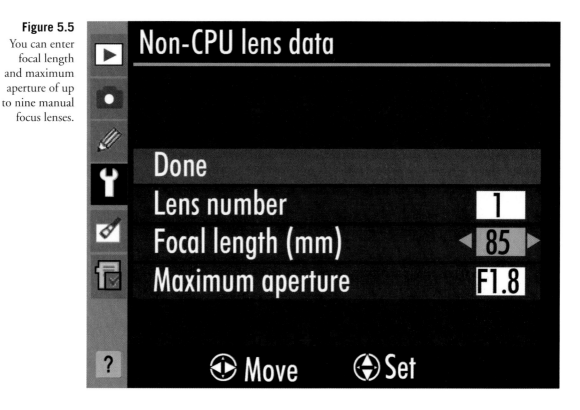

3. Scroll down to **Focal length (mm)** and use the multi-selector left/right buttons to choose a focal length between 6mm and 4000mm.

4. Scroll down to **Maximum aperture** and use the multi-selector left/right buttons to choose a maximum f/stop between f/1.2 and f/22.

5. Choose **Done.** You can now select the lens number using any of several controls you can define for the FUNC. button, depth-of-field preview button, or AE-L/AF-L buttons as described in Chapter 4 under **CSM #f4**, **CSM #f5**, or **CSM #f6.**

AF Fine-Tune

Troubled by lenses that don't focus exactly where they should, producing back-focus or front-focus problems? No need to send your lens and/or camera into Nikon for servicing. The Nikon D300 allows you to fine-tune focus for up to 12 different lenses. You'll probably never need to use this feature, but if you do, it's priceless. To fine-tune your lenses, first perform some tests to see just how much fine-tuning is required. The only problem I've run into is that with some lenses, particularly short-focal length lenses, using large negative values (–10 to –20) to move the focal point closer to the camera sometimes results in being unable focus to infinity. If you run into that, you may be better off sending the lens to Nikon so they can recalibrate the focus for you.

If you want to do it yourself, follow these steps:

1. Mount the CPU-equipped lens you want to fine-tune on the Nikon D300. The camera will automatically recognize the lens you are using during the "calibration" process.

2. Choose **AF fine tune (On/Off)** and turn it **ON**.

3. Select **Saved value**.

4. Press the multi-selector up/down buttons to tell the D300 to adjust the autofocus from +20 (move the focal point away from the camera to fix front-focus problems) to –20 values (move the focal point toward the camera to fix back-focus).

5. Press **OK** when the value you want is entered. You may have to use some trial and error to determine the correct adjustment.

6. Choose **List saved values** to see the lenses you've fine-tuned.

7. Assign a lens identifier from **00** to **27** to the lens you've just calibrated. This identifier can be used to differentiate a particular lens from other lenses of the same type.

8. Press **Menu** to exit.

Firmware Version

You can see the current firmware release in use in the menu listing. You can learn how to update firmware in Chapter 11.

Retouch Menu

The Retouch Menu (see Figure 5.6) allows you to create a new copy of an existing image with trimmed or retouched characteristics. You can apply D-lighting, remove red-eye, create a monochrome image, apply filter effects, rebalance color, overlay one image on another, and compare two images side-by-side. Just select a picture during Playback mode, and then scroll down to one of the retouching options. You can also go directly to the Retouch menu, select a retouching feature, and then choose a picture from the standard D300 picture selection screen shown multiple times in Chapter 2.

The Retouch menu is most useful when you want to create a modified copy of an image on the spot, for immediate printing or e-mailing without first importing into your computer for more extensive editing. You can also use it to create a JPEG version of an image in the camera when you are shooting RAW-only photos.

- D-Lighting
- Red-eye correction
- Trim

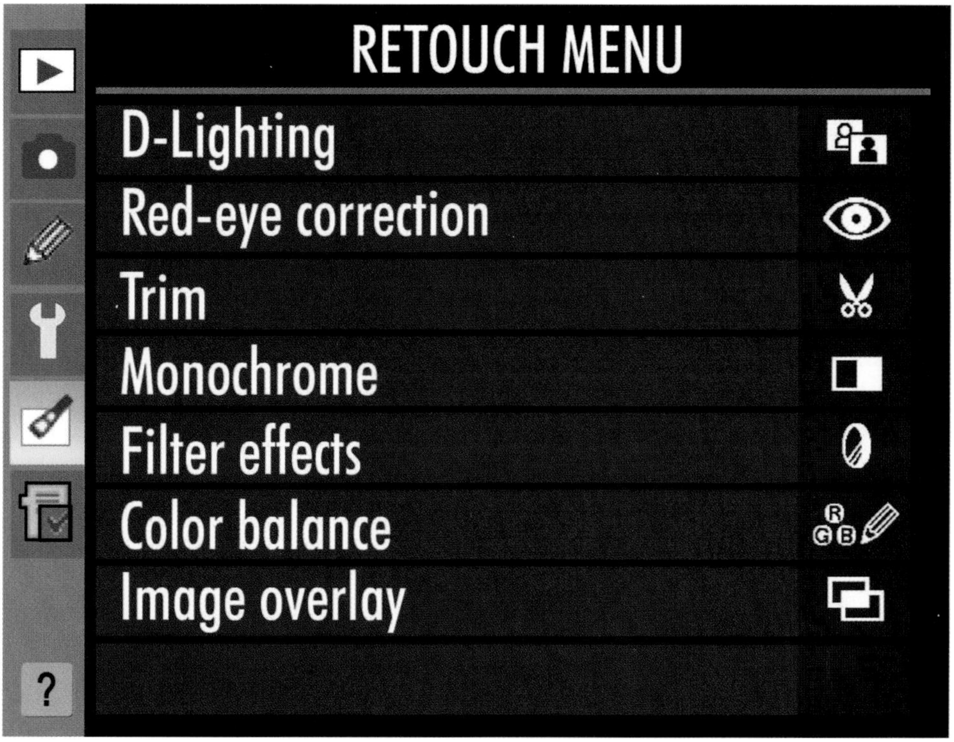

Figure 5.6
The Retouch menu allows simple in-camera editing.

- Monochrome
- Filter effects
- Color balance
- Image overlay

D-Lighting

This option brightens the shadows of pictures that have already been taken. Once you've selected your photo for modification, you'll be shown side-by-side images with the unaltered version on the left, and your adjusted version on the right. Press the multi-selector's up/down buttons to choose from **High**, **Normal**, or **Low** corrections. Press the Zoom button to magnify the image. When you're happy with the corrected image on the right, compared to the original on the left, press **OK** to save the copy to your memory card.

Red-Eye Correction

Your Nikon D300 has a fairly effective red-eye reduction flash mode. Unfortunately, your camera is unable, on its own, to totally *eliminate* the red-eye effects that occur when an electronic flash (or, rarely, illumination from other sources) bounces off the retinas of the eye and into the camera lens. Animals seem to suffer from yellow or green glowing pupils, instead; the effect is equally undesirable. The effect is worst under low-light conditions (exactly when you might be using a flash) as the pupils expand to allow more light to reach the retinas. The best you can hope for is to *reduce* or minimize the red-eye effect.

The best way to truly eliminate red-eye is to raise the flash up off the camera so its illumination approaches the eye from an angle that won't reflect directly back to the retina and into the lens. The extra height of the built-in flash may not be sufficient, however. That alone is a good reason for using an external flash. If you're working with your D300's built-in flash, your only recourse may be to switch to the red-eye reduction flash mode. That causes a lamp on the front of the camera to illuminate with a half-press of the shutter release button, which may result in your subjects' pupils contracting, decreasing the amount of the red-eye effect. (You may have to ask your subject to look at the lamp to gain maximum effect.) Figure 5.7 shows the effects of wider pupils (left) and those that have been contracted using the D300's red-eye reduction flash mode.

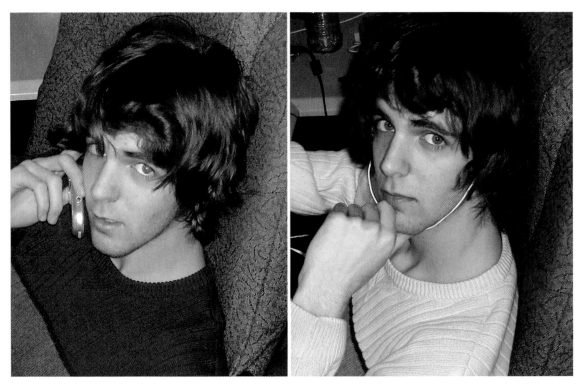

Figure 5.7 Wider pupils (left) can lead to red-eye effects; the Nikon D300's red-eye reduction lamp can cause pupils to contract (right).

The Retouch menu can be used to remove the residual red-eye look (or you can use the red-eye tools found in most image editors). After you've selected the picture to process, press **OK**. The D300 will look for red-eye, and, if detected, create a copy that has been processed to reduce the effect. If no red-eye is found, a copy is not created.

Trim

This option creates copies in specific sizes based on proportions you select. Once you've selected the photo you want to trim, use these options to create the trimmed duplicate image:

- **Crop in on your photo.** Press the Zoom Out/Thumbnail button to crop in on your picture using the selected aspect ratio (proportions) of 3:2, 4:3, or 5:4. The pixel dimensions of the image as cropped appears in the upper-left corner of the screen, and the current framed size is outlined in yellow (see Figure 5.8).

- **Enlarge the cropped area.** Press the Zoom button to increase the size of the cropped picture at the current aspect ratio. The pixel dimensions of the image as cropped appears in the upper-left corner of the screen, and the current framed size is outlined in yellow.

Figure 5.8
The Trim feature of the Retouch menu allows in-camera cropping.

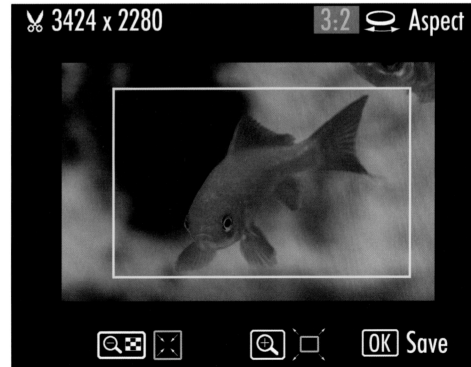

- **Change proportions.** Rotate the main command dial to cycle among 3:2, 4:3, and 5:4 aspect ratios. The proportions of the yellow frame will change as the aspect ratio is modified.

- **Move cropped area within the image.** Use the multi-selector left/right and up/down buttons to relocate the yellow cropping border within the frame.

- **View a preview.** Press the multi-selector center button to see a preview of the cropped image.

- **Save the cropped image.** Press **OK** to save a copy of the image using the current crop.

Monochrome

This Retouch choice allows you to produce a copy of the selected photo as a black-and-white image, sepia-toned image, or cyanotype (blue-and-white). You can fine-tune the color saturation of the previewed Sepia or Cyanotype version by pressing the multi-selector up button to increase color richness, and the down button to decrease saturation. When satisfied, press **OK** to create the monochrome duplicate.

Filter Effects

Add a warmer tone to your images using this Retouch option. You have two choices: **Skylight**, which makes the picture slightly less blue, and **Warm filter**, which adds a rich warm cast to the duplicate. Preview either effect in the color LCD before pressing **OK** to create the modified copy.

Color Balance

This Retouch effect allows you to create a copy with modified color balance. A screen like the one shown in Figure 5.9 appears with the selected photo shown in thumbnail size at the upper-left corner, and red/green/blue histograms at the right. You can bias the image along the magenta/green axis or blue/yellow (amber) axis based on your perception of the thumbnail or, as you gain experience, from your estimation of the distribution of tones as shown by the histograms.

Press the multi-selector up button to increase the amount of green, the down button to increase the amount of magenta, the right button to increase the bias towards yellow/amber, and the left button to increase the amount of blue. As you make these modifications, the changes will be reflected in the histograms.

There is one extra thing you can do with this capability: it can be used to create a JPEG Fine file when you have been shooting only RAW. Just select your NEF (RAW) image

Figure 5.9
Fine-tune color balance in the camera using this Retouch menu screen.

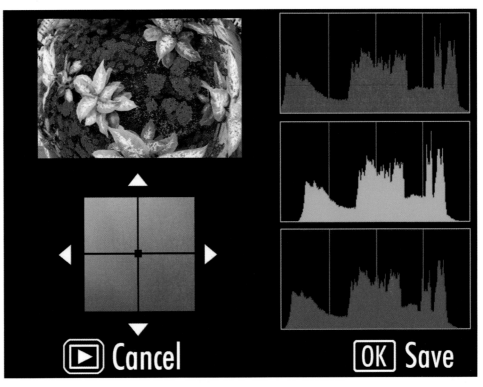

in the Color balance Retouch feature, then immediately press the OK button. The copy will be saved as a JPEG. This is a useful capability if you have been shooting RAW and need a JPEG image (say, to send by e-mail to someone who can't process RAW images) before you've had the chance to transfer the images from the camera to your computer.

Image Overlay

This feature allows you to combine two RAW photos (only NEF files can be used) in a composite image that Nikon claims is better than a "double exposure" created in an image editing application because the overlays are made using RAW data. To produce this composite image, follow these steps:

1. Choose **Image overlay**. The screen shown in Figure 5.10 will be displayed, with the Image 1 box highlighted.

2. Press **OK** and the Nikon D300's image selection screen appears. Choose the first image for the overlay and press **OK**.

3. Press the multi-selector right button to highlight the Image 2 box, and press **OK** to produce the image selection screen. Choose the second image for the overlay.

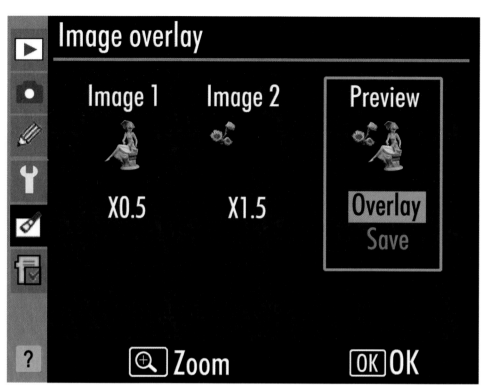

Figure 5.10
Overlay two
RAW images to
produce a
"double expo-
sure."

4. By highlighting either the **Image 1** or **Image 2** boxes and pressing the multi-selector up/down buttons, you can adjust the "gain," or how much of the final image
will be "exposed" from the selected picture. You can choose from X0.5 (half-expo-
sure) to X2.0 (twice the exposure) for each image. The default value is 1.0 for each,
so that each image will contribute equally to the final exposure.

5. Use the multi-selector right button to highlight the Preview box and view the combined picture. Press the Zoom button to enlarge the view.

6. When you're ready to store your composite copy, press the multi-selector down button when the Preview box is highlighted to select **Save**, and press **OK**. The combined image is stored on the memory card.

Side-by-Side Comparison

Use this to compare a retouched photo with the original. This Retouch option does not
appear on the menu unless you are viewing a retouched image. To use it, press the
Playback button and review images until you encounter a retouched version you want
to compare. The retouched copy will have the retouching icon in the upper-left corner.
Press **OK**. The Retouch Menu with **Trim**, **Monochrome**, **Filter effects**, and **Side-by-
Side comparison** appears (these are the only options that can be applied to an image

that has already been retouched). Scroll down to **Side-by-Side comparison** and press **OK**. The original and retouched image will appear next to each other, with the retouching options you've made shown as a label above the images. Highlight the original or the copy and press the Zoom button to magnify the image. When done comparing, press the Playback button.

My Menu

The Nikon D300 has a great new feature that allows you to define your own menu, with just the items listed that you want. Remember that the D300 always returns to the last menu and menu entry accessed when you press the Menu button. So you can set up My Menu (see Figure 5.11) to include just the items accessed most frequently, and (as long as you haven't used another menu) jump to those items instantly by pressing the Menu button.

I tend to include frequently used functions that aren't available using direct access buttons in My Menu. For example, I include Shooting menu bank, High ISO NR and Long Exp. NR, and Battery info. there, because I may want to change banks, turn noise reduction on or off, or check the status of my battery during shooting. I *don't* include ISO, QUAL, or WB changes in My Menu, even though they are available in the menu

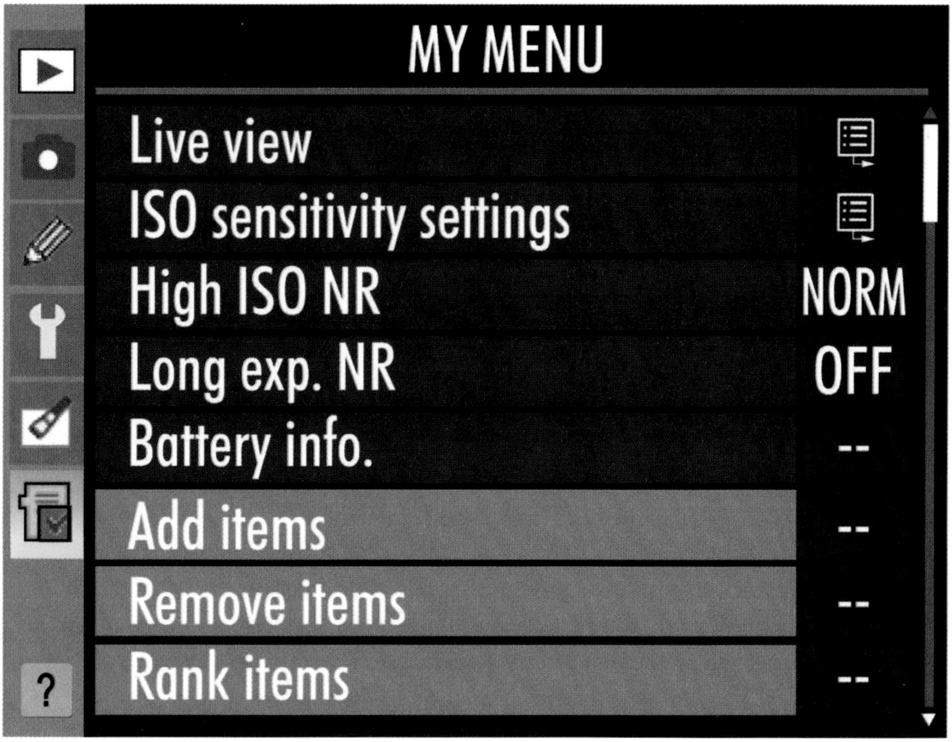

Figure 5.11

You can include your favorite menu items in the fast-access My Menu.

system, because I can quickly change those values by pressing their dedicated buttons and rotating the main command dial.

You can add or subtract entries on My Menu at any time, and reorder (or rank) the entries so the ones you access most often are shown at the top of the list. Here's all you need to know to work with My Menu. To add entries to My Menu:

1. Select My Menu and choose **Add items**.

2. A list of the available menus will appear (Playback, Shooting, Custom Setting, Setup, and Retouch menus). Highlight one and press the multi-selector's right button.

3. Within the selected menu, choose the menu item you want to add and press **OK**.

4. The label **Choose position** appears at the top of the My Menu screen. Use the up/down buttons to select a rank among the entries, and press **OK** to confirm and add the new item.

5. Repeat steps 1-4 if you want to add more entries to My Menu.

To reorder the menu listings:

1. Within the My Menu screen, choose **Rank items**.

2. Use the up/down buttons to select the item to be moved, and press **OK**.

3. Use the up/down buttons to relocate the selected item and press **OK**.

4. Repeat steps 2-3 to move additional entries.

To remove entries from the list you can simply press the Trash button while an item is highlighted in the My Menu screen. To remove multiple items, follow these steps:

1. Within the My Menu screen, choose **Remove items**.

2. A list with checkboxes next to the menu items appears. Scroll down to an item you want to remove and press the multi-selector right button to mark its box. If you change your mind, highlight the item and press the right button again to unmark the box.

3. When finished, highlight **Done** and press the OK button.

4. Press **OK** to confirm the deletion.

6

Getting the Right Exposure

Correct exposure is one of the foundations of good photography, along with accurate focus and sharpness, appropriate color balance, freedom from unwanted noise and excessive contrast, as well as pleasing composition. The Nikon D300 gives you a great deal of control over all of these, although composition is entirely up to you: there are no "automated" short cuts. You must still frame the photograph to create an interesting arrangement of subject matter, but all the other parameters are basic functions of the camera. You can let your D300 set them for you automatically, you can fine-tune how the camera applies its automatic settings, or you can make them yourself, manually. The amount of control you have over exposure, sensitivity (ISO settings), color balance, focus, and image parameters like sharpness and contrast make the D300 a versatile tool for creating images.

This chapter deals with just one of those foundations, and explains the shooting basics of exposure, either as an introduction or as a refresher course, depending on your current level of expertise. When you finish this chapter, you'll understand most of what you need to know to take well-exposed photographs in a broad range of situations.

Getting a Handle on Exposure

Exposure can make or break your photo. Correct exposure brings out the detail in the areas you want to picture, providing the range of tones and colors you need to create the desired image. Poor exposure can cloak important details in shadow, or wash them out in glare-filled featureless expanses of white. However, getting the perfect exposure can be tricky, because digital sensors can't capture all the tones we are able to see. If the range of tones in an image is extensive, embracing both inky black shadows and bright highlights, we often must settle for an exposure that renders most of those tones—but not all—in a way that best suits the photo we want to produce.

There are four things within our control that affect exposure, listed in "chronological" order (that is, as the light moves from the subject to the sensor):

- **Reflected, transmitted, or emitted light.** We see and photograph objects by light that is reflected from our subjects, transmitted (say, from translucent objects that are lit from behind), or emitted (by a candle or television screen). When more or less light reaches the lens from the subject, we need to adjust the exposure. This part of the equation is under our control to the extent we can increase the amount of light falling on or passing through the subject (by adding extra light sources or using reflectors), or by pumping up the light that's emitted (by increasing the brightness of the glowing object).

- **Light transmitted by the lens.** Not all the illumination that reaches the front of the lens makes it all the way through. Filters can remove some of the light before it enters the lens. Inside the lens barrel is a variable-sized diaphragm called an *aperture* that dilates and contracts to control the amount of light that enters the lens. You, or the D300's autoexposure system, can control exposure at this point by varying the size of the aperture. The relative size of the aperture is called the *f/stop*.

- **Light passing through the shutter.** Once light passes through the lens, the amount of time the sensor receives it is determined by the D300's shutter, which can remain open for as long as 30 seconds (or even longer if you use the Bulb setting) or as briefly as 1/8,000th second.

- **Light captured by the sensor.** All the light falling onto the sensor is captured. If the number of photons reaching a particular photosite doesn't pass a set threshold, no information is recorded. Similarly, if too much light illuminates a pixel in the sensor, then the excess isn't recorded or, worse, spills over to contaminate adjacent pixels. We can modify the minimum and maximum number of pixels that contribute to image detail by adjusting the ISO setting. At higher ISOs, the incoming light is amplified to boost the effective sensitivity of the sensor.

These four factors—quantity of light, light passed by the lens, the amount of time the shutter is open, and the sensitivity of the sensor—all work proportionately and reciprocally to produce an exposure. That is, if you double the amount of light, increase the aperture by one stop, make the shutter speed twice as long, or boost the ISO setting 2X, you'll get twice as much exposure. Similarly, you can increase any of these factors while decreasing one of the others by a similar amount to keep the same exposure.

F/STOPS AND SHUTTER SPEEDS

If you're *really* new to more advanced cameras (and I realize that some ambitious amateurs do purchase the D300 as their first digital SLR), you might need to know that the lens aperture, or f/stop, is a ratio, much like a fraction, which is why f/2 is larger than f/4, just as 1/2 is larger than 1/4. However, f/2 is actually *four times* as large as f/4. (If you remember your high school geometry, you'll know that to double the area of a circle, you multiply its diameter by the square root of two: 1.4.)

Lenses are usually marked with intermediate f/stops that represent a size that's twice as much/half as much as the previous aperture. So, a lens might be marked:

f/2, f/2.8, f/4, f/5.6, f/8, f/11, f/16, f/22, with each larger number representing an aperture that admits half as much light as the one before, as shown in Figure 6.1.

Shutter speeds are actual fractions (of a second), but the numerator is omitted, so that 60, 125, 250, 500, 1,000, and so forth represent 1/60th, 1/125th, 1/250th, 1/500th, and 1/1,000th second. To avoid confusion, Nikon uses quotation marks to signify longer exposures: 2", 2"5, 4", and so forth representing 2.0, 2.5, and 4.0-second exposures, respectively.

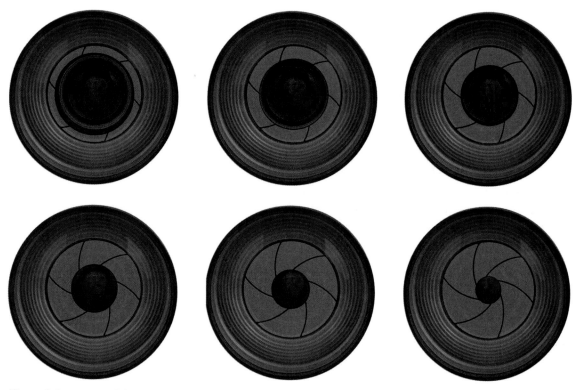

Figure 6.1 Top row (left to right): f/2, f/2.8, f/4; bottom row, f/5.6, f/8, f11.

Most commonly, exposure settings are made using the aperture and shutter speed, followed by adjusting the ISO sensitivity if it's not possible to get the preferred exposure (that is, the one that uses the "best" f/stop or shutter speed for the depth-of-field or action stopping we want). Table 6.1 shows equivalent exposure settings using various shutter speeds and f/stops.

Table 6.1 Equivalent Exposures	
Shutter speed	**f/stop**
1/30th second	f/22
1/60th second	f/16
1/125th second	f/11
1/250th second	f/8
1/500th second	f/5.6
1/1,000th second	f/4
1/2,000th second	f/2.8
1/4,000th second	f/2
1/8,000th second	f/1.4

When the D300 is set for P mode, the metering system selects the correct exposure for you automatically, but you can change quickly to an equivalent exposure by holding down the shutter release button halfway ("locking" the current exposure), and then spinning the main command dial until the desired equivalent exposure combination is displayed. You can use this Flexible Program feature more easily if you remember that you need to rotate the command dial towards the left when you want to increase the amount of depth-of-field or use a slower shutter speed; rotate to the right when you want to reduce the depth-of-field or use a faster shutter speed. The need for more/less DOF and slower/faster shutter speed are the primary reasons you'd want to use Flexible Program. This program shift mode does not work when you're using flash.

In Aperture Priority (A) and Shutter Priority (S) modes, you can change to an equivalent exposure, but only by either adjusting the aperture (the camera chooses the shutter speed) or shutter speed (the camera selects the aperture). I'll cover all these exposure modes later in the chapter.

How the D300 Calculates Exposure

Your Nikon D300 calculates exposure by measuring the light that passes through the lens and is bounced up by the mirror to a 1005-segment RGB sensor located near the focusing surface, using a pattern you can select (more on that later) and based on the assumption that each area being measured reflects about the same amount of light as a neutral gray card with 18 percent reflectance. That assumption is necessary, because different subjects reflect different amounts of light. In a photo containing a white cat and a dark gray cat, the white cat might reflect five times as much light as the gray cat. An exposure based on the white cat will cause the gray cat to appear to be black, while an exposure based only on the gray cat will make the white cat washed out. Light-measuring devices handle this by assuming that the areas measured average a standard value of 18 percent gray, a figure that's been used as a rough standard (not all vendors calibrate their metering for exactly 18 percent gray) for many years.

You could, in many cases, arrive at a reasonable exposure by pointing your D300 at an evenly lit object, such as an actual gray card or the palm of your hand (the backside of the hand is too variable). You'll need to increase the exposure by one stop in the latter case, because the human palm—of any ethnic group—reflects about twice as much light as a gray card. It's more practical though, to use your D300's system to meter the actual scene.

F/STOPS VERSUS STOPS

In photography parlance, *f/stop* always means the aperture or lens opening. However, for lack of a current commonly used word for one exposure increment, the term *stop* is often used. (In the past, EV served this purpose, but Exposure Value and its abbreviation has been inextricably intertwined with its use in describing Exposure Compensation.) In this book, when I say "stop" by itself (no *f*), I mean one whole unit of exposure, and am not necessarily referring to an actual f/stop or lens aperture. So, adjusting the exposure by "one stop" can mean both changing to the next shutter speed increment (say, from 1/125th second to 1/250th second) or the next aperture (such as f/4 to f/5.6). Similarly, 1/3 stop or 1/2 stop increments can mean either shutter speed or aperture changes, depending on the context. Be forewarned.

In most cases, your camera's light meter will do a good job of calculating the right exposure, especially if you use the exposure tips in the next section. But if you want to double-check, or feel that exposure is especially critical, take the light reading off an object of known reflectance. Photographers sometimes carry around an 18 percent gray card (available from any camera store) and, for critical exposures, actually use that card, placed in the subject area, to measure exposure (or to set a custom white balance if needed).

To meter properly, you'll want to choose both the *metering method* (how light is evaluated) and *exposure method* (how the appropriate shutter speeds and apertures are chosen based on the metered information). I'll describe both in the following sections.

Choosing a Metering Method

The D300 has three different schemes for evaluating the light received by its exposure sensors, Matrix (with several variations, depending on what lens you have attached); Center-Weighted, and Spot metering. Select the mode you want to use by rotating the metering method dial immediately to the right of the viewfinder window. Here is what you need to know about each metering method:

Matrix Metering

For its various Matrix metering modes, the D300 slices up the frame into 1,005 different zones, arrayed in 67 rows of 15 columns that cover most of the sensor area, shown in Figure 6.2. When Matrix metering is active, an icon appears in the viewfinder (lower left) and in the monochrome status LCD (enlarged in the upper-right corner). In all cases, the D300 evaluates the differences between the zones, and compares them with

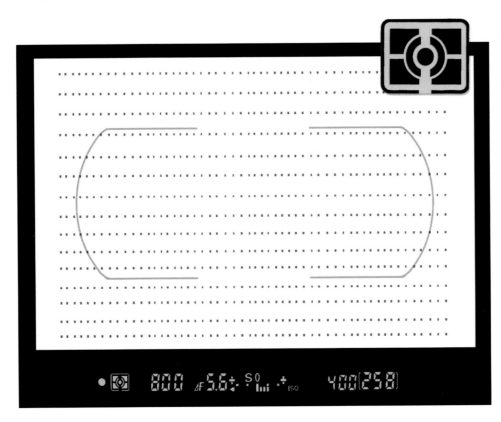

Figure 6.2

Matrix metering calculates exposure based on 1005 points in the frame.

a built-in database of several hundred thousand images to make an educated guess about what kind of picture you're taking. For example, if the top sections of a picture are much lighter than the bottom portions, the algorithm can assume that the scene is a landscape photo with lots of sky. An image that includes most of the lighter portions in the center area may be a portrait. The Nikon D300 also uses information other than brightness to make its evaluation:

- **3D Color Matrix metering II.** This metering mode is used by default when the D300 is equipped with a lens that has a type G or type D designator in its name, such as the AF-S DX Nikkor 16-85mm f/3.5-5.6G ED VR lens. The G after the f/5.6 is the giveaway. (More on lens nomenclature in Chapter 8.) The camera calculates exposure based on brightness, colors of the subject matter (that is, blue pixels in the upper part of the image are probably sky; green pixels in the lower half probably foliage), focus point, and distance information. The D300 is able to use that additional distance data to better calculate what kind of scene you have framed. For example, if you're shooting a portrait with a longer focal-length lens focused to about 5 to 12 feet from the camera, and the upper half of the scene is very bright, the camera assumes you would prefer to meter for the rest of the image, and discount the bright area. However, if the camera has a wide-angle lens attached and is focused at infinity, the D300 can assume you're taking a landscape photo and take the bright upper area into account to produce better looking sky and clouds.

- **Color Matrix metering II.** If you have a non-G or non-D lens equipped with a CPU chip (these are generally older lenses, although chips can be added to optics that lack them), the distance range is not used. Instead, only focus, brightness, and color information is taken into account to calculate an appropriate exposure.

- **Color Matrix metering.** If you're using a non-CPU lens (such as an older manual focus lens) and have specified the focal length and maximum aperture in the Shooting menu (as described in Chapter 5), then the D300 uses plain old color Matrix metering, which evaluates exposure based only on brightness and color information detected in the scene.

- **With other lenses.** If you don't specify focal length or maximum aperture for a non-CPU lens, the D300 defaults to Center-Weighted metering.

Matrix metering is best for most general subjects, because it is able to intelligently analyze a scene and make an excellent guess of what kind of subject you're shooting a great deal of the time. The camera can tell the difference between low-contrast and high-contrast subjects by looking at the range of differences in brightness across the scene. Because the D300 has a fairly good idea about what kind of subject matter you are shooting, it can underexpose slightly when appropriate to preserve highlight detail when image contrast is high. (It's often possible to pull detail out of shadows that are too dark using an image editor, but once highlights are converted to white pixels, they are gone forever.)

CAUTION

If you're using a strong filter, including a polarizing filter, split-color filter, or neutral density filter (particularly a graduated neutral density filter), you should switch from Matrix metering to Center-Weighted, because the filter can affect the relationships between the different areas of the frame used to calculate a Matrix exposure. For example, a polarizing filter produces a sky that is darker than usual, hindering the Matrix algorithm's recognition of a landscape photo. Extra dark or colored filters disturb the color relationships used for color Matrix metering, too.

Center-Weighted Metering

In this mode, the exposure meter emphasizes a zone in the center of the frame to calculate exposure, as shown in Figure 6.3. About 75 percent of the exposure is based on that central area, and the remaining exposure is based on the rest of the frame. The theory, here, is that, for most pictures, the main subject will be located in the center. So, if

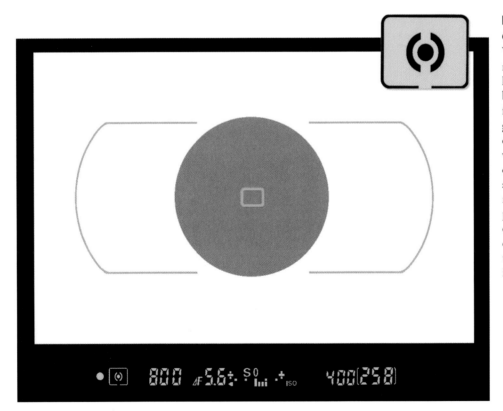

Figure 6.3
Center-Weighted metering calculates exposure based on the full frame, but gives 75 percent of the weight to the center area shown; the remaining 25 percent of the exposure is determined by the rest of the image area.

the D300 reads the center portion and determines that the exposure for that region should be f/8 at 1/250 second, while the outer area, which is a bit darker, calls for f/4 at 1/125 second, the camera will give the center portion the most weight and arrive at a final exposure of f/5.6 at 1/250 second. (Bet you're wondering how I calculated that! On an Exposure Value scale, the center-weighted section has a value of EV14, while the rest of the frame has an EV11 value. A simple 75:25 (3:1) ratio produces a weighted average of EV13.25, which translates into the f/5.6 at 1/250 second final exposure.)

Center-Weighting works best for portraits, architectural photos, backlit subjects with extra-bright backgrounds (such as snow or sand), and other pictures in which the most important subject is located in the middle of the frame. As the name suggests, the light reading is *weighted* towards the central portion, but information is also used from the rest of the frame. If your main subject is surrounded by very bright or very dark areas, the exposure might not be exactly right. However, this scheme works well in many situations if you don't want to use one of the other modes. This mode can be useful for close-ups of subjects like flowers, or for portraits. You can adjust the size of the center area assigned the greatest weight using **CSM #b5**, as described in Chapter 4.

Spot Metering

Spot metering is favored by those of us who used to use a hand-held light meter to measure exposure at various points (such as metering highlights and shadows separately). However, you can use Spot metering in any situation where you want to individually measure the light reflecting from light, midtone, or dark areas of your subject—or any combination of areas.

This mode confines the reading to a limited 3mm area in the center of the viewfinder, making up only two percent of the image, as shown in Figure 6.4. The circle is centered on the current focus point, *but is larger than the focus point*, so don't fall into the trap of believing that exposure is being measured only within the brackets that represent the active focus point. This is the only metering method you can use to tell the D300 exactly where to measure exposure. However, if a non-CPU lens is mounted, or you have selected Auto-area AF, only the center focus point is used to spot meter.

You'll find spot metering useful when you want to base exposure on a small area in the frame. If that area is in the center of the frame, so much the better. If not, you'll have to make your meter reading for an off-center subject and then lock exposure by pressing the shutter release halfway, or by pressing the AE-Lock button. This mode is best for subjects where the background is significantly brighter or darker.

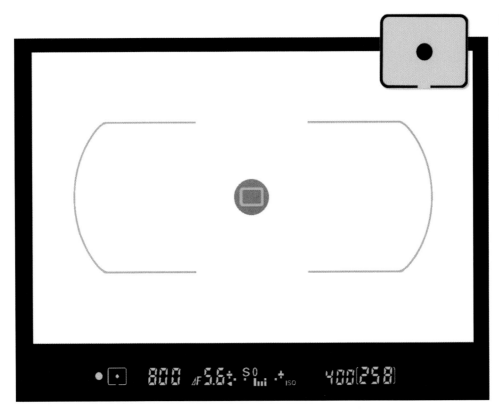

Figure 6.4
Spot metering calculates exposure based on a center spot that's only two percent of the image area.

Choosing an Exposure Method

You'll find four methods for choosing the appropriate shutter speed and aperture. You can choose among them by pressing the Mode button on the top panel, and using the main command dial until the icon for the mode you want appears in the monochrome status LCD. Your choice of which is best for a given shooting situation will depend on things like your need for lots of (or less) depth-of-field, a desire to freeze action or allow motion blur, or how much noise you find acceptable in an image. Each of the D300's exposure methods emphasizes one aspect of image capture or another. This section introduces you to all four.

Aperture Priority

In A mode, you specify the lens opening used, and the D300 selects the shutter speed. Aperture Priority is especially good when you want to use a particular lens opening to achieve a desired effect. Perhaps you'd like to use the smallest f/stop possible to maximize depth-of-field in a close-up picture. Or, you might want to use a large f/stop to throw everything except your main subject out of focus, as in Figure 6.5. Maybe you'd

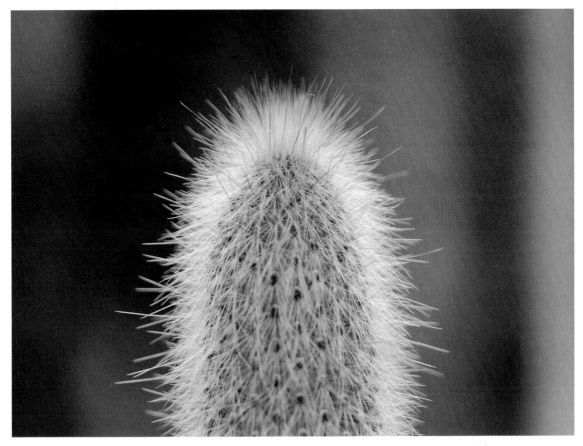

Figure 6.5 Use Aperture Priority to "lock in" a large f/stop when you want to blur the background.

just like to "lock in" a particular f/stop because it's the sharpest available aperture with that lens. Or, you might prefer to use, say, f/2.8 on a lens with a maximum aperture of f/1.4, because you want the best compromise between speed and sharpness.

Aperture Priority can even be used to specify a *range* of shutter speeds you want to use under varying lighting conditions, which seems almost contradictory. But think about it. You're shooting a soccer game outdoors with a telephoto lens and want a relatively high shutter speed, but you don't care if the speed changes a little should the sun duck behind a cloud. Set your D300 to A, and adjust the aperture until a shutter speed of, say, 1/1,000th second is selected at your current ISO setting. (In bright sunlight at ISO 400, that aperture is likely to be around f/11.) Then, go ahead and shoot, knowing that your D300 will maintain that f/11 aperture (for sufficient DOF as the soccer players move about the field), but will drop down to 1/750th or 1/500th second if necessary should the lighting change a little.

A **Lo** or **HI** indicator in the viewfinder and the top-panel monochrome LCD indicates that the D300 is unable to select an appropriate shutter speed at the selected aperture and that over- and underexposure will occur at the current ISO setting. That's the major pitfall of using A: you might select an f/stop that is too small or too large to allow an optimal exposure with the available shutter speeds. For example, if you choose f/2.8 as your aperture and the illumination is quite bright (say, at the beach or in snow), even your camera's fastest shutter speed might not be able to cut down the amount of light reaching the sensor to provide the right exposure. Or, if you select f/8 in a dimly lit room, you might find yourself shooting with a very slow shutter speed that can cause blurring from subject movement or camera shake. Aperture Priority is best used by those with a bit of experience in choosing settings. Many seasoned photographers leave their D300 set on A all the time.

Shutter Priority

Shutter Priority (S) is the inverse of Aperture Priority: you choose the shutter speed you'd like to use, and the camera's metering system selects the appropriate f/stop. Perhaps you're shooting action photos and you want to use the absolute fastest shutter speed available with your camera; in other cases you might want to use a slow shutter speed to add some blur to a sports photo that would be mundane if the action were completely frozen. (See Figure 6.6.) Shutter Priority mode gives you some control over how much action-freezing capability your digital camera brings to bear in a particular situation.

You'll also encounter the same problem as with Aperture Priority when you select a shutter speed that's too long or too short for correct exposure under some conditions. I've shot outdoor soccer games on sunny Fall evenings and used Shutter Priority mode to lock in a 1/1,000th second shutter speed, only to find my D300 refused to shoot when the sun dipped behind some trees and there was no longer enough light to shoot at that speed, even with the lens wide open.

Like A mode, it's possible to choose an inappropriate shutter speed. If that's the case, the maximum aperture of your lens (to indicate underexposure) or the minimum aperture (to indicate overexposure) will blink.

Program Mode

Program mode (P) uses the D300's built-in smarts to select the correct f/stop and shutter speed using a database of picture information that tells it which combination of shutter speed and aperture will work best for a particular photo. If the correct exposure cannot be achieved at the current ISO setting, the **Lo** or **HI** indicator in the viewfinder and monochrome LCD will appear. You can then boost or reduce the ISO to increase or decrease sensitivity.

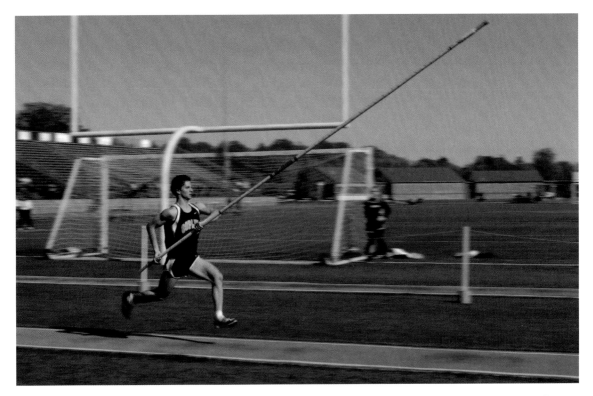

Figure 6.6 Lock the shutter at a slow speed to introduce blur into an action shot, as with this panned image of a pole vaulter.

The D300's recommended exposure can be overridden if you want. Use the EV setting feature (described later, because it also applies to S and A modes) to add or subtract exposure from the metered value. And, as I mentioned earlier in this chapter, in Program mode you can rotate the main command dial to change from the recommended setting to an equivalent setting (as shown in Table 6.1) that produces the same exposure, but using a different combination of f/stop and shutter speed.

This is called "Flexible Program" by Nikon. Rotate the main command dial counter-clockwise to reduce the size of the aperture (going from, say, f/4 to f/5.6), so that the D300 will automatically use a slower shutter speed (going from, say, 1/250 second to 1/125 second). Rotate the main command dial clockwise to use a larger f/stop, while automatically producing a shorter shutter speed that provides the same equivalent exposure as metered in P mode. An asterisk appears next to the P in the monochrome LCD and viewfinder so you'll know you've over-ridden the D300's default program setting. Your adjustment remains in force until you rotate the main command dial until the asterisk disappears, or you switch to a different exposure mode, or turn the D300 off.

MAKING EV CHANGES

Sometimes you'll want more or less exposure than indicated by the D300's metering system. Perhaps you want to underexpose to create a silhouette effect, or overexpose to produce a high key look. It's easy to use the D300's exposure compensation system to override the exposure recommendations. Press the EV button on the top of the camera (just southeast of the shutter release). Then rotate the main command dial counter-clockwise to add exposure, and clockwise to subtract exposure. The EV change you've made remains for the exposures that follow, until you manually zero out the EV setting. The EV plus/minus icon appears in the viewfinder and monochrome status panel to warn you that an exposure compensation change has been entered.

Manual Exposure

Part of being an experienced photographer comes from knowing when to rely on your D300's automation (with P mode), when to go semiautomatic (with S or A), and when to set exposure manually (using M). Some photographers actually prefer to set their exposure manually, as the D300 will be happy to provide an indication of when its metering system judges your manual settings provide the proper exposure, using the analog exposure scale at the bottom of the viewfinder and on the status LCD.

Manual exposure can come in handy in some situations. You might be taking a silhouette photo and find that none of the exposure modes or EV correction features give you exactly the effect you want. Set the exposure manually to use the exact shutter speed

METERING WITH OLDER LENSES

Older lenses that lack the CPU chip that tells the Nikon D300 what kind of lens is mounted can be used with Aperture Priority and Manual exposure modes only, assuming you've entered the Non-CPU Lens information in the Setup menu, as described in Chapter 5. If the D300 knows the maximum aperture of the lens, you can set the aperture using the lens's aperture ring, and, in A mode, the camera will automatically select an appropriate shutter speed. In Manual mode, you can set the aperture, and the analog exposure scale in the viewfinder and monochrome LCD status panel will indicate when you've set the correct shutter speed manually. If a non-CPU lens is mounted and you try to set Program or Shutter Priority modes, the D300 switches to Aperture Priority automatically. The process works because the D300 camera body (as well as the earlier D200) and "pro" bodies like the D2Xs and D3 have a mechanical linkage built into the lens mount that tells the camera when the f/stop has been changed. Amateur cameras like the Nikon D40/D40x, D50, D60, D70/D70s, and D80 lack this linkage and cannot meter with non-CPU lenses.

and f/stop you need. Or, you might be working in a studio environment using multiple flash units. The additional flash are triggered by slave devices (gadgets that set off the flash when they sense the light from another flash, or, perhaps from a radio or infrared remote control). Your camera's exposure meter doesn't compensate for the extra illumination, so you need to set the aperture manually.

Because, depending on your proclivities, you might not need to set exposure manually very often, you should still make sure you understand how it works. Fortunately, the D300 makes setting exposure manually very easy. Just press the Mode button and rotate the main command dial to change to Manual mode, and then turn the main command dial to set the shutter speed, and the sub-command dial to adjust the aperture. Press the shutter release halfway or press the AE-Lock button, and the exposure scale in the viewfinder shows you how far your chosen setting diverges from the metered exposure.

Adjusting Exposure with ISO Settings

Another way of adjusting exposures is by changing the ISO sensitivity setting. Sometimes photographers forget about this option, because the common practice is to set the ISO once for a particular shooting session (say, at ISO 200 for bright sunlight outdoors, or ISO 800 when shooting indoors) and then forget about ISO. The reason for that is that ISOs higher than ISO 200 or 400 are seen as "bad" or "necessary evils." However, changing the ISO is a valid way of adjusting exposure settings, particularly with the Nikon D300, which produces good results at ISO settings that create grainy, unusable pictures with some other camera models.

Indeed, I find myself using ISO adjustment as a convenient alternate way of adding or subtracting EV when shooting in Manual mode, and as a quick way of choosing equivalent exposures when in Program or Shutter Priority or Aperture Priority modes. For example, I've selected a Manual exposure with both f/stop and shutter speed suitable for my image using, say, ISO 200. I can change the exposure in 1/3 stop increments by pressing the ISO button on the left side of the top surface of the camera, and spinning the main command dial one click at a time. The difference in image quality/noise at the base setting of ISO 200 is negligible if I dial in L 0.3 or L 0.7 (ISO 160 or 125 equivalents) to reduce exposure a little, or change to ISO 250 or 320 to increase exposure. I keep my preferred f/stop and shutter speed, but still adjust the exposure.

Or, perhaps, I am using S mode and the metered exposure at ISO 200 is 1/500th second at f/11. If I decide on the spur of the moment I'd rather use 1/500th second at f/8, I can press the ISO button and spin the main command dial three clicks counter-clockwise to switch to LO 1.0 (ISO 100 equivalent). Of course, it's a good idea to monitor your ISO changes, so you don't end up at ISO 6400 accidentally. An ISO indicator appears in the monochrome control panel and in the viewfinder to remind you what sensitivity setting has been dialed in.

ISO settings can, of course, also be used to boost or reduce sensitivity in particular shooting situations. The D300 can use ISO settings from L 1.0 (ISO 100) up to H 1.0 (6,400 equivalent). The camera can also adjust the ISO automatically as appropriate for various lighting conditions. When you choose the Auto ISO setting in the Shooting menu, as described in Chapter 3, the D300 adjusts the sensitivity dynamically to suit the subject matter, based on minimum shutter speed and ISO limits you have prescribed. As I noted in Chapter 3, you should use Auto ISO cautiously if you don't want the D300 to use an ISO higher than you might otherwise have selected.

Bracketing

Bracketing is a method for shooting several consecutive exposures using different settings, as a way of improving the odds that one will be exactly right. Alternatively, bracketing can be used to create a series of photos with slightly different exposures (or white balances) in anticipation that one of the exposures will be a "better" frame from a creative standpoint. For example, bracketing can supply you with a normal exposure of a backlit subject, one that's "underexposed", producing a silhouette effect, and a third that's "overexposed" to create still another look.

Before digital cameras took over the universe, it was common to bracket exposures, shooting, say, a series of three photos at 1/125th second, but varying the f/stop from f/8 to f/11 to f/16. In practice, smaller than whole-stop increments were used for greater precision, and lenses with apertures that were set manually commonly had half-stop detents on their aperture rings, or could easily be set to a mid-way position between whole f/stops. It was just as common to keep the same aperture and vary the shutter speed, although in the days before electronic shutters, film cameras often had only whole increment shutter speeds available.

Today, cameras like the D300 can bracket exposures much more precisely, and bracket white balance as well. While WB bracketing is sometimes used when getting color absolutely correct in the camera is important, auto exposure bracketing is used much more often. When this feature is activated, the D300 takes three consecutive photos: one at the metered "correct" exposure, one with less exposure, and one with more exposure, using an increment of your choice up to +2/-2 stops. (Choose between increments by setting Custom Function **CSM #b2**.) In A mode, the aperture will change, while in S mode, the shutter speed will change.

Using autoexposure bracketing is trickier than it needs to be, but you can follow these steps to get results like those shown in Figure 6.7:

1. **Choose type of bracketing.** First, select the type of bracketing you want to do, using **CSM #e5**, as explained in Chapter 4. You can select autoexposure and flash, autoexposure only, flash only, and white balance. If you plan on shooting in Manual exposure mode, you can specify how bracketing is performed using **CSM #e6.**

2. **Press bracketing setting button.** Press the button you defined as the bracketing setting button in **CSM #f4** (**Fn** button+command dial), **CSM #f5** (**Preview** button+command dial), or **CSM #f6** (**AE-L/AF-L** button+command dial)**,** as described in Chapter 4. The Fn+command dial button is the most convenient for most and is the default value when the D300 comes from the factory, but you can choose one of the others if you prefer.

3. **Select number of bracketed exposures.** With the setting button held down, rotate the main command dial to choose the number of shots in the sequence, either **0** (which turns bracketing off), **2, 3, 5, 7**, or **9** bracketed shots. Rotate the main command dial counter-clockwise to center the bracketed shots around the metered exposure (the 2 value is not available if you do this), and rotate it clockwise to choose 2 or 3 bracketed exposures concentrated either over or under the metered exposure. This is the most confusing aspect of bracketing, so I'll explain how this works in more detail next.

4. **Choose bracket increment.** With the setting button still held down, rotate the sub-command dial to choose the exposure increment, either **1/3, 2/3**, or **1** EV (unless you've redefined the exposure compensation increment in **CSM #b2**).

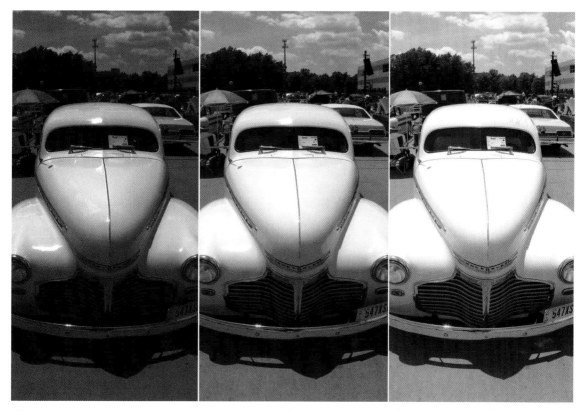

Figure 6.7 Bracketing can give you three different exposures of the same subject.

5. **Frame and shoot.** As you take your photos the camera will vary exposure, flash level, or white balance for each image, based on the bracketing "program" you selected, and in the order you specified in **CSM #e7**. In single-shot mode, you'll need to press the shutter release button the number of times you specified for the exposures in your bracketed burst (2, 3, 5, 7, or 9 shots). I've found it easy to forget that I am shooting bracketed pictures, stop taking my sequence, and then wonder why the remaining pictures in my defined burst are "incorrectly" exposed. To avoid that, I often set the D300 to one of the two continuous shooting modes, so that all my bracketed pictures are taken at once. The D300 does provide indicators on the monochrome LCD (a BKT indicator as well as a bracketing progress indicator), but they may be overlooked.

6. **Turn bracketing off.** When you're finished bracketing shots, remember to press the bracket setting button and rotate the main command dial until the number of shots in the sequence is 0F, and the BKT indicator is no longer displayed.

More on Bracketing

Unless you have previous experience with Nikon's bracketing procedures, the process can seem a little confusing, particularly when it comes time to select the number of bracketed exposures. That's because Nikon combines two functions in one setting: *how many actual shots in the burst* and *where those shots are placed within the overall scheme of exposure.* Both those parameters are set when you hold down your bracket setting button (usually the **Fn** button) and spin the main command dial. That's an entirely different operation than setting the exposure increment, which is accomplished by holding down the setting button and spinning the sub-command dial.

Here's what happens. When you go to set the number of bracketed exposures, there are two "modes" based on which direction you rotate the command dial. Rotate the dial counter-clockwise, and the number of exposures increases from 0 to 3, 5, 7, or 9 images. In *all* cases, the bracketed exposure values will be evenly spaced on either side of the metered exposure, using the increment you have selected separately (with the sub-command dial). Suppose you have already chosen 1/3 EV as your increment, and then rotate the main command dial counter-clockwise. At the **3F 0.3** position, the exposures will be taken at the metered exposure, plus 1/3 stop less and 1/3 stop more (three shots in all). At the **5F 0.3** position, the exposures will be taken at the metered exposure, plus 1/3 stop and 2/3 stop less, as well as 1/3 stop and 2/3 stop more (five shots in all). The bracketed exposures are evenly spread on either side of the metered exposure.

Now rotate the main dial in the clockwise direction instead. In that case, the first setting that appears on the LCD is **–2F 0.3**, which will tell the D300 to shoot one picture at the measured exposure, and one at 1/3 stop less (two shots). The next click produces a readout of **+2F 0.3,** which produces one shot at the metered exposure, and one at 1/3 stop *more.* You can also select **–3F 0.3** or **+3F 0.3**. In all cases, the additional bracketed shots are biased either towards under- or overexposure. That's as far as the clockwise spin will take you. There are no –5F or +5F or larger numeric settings available.

A lot of people find this concept confusing, because the Nikon manual discusses these variations (which it calls "bracketing programs") in the section that follows the description of exposure increments, set with the *sub*-command dial. Yes, the exposure increment you select does affect the "program," but the number of shots and distribution of the bracketed exposures is an entirely different concept, and is controlled by spinning the *main* command dial.

Bracketing and Merge to HDR

While my goal in this book is to show you how to take great photos *in the camera* rather than how to fix your errors in Photoshop, the **Merge to HDR** (high dynamic range) feature in Adobe's flagship image editor is too cool to ignore. The ability to have a bracketed set of exposures that are identical except for exposure is key to getting good results with this Photoshop feature, which allows you to produce images with a full, rich dynamic range that includes a level of detail in the highlights and shadows that is almost impossible to achieve with digital cameras. In contrasty lighting situations, even the Nikon D300 has a tendency to blow out highlights when you expose solely for the shadows or midtones.

Suppose you wanted to photograph a dimly-lit room that had a bright window showing an outdoors scene. Proper exposure for the room might be on the order of 1/60th second at f/2.8 at ISO 200, while the outdoors scene probably would require f/11 at 1/400th second. That's almost a 7 EV step difference (approximately 7 f/stops) and well beyond the dynamic range of any digital camera, including the Nikon D300.

When you're using Merge to HDR, you'd take two to three pictures, one for the shadows, one for the highlights, and perhaps one for the midtones. Then, you'd use the Merge to HDR command to combine all of the images into one HDR image that integrates the well-exposed sections of each version. You can use the Nikon D300's bracketing feature to produce those images.

The images should be as identical as possible, except for exposure. So, it's a good idea to mount the D300 on a tripod, use a remote release like the Nikon MC-30, and take all the exposures in one burst. Just follow these steps:

1. Mount the D300 on a tripod and connect the remote release cable.

2. Press the bracketing setting button (usually the Fn button) and rotate the sub-command dial to set the increment to **1EV**. Merge to HDR works best with a significant difference in exposure between the bracketed shots; subtle changes are not better here.

3. Still holding down the bracketing setting button, rotate the main dial until the **3F 1.0** setting is made. This will take a total of three exposures, one at the metered exposure, one 1 stop under and one 1 stop over.

4. Rotate the release mode dial to one of the continuous shooting modes. This will ensure that all three bracketed shots are taken consecutively once you've triggered the shutter with the remote release.

5. Set the D300 to A (Shutter Priority). This forces the D300 to bracket the exposures by changing the shutter speed. You don't want the bracketed exposures to have different aperture settings, because the depth-of-field will change, perhaps enough to disturb a smooth merger of the final shots.

6. Hold down the QUAL button and choose RAW exposures. You'll need RAW files to give you the 16-bit high dynamic range images that the Merge to HDR feature processes best.

7. Manually focus or autofocus the D300.

8. Trigger the remote release to take all the exposures in the bracketed set. Repeat if you like.

9. Copy your images to your computer and continue with the Merge to HDR steps listed next.

The next steps show you how to combine the separate exposures into one merged high dynamic range image. The sample images shown in Figures 6.8, 6.9, and 6.11 show the results you can get from a two-shot bracketed sequence. I merged only two pictures for simplicity, because the differences between three or more bracketed exposures, even when taken at exposures that are 1 stop apart, can be too subtle to show up well on the printed page. My two examples were taken from a longer sequence, and actually have a two-stop difference.

1. If you use an application to transfer the files to your computer, make sure it does not make any adjustments to brightness, contrast, or exposure. You want the real raw information for Merge to HDR to work with. If you do everything correctly, you'll end up with at least two photos like the ones shown in Figures 6.8 and 6.9.

2. Load the images into Photoshop using your preferred RAW converter. Make sure the 16-bits-per-channel depth is retained (don't reduce them to 8-bit files). You can load them ahead of time and save as 16-bit Photoshop .PSD files, as I did for my example photos.

3. Activate Merge to HDR by choosing File > Automate > Merge to HDR.

4. Select the photos to be merged, as shown in Figure 6.10, where I have specified the two 16-bit PSD files. You'll note a checkbox that can be used to automatically align the images if they were not taken with the D300 mounted on a rock-steady support.

5. Once HDR merge has done its thing, you must save in .PSD, .PFM, .TIFF, or .EXR formats to retain the 16-bit file's floating-point data, in case you want to work with the HDR image later. Otherwise, you can convert to a normal 24-bit file and save in any compatible format.

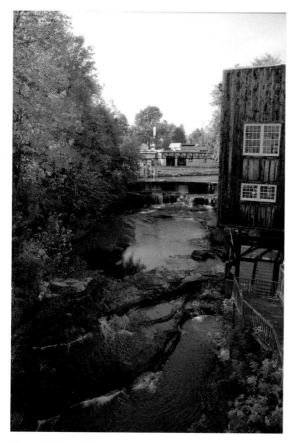

Figure 6.8 Make one exposure for the shadow areas.

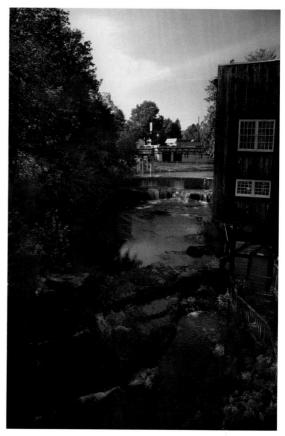

Figure 6.9 Make a second exposure for the highlights, such as the sky.

Figure 6.10
Use the Merge
to HDR com-
mand in
Photoshop to
combine the
two images.

Merge to HDR

Source Files

Choose two or more files from a set of exposures to
merge and create a High Dynamic Range image.

OK

Cancel

Use: Files

river02.psd
river01.psd

Browse...

Remove

Add Open Files

☑ Attempt to Automatically Align Source Images

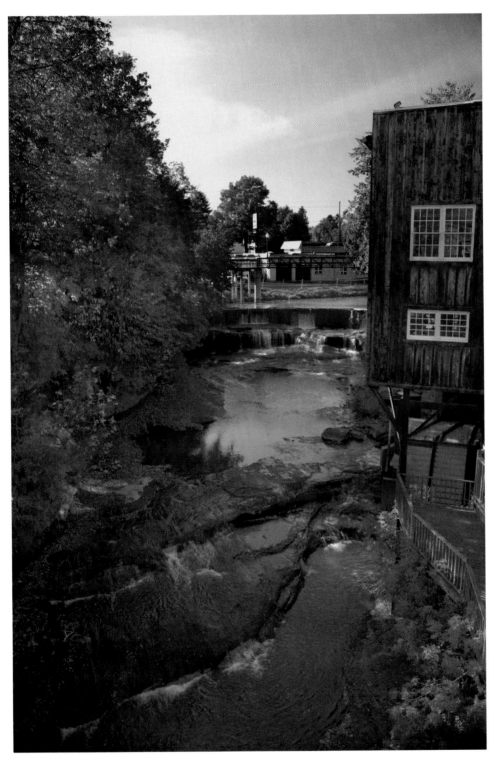

Figure 6.11
You'll end up with an extended dynamic range photo like this one.

If you do everything correctly, you'll end up with a photo like the one shown in Figure 6.11, which has the properly exposed foreground of the first shot, and the well-exposed sky of the second image. Note that, ideally, nothing should move between shots. In the example pictures, the river is moving, but the exposures were made so close together that, after the merger, you can't really tell.

What if you don't have the opportunity, inclination, or skills to create several images at different exposures, as described? If you shoot in RAW format, you can still use Merge to HDR, working with a *single* original image file. What you do is import the image into Photoshop several times, using Adobe Camera Raw to create multiple copies of the file at different exposure levels.

For example, you'd create one copy that's too dark, so the shadows lose detail, but the highlights are preserved. Create another copy with the shadows intact and allow the highlights to wash out. Then, you can use Merge to HDR to combine the two and end up with a finished image that has the extended dynamic range you're looking for. (This concludes the image editing portion of the chapter. We now return you to our alternate sponsor: photography.)

Dealing with Noise

Image noise is that random grainy effect that some like to use as a visual effect, but which, most of the time, is objectionable because it robs your image of detail even as it adds that "interesting" texture. Noise is caused by two different phenomena: high ISO settings and long exposures.

High ISO noise commonly appears when you raise your camera's sensitivity setting above ISO 800. The Nikon D300 is a huge leap forward, noise-wise, from the earlier D200, and has very good ISO noise characteristics, but noise is likely to be visible at ISO 800, and is usually fairly noticeable at ISO 1,600. At ISO 3,200 noise is still quite good, and I've gotten excellent results shooting sports at the maximum ISO 6,400 setting. High ISO noise appears as a result of the amplification needed to increase the sensitivity of the sensor. While higher ISOs do pull details out of dark areas, they also amplify non-signal information randomly, creating noise. You can counter much of this noise by activating the D300's **High ISO NR** feature, found in the Shooting menu and described in Chapter 3.

A similar noisy phenomenon occurs during long time exposures, which allow more photons to reach the sensor, increasing your ability to capture a picture under low-light conditions. However, the longer exposures also increase the likelihood that some pixels will register random phantom photons, often because the longer an imager is "hot" the warmer it gets, and that heat can be mistaken for photons. There's also a special kind of noise that CMOS sensors like the one used in the D300 are potentially susceptible to. With a CCD, the entire signal is conveyed off the chip and funneled through a single amplifier and analog-to-digital conversion circuit. Any noise introduced there is, at least, consistent. CMOS imagers, on the other hand, contain millions of individual amplifiers and A/D converters, all working in unison. Because all these circuits don't necessarily all process in precisely the same way all the time, they can introduce something called fixed-pattern noise into the image data.

Fortunately, Nikon's electronics geniuses have done an exceptional job minimizing noise from all causes in the D300. Even so, you might still want to apply the optional long exposure noise reduction that can be activated using the Shooting menu's **Long exp. NR entry**, as described in Chapter 3. This type of noise reduction involves the D300 taking a second, blank exposure, and comparing the random pixels in that image with the photograph you just took. Pixels that coincide in the two represent noise and can safely be suppressed. This noise reduction system, called *dark frame subtraction,* effectively doubles the amount of time required to take a picture, and is used only for exposures longer than eight seconds.

Noise reduction can reduce the amount of detail in your picture, as some image information may be removed along with the noise. So, you might want to use this feature with moderation. You can also apply noise reduction to a lesser extent using Nikon Capture NX, Photoshop, and when converting RAW and sRAW files to some other format, using your favorite RAW converter, or an industrial-strength product like Noise Ninja (**www.picturecode.com**) to wipe out noise after you've already taken the picture.

Fixing Exposures with Histograms

While you can often recover poorly exposed photos in your image editor, your best bet is to arrive at the correct exposure in the camera, minimizing the tweaks that you have to make in post-processing. However, you can't always judge exposure just by viewing the image on your D300's LCD after the shot is made. Nor can you get a 100 percent accurately exposed picture by using the D300's Live View feature. Ambient light may make the LCD difficult to see, and the brightness level you've set can affect the appearance of the playback image.

Instead, you can use a histogram, which is a chart displayed on the D300's LCD that shows the number of tones being captured at each brightness level. You can use the information to provide correction for the next shot you take. The D300 offers four histogram variations in three screens: three histograms that show overall brightness levels for an image and an alternate version that separates the red, green, and blue channels of your image into separate histograms.

The most basic histogram is displayed during Playback when you press the multi-selector up/down buttons to produce the Overview Data screen, as described in Chapter 2, and shown in Figure 6.12. This screen provides a small histogram at the right side that displays the distribution of luminance or brightness. You can also view a larger luminance histogram, like the one shown in Figure 6.13, by pressing the multi-selector center button when CSM #f1 is properly set up, as mentioned above. The final histogram screen is the one shown in Figure 6.14, which displays both a luminance chart and separate red, green, and blue charts.

DISPLAYING HISTOGRAMS

To view all the available histograms on your screen, you must have the D300 set up properly. First, you'll need to mark **Histograms** using the Display mode entry in the Playback menu, as described in Chapter 3. That will make the Histograms screen visible when you cycle among the informational screens while pressing the multi-selector up/down buttons while an image is displayed.

If you also want to view a larger brightness/luminance histogram overlaid on your image at the press of the multi-selector center button, you'll need to specify that behavior using **CSM #f1**, as described in Chapter 4.

Figure 6.12
A histogram shows the relationship of tones in an image.

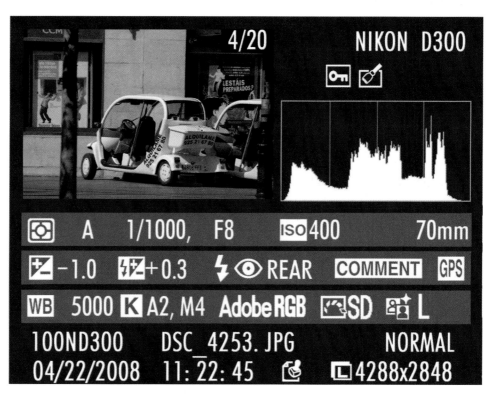

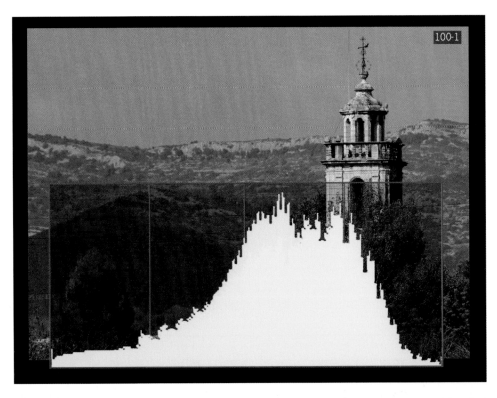

Figure 6.13
A large histogram can be overlaid on the image when you press the multi-selector center button.

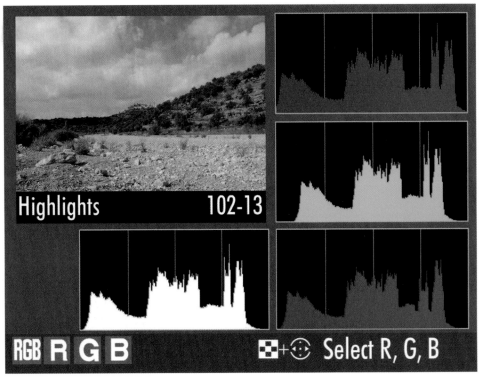

Figure 6.14
The D300's most complete histogram screen shows both luminance and separate red, green, and blue histograms.

Both luminance and RGB histograms are charts that include a representation of up to 256 vertical lines on a horizontal axis that show the number of pixels in the image at each brightness level, from 0 (black) on the left side to 255 (white) on the right. (The 3-inch LCD doesn't have enough pixels to show each and every one of the 256 lines, but, instead provides a representation of the shape of the curve formed.) The more pixels at a given level, the taller the bar at that position. If no bar appears at a particular position on the scale from left to right, there are no pixels at that particular brightness level.

As you can see, a typical histogram produces a mountain-like shape, with most of the pixels bunched in the middle tones, with fewer pixels at the dark and light ends of the scale. Ideally, though, there will be at least some pixels at either extreme, so that your image has both a true black and a true white representing some details. Learn to spot histograms that represent over- and underexposure, and add or subtract exposure using an EV modification to compensate.

For example, Figure 6.15 shows the histogram for an image that is badly underexposed. You can guess from the shape of the histogram that many of the dark tones to the left

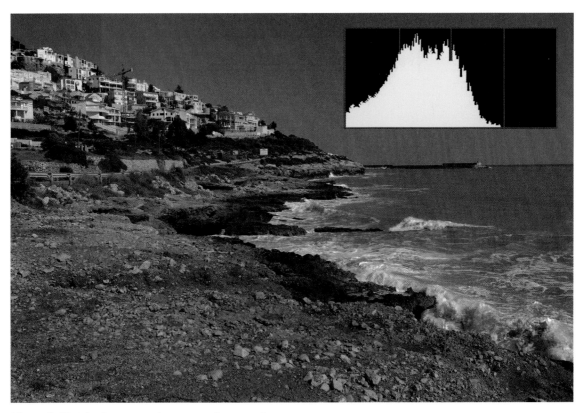

Figure 6.15 This histogram shows an underexposed image.

of the graph have been clipped off. There's plenty of room on the right side for additional pixels to reside without having them become overexposed. Or, a histogram might look like Figure 6.16, which is overexposed. In either case, you can increase or decrease the exposure (either by changing the f/stop or shutter speed in Manual mode or by adding or subtracting an EV value in A or S modes) to produce the corrected histogram shown in Figure 6.17, in which the tones "hug" the right side of the histogram to produce as many highlight details as possible. See "Making EV Changes" above for information on dialing in exposure compensation.

The histogram can also be used to aid in fixing the contrast of an image, although gauging incorrect contrast is more difficult. For example, if the histogram shows all the tones bunched up in one place in the image, the photo will be low in contrast. If the tones are spread out more or less evenly, the image is probably high in contrast. In either case, your best bet may be to switch to RAW (if you're not already using that format) so you can adjust contrast in post processing. However, you can also change to a user-defined Picture Control with contrast set lower (–1 to –3) or higher (+1 to +3) as required. You'll find instructions for creating Picture Controls in Chapter 3.

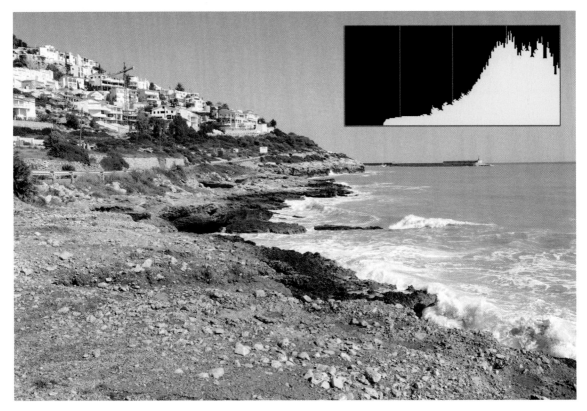

Figure 6.16 This histogram reveals that the image is overexposed.

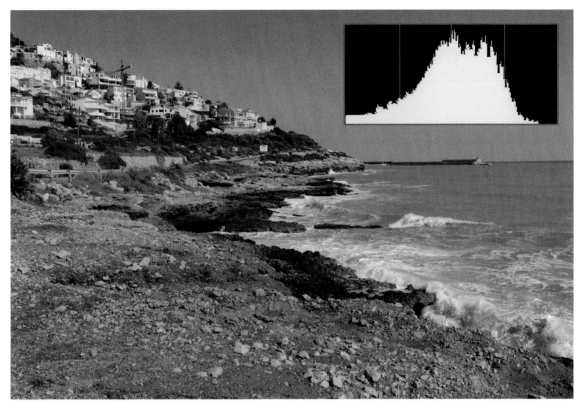

Figure 6.17 A histogram for a properly exposed image should look like this.

One useful, but often overlooked tool in evaluating histograms is the Highlights display, which shows blown out highlights in the thumbnail with a black blinking border. Highlights can give you a better picture of what information is being lost to overexposure. By default, the Highlights display shows "blinkies" for the luminance channel, but you can separately view highlights for the red, green, and blue channels. Just follow these steps:

1. With an image displayed, and the highlights/histogram screen shown, hold down the Thumbnail/Zoom button.

2. Press the multi-selector left/right buttons to cycle among RGB (all channels), R, G, and B.

3. When a channel is framed in an orange outline, the Highlight information for that channel is shown in the thumbnail image in the upper-left corner. At the bottom left of the screen, either RGB, R, G, or B will be highlighted to show the currently active channel.

In working with histograms, your goal should be to have all the tones in an image spread out between the edges, with none clipped off at the left and right sides. Underexposing (to preserve highlights) should be done only as a last resort, because retrieving the underexposed shadows in your image editor will frequently increase the noise, even if you're working with RAW files. A better course of action is to expose for the highlights, but, when the subject matter makes it practical, fill in the shadows with additional light, using reflectors, fill flash, or other techniques rather than allowing them to be seriously underexposed.

The more you work with histograms, the more useful they become. One of the first things that histogram veterans notice is that it's possible to overexpose one channel even if the overall exposure appears to be correct. For example, flower photographers soon discover that it's really, really difficult to get a good picture of a rose, like the one shown in Figure 6.18. The exposure looks okay—but there's no detail in the rose's petals. Looking at the histogram (see Figure 6.19) shows why: the red channel is blown out. If

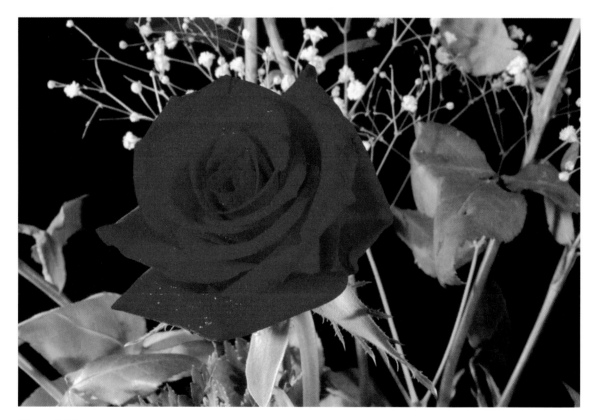

Figure 6.18 It's common to lose detail in bright red flowers because the red channel becomes overexposed even when the other channels are properly exposed.

Figure 6.18

The RGB histograms show that both the red and green channels are overexposed.

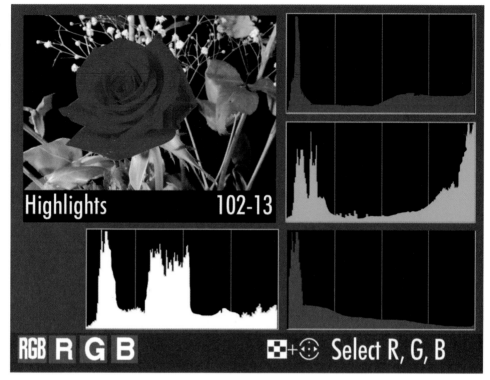

you look at the red histogram, there's a peak at the right edge that indicates that highlight information has been lost. In fact, the green channel has been blown, too, and so the green parts of the flower also lack detail. Only the blue channel's histogram is entirely contained within the boundaries of the chart, and, on first glance, the white luminance histogram at the lower left seems fairly normal.

Any of the primary channels, red, green, or blue, can blow out all by themselves, although bright reds seem to be the most common problem area. More difficult to diagnose are overexposed tones in one of the "in-between" hues on the color wheel. Overexposed yellows (which are very common) will be shown by blow-outs in *both* the red and green channels. Too-bright cyans will manifest as excessive blue and green highlights, while overexposure in the red and blue channels reduces detail in magenta colors. As you gain experience, you'll be able to see exactly how anomalies in the RGB channels translate into poor highlights and murky shadows.

The only way to correct for color channel blowouts is to reduce exposure. As I mentioned earlier, you might want to consider filling in the shadows with additional light to keep them from becoming too dark when you decrease exposure. In practice, you'll want to monitor the red channel most closely, followed by the blue channel, and slightly decrease exposure to see if that helps. Because of the way our eyes perceive color, we are more sensitive to variations in green, so green channel blowouts are less of a problem, unless your main subject is heavily colored in that hue. If you plan on photographing a frog hopping around on your front lawn, you'll want to be extra careful to preserve detail in the green channel, using bracketing or other exposure techniques outlined in this chapter.

7

Advanced Shooting Tips for Your Nikon D300

Getting the right exposure is one of the foundations of a great photograph, but a lot more goes into a compelling shot than good tonal values. A sharp image, proper white balance, good color, and other factors all can help elevate your image from good to exceptional. So, now that you've got a good understanding of exposure tucked away, you'll want to learn how to work with additional exposure options available with the Nikon D300, explore some of the intricacies of automatic focus (including the ability to focus anywhere on the image with Live View), and master some of the many ways you can fine-tune your images through a few useful tables of recommended settings for the four banks in the Shooting and Custom Setting menus.

This chapter is a bit of a grab-bag, because I'm including some specific advanced shooting techniques that didn't quite fit into the other chapters. If you master these concepts, you can be confident that you're well on your way towards mastering your Nikon D300. In fact, you'll be ready for the discussions of using lenses (Chapter 8) and working with light (Chapter 9).

A Tiny Slice of Time

Exposures that seem impossibly brief can reveal a world we didn't know existed. In the 1930s, Dr. Harold Edgerton, a professor of electrical engineering at MIT, pioneered high-speed photography using a repeating electronic flash unit he patented called the *stroboscope*. As the inventor of the electronic flash, he popularized its use to freeze objects in motion, and you've probably seen his photographs of bullets piercing balloons and drops of milk forming a coronet-shaped splash.

Electronic flash freezes action by virtue of its extremely short duration—as brief as 1/50,000th second or less. Although the D300's built-in flash unit can give you these ultra-quick glimpses of moving subjects, an external flash, such as one of the Nikon Speedlights, offers even more versatility. You can read more about using electronic flash to stop action in Chapter 9.

Of course, the D300 is fully capable of immobilizing all but the fastest movement using only its shutter speeds, which range all the way up to an astonishing 1/8,000th second. Indeed, you'll rarely have need for such a brief shutter speed in ordinary shooting. If you wanted to use an aperture of f/1.8 at ISO 200 outdoors in bright sunlight, for some reason, a shutter speed of 1/8,000th second would more than do the job. You'd need a faster shutter speed only if you moved the ISO setting to a higher sensitivity (but why would you do that?). Under less than full sunlight, 1/8,000th second is more than fast enough for any conditions you're likely to encounter.

Most sports action can be frozen at 1/2,000th second or slower, and for many sports a slower shutter speed is actually preferable—for example, to allow the wheels of a racing automobile or motorcycle, or the propeller on a classic aircraft to blur realistically. Figure 7.1 is another example. The 1/500 second shutter speed effectively stopped the football players in mid-tackle but allowed the fastest moving things, such as the ball carrier's feet, to blur slightly. The blur tells us that this shot is a true action picture.

But if you want to do some exotic action-freezing photography without resorting to electronic flash, the D300's top shutter speed is at your disposal. Here are some things to think about when exploring this type of high-speed photography:

- **You'll need a lot of light.** High shutter speeds cut very fine slices of time and sharply reduce the amount of illumination that reaches your sensor. To use 1/8,000th second at an aperture of f/6.3, you'd need an ISO setting of 1,600—even in full daylight. To use an f/stop smaller than f/6.3 or an ISO setting lower than 1,600, you'd need *more* light than full daylight provides. (That's why electronic flash units work so well for high-speed photography when used as the sole illumination; they provide both the effect of a brief shutter speed and the high levels of illumination needed.)

- **Forget about reciprocity failure.** If you're an old-time film shooter, you might recall that very brief shutter speeds (as well as very high light levels and very *long* exposures) produced an effect called *reciprocity failure,* in which given exposures ended up providing less than the calculated value because of the way film responded to very short, very intense, or very long exposures of light. Solid-state sensors don't suffer from this defect, so you don't need to make an adjustment when using high shutter speeds (or brief flash bursts).

Figure 7.1

A little blur can be a good thing, as the blurry feet and hands of some players add excitement to this action shot.

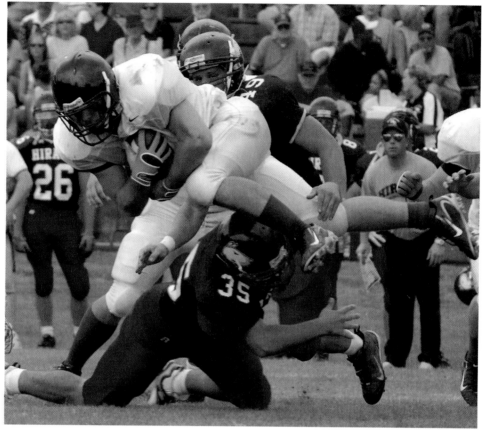

- **No elongation effect.** This is another old bugaboo that has largely been solved through modern technology, but I wanted to bring it to your attention anyway. In olden times, cameras used shutters that traveled horizontally. To achieve faster shutter speeds, focal plane shutters (located just in front of the plane of the sensor) open only a smaller-than-frame-sized slit so that, even though the shutter is already traveling at its highest rate of speed, the film/sensor is exposed for a briefer period of time as the slit moves across the surface. At very short shutter speeds, and with subjects moving horizontally at very fast velocities, it was possible for the subject to partially "keep up" with the shutter if it were traveling in the same direction as the slit, producing an elongated or slanted effect. Conversely, subjects moving in the opposite direction of shutter motion could be compressed. Today, shutters like those in the D300 move vertically and at a higher maximum rate of speed. So, unless you're photographing a rocket blasting into space, and holding the camera horizontally to boot (or shooting a racing car in vertical orientation), it's almost impossible to produce unwanted elongation/compression.

- **High shutter speeds with electronic flash.** You might be tempted to use an electronic flash with a high shutter speed. Perhaps you want to stop some action in daylight with a brief shutter speed and use electronic flash only as supplemental illumination to fill in the shadows. Unfortunately, under most conditions you can't use flash in subdued illumination with your D300 at any shutter speed faster than 1/250th second. That's the fastest speed at which the camera's focal plane shutter is fully open: at shorter speeds, the "slit" described above comes into play, so that the flash will expose only the small portion of the sensor exposed by the slit during its duration. (Check out "High Speed Sync" in Chapter 9 if you want to see how you *can* use shutter speeds shorter than 1/250th second, albeit at much-reduced effective power levels.)

Working with Short Exposures

You can have a lot of fun exploring the kinds of pictures you can take using very brief exposure times, whether you decide to take advantage of the action-stopping capabilities of your built-in or external electronic flash or work with the Nikon D300's faster shutter speeds. Here are a few ideas to get you started:

- **Take revealing images.** Fast shutter speeds can help you reveal the real subject behind the façade, by freezing constant motion to capture an enlightening moment in time. Legendary fashion/portrait photographer Philippe Halsman used leaping photos of famous people, such as the Duke and Duchess of Windsor, Richard Nixon, and Salvador Dali to illuminate their real selves. Halsman said, "*When you ask a person to jump, his attention is mostly directed toward the act of jumping and the mask falls so that the real person appears.*" Try some high-speed portraits of people you know in motion to see how they appear when concentrating on something other than the portrait.

- **Create unreal images.** High-speed photography can also produce photographs that show your subjects in ways that are quite unreal. A helicopter in mid-air with its rotors frozen or a motocross cyclist leaping over a ramp, but with all motion stopped so that the rider and machine look as if they were frozen in mid-air, make for an unusual picture. When we're accustomed to seeing subjects in motion, seeing them stopped in time can verge on the surreal.

- **Capture unseen perspectives.** Some things are *never* seen in real life, except when viewed in a stop-action photograph. Edgerton's balloon bursts were only a starting point. Freeze a hummingbird in flight for a view of wings that never seem to stop. Or, capture the splashes as liquid falls into a bowl, as shown in Figure 7.2. No electronic flash was required for this image (and wouldn't have illuminated the water in the bowl as evenly). Instead, a clutch of high intensity lamps and an ISO setting of 1,600 allowed the D300 to capture this image at 1/2,000th second.

Figure 7.2

A large amount of artificial illumination and an ISO 1,600 sensitivity setting allowed capturing this shot at 1/2,000th second without use of an electronic flash.

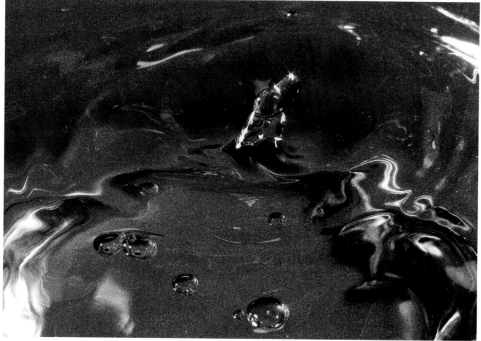

■ **Vanquish camera shake and gain new angles.** Here's an idea that's so obvious it isn't always explored to its fullest extent. A high enough shutter speed can free you from the tyranny of a tripod, making it easier to capture new angles, or to shoot quickly while moving around, especially with longer lenses. I tend to use a mono-pod or tripod for almost everything when I'm not using an image-stabilized lens, and I end up missing some shots because of a reluctance to adjust my camera support to get a higher, lower, or different angle. If you have enough light and can use an f/stop wide enough to permit a high shutter speed, you'll find a new freedom to choose your shots (see Figure 7.3). I have a favored 170mm-500mm lens that I use for sports and wildlife photography, almost invariably with a tripod, as I don't find the "reciprocal of the focal length" rule particularly helpful in most cases. I would *not* hand-hold this hefty lens at its 500mm setting with a 1/500th second shutter speed under most circumstances. Nor, if you want to account for the crop factor, would I use 1/750 second. However, at 1/2,000th second or faster, it's entirely pos-sible for a steady hand to use this lens without a tripod or monopod's extra support, and I've found that my whole approach to shooting animals and other elusive sub-jects changes in high-speed mode. Selective focus allows dramatically isolating my prey wide open at f/6.3, too.

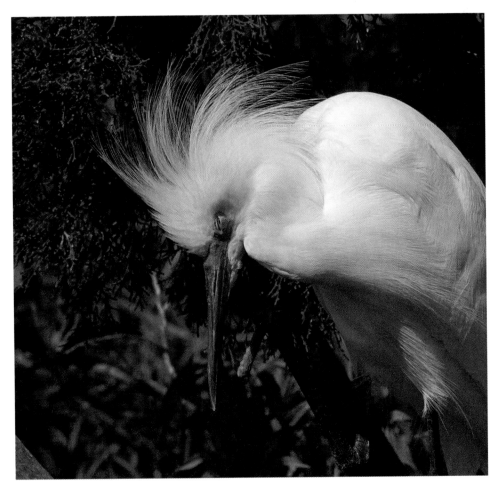

Figure 7.3
Outdoors, you may need a shutter speed of 1/2,000th second to hand-hold a 500mm lens to capture distant wildlife.

Long Exposures

Longer exposures are a doorway into another world, showing us how even familiar scenes can look much different when photographed over periods measured in seconds. At night, long exposures produce streaks of light from moving, illuminated subjects like automobiles or amusement park rides. Extra-long exposures of seemingly pitch-dark subjects can reveal interesting views using light levels barely bright enough to see by. At any time of day, including daytime (in which case you'll often need the help of neutral density filters to make the long exposure practical), long exposures can cause moving objects to vanish entirely, because they don't remain stationary long enough to register in a photograph.

Three Ways to Take Long Exposures

There are actually three common types of lengthy exposures: *timed exposures, bulb exposures*, and *time exposures*. The D300 offers only the first two, but once you understand all three, you'll see why Nikon made the choices it did. Because of the length of the exposure, all of the following techniques should be used with a tripod to hold the camera steady.

- **Timed exposures.** These are long exposures from 1 second to 30 seconds, measured by the camera itself. To take a picture in this range, simply use Manual or S modes and use the main command dial to set the shutter speed to the length of time you want, choosing from preset speeds of 1.0, 1.5, 2.0, 3.0, 4.0, 6.0, 8.0, 10.0, 15.0, 20.0, or 30.0 seconds (if you've specified 1/2 stop increments for exposure adjustments), or 1.0, 1.3, 1.6, 2.0, 2.5, 3.2, 4.0, 5.0, 6.0, 8.0, 10.0, 13.0, 15.0, 20.0, 25.0, and 30.0 seconds (if you're using 1/3 stop increments). The advantage of timed exposures is that the camera does all the calculating for you. There's no need for a stop-watch. If you review your image on the LCD and decide to try again with the exposure doubled or halved, you can dial in the correct exposure with precision. The disadvantage of timed exposures is that you can't take a photo for longer than 30 seconds.

- **Bulb exposures.** This type of exposure is so-called because in the olden days the photographer squeezed and held an air bulb attached to a tube that provided the force necessary to keep the shutter open. Traditionally, a bulb exposure is one that lasts as long as the shutter release button is pressed; when you release the button, the exposure ends. To make a bulb exposure with the D300, set the camera on Manual mode and use the main command dial to select the shutter speed immediately after 30 seconds—bulb. Then, press the shutter to start the exposure, and press it again to close the shutter. If you'd like to simulate a time exposure (described below), you can use the Nikon MC-30 remote control cable (about $60), MC-36 remote shutter release ($130), or ML-3 wireless remote control that attach to the 10-pin terminal on the left side of the camera under the rubber cover.

- **Time exposures.** This is a setting found on some cameras to produce longer exposures. With cameras that implement this option, the shutter opens when you press the shutter release button, and remains open until you press the button again. With the Nikon D300, you can produce this effect with a locking cable release, like the Nikon MC-30 and other remote releases just mentioned. You can press the shutter release button, go off for a few minutes, and come back to close the shutter (assuming your camera is still there). The disadvantages of this mode are exposures must be timed manually, and with shorter exposures it's possible for the vibration of manually opening and closing the shutter to register in the photo. For longer exposures, the period of vibration is relatively brief and not usually a problem.

Working with Long Exposures

Because the D300 produces such good images at longer exposures, and there are so many creative things you can do with long-exposure techniques, you'll want to do some experimenting. Get yourself a tripod or another firm support and take some test shots with long exposure noise reduction both enabled and disabled (to see whether you prefer low noise or high detail) and get started. Here are some things to try:

- **Make people invisible.** One very cool thing about long exposures is that objects that move rapidly enough won't register at all in a photograph, while the subjects that remain stationary are portrayed in the normal way. That makes it easy to produce people-free landscape photos and architectural photos at night or, even, in full daylight if you use a neutral density filter (or two) (or three) to allow an exposure of at least a few seconds. At ISO 100 (actually **LO 1.0**), f/22, and a pair of 8X (three-stop) neutral density filters you can use exposures of nearly two seconds; overcast days and/or even more neutral density filtration would work even better if daylight people-vanishing is your goal. They'll have to be walking *very* briskly and across the field of view (rather than directly toward the camera) for this to work. At night, it's much easier to achieve this effect with the 20- to 30-second exposures that are possible, as you can see in Figure 7.4.

- **Create streaks.** If you aren't shooting for total invisibility, long exposures with the camera on a tripod can produce some interesting streaky effects. Even a single 8X ND filter will let you shoot at f/22 and 1/6th second in daylight.

- **Produce light trails.** At night, car headlights and taillights and other moving sources of illumination can generate interesting light trails, as shown in Figure 7.5. Your camera doesn't even need to be mounted on a tripod; hand-holding the D300 for longer exposures adds movement and patterns to your trails. If you're shooting fireworks, a longer exposure may allow you to combine several bursts into one picture.

- **Blur waterfalls, etc.** You'll find that waterfalls and other sources of moving liquid produce a special type of long-exposure blur, because the water merges into a fantasy-like veil that looks different at different exposure times, and with different waterfalls. Cascades with turbulent flow produce a rougher look at a given longer exposure than falls that flow smoothly. Although blurred waterfalls have become almost a cliché, there are still plenty of variations for a creative photographer to explore.

■ **Show total darkness in new ways.** Even on the darkest, moonless nights, there is enough starlight or glow from distant illumination sources to see by, and, if you use a long exposure, there is enough light to take a picture, too. I was visiting a lakeside park about an hour after sunset and the sky was almost pitch black, with only a faint glow at the horizon. Yet, with a 20-second exposure the scene appears as if sunset were only minutes past, as you can see in Figure 7.6.

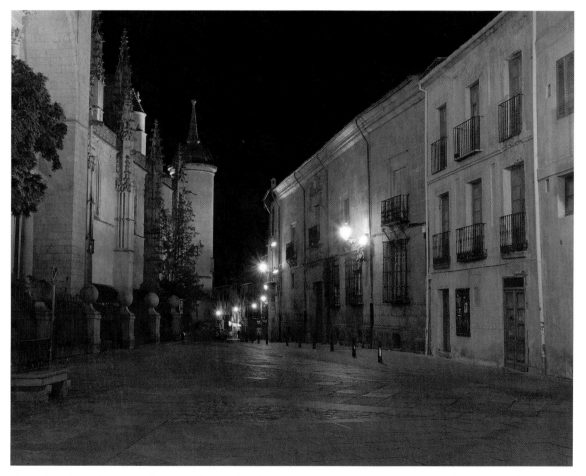

Figure 7.4 This European alleyway is thronged with people, but with the camera on a tripod, a 30-second exposure rendered the passersby almost invisible.

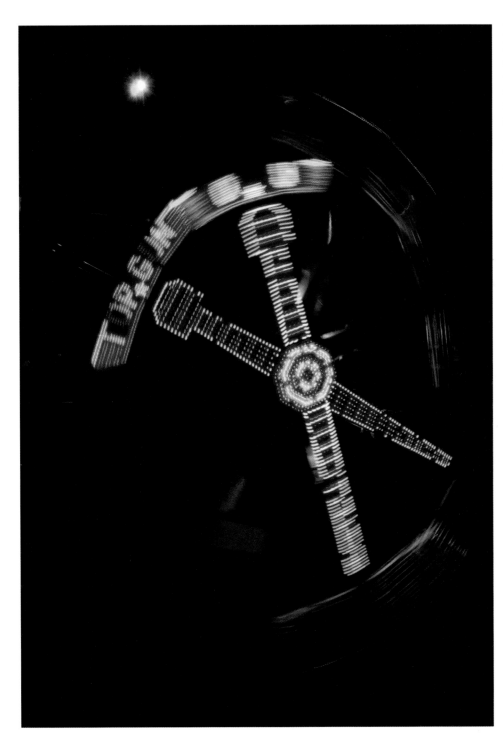

Figure 7.5
Long exposures
can transform
the most mun-
dane nighttime
subjects, such
as this amuse-
ment park ride,
into an inter-
esting light-
trails display.

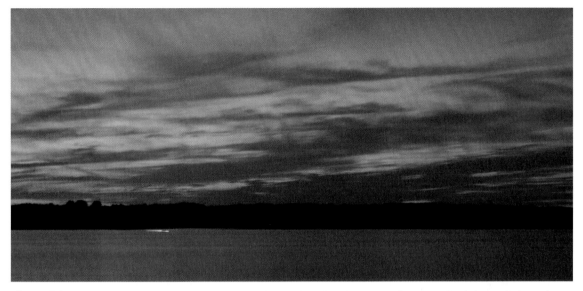

Figure 7.6 A 20-second exposure on a dark night revealed this lakeside setting, illuminated only by starlight and a waning sunset that had taken place more than an hour ago.

Delayed Exposures

Sometimes it's desirable to have a delay of some sort before a picture is actually taken. Perhaps you'd like to get in the picture yourself, and would appreciate it if the camera waited 10 seconds after you press the shutter release to actually take the picture. Maybe you want to give a tripod-mounted camera time to settle down and damp any residual vibration after the release is pressed to improve sharpness for an exposure with a relatively slow shutter speed. It's possible you want to explore the world of time-lapse photography. The next sections present your delayed exposure options.

Self-Timer

The D300 has a built-in self-timer with a user-selectable delay. Activate the timer by rotating the release mode dial to the self-timer icon. Press the shutter release button halfway to lock in focus on your subjects (if you're taking a self-portrait, focus on an object at a similar distance and use focus lock). When you're ready to take the photo, continue pressing the shutter release the rest of the way. The lamp on the front of the camera will blink slowly for eight seconds (when using the 10-second timer) and the beeper will chirp (if you haven't disabled it in the Shooting menu, as described in Chapter 3). During the final two seconds, the beeper sounds more rapidly and the lamp remains on until the picture is taken.

Another way to use the self-timer is with the **M-Up** mirror lockup. This is something you might want to do if you're shooting close-ups, landscapes, or other types of pictures using the self-timer only to trip the shutter in the most vibration-free way possible. Forget to bring along your tripod, but still want to take a close-up picture with a precise focus setting? That happened to me when I encountered this orchid (see Figure 7.7) in a greenhouse when picking up some potted plants. I wheeled a planting cart over to the blossom, rested the D300 on a soft bag of potting soil (a beanbag would have been better!), carefully focused, and let the self-timer trip the shutter at the appropriate moment. In such situations, the camera might teeter back and forth for a second or two, but it will settle back to its original position before the self-timer activates the shutter. The self-timer remains the active mode until you turn it off—even if you power down the D300—so remember to turn the release mode dial back to single frame mode when you're finished.

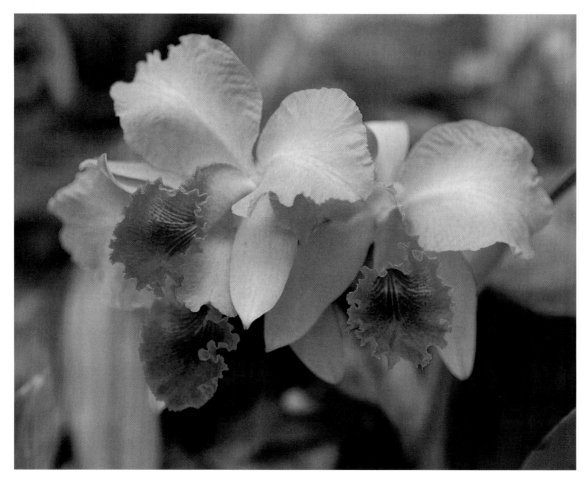

Figure 7.7 With the camera resting on a bag of potting soil on a cart, the self-timer triggered this vibration-free image of an orchid.

Remote Control

As outlined in the "Bulb Exposure" description earlier, your Nikon D300 can be triggered using a plug-in remote control with an electronic or infrared connection. For example, Nikon MC-36 is a remote switch with a 2.6-foot cord (you can add a 33-foot extension cable) and includes a flexible self-timer that can be set to trip the camera after a delay of anywhere from 1 second to 99 hours, 59 minutes, and 59 seconds (in other words, one second less than 100 hours). It can be used for interval shooting (time-lapse photography) for up to 999 shots with up to 99 hours, 99 minutes, and 99 seconds between shots. (I'll describe applications for time-lapse photography in the next section.)

The ML-3 is a two-channel infrared remote for operating Nikon film and digital cameras that have a 10-pin terminal like the one found on the front of the D300. Its features include automatic triggering, a three-second shutter release and either single shot or continuous shooting modes that can be selected from the remote position.

Your final remote control option is the coolest of all: the WT-4a wireless transmitter. This is the gadget for wireless remote control operation with Nikon Camera Control Pro 2 software, which I'll describe in Chapter 10. It allows communications from your camera to your computer (to transmit photos to, say, a laptop as they are taken) or to let your computer have near-total control over your D300's operation from a remote location. In photo-transmit mode, wedding and event photographers can get a lot of use out of this accessory, and studio photographers can benefit from it, too. Not only can you back up all your photos to a laptop or desktop computer as they are taken, you or an assistant can be viewing, editing, and displaying them virtually simultaneously to clients, art directors, or anyone else. When used to control the camera remotely with Camera Control Pro, the WT-4a is useful for photographing easily spooked wildlife, while the photographer remains hidden with a laptop.

Time-Lapse/Interval Photography

Who hasn't marveled at a time-lapse photograph of a flower opening, a series of shots of the moon marching across the sky, or one of those extreme time-lapse picture sets showing something that takes a very, very long time, such as a building under construction.

You probably won't be shooting such construction shots, unless you have a spare D300 you don't need for a few months (or are willing to go through the rigmarole of figuring out how to set up your camera in precisely the same position using the same lens settings to shoot a series of pictures at intervals). However, other kinds of time-lapse photography are entirely within reach.

The D300 can take time-lapse/interval photographs all by itself, using the **Interval timer shooting** entry found in the Shooting menu. If you're willing to tether the camera to a computer (a laptop will do) using the USB cable, you can take time-lapse photos using the optional Nikon Camera Control Pro.

If you want freedom to shoot anywhere, the Nikon MC-36 is an affordable add-on (around $135) with much more than the self-timer and remote control features mentioned previously. In fact, it has many different modes with an interesting array of delay/interval combinations. For example, you can set the self-timer for a specific period of time, then take a specified number of exposures at one-second intervals. Or, you can set a delay period that must elapse before the D300 begins a long exposure. Finally, you can choose to shoot a set number of pictures at intervals from 1 second to 99 hours, 59 minutes, and 59 seconds.

Here is a recap of essential tips for effective time-lapse photography:

- **Use AC power.** If you're shooting a long sequence, consider connecting your camera to an AC adapter, as leaving the D300 on for long periods of time will rapidly deplete the battery.

- **Make sure you have enough storage space.** Unless your memory card has enough capacity to hold all the images you'll be taking, you might want to change to a higher compression rate or reduced resolution to maximize the image count.

- **Make a movie.** While time-lapse stills are interesting, you can increase your fun factor by compiling all your shots into a motion picture using your favorite desktop movie-making software.

- **Protect your camera.** If your camera will be set up for an extended period of time (longer than an hour or two), make sure it's protected from weather, earthquakes, animals, young children, innocent bystanders, and theft.

- **Vary intervals.** Experiment with different time intervals. You don't want to take pictures too often or less often than necessary to capture the changes you hope to image.

How Focus Works

Although Nikon added autofocus capabilities in the 1980s, back in the day of film cameras, prior to that focusing was always done manually. Honest. Even though viewfinders were bigger and brighter than they are today, special focusing screens, magnifiers, and other gadgets were often used to help the photographer achieve correct focus. Imagine what it must have been like to focus manually under demanding, fast-moving conditions such as sports photography.

Focusing was problematic because our eyes and brains have poor memory for correct focus, which is why your eye doctor must shift back and forth between sets of lenses and ask "Does that look sharper—or was it sharper before?" in determining your correct prescription. Similarly, manual focusing involves jogging the focus ring back and forth as you go from almost in focus, to sharp focus, to almost focused again. The little clockwise and counterclockwise arcs decrease in size until you've zeroed in on the point of correct focus. What you're looking for is the image with the most contrast between the edges of elements in the image.

The camera also looks for these contrast differences among pixels to determine relative sharpness. There are two ways that sharp focus is determined:

■ **Phase detection.** In this mode, the autofocus sampling area is divided into two halves by a lens in the sensor. The two halves are compared, much like (actually, exactly like) a two-window rangefinder used in surveying, weaponry—and non-SLR cameras like the venerable Leica M film models. The contrast between the two images changes as focus is moved in or out, until sharp focus is achieved when the images are "in phase," or lined up. Phase detection is the normal mode used by the D300 (and is applied when using Live View in **Hand-held** mode, discussed later in this chapter). As with any rangefinder-like function, accuracy is better when the "base length" between the two images is larger. (Think back to your high school trigonometry; you could calculate a distance more accurately when the separation between the two points where the angles were measured was greater.) For that reason, phase detection autofocus is more accurate with larger (wider) lens openings than with smaller lens openings, and may not work at all when the f/stop is smaller than f/5.6. The D300 is able to perform these comparisons very quickly.

■ **Contrast detection.** This is a slower mode, suitable for static subjects, and used by the Nikon D300 with Live View in **Tripod** mode. It's a bit easier to understand and is illustrated by Figure 7.8. At left in the extreme enlargement of a clay-tiled roof, the transitions between pixels are soft and blurred. Even the boundary between the bright sky and the tiles is smudged. When the image is brought into focus (right), the transitions are sharp and clear. Although this example is a bit exaggerated so you can see the results on the printed page, it's easy to understand that when maximum contrast in a subject is achieved, it can be deemed to be in sharp focus.

The D300's autofocus mechanism, like all such systems found in SLR cameras, evaluates the degree of focus, but, unlike the human eye, it is able to remember the progression perfectly, so that autofocus can lock in much more quickly and, with an image that has sufficient contrast, more precisely. Unfortunately, while the D300's focus system finds it easy to measure degrees of apparent focus at each of the focus points in the viewfinder, it doesn't really know with any certainty *which* object should be in sharpest focus. Is it the closest object? The subject in the center? Something lurking *behind* the closest subject? A person standing over at the side of the picture? Many of the techniques for using autofocus effectively involve telling the D300 exactly what it should be focusing on, by choosing a focus zone or by allowing the camera to choose a focus zone for you. I'll address that topic shortly. But first, some confusion…

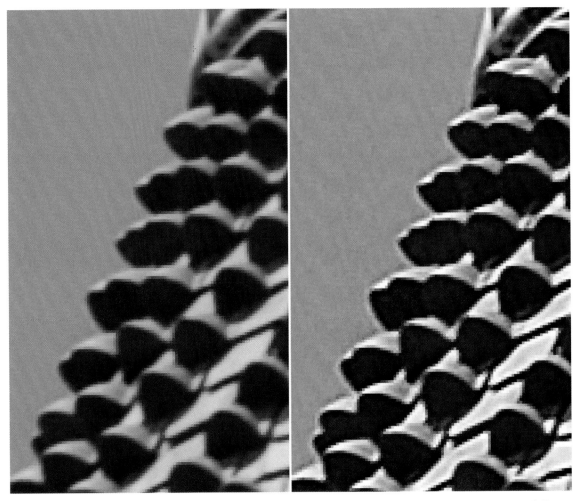

Figure 7.8 Focus sensors detect the increase in contrast in the edges of subjects, starting with a blurry image (left) and producing a sharp, contrasty image (right).

Adding Circles of Confusion

But there are other factors in play, as well. You know that increased depth-of-field brings more of your subject into focus. But more depth-of-field also makes autofocusing (or manual focusing) more difficult because the contrast is lower between objects at different distances. So, autofocus with a 200mm lens (or zoom setting) may be easier than at a 28mm focal length (or zoom setting) because the longer lens has less apparent depth-of-field. By the same token, a lens with a maximum aperture of f/1.8 will be easier to autofocus (or manually focus) than one of the same focal length with an f/4 maximum aperture, because the f/4 lens has more depth-of-field *and* a dimmer view. That's why lenses with a maximum aperture smaller than f/5.6 can give your D300's autofocus system fits.

To make things even more complicated, many subjects aren't polite enough to remain still. They move around in the frame, so that even if the D300 is sharply focused on your main subject, it may change position and require refocusing. An intervening subject may pop into the frame and pass between you and the subject you meant to photograph. You (or the D300) have to decide whether to lock focus on this new subject, or remain focused on the original subject. Finally, there are some kinds of subjects that are difficult to bring into sharp focus because they lack enough contrast to allow the D300's AF system (or our eyes) to lock in. Blank walls, a clear blue sky, or other subject matter may make focusing difficult.

If you find all these focus factors confusing, you're on the right track. Focus is, in fact, measured using something called a *circle of confusion.* An ideal image consists of zillions of tiny little points, which, like all points, theoretically have no height or width. There is perfect contrast between the point and its surroundings. You can think of each point as a pinpoint of light in a darkened room. When a given point is out of focus, its edges decrease in contrast and it changes from a perfect point to a tiny disc with blurry edges (remember, blur is the lack of contrast between boundaries in an image). (See Figure 7.9.)

Figure 7.9

When a pinpoint of light (left) goes out of focus, its blurry edges form a circle of confusion (center and right).

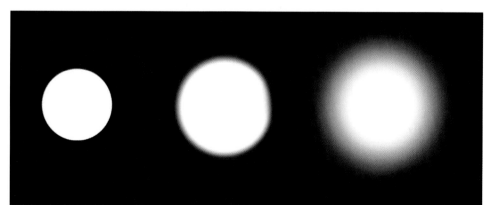

If this blurry disc—the circle of confusion—is small enough, our eye still perceives it as a point. It's only when the disc grows large enough that we can see it as a blur rather than a sharp point that a given point is viewed as out of focus. You can see, then, that enlarging an image, either by displaying it larger on your computer monitor or by making a large print, also enlarges the size of each circle of confusion. Moving closer to the image does the same thing. So, parts of an image that may look perfectly sharp in a 5 × 7-inch print viewed at arm's length, might appear blurry when blown up to 11 × 14 and examined at the same distance. Take a few steps back, however, and it may look sharp again.

To a lesser extent, the viewer also affects the apparent size of these circles of confusion. Some people see details better at a given distance and may perceive smaller circles of confusion than someone standing next to them. For the most part, however, such differences are small. Truly blurry images will look blurry to just about everyone under the same conditions.

Technically, there is just one plane within your picture area, parallel to the back of the camera (or sensor, in the case of a digital camera), that is in sharp focus. That's the plane in which the points of the image are rendered as precise points. At every other plane in front of or behind the focus plane, the points show up as discs that range from slightly blurry to extremely blurry (see Figure 7.10). In practice, the discs in many of these planes will still be so small that we see them as points, and that's where we get depth-of-field. Depth-of-field is just the range of planes that include discs that we perceive as points rather than blurred splotches. The size of this range increases as the aperture is reduced in size and is allocated roughly one-third in front of the plane of sharpest focus, and two-thirds behind it. The range of sharp focus is always greater behind your subject than in front of it.

Autofocus Simplifies Our Lives... Doesn't It?

Manual focus is tricky, requires judgment, and fast reflexes. So, we're all better off now that autofocus has become almost universal, right? On the one hand, AF does save time and allows us to capture subjects (particularly fast-moving sports) that are difficult to image sharply using manual focusing (unless you have training and know certain techniques). On the other hand, learning to apply the Nikon D300's autofocus system most effectively requires a bit of study and some practice. Then, once you're comfortable with autofocus, you'll know when it's appropriate to use the manual focus option, too.

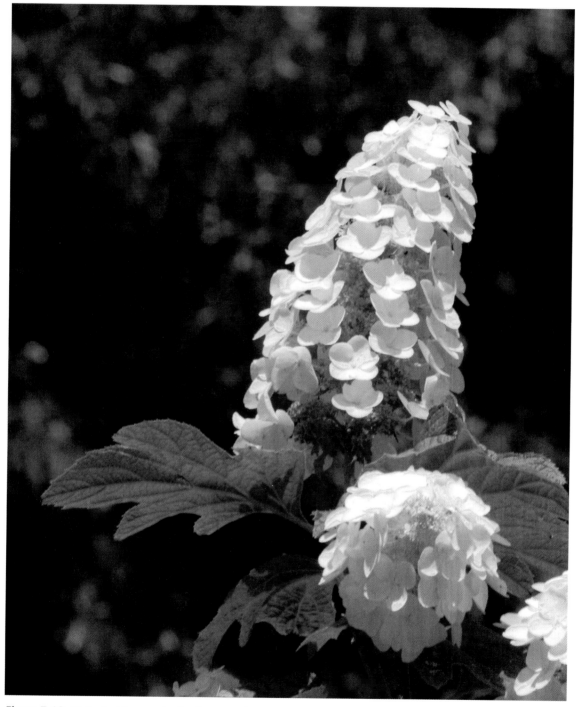

Figure 7.10 Only the blossoms in the foreground are in focus—the area behind them appears blurry because the depth-of-field is limited.

The important thing to remember is that focus isn't absolute. For example, some things that look in sharp focus at a given viewing size and distance might not be in focus at a larger size and/or closer distance. In addition, the goal of optimum focus isn't always to make things look sharp. Not all of an image will be or should be sharp. Controlling exactly what is sharp and what is not is part of your creative palette. Use of depth-of-field characteristics to throw part of an image out of focus while other parts are sharply focused is one of the most valuable tools available to a photographer. But selective focus works only when the desired areas of an image are in focus properly. For the digital SLR photographer, correct focus can be one of the trickiest parts of the technical and creative process.

As you'll learn in the following sections, the autofocus system used in the Nikon D300 is considerably different from what you might have been accustomed to if you have migrated from a Nikon D200 (or even a D2xs). The earlier cameras used a system that let you choose various "patterns" for autofocus when using the multi-zone shifting AF mode ("Group Dynamic"). You could also select attributes like "Closest Subject" to help the camera decide what to focus on. With all the options available, autofocus was still not perfect. If anything, the camera (and photographer) had *too many* choices, which, if not selected appropriately, could lead to poor focus.

The D300 now uses Nikon's new Multi-CAM 3500DX autofocus system that's very similar to the Multi-CAM 3500FX AF system used in the top-of-the-line Nikon D3—with one key difference: how the "zones" used to evaluate focus are allocated. The D300's DX AF sensor covers a larger percentage of the frame, as you can see in Figure 7.11. Both systems deploy an intelligent array of 15 cross-type sensors and 36 horizontal sensors in the viewing system (I'll explain how they work shortly). All 51 autofocus sensors can be used individually or in groups of 9, 21, or all 51 focus zones. The AF system uses the color and light values found in the focus zone array to accurately track moving objects, and to classify subjects into what Nikon calls a "scene recognition system." The new autofocus system uses a separate sensor in the viewing system to measure the contrast of the image. That's Nikon's autofocus system in a nutshell.

Like all camera autofocus sensors, those in your D300 require a minimum amount of light as well as a minimum aperture size to operate, which is why autofocus capabilities are possible only with lenses having an f/5.6 or larger maximum aperture. While there's not a lot you can do to "fix" a lens that has a maximum aperture that's too small, if your subject's contrast is difficult to detect because of waning light levels, the AF assist beam built into the D300 and Nikon's dedicated flash units provide additional light that helps assure enough illumination for autofocus.

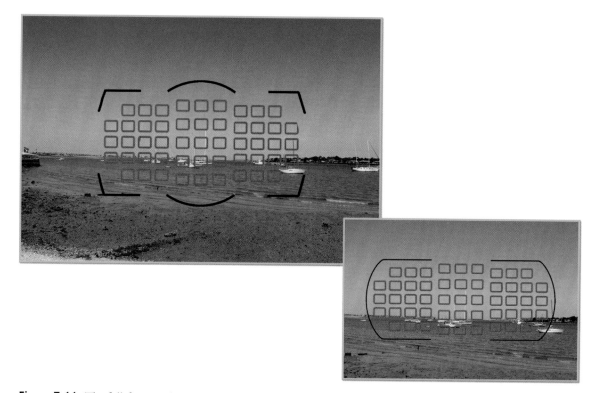

Figure 7.11 The full-frame Nikon D3's autofocus sensors (upper left) are spread out over a smaller percentage of the entire image compared to the Nikon D300's layout (lower right).

Bringing the Multi-CAM 3500DX AF System into Focus

I've explained individual bits and pieces of the Nikon D300's autofocus system earlier in this book, particularly in the "roadmap" sections that showed you where all the controls were located, and the "setup" chapters that explained the key autofocus options. Now it's time to round out the coverage as we tie everything together. There are three aspects of autofocus that you need to understand to use this essential feature productively:

- **Autofocus point selection.** This aspect controls how the D300 selects which areas of the frame are used to evaluate focus. Point selection allows the camera (or you) to specify a subject and lock focus in on that subject.

- **Autofocus mode and priority.** This governs *when* during the framing and shooting process autofocus is achieved. Should the camera focus once when activated, or continue to monitor your subject and refocus should the subject move? Is it okay to take a picture even if sharp focus isn't yet achieved, or should the camera lock out the shutter release until the image is sharp?

■ **Autofocus activation.** When should the autofocus process begin, and when should it be locked? This aspect is related to the autofocus mode, but uses controls that you can specify to activate and/or lock the autofocus process.

Autofocus Point Selection Overview

I'm discussing this aspect of autofocus first, because, in many ways, it is the most important. If your D300 isn't focusing on the correct subject, autofocus speed and activation are pretty much wasted effort. As you've learned, the D300 has up to 51 different points on the screen that can be individually selected by you or the camera as the active focus zone. One improvement that new Nikon D300 owners sometimes overlook is the upgrade to cross-type focus sensors at 15 of the central focus zone positions. (See Figure 7.12.) Why is this important? It helps to review exactly how the D300 determines focus.

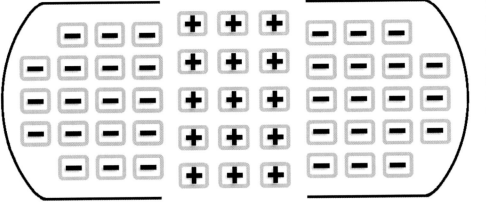

Figure 7.12
Fifteen central focus zones use cross-type sensors; the other 36 use horizontal focus sensors.

The cross-type and horizontal focus points don't really look like the coarse crosses and horizontal lines shown in the figure. In practice, each focus point is actually composed of short lines of pixels, arranged in either a horizontal row or an intersecting set of horizontal and vertical pixels in a cross shape. The D300 can interpret the horizontal focus sensors quickly under all lighting conditions; the cross-shaped focus sensors require a little more effort and a bit more light to operate effectively. That's why *all* the focus sensors in the D300 aren't of the cross variety.

The value of cross-type focus sensors, which can interpret contrast in both horizontal and vertical directions, can be seen in Figure 7.13. The two upper photos show a horizontal-type sensor evaluating a subject, which happens to be a piece of aged wood siding heavily creased with horizontal lines. At upper left, the sensor sees blurry lines, which become sharper when the wood is brought into focus. This type of subject is of average

Figure 7.13

Horizontal (and vertical) focus sensors can interpret image contrast in only one direction (top), while cross-type sensors can evaluate contrast in both horizontal and vertical directions.

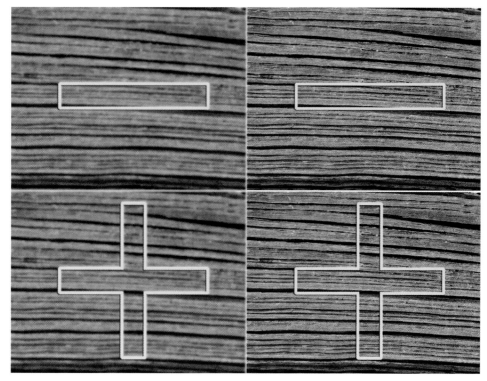

difficulty for a horizontal sensor: easier to interpret than an image with no pattern at all, and harder to focus than, say, vertical lines, which would stand out more clearly. You can see that a horizontal focus sensor does a good job but has some weaknesses. (A vertical-only focus sensor would have the same reduced performance with vertical lines and better focusing with horizontal lines.)

At the bottom of the figure you'll see the same subject being evaluated by a cross-type sensor. The horizontal lines are still more difficult to interpret with the horizontal arm of the cross, but they stand out in sharp contrast (even in the blurry version at lower left) and allow the camera to snap the image into focus easily, as you can see at lower right. In this example, both the horizontal and cross-type sensors were able to produce an equally sharp focus (upper and lower right), but the cross-type sensor probably focused the image a tad faster. And, in lower light levels, with subjects that were moving, or with subjects that have no pattern and less contrast to begin with, the cross-type sensor not only works faster but can focus subjects that a horizontal- or vertical-only sensor can't handle at all. So, you can see that having 15 cross-type focus sensors is a definite advantage.

The number and type of autofocus sensors in use can affect how well the system operates. As I mentioned, the Nikon D300 has 51 AF points. These focus sensors can consist of vertical or horizontal lines of pixels, cross-shapes, and/or a mixture of these types within a single camera, as with the D300. The more AF points available, the more easily the camera can differentiate among areas of the frame, and the more precisely you can specify the area you want to be in focus if you're manually choosing a focus spot.

But, there's another side of the coin. There is such a thing as *too many* focus zones for some types of subjects. For example, when using 51 focus points to select a zone for large, evenly illuminated subjects, you can waste a lot of time thumbing the multi-selector among the four-dozen (plus) focus points. That's why **CSM #a8** lets you switch the D300 to a more widely spaced set of 11 focus zones that you can select quickly. (Flip back to Figure 4.4 for a comparison.)

As the camera collects contrast information from the sensors, it then evaluates the data to determine whether the desired sharp focus has been achieved. The calculations may include whether the subject is moving, and whether the camera needs to "predict" where the subject will be when the shutter release button is fully depressed and the picture is taken. The speed with which the camera is able to evaluate focus and then move the lens elements into the proper position to achieve the sharpest focus determines how fast the autofocus mechanism is.

Although your D300 will almost always focus more quickly than a human, there are types of shooting situations where that's not fast enough. For example, if you're having problems shooting sports because the D300's autofocus system manically follows each moving subject, a better choice might be to switch autofocus modes or shift into manual and prefocus on a spot where you anticipate the action will be, such as a goal line or soccer net. At night football games, for example, when I am shooting with a telephoto lens almost wide open, I often focus manually on one of the referees who happens to be standing where I expect the action to be taking place (say, a halfback run or a pass reception). I also use *trap focus*, which is a technique discussed in a sidebar later in this chapter.

Choosing Autofocus Point Selection Mode

The Nikon D200 has four different focus point selection modes; the D300 has only three, which operate somewhat differently, faster, and more logically than the earlier camera's modes. I'm going to describe the three "surviving" modes, and explain how to use them. You can set any of the three modes using the AF-area mode selector switch, shown in Figure 7.14.

Figure 7.14
Autofocus
mode selector
switch is used
to choose how
autofocus
points are allocated.

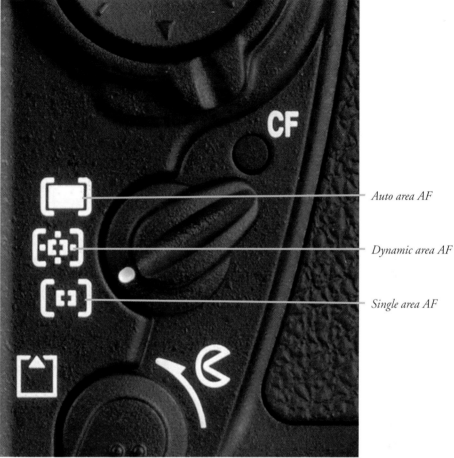

Auto area AF

Dynamic area AF

Single area AF

Single Point AF

In this mode, you always select the focus point manually, using the multi-selector button (which, helpfully, will respond to your thumb-presses not only in the left/right and up/down directions, but diagonally, as well). The D300 evaluates focus based solely on the point you select, making this a good choice for subjects that don't move much. As I mentioned earlier, you can use **CSM #a8** to choose whether the selected focus point resides in an 11-point widely spaced distribution, or within the full 51 point array. This choice is similar to the equivalent mode with the D200, except that camera offered only 11-point (normal) and 7-point (wide) zone arrays. In either Single Point AF or Dynamic AF, if you want to lock the focus point you've selected for a series of shots, rotate the focus selector lock lever back to the L position. You can also temporarily lock the focus point by partially depressing the shutter release, or pressing the AE-L/AF-L button (unless you've redefined this behavior to some other controls in the Custom Setting menu).

Dynamic AF

In this mode, you still select the focus point yourself using the multi-selector button, and when using Single-Servo autofocus (AF-S, discussed later), the D300 will evaluate focus solely based on that point. In that respect, the D300 behaves exactly as it does in Single Point AF mode. However, if you have chosen Continuous-Servo autofocus (AF-C), the D300's "smarts" spring to life if your subject leaves the selected focus zone. When that happens, the camera re-evaluates focus based on the other focus points surrounding the one you chose, as I originally described in Chapter 4 in the discussion of **CSM #a4** (where you specify which points are used). To recap, you can set the D300 so that it will use 9, 21, 51 points, or 51 points with 3D tracking. You can view what pattern is currently being used by pressing the Info button and viewing the autofocus array representation in the screen that pops up.

- **9 points.** Only eight surrounding focus points will be used, allowing the D300 to respond quickly to subjects that are moving in a predictable way. (See Figure 7.15; the eight additional points are highlighted in green.)

- **21 points.** Should the subject leave the selected focus point, the D300 will refocus based on information from 20 surrounding focus points (highlighted in blue in Figure 7.15). This mode is best for subjects that are moving erratically. Autofocus may take slightly longer because more points are considered. I prefer this mode most of the time.

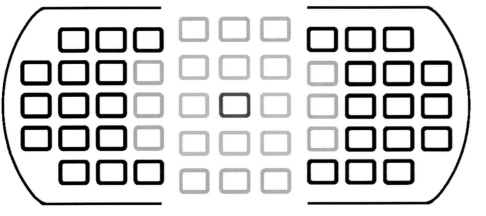

Figure 7.15
You can select from 9 (red/green), 21 (red/green/blue), or 51 (red/green/blue/black) active focus points.

> **Note**
>
> The active focus points surrounding the red highlighted focus zone will shift around the array as you move the manually-chosen focus point. The highlighting shown in Figure 7.15 applies to the 9-point and 21-point options *only* when the center point is selected as the active focus point.

- **51 points.** Should the subject leave your selected focus point, the camera will refocus based on information from all 50 surrounding focus points, which may be best for fast moving subjects.
- **51 points (3D-tracking).** Should the subject leave your selected focus zone, the D300 uses distance information to calculate the path of the subject and select a new focus point. Nikon recommends using this setting to focus subjects that move erratically from side to side, because the camera can use the distance information to differentiate the original subject from objects that are closer or farther away.

The Dynamic Area autofocus option was available in a rudimentary form in the D200; the camera would shift focus points if the subject moved outside the area you selected. However, the D200 didn't provide the choice of how many additional points would be considered.

Automatic Area AF

In this mode, autofocus point selection is out of your hands; the D300 performs the task for you using its own intelligence. If you are using a type G or D lens, the camera can even work with the supplied distance information to distinguish humans from their background, so a person standing at the side of the frame will be detected and used to evaluate focus, while the camera ignores the background area in the frame.

The D300 tends to keep the active focus point somewhat of a mystery (although it will be displayed during picture review if you've activated that option). In AF-S mode, the active focus point is highlighted in the viewfinder for about one second after focus is achieved. In AF-C mode, the active focus point is not shown.

Automatic Area and Dynamic Area autofocus effectively replace two clumsier and confusing modes offered in the D200 (as well as the D2xs): Group Dynamic and Dynamic Area (Closest Subject) options. In Group Dynamic mode you had to select from among two group patterns offered, with center area or closest subject priority options available for both. Dynamic area (Closest Subject) supposedly was the best choice if you always knew your subject would be the nearest object to the camera. I'm glad these two variations are gone.

Autofocus Mode and Priority

Choosing the right autofocus mode (AF-S, AF-C, or Manual) is another key to focusing success. To save battery power, your D300 doesn't start to focus the lens until you partially depress the shutter release or press the AF-ON button on the back of the camera or on the MB-D10 battery pack/grip (unless you've reprogrammed the AF-ON button for some other function or have specified another control to activate autofocus, as described in Chapter 4). But, autofocus isn't some mindless beast out there snapping your pictures in and out of focus with no feedback from you after you press that button. There are several settings you can modify that return at least a modicum of control to you. Your first decision should be whether you set the D300 to AF-S, AF-C, or Manual. There's a switch on the side of the lens mount that allows you to do that.

Single-Servo Autofocus

In this mode, also called *AF-S*, focus is set once and remains at that setting until the button is fully depressed, taking the picture, or until you release the shutter button without taking a shot. For non-action photography, this setting is usually your best choice, as it minimizes out-of-focus pictures (at the expense of spontaneity). The drawback here is that you might not be able to take a picture at all while the camera is seeking focus; you're locked out until the autofocus mechanism is happy with the current setting. As described in Chapter 4, you can set AF-S mode to use either focus priority (the default) or release priority using **CSM #a2**.

When sharp focus is achieved, the selected focus point will flash red in the viewfinder, and the focus confirmation light at the lower left will flash green. If you're using Matrix metering, the exposure will be locked at the same time. By keeping the shutter button depressed halfway, you'll find you can reframe the image while retaining the focus (and exposure) that's been set. You can also use the AE-L/AF-L button, as described in Chapter 4, if you've set that button to lock focus when pressed. Because of the small delay while the camera zeroes in on correct focus, you might experience slightly more shutter lag. This mode uses less battery power.

Continuous-Servo Autofocus

This mode, also known as *AF-C* is the mode to use for sports and other fast-moving subjects. In this mode, once the shutter release is partially depressed, the camera sets the focus but continues to monitor the subject, so that if it moves or you move, the lens will be refocused to suit. Focus and exposure aren't really locked until you press the shutter release down all the way to take the picture. You'll find that AF-C produces the least amount of shutter lag of any autofocus mode when set to release priority: press the button and the camera fires. It also uses the most battery power, because the autofocus system operates as long as the shutter release button is partially depressed.

Continuous-Servo autofocus uses a technology called *predictive AF*, which allows the D300 to calculate the correct focus if the subject is moving toward or away from the camera at a constant rate. It uses either the automatically selected AF point or the point you select manually to set focus. As described in Chapter 4, you can set AF-C mode to use either release priority (the default), release priority+focus (which slows continuous shooting slightly to give the D300 additional time to focus), or focus priority using **CSM #a1**.

If you want to lock the focus point you've selected for a series of shots, rotate the focus selector lock lever back to the L position. You can also temporarily lock the focus point by partially depressing the shutter release, or pressing the AE-L/AF-L button (unless you've redefined this behavior to some other controls in the Custom Setting menu).

Autofocus Activation... and More

The final considerations in using autofocus are the control or controls used to activate and lock autofocus, plus a few odds and ends. I've explained them in ample detail earlier in the book, but here are some cross references if you feel you need some review.

- **Which controls activate/lock autofocus.** You can use a half-press of the shutter release or a press of the AF-ON button (or both). See the instructions for **CSM #a5** in Chapter 4.

- **AF point illumination.** Do you want the active autofocus point illuminated when that is an option? Look up **CSM #a6** in Chapter 4.

- **Focus tracking with lock-on.** Intervening subjects passing in front of your main area of interest can interfere with autofocus. Set a delay time before the camera refocuses using **CSM #a4**, as described in Chapter 4.

- **Focus point wrap-around.** Do you want the focus point to wrap around to the opposite side during manual selection? Use **CSM #a7**.

- **AF illuminator.** Need to turn off the autofocus illuminator aid on your camera, flash, or SC-29 connecting cable? Use **CSM #a9**.

- **Center/show focus point.** You can program the multi-selector center button to either jump the active focus point to the center or to highlight the active focus point, using **CSM #f1**, as described in Chapter 4.

- **Lock focus with Fn, DOF Preview, or AE-L/AF-L buttons.** Check out **CSM #f4**, **CSM #f5**, or **CSM #f6**, as outlined in Chapter 4.

TRAP (AUTO) FOCUS

This technique comes in handy when you know where the action is going to take place (such as at the finish line of a horse race), but you don't know exactly *when*. The solution is to prefocus on the point where the action will occur, and then tell your D300 not to actually take the photo until something moves into the prefocus spot. That's not as difficult as you might think. The key is to decouple the focusing operation from the shutter release function. Just follow these steps:

1. Set **CSM #a5** to **AF-ON Only**. At that setting, pressing the shutter release halfway down does *not* activate autofocus. That happens only when you press the AF-ON button.

2. Set **CSM #a2** to **Focus** priority.

3. Set your point selection mode to **Single Area** (at the 7 o'clock position on the dial to the lower right of the LCD).

4. Make sure your lens is set to autofocus (either A or M/A).

5. Prefocus on the spot where the action will occur, or an equivalent distance.

6. Reframe your picture, if necessary, so that nothing is at the prefocused distance. (If an object occupies that spot, the D300 will take the photo immediately when you press the shutter release.)

7. Press and hold down the shutter release. The camera will not refocus, because you've disconnected the autofocus function from the shutter release.

8. The picture will be taken when a subject moves into the prefocused area.

Working with Live View

Live View is one of those features that experienced SLR users (especially those dating from the film era) sometimes think they don't need—until they try it. It's also one of those features (like truly "silent" shooting, without any shutter click) that point-and-shoot refugees are surprised that digital SLRs (until recently) have lacked. As I noted earlier, SLRs have actual, mechanical shutters that can't be completely silenced, as can be done with point-and-shoot cameras. I've fielded almost as many queries from those who want to know how to preview their images on the LCD—just as they did with their point-and-shoot cameras. Indeed, many P & S models don't even *have* optical viewfinders, engendering a whole generation of amateur photographers who think the only way to frame and compose an image is to hold the camera out at arm's length so the back panel LCD can be viewed more easily.

While dSLR veterans didn't really miss what we've come to know as Live View, it was at least, in part, because they didn't have it and couldn't miss what they never had. After all, why would you eschew a big, bright, magnified through-the-lens optical view that showed depth-of-field fairly well, and which was easily visible under virtually all ambient light conditions? LCD displays, after all, were small, tended to wash out in bright light, and didn't really provide you with an accurate view of what your picture was going to look like.

There were technical problems, as well. Real-time previews theoretically disabled a dSLR's autofocus system, as focus was achieved by measuring contrast through the optical viewfinder, which is blocked when the mirror is flipped up for a live view. Extensive previewing had the same effect on the sensor as long exposures: the sensor heated up, producing excess noise. Pointing the camera at a bright light source when using a real-time view could damage the sensor. The list of potential problems goes on and on.

That was then. This is now.

The Nikon D300 has a gorgeous three-inch LCD that can be viewed under a variety of lighting conditions and from wide-ranging angles, so you don't have to be exactly behind the display to see it clearly. It offers a 100-percent view of the sensor's capture area (the optical viewfinder shows 100 percent of the sensor's field of view). It's large enough to allow manual focusing—but there is an automatic focus option, too. You still have to avoid pointing your D300 at bright light sources (especially the Sun) when using Live View, but the real-time preview can be used for fairly long periods without frying the sensor.

Unlike some of the previous attempts at a Live View-type mode by other sensors, the D300's Live View works. No beam-splitting prisms that divert some light to the sensor, no grainy black-and-white real-time preview, no need for a spare sensor to provide a simulated Live View. Nikon's system works just like you'd want it to: the mirror flips up, the shutter opens, and what the sensor sees is displayed in full color on the LCD on the back of the camera, as shown in Figure 7.16.

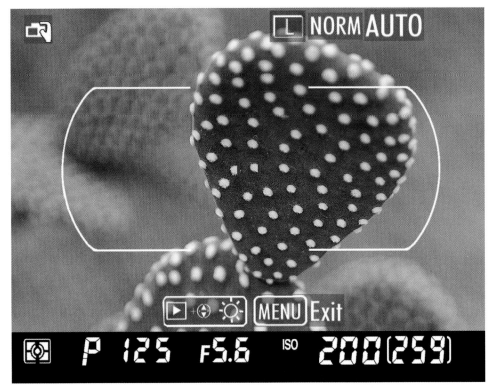

Figure 7.16
Live View
really shines on
the Nikon
D300's large 3
inch LCD.

What You Can Do with Live View

You may not have considered just what you can do with Live View, because the capability is so novel. But once you've played with it, you'll discover dozens of applications for this capability, as well as a few things that you can't do. Here's a list of Live View Dos/Don'ts/Cans/Can'ts.

- **Preview your images on a TV.** Connect your D300 to a television using the video cable, and you can preview your image on a large screen.

- **Preview remotely.** Extend the cable between the camera and TV screen, and you can preview your images some distance away from the camera.

- **Shoot from your computer.** With Camera Control Pro 2, you can control your camera from your computer, so you can preview images and take pictures without physically touching the D300.

- **Continuous shooting.** You can shoot bursts of images using Live View, but all shots will use the focus and exposure setting established for the first picture in the series.

■ **Shoot from tripod or hand-held.** Of course, holding the camera out at arms length to preview an image is poor technique, and will introduce a lot of camera shake. If you want to use Live View for hand-held images, use an image-stabilized lens and/or a high shutter speed in **Hand-Held** mode. A tripod and **Tripod** mode is a better choice if you can use one.

■ **Watch your power.** Live View uses a lot of juice and will deplete your battery rapidly. The optional AC adapter is a useful accessory.

■ **Watch your usage times.** Nikon says Live View can be used continuously for as long as one hour, but notes that after periods of more than a few minutes, the sensor warms up and increases image noise and color artifacts. Your D300 will shut down before your camera seriously overheats, and will give you a warning on the monitor 30 seconds before shut-off.

■ **MicroDrives not recommended.** Because they use up a lot of power on their own, mini hard drives are not recommended as a storage medium for Live View sessions. Use a Compact Flash card instead.

Enabling Live View

Activating Live View is easy. All you need to do ahead of time is decide whether you want to use Hand-Held mode or Tripod mode. The default is Hand-Held mode, which gives you the most flexibility when photographing moving subjects and when composing images from angles that are difficult to achieve when looking through the viewfinder. The D300 flips the mirror back down to focus normally just before you take the picture. Tripod mode is preferred for shooting non-moving subjects (especially macro shots) and focus is achieved by detecting the contrast of the image on the sensor, based on any point in the frame that you choose (not just the 51 autofocus points).

To start Live View follow these steps:

1. Press the Menu button, and navigate through the Shooting menu to the **Live view** choice. There, you'll be given two options: Live View Mode and Release Mode. Select **Live View Mode**.

2. Select either **Hand-Held** or **Tripod** modes. I'll describe these next.

3. Press **OK** to confirm your selection.

4. In the Live View screen, choose **Release Mode**.

5. Select **Single Frame, Continuous low-speed,** or **Continuous high-speed**. You need to select a release mode here, because you cannot do so when the release mode dial is set to the Live View position.

6. Press **OK** to confirm your choice.

7. Press the Menu button twice to exit the menu system.

8. Press the release mode dial lock button to free the release mode dial.

9. Spin the release mode dial to the **Lv** (Live View) position.

10. Press the shutter release. The mirror will flip up and the LCD will display the image that the sensor sees. You're in Live View mode!

Using Hand-Held Mode

This mode turns your D300 into a point-and-shoot camera, at least from an image preview standpoint. You can see the exact image produced by the sensor, and take pictures using your camera's autofocus and autoexposure features. If you like, you can even hold the camera out at arm's length to compose a photo, just like the tourists you saw during your last visit to Niagara Falls. To take a picture in Hand-Held mode, just follow these steps:

1. **Flip up the mirror and view.** Press the shutter release button all the way down (if you didn't already do so in Step 10 above). The mirror flips up and the sensor image appears on the color LCD. (To exit Live View, press the Menu button, or rotate the release mode dial to another setting.)

2. **Adjust LCD brightness.** If you'd like to adjust the brightness of the monitor, press the Playback button and use the multi-selector up/down buttons to increase/decrease brightness. Note that this only changes the display on the screen; it does not adjust the exposure of your image.

3. **Zoom image.** Press the Zoom button on the left side of the back of the camera to zoom in up to 3X. Use the multi-selector to scroll the zoomed area around within the full image. A navigational window in the lower right of the LCD shows your view's relative position in the frame.

4a. **Autofocus.** Select a focus point with the multi-selector pad. If you've chosen AF-S or AF-C modes, you can then focus automatically by pressing the shutter release button halfway, or by pressing the AF-ON button. The mirror will flip down to its normal position (obscuring your Live View) while the D300 calculates focus and exposure. Release the button to lock focus and exposure and return to Live View. This mode uses the D300's normal phase detection autofocus mode, as described earlier in this chapter.

or

4b. **Manually focus.** If you've chosen Manual focus, select a focus point with the multi-selector pad if you'd like feedback from the camera's focus confirmation indicator. Then, focus by rotating the lens's focus ring, using the sharpness of the image on the LCD as your focus guide.

5. **Take the photo.** Press the shutter release button all the way down to take the picture(s) using the release mode you selected in the menu (Single frame, Continuous low speed, or Continuous high speed).

Using Tripod Mode

Although Hand-Held mode is fun, Tripod mode is the way Live View was meant to be used for serious photography. You'll find that the extra control this mode gives you over the picture-taking process will lead to superior photos. Activate Live View mode as before, but with the D300 mounted on a tripod. Then, follow these steps:

1. **Mount the camera on a tripod.** Attach a remote release, like the Nikon MC-30 to allow you to trigger the camera without vibration.

2. **Set the camera to Live View mode.** Use the release mode dial.

3. **Autofocus in viewfinder.** If you'd like to use the D300's phase detect autofocus system, do so before activating the Live View preview image. With the camera and lens set for autofocus (AF-S or AF-C, and the lens set for autofocus), frame the picture in the optical viewfinder and press the **AF-ON** button. That will set the focus and exposure. (Pressing the shutter release halfway will not work in this mode.)

4. **Flip up the mirror and view.** Press the shutter release button all the way down. The mirror flips up and the sensor image appears on the color LCD. (To exit Live View, press the Menu button, or rotate the release mode dial to another setting.)

5. **Adjust LCD brightness.** If you'd like to adjust the brightness of the monitor, press the Playback button and use the multi-selector up/down buttons to increase/decrease brightness. Note that this only changes the display on the screen; it does not adjust the exposure of your image.

6. **Zoom image.** Press the Zoom button on the left side of the back of the camera to zoom in up to 13X. Use the multi-selector to scroll the zoomed area around within the full image. A navigational window in the lower right of the LCD shows your view's relative position in the frame. Press **OK** to exit Zoom mode.

7a. **Autofocus on LCD.** If you'd prefer to autofocus using the LCD, you can do so now using contrast-detect autofocus. Select a focus point with the multi-selector pad. Note that you can use *any* zone on the screen, not just the 51 autofocus points. Press the AF-ON button to autofocus. If the D300 is unable to focus in this mode, the focus point will blink red; if focus was successful, it will blink green. Note that even in AF-C mode, the D300 will focus just once and not refocus if your subject moves. Moreover, whether you're using AF-S or AF-C, in Tripod mode the camera is in "release priority" mode.

> ### Note
>
> If you have difficulty autofocusing in contrast-detect mode, you may have to focus manually (using Step 7b). Contrast-detect mode is slower than phase-detect autofocus, will not work if the camera is not mounted on a tripod, and may have difficulty with some subjects, especially those with low contrast or which are moving.

> ### Note
>
> To activate contrast-detect autofocus when using a remote cord, press the cord's release button halfway for longer than one second.

or

7b. **Manually focus on the LCD.** If you've chosen Manual focus, you can zoom in on the LCD screen with the Zoom button and multi-selector button, and focus manually using the lens's focus ring.

8. **Take the photo.** Press the shutter release button all the way down to take the picture(s) using the release mode you selected in the menu (Single frame, Continuous low speed, or Continuous high speed).

Continuous Shooting

The Nikon D300's pair of Continuous Shooting modes remind me how far digital photography has brought us. The first accessory I purchased when I worked as a sports photographer some years ago was a motor drive for my film SLR. It enabled me to snap off a series of shots in rapid succession, which came in very handy when a fullback broke through the line and headed for the end zone. Even a seasoned action photographer can miss the decisive instant when a crucial block is made, or a baseball superstar's bat shatters and pieces of cork fly out. Continuous shooting simplifies taking a series of pictures, either to ensure that one has more or less the exact moment you want to capture or to capture a sequence that is interesting as a collection of successive images.

The D300's "motor drive" capabilities are, in many ways, much superior to what you get with a film camera. For one thing, a motor-driven film camera can eat up film at an incredible pace, which is why many of them are used with cassettes that hold hundreds of feet of film stock. At three frames per second (typical of film cameras), a short burst of a few seconds can burn up as much as half of an ordinary 36 exposure roll of film. Digital cameras, in contrast, have reusable "film," so if you waste a few dozen shots on non-decisive moments, you can erase them and shoot more.

The increased capacity of digital film cards gives you a prodigious number of frames to work with. At a baseball game I covered earlier this year, I took more than 1,000 images in a couple hours. Yet, even shooting RAW+JPEG Fine I could fit more than 200 images on a single 4GB Compact Flash card. If I'd switched to JPEG, I could have taken about 900 different images without switching cards. Even at the top speed of 6 frames per second that the D300 is capable of (without the MB-D10 battery grip), that's a lot of shooting. Given an average burst of about eight frames per sequence (nobody really takes 15-20 shots or more of one play in a baseball game), I was able to capture 32 different sequences before I needed to swap cards.

On the other hand, at a football game I covered later in the same month (there are some weird sports overlaps in early September!), the longer bursts came in handy, because running and passing plays often lasted 5 to 10 seconds, and changed in character as the action switched from the quarterback dropping back to pass or hand off the ball, then the receiver or running back trying to gain as much yardage as possible. Even simple plays, like a punt, seemed more exciting when captured in a sequence of shots, as in Figure 7.17.

To use the D300's Continuous Shooting modes, hold down the release mode dial's unlock button and rotate the dial until either C_L or C_H appear. When you partially depress the shutter button, the viewfinder will display at the right side a number representing the maximum number of shots you can take at the current quality settings. The large buffer in the D300 will generally allow you to take as many as 75 JPEG shots in a single burst, or 17 RAW photos.

To increase this number, reduce the image-quality setting by switching to JPEG only (from JPEG+RAW), to a lower JPEG quality setting, or by reducing the D300's resolution from L to M or S. The reason the size of your bursts is limited is that continuous images are first shuttled into the D300's internal memory buffer, then doled out to the Compact Flash card as quickly as they can be written to the card. Technically, the

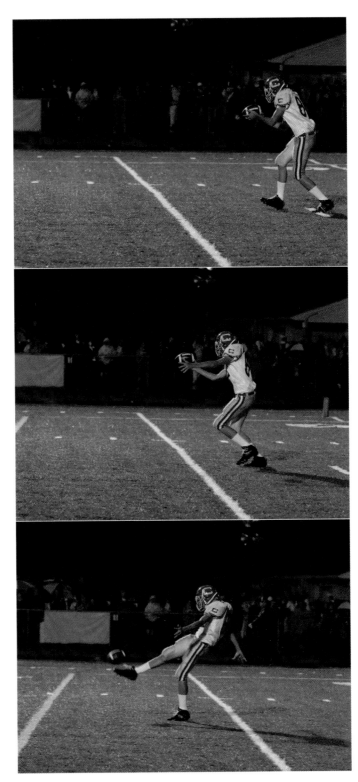

Figure 7.17
Continuous shooting allows you to capture an entire sequence of exciting moments as they unfold.

D300 takes the RAW data received from the digital image processor and converts it to the output format you've selected—either .jpg or .nef (raw)—and deposits it in the buffer ready to store on the card.

This internal "smart" buffer can suck up photos much more quickly than the CF card and, indeed, some memory cards are significantly faster or slower than others. When the buffer fills, you can't take any more continuous shots until the D300 has written some of them to the card, making more room in the buffer. (You should keep in mind that faster CF cards write images more quickly, freeing up buffer space faster.)

Recommended Customized Settings

I'm going to finish off this chapter with some tables listing recommended settings for your Shooting and Custom Setting banks. I outlined how to set the four Shooting Menu Banks, A, B, C, and D in Chapter 3, and showed you how to assign each of them a suitable name so you could more easily remember the shooting situations the customized settings were tailored for. In Chapter 4, I explained the four Custom Setting Banks (also named A, B, C, and D by default), and some of the ways you could set up groups of settings for different kinds of picture-taking opportunities.

Because those two chapters had already ballooned to nearly 100 pages, it didn't really make sense to try and cram in some recommended settings there, as that level of detail would tend to confound those who were simply trying to get their cameras set up properly. So, I've deposited my recommended "starter" settings in this chapter, which has become something of a catch-all, anyway.

I've divided the recommended settings into a group of tables, rather than one or two huge tables that would be more difficult to read. The tables show the "default" settings for the Shooting Menu Banks and Custom Setting Banks, as they come from the factory, plus eight groups intended for Basic, Studio Flash, Portrait, Long Exposure, Sports—Indoors, Sports—Outdoors, Landscapes, and Portraits. For the Custom Setting menu, I added one more group of settings, for exposure bracketing.

Each setting includes options that I consider best-suited for their particular shooting situations. For example, when I am bracketing exposures, I like to shoot off a single bracket burst fairly quickly, so I choose C_L release mode, with the shooting speed set to 4 frames per second. When I press the shutter release, all the exposures are taken consecutively in a brief period of time. Similarly, when I am shooting indoor sports, I like to use ISO 1600 and set my autofocus priority to Release+Focus. That lets me shoot bursts of pictures with minimal shutter lag when I press the shutter release button, but still gives the D300 a little extra time to get that first picture in sharp focus. I understand that the continuous shooting speed may be a little slower in that mode, but it works for me.

Now, obviously, your D300 has only four Shooting Banks and four Custom Setting Banks, so you'll have to choose which of my recommendations to "install" in your camera. I also suggest further customizing these settings to best suit your own habits and needs. In addition, there are some settings that I do not suggest changes for, but which can easily be modified by you, if you like.

For example, you may not have known that you can select both a folder name and file naming scheme for *each* Shooting Menu Bank. So, you can deposit your image files in a different folder, if you like, based on which Shooting Menu Bank you've selected. Similarly, you could conceivably use different file name prefixes for each bank (say, to separate SPT_ [sports] shots from LND_ [landscape] pictures). That seems a lot of trouble to me, but you can do it.

Shooting Menu Bank Recommendations

I'll list my Shooting Menu Bank suggestions first. The Custom Setting Menu Bank recommendations are divided into the exact same categories but, of course, deal with different options. In the first table, the second column shows the default settings, as the D300 comes from the factory.

Table 7.1 Shooting Menu Recommendations #1

Option	Camera Default	Basic Setting	Studio Flash	Portrait
Active Folder	Default	Your choice	Your choice	Your choice
File Naming	DSC/_DSC	Your choice	Your choice	Your choice
Image Format/ Quality	JPEG Normal	NEF(RAW)+ JPEG Fine	NEF	NEF+JPEG Fine
Image Size	Large	Large	Large	Large
JPEG Compression	Size Priority	Optimal Quality	Optimal Quality	Optimal Quality
NEF (RAW) recording:				
>*Type*	Lossless Compressed	Lossless Compressed	Lossless Compressed	Lossless Compressed
>*NEF(RAW) bit depth*	12-bit	12-bit	14-bit	12-bit
White Balance	Auto	Auto	Preset Manual	Auto
Set Picture Control	Standard	C-1 (Standard+ Sharp 7)	Standard	C-3 (Neutral+ Sharp -2)

Option	Camera Default	Basic Setting	Studio Flash	Portrait
Color Space	sRGB	Adobe RGB	Adobe RGB	Adobe RGB
Active D-Lighting	Off	Off	Off	Off
Long Exp. NR	Off	Off	Off	Off
High ISO NR - ISO 800+	Normal	Low	Low	Low
ISO sensitivity settings:				
>ISO Sensitivity	200	200	200	200
> ISO sensitivity auto control:	Off	On	Off	Off
Maximum sensitivity	3200	800	1600	1600
Minimum shutter speed	1/30 s	1/60 s	1/60 s	1/60 s
Live View				
>Live View Mode	Hand-held	Hand-held	Hand-held	Hand-held
>Release Mode	Single-frame	Single-frame	Single-frame	Single-frame
Multiple Exposure:				
> Number of Shots	2	2	Applies to All Banks	Applies to All Banks
>Auto gain	On	Off	Applies to All Banks	Applies to All Banks
Interval Timer Shooting:				
> Start Time	Now	Now/Set time	Applies to All Banks	Applies to All Banks
> Interval	00:00':00"	Select	Applies to All Banks	Applies to All Banks
> No. of Intervals	1	Select	Applies to All Banks	Applies to All Banks
> No. of Shots	1	Select	Applies to All Banks	Applies to All Banks
> Start	Off	Turn On/Off	Applies to All Banks	Applies to All Banks

Table 7.2 Shooting Menu Recommendations #2

Option	Long Exposure	Sports Indoors	Sports Outdoors	Landscape
Active Folder	Your choice	Your choice	Your choice	Your choice
File Naming	Your choice	Your choice	Your choice	Your choice
Image Format/ Quality	NEF	JPEG Fine	JPEG Fine	NEF+JPEG Fine
Image Size	Large	Large	Large	Large
JPEG Compression	Optimal Quality	Optimal Quality	Optimal Quality	Optimal Quality
NEF (RAW) recording:				
>Type	Lossless Compressed	Lossless Compressed	Lossless Compressed	Lossless Compressed
>NEF(RAW) bit depth	12-bit	12-bit	12-bit	12-bit
White Balance	Auto	Auto	Auto	Auto
Set Picture Control	Standard	Standard	Standard	C-2 (Vivid+ Sharp 5)
Color Space	Adobe RGB	Adobe RGB	Adobe RGB	Adobe RGB
Active D-Lighting	Off	Off	Off	Off
Long Exp. NR	On	Off	Off	Off
High ISO NR - ISO 800+	Low	Normal	Low	Low
ISO sensitivity settings:				
>ISO Sensitivity	400	1600	400	200
> ISO sensitivity auto control:	Off	Off	Off	Off
Maximum sensitivity	1600	1600	1600	1600
Minimum shutter speed	1/60 s	1/60 s	1/60 s	1/60 s
Live View				
>*Live View Mode*	Hand-held	Hand-held	Hand-held	Hand-held
>*Release Mode*	Single-frame	Single-frame	Single-frame	Single-frame

Option	Long Exposure	Sports Indoors	Sports Outdoors	Landscape
Multiple Exposure:				
> *Number of Shots*	Applies to All Banks	Applies to All Banks	Applies to All Banks	Applies to All Banks
>*Auto gain*	Applies to All Banks	Applies to All Banks	Applies to All Banks	Applies to All Banks
Interval Timer Shooting:				
> *Start Time*	Applies to All Banks	Applies to All Banks	Applies to All Banks	Applies to All Banks
> *Interval*	Applies to All Banks	Applies to All Banks	Applies to All Banks	Applies to All Banks
> *No. of Intervals*	Applies to All Banks	Applies to All Banks	Applies to All Banks	Applies to All Banks
> *No. of Shots*	Applies to All Banks	Applies to All Banks	Applies to All Banks	Applies to All Banks
> *Start*	Applies to All Banks	Applies to All Banks	Applies to All Banks	Applies to All Banks

Custom Setting Menu Bank Recommendations

Next come the Custom Setting Menu Bank recommendations. They are divided into the exact same categories, but with the addition of a new category for bracketed shots. And, of course, they all deal with different options.

Table 7.3 Custom Setting Menu Bank Recommendations #1

Item	Option	Camera Default	Basic Setting	Studio Flash	Portrait	Long Exposure
	Autofocus					
a1	AF-C priority selection	Release	Release	Release	Release	Release
a2	AF-S priority selection	Focus	Focus	Focus	Focus	Focus
a3	Dynamic AF area	9 Points	51 points 3D	51 points 3D	51 points 3D	21 points

Table 7.3 Custom Setting Menu Bank Recommendations #1 (continued)

Item	Option	Camera Default	Basic Setting	Studio Flash	Portrait	Long Exposure
a4	Focus tracking with lock-on	Normal	Normal	Normal	Normal	Normal
a5	AF activation	Shutter/AF-ON (ON)	Shutter/AF-ON (ON)	Shutter/AF-ON (ON)	Shutter/AF-ON (ON)	Shutter/AF-ON (ON)
a6	AF point illumination	Auto	Auto	Auto	Auto	Auto
a7	Focus point wrap-around	No wrap (OFF)	No wrap (OFF)	No wrap (OFF)	No wrap (OFF)	No wrap (OFF)
a8	AF point selection	51 points	51 points	11 points	51 points	51 points
a9	AF assist illuminator	On	On	Off	Off	On
a10	AF-On for MB-D10	AF-ON	AF-ON	AF-ON	AF-ON	AF-ON
	Metering/exposure					
b1	ISO sensitivity step value	1/3 step	1/3 step	1/3 step	1/3 step	1/3 step
b2	EV steps for exposure control	1/3 step	1/3 step	1/3 step	1/3 step	1/3 step
b3	Exp comp/ fine tune	1/3 step	1/3 step	1/3 step	1/3 step	1/3 step
b4	Easy exposure compensation	Off	Off	Off	Off	Off
b5	Center-weighted area	8mm	8mm	8mm	8mm	8mm

Item	Option	Camera Default	Basic Setting	Studio Flash	Portrait	Long Exposure
b6	Fine-tune optimal exposure:					
	> Matrix metering	0	0	0	0	0
	> Center Weighted	0	0	0	0	0
	> Spot metering	0	0	0	0	0
	Timers/AE Lock					
c1	Shutter-release button AE-L	Off	Off	Off	Off	Off
c2	Auto meter-off delay	6 sec	6 sec	6 sec	6 sec	6 sec
c3	Self-timer delay	10 sec	20 sec	10 sec	10 sec	2 sec
c4	Monitor off delay	20 sec	20 sec	20 sec	20 sec	20 sec
	Shooting/display					
d1	Beep	High	Off	Off	Off	High
d2	Viewfinder grid display	Off	Off	Off	On	Off
d3	Viewfinder warning display	On	On	On	On	On
d4	CL mode shooting speed	3 fps	3 fps	3 fps	3 fps	3 fps
d5	Max. continuous release	100	20	20	20	20
d6	File No. Sequence	On	On	On	On	On

Table 7.3 Custom Setting Menu Bank Recommendations #1 (continued)

Item	Option	Camera Default	Basic Setting	Studio Flash	Portrait	Long Exposure
d7	Shooting Info Display	Auto	Auto	Auto	Auto	Auto
d8	LCD Illumination	Off	Off	Off	Off	Off
d9	Exposure Delay Mode	Off	Off	Off	Off	Off
d10	MB-D10 Battery Type	AA Alkaline	AA Alkaline	AA Alkaline	AA Alkaline	AA Alkaline
d11	Battery Order	MB-D10 First	MB-D10 First	MB-D10 First	MB-D10 First	MB-D10 First
	Bracketing/Flash					
e1	Flash sync speed	1/250	1/250	1/250	1/250	1/250
e2	Flash shutter speed	1/60	1/60	1/60	1/60	1/60
e3	Flash control for built-in flash	TTL	TTL	Commander	Commander	TTL
	> Commander Only - Built In	TTL 0	TTL 0	TTL 0	TTL 0	TTL 0
	> Commander Only - Group A	TTL 0	TTL 0	TTL 0	TTL 0	TTL 0
	> Commander Only - Group B	TTL 0	TTL 0	TTL 0	TTL 0	TTL 0
	> Commander Only - Channel#	1	1	1	1	1
e4	Modeling Flash	ON	ON	ON	ON	ON

Item	Option	Camera Default	Basic Setting	Studio Flash	Portrait	Long Exposure
e5	Auto Bracket Set	AE & Flash	AE & Flash	AE & Flash	AE & Flash	AE & Flash
e6	Auto Bracketing Manual Mode	Flash/Speed	Flash/Speed	Flash/Speed	Flash/Speed	Flash/Speed
e7	Auto Bracket Order	Meter> Under>Over	Meter> Under>Over	Meter> Under>Over	Meter> Under>Over	Meter> Under>Over
Controls						
f1	Multi Selector Center Button > Shooting Mode > Playback Mode	Select center focus point Thumbnail On/Off	Select center focus point View histograms	Select center focus point View histograms	Select center focus point View histograms	Select center focus point View histograms
f2	Multi-selector	Do nothing (OFF)	Do nothing (OFF)	Do nothing (OFF)	Do nothing (OFF)	Do nothing (OFF)
f3	Photo info/ playback	Info __/ Playback__	Info __/ Playback__	Info __/ Playback__	Info __/ Playback__	Info __/ Playback__
f4	Assign FUNC Button >FUNC. button press >FUNC. button + dials	None Auto bracketing	Flash Off Auto bracketing	FV Lock Auto bracketing	FV Lock None	None Auto bracketing
f5	Assign Preview Button >Preview button press >Preview button + dials	Preview None	Preview None	Preview None	Preview None	Preview None
f6	Assign AE-L/AF-L Button >AE-L/AF-L button press >AE-L/AF-L button + dials	AE-AF lock None	AE-AF lock None	AE-AF lock None	AE-AF lock None	AE-AF lock None

Table 7.3 Custom Setting Menu Bank Recommendations #1 (continued)

Item	Option	Camera Default	Basic Setting	Studio Flash	Portrait	Long Exposure
f7	Customize Command Dials					
	> Reverse rotation	No (OFF)	No (OFF)	No (OFF)	No (OFF)	No (OFF)
	> Change main/sub	No (OFF)	No (OFF)	No (OFF)	No (OFF)	No (OFF)
	> Aperture setting	ON (Sub-command Dial)	ON (Sub-command Dial)	ON (Sub-command Dial)	ON (Sub-command Dial)	ON (Sub-command Dial)
	> Menus and playback	Off	Off	Off	Off	Off
f8	Release Button to Use Dial	No (OFF)	No (OFF)	No (OFF)	No (OFF)	No (OFF)
f9	No Memory Card	Enable Release (OK)	Release locked (LOCK)	Release locked (LOCK)	Release locked (LOCK)	Release locked (LOCK)
f10	Reverse Indicators for Exposure	+ 0 -	+ 0 -	+ 0 -	+ 0 -	+ 0 -

Table 7.4 Custom Setting Menu Bank Recommendations #2

Item	Option	Sports Indoors	Sports Outdoors	Landscape	Bracketing
	Autofocus				
a1	AF-C priority selection	Release+focus	Release+focus	Release	Release+focus
a2	AF-S priority selection	Focus	Focus	Focus	Focus
a3	Dynamic AF area	21 points	21 points	21 points	51 points
a4	Focus tracking with lock-on	Normal	Long	Normal	Normal

Item	Option	Sports Indoors	Sports Outdoors	Landscape	Bracketing
a5	AF activation	Shutter/AF-ON (ON)	Shutter/AF-ON (ON)	Shutter/AF-ON (ON)	Shutter/AF-ON (ON)
a6	AF point illumination	Auto	Auto	Auto	Auto
a7	Focus point wrap-around	No wrap (OFF)	No wrap (OFF)	No wrap (OFF)	No wrap (OFF)
a8	AF point selection	51 points	51 points	51 points	51 points
a9	AF assist illuminator	Off	Off	Off	Off
a10	AF-On for MB-D10	AF-ON	AF-ON	AF-ON	AF-ON
	Metering/exposure				
b1	ISO sensitivity step value	1/3 step	1/3 step	1/3 step	1/3 step
b2	EV steps for exposure control	1/3 step	1/3 step	1/3 step	1/3 step
b3	Exp comp/fine tune	1/3 step	1/3 step	1/3 step	1/3 step
b4	Easy exposure compensation	Off	Off	Off	Off
b5	Center-weighted area	8mm	8mm	8mm	8mm
b6	Fine-tune optimal exposure:				
	> Matrix metering	0	0	0	0
	> Center Weighted	0	0	0	0
	> Spot metering	0	0	0	0
	Timers/AE Lock				
c1	Shutter-release button AE-L	Off	Off	Off	Off
c2	Auto meter-off delay	6 sec	6 sec	6 sec	6 sec
c3	Self-timer delay	10 sec	10 sec	2 sec	2 sec
c4	Monitor off delay	20 sec	20 sec	20 sec	20 sec

Table 7.4 Custom Setting Menu Bank Recommendations #2 (continued)

Item	Option	Sports Indoors	Sports Outdoors	Landscape	Bracketing
	Shooting/display				
d1	Beep	Off	Off	High	High
d2	Viewfinder grid display	Off	Off	On	Off
d3	Viewfinder warning display	On	On	On	On
d4	CL mode shooting speed	4 fps	4 fps	3 fps	5 fps
d5	Max. continuous release	35	35	20	100
d6	File No. Sequence	On	On	On	On
d7	Shooting Info Display	Auto	Auto	Auto	Auto
d8	LCD Illumination	Off	Off	Off	Off
d9	Exposure Delay Mode	Off	Off	Off	Off
d10	MB-D10 Battery Type	AA Alkaline	AA Alkaline	AA Alkaline	AA Alkaline
d11	Battery Order	MB-D10 First	MB-D10 First	MB-D10 First	MB-D10 First
	Bracketing/Flash				
e1	Flash sync speed	1/250	1/250	1/250	1/250
e2	Flash shutter speed	1/60	1/60	1/60	1/60
e3	Flash control for built-in flash	TTL	TTL	TTL	TTL
	> Commander Only - Built In	TTL 0	TTL 0	TTL 0	TTL 0
	> Commander Only - Group A	TTL 0	TTL 0	TTL 0	TTL 0
	> Commander Only - Group B	TTL 0	TTL 0	TTL 0	TTL 0
	> Commander Only - Channel#	1	1	1	1

Item	Option	Sports Indoors	Sports Outdoors	Landscape	Bracketing
e4	Modeling Flash	ON	ON	ON	ON
e5	Auto Bracket Set	AE & Flash	AE & Flash	AE & Flash	AE & Flash
e6	Auto Bracketing Manual Mode	Flash/Speed	Flash/Speed	Flash/Speed	Flash/Speed
e7	Auto Bracket Order	Meter> Under>Over	Meter> Under>Over	Meter> Under>Over	Under> Meters>Over
	Controls				
f1	Multi Selector Center Button				
	> Shooting Mode	Select center focus point	Select center focus point	Select center focus point	Select center focus point
	> Playback Mode	View histograms	View histograms	View histograms	View histograms
f2	Multi-selector	Do nothing (OFF)	Do nothing (OFF)	Do nothing (OFF)	Do nothing (OFF)
f3	Photo info/playback	Info __/ Playback__	Info __/ Playback__	Info __/ Playback__	Info __/ Playback__
f4	Assign FUNC Button				
	>FUNC. button press	Spot metering	Spot metering	Bracketing burst	Bracketing burst
	>FUNC. button + dials	Auto bracketing	Auto bracketing	Auto bracketing	Auto bracketing
f5	Assign Preview Button				
	>Preview button press	Preview	Preview	Preview	Preview
	>Preview button + dials	None	None	None	None
f6	Assign AE-L/AF-L Button				
	>AE-L/AF-L button press	AE-AF lock	AE-AF lock	AE-AF lock	AE-AF lock
	>AE-L/AF-L button + dials	None	None	None	None

Table 7.4 Custom Setting Menu Bank Recommendations #2 (continued)

Item	Option	Sports Indoors	Sports Outdoors	Landscape	Bracketing
f7	Customize Command Dials				
	> Reverse rotation	No (OFF)	No (OFF)	No (OFF)	No (OFF)
	> Change main/sub	No (OFF)	No (OFF)	No (OFF)	No (OFF)
	> Aperture setting	ON (Sub-command Dial)	ON (Sub-command Dial)	ON (Sub-command Dial)	ON (Sub-command Dial)
	> Menus and playback	Off	Off	Off	Off
f8	Release Button to Use Dial	No (OFF)	No (OFF)	No (OFF)	No (OFF)
f9	No Memory Card	Release locked (LOCK)	Release locked (LOCK)	Release locked (LOCK)	Release locked (LOCK)
f10	Reverse Indicators for Exposure	+ 0 -	+ 0 -	+ 0 -	+ 0 -

8

Working with Lenses

If Nikon has one advantage over many of the other vendors of digital SLRs (other than making great, affordable cameras), it's the mind-bending assortment of high-quality lenses available to enhance the capabilities of cameras like the Nikon D300. You can use thousands of current and older lenses introduced by Nikon and third-party vendors since 1959 (although lenses made before 1977 may need an inexpensive modification). These can give you a wider view, bring distant subjects closer, let you focus closer, shoot under lower light conditions, or provide a more detailed, sharper image for critical work. Other than the sensor itself, the lens you choose for your dSLR is the most important component in determining image quality and perspective of your images.

This chapter explains how to select the best lenses for the kinds of photography you want to do.

But First, a Word from Our Sensor

One pervasive consideration that will trip us up in this chapter (and throughout this book) is the omnipresent *lens crop factor*. If the sensor is smaller than the standard 35mm film frame (24mm x 36mm), then any given lens will produce a field of view that's *cropped* from that full frame. To express the "real" field of view in 35mm terms, you must multiply a lens's focal length by the crop factor, which in the case of the Nikon D300 is 1.5X. Nikon also sells dSLRs with 1X (full-frame) sensors (currently only the Nikon D3), which provide the field of view shown in Figure 8.1.

If you're accustomed to using full-frame film cameras, you might find it helpful to use the crop factor "multiplier" to translate a lens's real focal length into the full-frame equivalent, even though nothing is actually being multiplied. Throughout most of this book

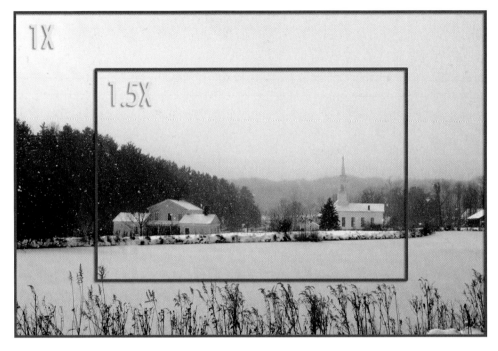

Figure 8.1

Most Nikon digital SLRs offer a 1.5X crop like the D300, but the company has begun offering full-frame (1X crop) cameras such as the Nikon D3.

I've been using actual focal lengths and not equivalents, except when referring to specific wide-angle or telephoto focal length ranges and their fields of view.

Your First Lens

Some Nikon dSLRs are almost always purchased with a lens. The entry- and mid-level Nikon dSLRs, like the Nikon D40 and D60, are often bought by those new to digital photography, frequently by first-time SLR or dSLR owners who find the AF-S DX Zoom-Nikkor 18-55mm f/3.5-5.6G ED II autofocus lens or the newer VR version with vibration reduction an irresistible bargain. Other Nikon models, including the Nikon D300, D2xs, and D3, are generally purchased without a lens by veteran Nikon photographers who already have a complement of optics to use with their cameras.

I bought my D300 as a body-only, because I already had a (large) collection of lenses. But you might have purchased your D300 with a lens, because it's an excellent first Nikon camera for photographers experienced with another camera line, or for ambitious beginners. That makes an economical "kit" lens very attractive. When the D300 was first introduced, Nikon offered it as a kit with the AF-S DX Zoom-Nikkor 18-135mm f/3.5-5.6G IF-ED lens or the vibration resistant AF-S DX VR Zoom-Nikkor 18-200mm f/3.5-5.6G IF-ED zoom. However, the body was also readily available for many purchasers who, like me, fall into one of the following categories: Those who are upgrading from the Nikon D200, from a Nikon film camera; or who are buying the D300 as a second camera body to complement their Nikon D2xs, or even as an adjunct to their full-frame Nikon D3. These owners, too, generally have lenses they can use with their new D300.

So, depending on which category you fall into, you'll need to make a decision about what kit lens to buy, or decide what other kind of lenses you need to fill out your complement of Nikon optics. This section will cover "first lens" concerns, while later in the chapter we'll look at "add-on lens" considerations.

When deciding on a first lens, there are several factors you'll want to consider:

- **Cost.** You might have stretched your budget a bit to purchase your Nikon D300, so you might want to keep the cost of your first lens fairly low. Fortunately, there are excellent lenses available that will add from $100 to $300 to the price of your camera if purchased at the same time.

- **Zoom range.** If you have only one lens, you'll want a fairly long zoom range to provide as much flexibility as possible. Fortunately, the two most popular basic lenses for the D300 have 3X to 5X zoom ranges, extending from moderate wide-angle/normal out to medium telephoto. Either are fine for everyday shooting, portraits, and some types of sports.

- **Adequate maximum aperture.** You'll want an f/stop of at least f/3.5 to f/4 for shooting under fairly low light conditions. The thing to watch for is the maximum aperture when the lens is zoomed to its telephoto end. You may end up with no better than an f/5.6 maximum aperture. That's not great, but you can often live with it, particularly with a lens having vibration reduction (VR) capabilities, because you can often shoot at lower shutter speeds to compensate for the limited maximum aperture.

- **Image quality.** Your starter lens should have good image quality, because that's one of the primary factors that will be used to judge your photos. Even at a low price, several of the different lenses that can be packaged with the D300 kit include extra-low dispersion glass and aspherical elements that minimize distortion and chromatic aberration; they are sharp enough for most applications. If you read the user evaluations in the online photography forums, you know that owners of the kit lenses have been very pleased with its image quality.

- **Size matters.** A good walking-around lens is compact in size and light in weight.

- **Fast/close focusing.** Your first lens should have a speedy autofocus system (which is where the Silent Wave motor found in all but the bargain basement lenses is an advantage). Close focusing (to 12 inches or closer) will let you use your basic lens for some types of macro photography.

You can find comparisons of the lenses discussed in the next section, as well as third-party lenses from Sigma, Tokina, Tamron, and other vendors, in online groups and web-sites. I'll provide my recommendations, but more information is always helpful.

Buy Now, Expand Later

The D300 is commonly available with several good, basic lenses that can serve you well as a "walk-around" lens (one you keep on the camera most of the time, especially when you're out and about without your camera bag). The number of options available to you is actually quite amazing, even if your budget is limited to about $100-$350 for your first lens. One other vendor, for example, offers only 18mm-70mm and 18mm-55mm kit lenses in that price range, plus a 24mm-85mm zoom. Two of the most popular starter lenses Nikon offers are shown in Figure 8.2. Here's a list of Nikon's best-bet "first" lenses.

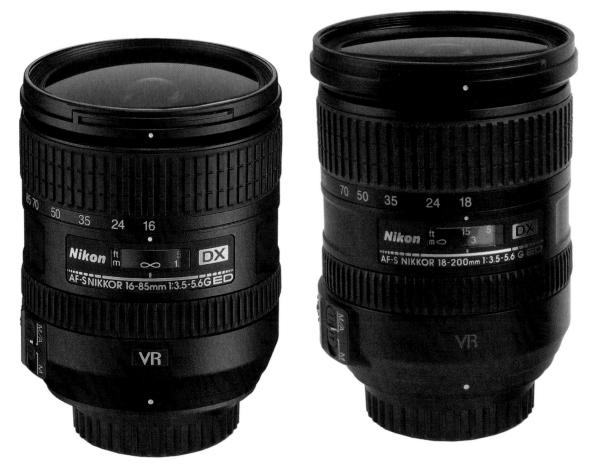

Figure 8.2 The AF-S DX Nikkor 16-85mm f/3.5-5.6G ED VR (left) and AF-S DX VR Zoom-Nikkor 18-200mm f/3.5-5.6G IF-ED (right), are two of the most popular basic lenses for the Nikon D300.

Don't worry about sorting out the alphabet soup right now; I provide a complete list of Nikon lens "codes" later in the chapter.

■ **AF-S DX Nikkor 16-85mm f/3.5-5.6G ED VR.** I've listed this lens first because the new 16-85mm VR lens is, in fact, the zoom that would make the most sense as a kit lens for the D300, given the typical user of that more advanced camera. It's not cheap; firm pricing hasn't been established yet as this is written, but it will be in the $600 range, which isn't out of line for a sophisticated camera like the Nikon D300. If you really want to use just a single lens with your camera, this one provides the best combination of focal lengths, image quality, and features. Its zoom range extends from a true wide angle (equivalent to a 24mm lens on a full-frame camera) to useful medium telephoto (about 128mm equivalent), and so can be used for everything from architecture to portraiture to sports. If you think vibration reduction is useful only with longer telephoto lenses, you may be surprised at how much it helps you hand-hold your D300 even at the widest focal lengths. The only disadvantages to this lens are its relatively slow speed (f/5.6) when you crank it out to the telephoto end, and that, as a DX lens, it can't be used to its full potential on a full-frame camera you might buy in the future.

■ **AF-S DX Zoom-Nikkor 18-55mm f/3.5-5.6G ED II.** This is the least expensive basic zoom Nikon offers, and suitable for the D300 only if you're really pinching pennies and plan to upgrade to better lenses in the near future. It's really intended for the amateur/entry-level dSLRs in the Nikon line, and you probably won't be happy with the very limited focal length range. Image quality is fine, but your D300 really deserves better.

■ **AF-S DX Nikkor 18-55mm f/3.5-5.6G VR.** This VR version of the 18-55 is a marginally better choice than the basic 18-55 optic, because the vibration reduction partially offsets the relatively slow maximum aperture of the lens at the telephoto position. It can be mated with Nikon's AF-S DX VR Zoom-Nikkor 55-200mm f/4-5.6G IF-ED to give you a two-lens VR pair that will handle everything from 18mm to 200mm, at a relatively low price. However, serious Nikon D300 users will probably prefer a different lens line up for that range.

■ **AF-S DX Zoom-Nikkor 18-70mm f/3.5-4.5G IF-ED.** If you don't plan on getting a longer zoom-range basic lens and can't afford the 16-85 zoom, I highly recommend this aging, but impressive lens. Originally introduced as the kit lens for the venerable Nikon D70, the 18-70mm zoom quickly gained a reputation as a very sharp lens at a bargain price. It doesn't provide a view that's as long or as wide as the 16-85, but it's a half-stop faster at its maximum zoom position. You may have to hunt around to find one of these, but they are available for $250-$300 and well worth it.

■ **AF-S DX Zoom-Nikkor 18-135mm f/3.5-5.6G IF-ED.** This lens has been sold as a kit lens for intermediate amateur-level Nikons, and is being packaged with the

D300 as well. While decent, it's really best suited for the crowd who buy one do-everything lens and then never purchase another. Available for less than $300, you won't tie up a lot of money in this lens.

■ **AF-S DX VR Zoom-Nikkor 18-200mm f/3.5-5.6G IF-ED.** I had this lens for about three months, and decided it really didn't meet my needs. It was introduced as an ideal "kit" lens for the Nikon D200, and, at the time had almost everything you might want. It's a holdover, more upscale kit lens for the D300. Its stunning 11X zoom range covers everything from the equivalent of 27mm to 300mm when the 1.5X crop factor is figured in, and its VR capabilities plus light weight let you use it without a tripod most of the time. However, I found the image quality to be good, but not outstanding, and the slow maximum aperture at 200mm to be limiting when a fast shutter speed is required to stop action. The "zoom creep" (a tendency for the lens to zoom when the camera is tilted up or down) found in many examples will drive you nuts after awhile. Today, when I need a 200mm focal length, I prefer my Nikon 70-200mm f2.8 VR lens when I require speed and vibration reduction, and my Nikon 28-200mm f3.5-5.6 zoom when I want compactness. Both lenses are described later.

■ **AF Zoom-Nikkor 28-200mm f/3.5-5.6G ED.** This lens is a neglected gem! It faded into obscurity when the sexier 18-200mm VR zoom was introduced, primarily because it didn't have the same wide-angle range as the newer lens. Don't confuse this series G lens with the older and less desirable D version (they can be readily told apart because, like all G lenses, the "good" version has no aperture ring). This lens has superb optical quality (incorporating three extra-low dispersion ED elements), is incredibly compact at 12.7 ounces and 2.8 x 2.7 inches (length/diameter), and focuses down to 1.3 feet. I've taken it to Europe twice on important shooting trips rather than lug around my legendary Nikon 70-200 VR optic (which costs more than five times as much), because I knew I wouldn't be sacrificing any image quality. It's available for about $300, and, unlike all but one of the lenses in this section, can be used with both DX and FX (full frame) Nikon bodies. Disadvantages? It's slow, lacks VR, and requires a focus motor built into the camera body (so it won't autofocus on the Nikon D40/40x and D60 camera bodies). But what do you want for $300?

■ **AF-S VR Zoom-Nikkor 24-120mm f/3.5-5.6G IF-ED.** I felt I had to mention this lens because I see a large number of them available used at low prices. There are two versions, an older non-VR lens, and this model, which added vibration reduction, internal focusing, and some extra low dispersion (ED) elements to improve image quality. Unfortunately, while image quality is very good at the maximum 120mm, the lens softens quite a bit at shorter focal lengths and at larger apertures, making it less suitable as an all-around tool. My guess is that the reason there are so many available at less than $300 on the used market is that the original owners dumped them for something better.

What Lenses Can You Use?

The previous section helped you sort out what lens you need to buy with your D300 (assuming you already didn't own any Nikon lenses). Now, you're probably wondering what lenses can be added to your growing collection (trust me, it will grow). You need to know which lenses are suitable and, most importantly, which lenses are fully compatible with your Nikon D300.

With the Nikon D300, the compatibility issue is a simple one: It accepts any lens with the AF or AF-S designation, with full availability of all autofocus, auto aperture, auto-exposure, and image-stabilization features (if present). You can also use any AI, AI-S, or AI-P lens, which are manual focus lenses produced starting in 1977 and effectively through the present day, because Nikon continues to offer a limited number of manual focus lenses for those who need them. Nikon lenses produced prior to 1977 must have a minor conversion done (John White at **www.aiconversions.com** will do the work for about $35) to be safely used on any Nikon digital camera (including the D300). It's comforting to know that almost any of the lenses sold since 1959 will work as designed with your camera.

Today, in addition to its traditional full-frame lenses, Nikon offers lenses with the DX designation, which is intended for use only on DX-format cameras (currently every Nikon digital camera except for the D3). While the lens mounting system is the same, DX lenses have a coverage area that fills only the smaller frame, allowing the design of more compact, less-expensive lenses especially for non-full-frame cameras.

Ingredients of Nikon's Alphanumeric Soup

Nikon has always been fond of appending cryptic letters and descriptors onto the names of its lenses. Some of the first Nikon lenses I purchased had names like 35mm f/2 Auto Nikkor-O, 85mm f/1.8 Auto Nikkor-H, 105mm Auto Nikkor-P, and 200mm f/4 Auto Nikkor-Q. At the time, I didn't know what the funny letters represented, but I did know that the "Auto" portion of the name meant that, when you pressed the shutter release button, the lens would actually *stop down automatically* to the aperture you'd selected for the exposure. Don't laugh. Many lenses required rotating a ring manually after focusing and before taking the picture in order to close the lens down to the so-called *pre-set* aperture.

I actually still own all those lenses, because they work just fine on my Nikon digital camera bodies, including my beloved D300. And I now know that the funny letters stood for the number of elements in the lens, which was apparently a more important attribute for a photographer to know than it is today. P stood for *penta* (five elements); H represented *hexa* (six elements); S stood for *septa* (seven elements), and so on through *octa, nona,* and *deca* (eight, nine, and ten). I'd finally found a use for my high-school

Latin, even though Nikon substituted penta for *quinta*, because Q was already taken by *quadra* (four elements).

In the years since, Nikon lens nomenclature has become considerably more complex. Even the basic name of the company's lenses can be a source of confusion. Back when Paul Simon wrote his hit *Kodachrome* it was always a "Nikon camera" and a "Nikkor lens." Today, *Nikkor* is still officially part of the name of each lens produced by Nikon, with the exception of the company's "budget" line of 30 years ago, which were called *Nikon Lens Series E* to differentiate them from all the other "top of the line" lenses. But it's become more common to informally refer to a Nikon lens without fear of being corrected.

Here's an alphabetical list of lens terms you're likely to encounter, either as part of the lens name, or in reference to the lens's capabilities. Not all of these are used as parts of a lens's name; but you may come across some of these terms in discussions of particular Nikon optics:

- **AF, AF-D, AF-I, AF-S.** In all cases, AF stands for *autofocus* when appended to the name of a Nikon lens. An extra letter is added to provide additional information. A plain-old **AF** lens is an autofocus lens that uses a slot-drive motor in the camera body to provide autofocus functions (and so cannot be used in AF mode on the Nikon D40, D40x, or D60, which lack the camera body motor). The **D** means that it's a D-type lens (described later in this listing); the **I** indicates that focus is through a motor inside the lens; and the **S** means that a super-special (Silent Wave) motor in the lens provides focusing. (Don't confuse a Nikon AF-S lens with the AF-S [Single-Servo Autofocus] mode). Nikon is currently upgrading its older AF lenses with AF-S versions, but it's not safe to assume that all newer Nikkors are AF-S, or even offer autofocus. For example, the brand-new PC-E Nikkor 24mm f/3.5D ED perspective control lens must be focused manually, and Nikon offers a surprising collection of other manual focus lenses to meet specialized needs.

- **AI, AI-S.** All Nikkor lenses produced after 1977 have either automatic aperture indexing (AI) or automatic indexing-shutter (AI-S) features that eliminate the previous requirement to manually align the aperture ring on the camera when mounting a lens. When AI/AI-S was introduced, Nikon included the designation in the lens name and offered a service to convert most older lenses to the new configuration. Within a few years, all Nikkors had this automatic aperture indexing feature (except for G-type lenses, which have no aperture ring at all), including Nikon's budget-priced Series E lenses, so the designation was dropped at the time the first autofocus (AF) lenses were introduced. The most important difference between AI and AI-S lenses is that the aperture action of the AI-S versions is *linear*, theoretically allowing for more efficient shutter priority and programmed exposure metering on cameras of the time. Current models make no distinction between AI and AI-S lenses. These lenses can be used for Aperture Priority and Manual mode metering on the Nikon D300 and other Nikon "pro" bodies.

- **AI-P.** A lens with an AI-P designation is an AI lens that has the CPU chip included, which allows the transfer of basic lens information to the camera. It was possible to add an appropriate chip to most AI and AI-S lenses, upgrading them to AI-P status, but there are few companies offering this service anymore. "Chipped" AI/AI-S/AI-P lenses are manual focus optics that can be used with the full range of metering options, the same as with autofocus lenses.

- **CRC (Close Range Correction).** The so-called "floating element" system allowed lens elements to shift position to reduce curvature of field and spherical aberrations at close-focusing distances. Available with certain lenses, including the AF Micro-Nikkor 60mm f/2.8D, which was recently replaced by the AF-S Micro-Nikkor 60mm f/2.8G ED.

- **E.** The E designation was used for Nikon's budget-priced E Series optics, five prime and three zoom manual focus lenses built using aluminum or plastic parts rather than the preferred brass, so they were less rugged. All are effectively AI-S lenses. They do have good image quality, which makes them a bargain for those who treat their lenses gently and don't need the latest autofocus features. They were available in 28mm f/2.8, 35mm f/2.5, 50mm f/1.8, 100mm f/2.8, and 135mm f/2.8 focal lengths, plus 36-72mm f/3.5, 75mm-150mm f/3.5, and 70-210mm f/4 zooms. (All these would be considered fairly "fast" today.)

- **D.** Appended to the maximum f/stop of the lens (as in f/2.8D), a D Series lens is able to send focus distance data to the camera, which uses the information for flash exposure calculation and 3D Color Matrix II matrix metering.

- **DC.** The DC stands for defocus control, which allows managing the out-of-focus parts of an image to produce better-looking portraits and close-ups.

- **DX.** The DX lenses are designed for use with digital cameras using the APS-C–sized sensor having the 1.5X crop factor. Their image circle isn't large enough to fill up a full 35mm frame at all focal lengths, but they can be used on Nikon's full-frame D3 model using the automatic/manual DX crop mode. Theoretically, these lenses can be built smaller and lighter than their full-frame counterparts, but there are some hefty DX lenses available, including the AF-S DX Zoom-Nikkor 17-55mm f/2.8G IF-ED.

- **ED (or LD/UD).** The ED (extra low dispersion) designation indicates that some lens elements are made of a special hard and scratch-resistant glass that minimizes the divergence of the different colors of light as they pass through, thus reducing chromatic aberration (color "fringing") and other image defects. A gold band around the front of the lens indicates an optic with ED elements. You sometimes find LD (low dispersion) or UD (ultra-low dispersion) designations.

- **FX.** When Nikon introduced the Nikon D3 full-frame camera, it coined the term "FX," representing the 23.9 x 36mm sensor format as a counterpart to "DX," which was used for its 15.8 x 23.6mm APS-C-sized sensors. Although FX hasn't been officially applied to any Nikon lenses so far, expect to see the designation used more often to differentiate between lenses that are compatible with any Nikon digital SLR (FX) and those that operate only on DX-format cameras, or in DX mode when used on an FX camera like the D3.

- **G.** G-type lenses have no aperture ring, and you can use them at other than the maximum aperture only with electronic cameras like the D300 that set the aperture automatically or by using the command dial while the Exposure Compensation/Aperture button is depressed. This includes all Nikon digital dSLRs.

- **IF.** Nikon's *internal focusing* lenses change focus by shifting only small internal lens groups with no change required in the lens's physical length, unlike conventional double helicoid focusing systems that move all lens groups toward the front or rear during focusing. IF lenses are more compact and lighter in weight, provide better balance, focus more closely, and can be focused more quickly.

- **IX.** These lenses were produced for Nikon's long-discontinued Pronea 6i and S APS film cameras. While the Pronea could use many standard Nikon lenses, IX lenses cannot be mounted on any Nikon digital SLR.

- **Micro.** Nikon uses the term *micro* to designate its close-up lenses. Most other vendors use *macro* instead.

- **NAI.** This is not an official Nikon term, but it is widely used to indicate that a manual focus lens is *Not-AI*, which means that it was manufactured before 1977, and therefore cannot be used safely on modern digital Nikon SLRs without modification.

- **NOCT (Nocturnal).** Used primarily to refer to the prized Nikkor AI-S Noct 58mm f/1.2, a "fast" (wide aperture) lens, with aspherical elements, capable of taking photographs in very low light.

- **PC (Perspective Control).** A PC lens is capable of shifting the lens from side to side (and up/down) to provide a more realistic perspective when photographing architecture and other subjects that otherwise require tilting the camera so that the sensor plane is not parallel to the subject. Older Nikkor PC lenses offered shifting only, but more modern models, such as the PC-E Nikkor 24mm f/3.5D ED lens introduced early in 2008, allow both shifting and tilting.

- **UV.** This term is applied to special (and expensive) lenses designed to pass ultraviolet light.

- **UW.** Lenses with this designation are designed for underwater photography with Nikonos camera bodies, and cannot be used with Nikon digital SLRs.

- **VR.** Nikon has an expanding line of vibration reduction (VR) lenses, including several very affordable models and the new AF-S DX Nikkor 16-85mm f/3.5-5.6G ED VR lens, which shifts lens elements internally to counteract camera shake. The VR feature allows using a shutter speed up to four stops slower than would be possible without vibration reduction.

What Lenses Can Do for You

I'm something of a lens nut. Because my work requires me to evaluate lots of different lenses and provide recommendations for specific lenses that may have overlapping focal lengths and features, I'm able to justify owning many more optics than the average person wants or needs. It probably wouldn't make sense for you to own 17-35mm, 24-70mm, 18-70mm, and 28-200mm zooms as I do. Indeed, a much saner approach to expanding your lens collection is to consider what each of your options can do for you and then choose the type of lens and specific model that will really boost your creative opportunities.

So, in the sections that follow, I'm going to provide a general guide to the sort of capabilities you can gain for your D300 by adding a lens to your repertoire. Then, at the end of the chapter, I'll provide a more detailed discussion of some specific lenses and how they might fit into your camera bag toolkit.

- **Wider perspective.** Your 18-55mm f/3.5-5.6 or 16-85mm f/4-5.6 lens has served you well for moderate wide-angle shots. Now you find your back is up against a wall and you *can't* take a step backwards to take in more subject matter. Perhaps you're standing on the rim of the Grand Canyon, and you want to take in as much of the breathtaking view as you can. You might find yourself just behind the baseline at a high school basketball game and want an interesting shot with a little perspective distortion tossed in the mix. There's a lens out there that will provide you with what you need, such as the 12-24mm Nikon zoom I'll describe later in this chapter.

- **Bring objects closer.** A long lens brings distant subjects closer to you, offers better control over depth-of-field, and avoids the perspective distortion that wide-angle lenses provide. They compress the apparent distance between objects in your frame. Don't forget that the Nikon D300's crop factor narrows the field of view of all these lenses, so your 70-300mm lens looks more like a 105mm-450mm zoom through the viewfinder. The image shown in Figure 8.3 was taken using a wide 16mm lens, while the image in Figures 8.4 and 8.5 were taken from the same position as Figure 8.3, but with focal lengths of 40mm and 85mm, respectively.

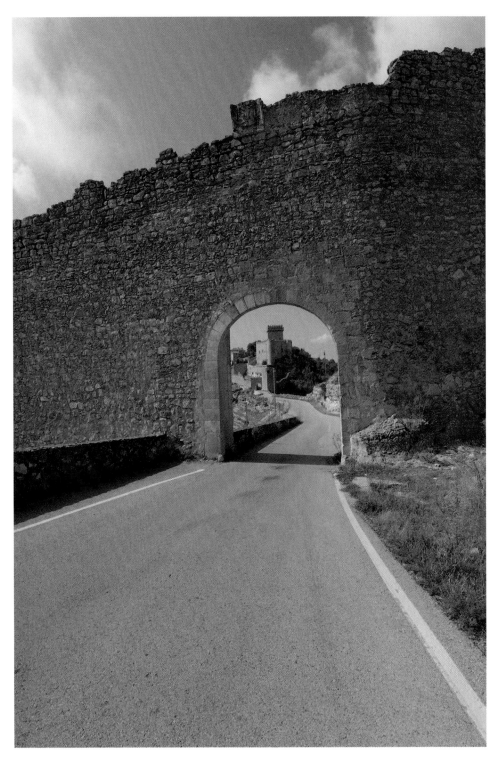

Figure 8.3
An ultra-wide-angle lens pro-vided this view of an 8th Century castle.

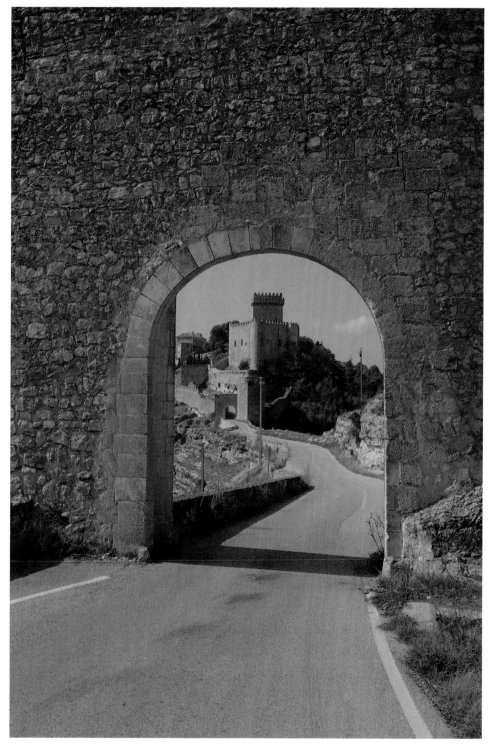

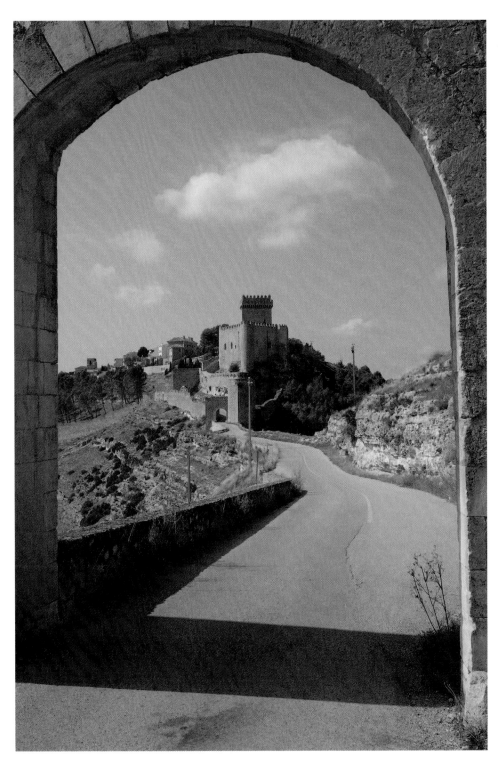

Figure 8.5
A medium tele-
photo lens cap-
tured this
closer view of
the castle from
approximately
the same shoot-
ing position.

- **Bring your camera closer.** Macro lenses allow you to focus to within an inch or two of your subject. Nikon's best close-up lenses are all fixed focal length optics in the 60mm to 200mm range, but you'll find good macro zooms available from Sigma and others. They don't tend to focus quite as close, but they provide a bit of flexibility when you want to vary your subject distance (say, to avoid spooking a skittish creature).

- **Look sharp.** Many lenses are prized for their sharpness and overall image quality. While your run-of-the-mill lens is likely to be plenty sharp for most applications, the very best optics are even better over their entire field of view (which means no fuzzy corners), are sharper at a wider range of focal lengths (in the case of zooms), and have better correction for various types of distortion.

- **More speed.** Your Nikon 70-300mm f/4.5-5.6 telephoto zoom lens might have the perfect focal length and sharpness for sports photography, but the maximum aperture won't cut it for night baseball or football games, or, even, any sports shooting in daylight if the weather is cloudy or you need to use some ungodly fast shutter speed, such as 1/4,000th second. You might be happier to gain a full f/stop with an AF-S Nikkor 300mm f/4D IF-ED for a little more than $1000, or even the pricier Nikon AF-S VR Zoom-Nikkor 70-200mm f/2.8G IF-E mated to a 1.4x teleconverter (giving you a 98-280mm f/4 lens). If money is no object, you can spring for Nikon's superfast 400mm f/2.8 and 600mm f/4 (both with vibration reduction and priced in the $6,500-and-up stratosphere). Or, maybe you just need the speed and can benefit from an f/1.8 or f/1.4 prime lens. They're all available in Nikon mounts (there's even an 85mm f/1.4 and 50mm f/1.4 for the real speed demons). With any of these lenses you can continue photographing under the dimmest of lighting conditions without the need for a tripod or flash.

- **Special features.** Accessory lenses give you special features, such as tilt/shift capabilities to correct for perspective distortion in architectural shots. You'll also find macro lenses, including the new AF-S Micro-Nikkor 60mm f/2.8G ED. Fisheye lenses like the AF DX Fisheye-Nikkor 10.5mm f/2.8G ED, and all VR (vibration reduction) lenses also count as special-feature optics.

Zoom or Prime?

Zoom lenses have changed the way serious photographers take pictures. One of the reasons that I own 12 SLR film bodies dating back to the pre-zoom days is that in ancient times it was common to mount a different fixed focal length prime lens on various cameras and take pictures with two or three cameras around your neck (or tucked in a camera case) so you'd be ready to take a long shot or an intimate close-up or wide-angle view on a moment's notice, without the need to switch lenses. It made sense (at the time) to have a half-dozen or so bodies (two to use, one in the shop, one in transit, and a couple backups). Zoom lenses of the time had a limited zoom range, were heavy, and not very sharp (especially when you tried to wield one of those monsters hand-held).

That's all changed today. Lenses like the razor-sharp AF-S VR Zoom-Nikkor 70-200mm f/2.8G IF-ED boast longer zoom ranges, in a package that's about 8.5-inches long, and while not petite at 3.2 pounds, quite usable hand-held (especially with VR switched on). Although such a lens might seem expensive at $1600-plus, it's actually much less costly than the six or so lenses it replaces. I'll explain more about this particular lens later in the chapter.

When selecting between zoom and prime lenses, there are several considerations to ponder. Here's a checklist of the most important factors. I already mentioned image quality and maximum aperture earlier, but those aspects take on additional meaning when comparing zooms and primes.

- **Logistics.** As prime lenses offer just a single focal length, you'll need more of them to encompass the full range offered by a single zoom. More lenses mean additional slots in your camera bag, and extra weight to carry. Just within Nikon's line alone you can choose from a good selection of general purpose prime lenses in 28mm, 35mm, 50mm, 85mm, 100mm, 135mm, and 200mm focal lengths, all of which are overlapped by the 28-200mm zoom I mentioned earlier. Even so, you might be willing to carry an extra prime lens or two in order to gain the speed or image quality that lens offers.

- **Image quality.** Prime lenses usually produce better image quality at their focal length than even the most sophisticated zoom lenses at the same magnification. Zoom lenses, with their shifting elements and f/stops that can vary from zoom position to zoom position, are in general more complex to design than fixed focal length lenses. That's not to say that the very best prime lenses can't be complicated as well. However, the exotic designs, aspheric elements, and low-dispersion glass can be applied to improving the quality of the lens, rather than wasting a lot of it on compensating for problems caused by the zoom process itself.

- **Maximum aperture.** Because of the same design constraints, zoom lenses usually have smaller maximum apertures than prime lenses, and the most affordable zooms have a lens opening that grows effectively smaller as you zoom in. The difference in lens speed verges on the ridiculous at some focal lengths. For example, the 18mm-55mm basic zoom gives you a 55mm f/5.6 lens when zoomed all the way out, while prime lenses in that focal length commonly have f/1.8 or faster maximum apertures. Indeed, the fastest f/2, f/1.8, f1/4, and f/1.2 lenses are all primes, and if you require speed, a fixed focal length lens is what you should rely on. Figure 8.6 shows an image taken with a Nikon 85mm f /1.8 lens.

■ **Speed.** Using prime lenses takes time and slows you down. It takes a few seconds to remove your current lens and mount a new one, and the more often you need to do that, the more time is wasted. If you choose not to swap lenses, when using a fixed focal length lens you'll still have to move closer or farther away from your subject to get the field of view you want. A zoom lens allows you to change magnifications and focal lengths with the twist of a ring and generally saves a great deal of time.

Figure 8.6
An 85mm f/1.8 lens was perfect for this hand-held photo of guitarist Bo Ramsey.

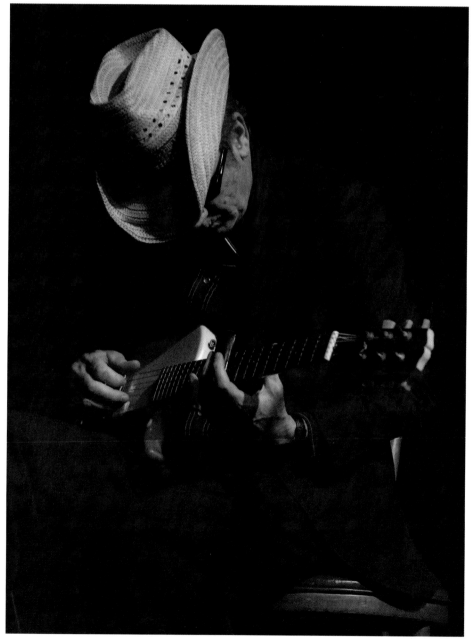

Categories of Lenses

Lenses can be categorized by their intended purpose—general photography, macro photography, and so forth—or by their focal length. The range of available focal lengths is usually divided into three main groups: wide-angle, normal, and telephoto. Prime lenses fall neatly into one of these classifications. Zooms can overlap designations, with a significant number falling into the catch-all wide-to-telephoto zoom range. This section provides more information about focal length ranges, and how they are used.

When the 1.5X crop factor (mentioned at the beginning of this chapter) is figured in, any lens with an equivalent focal length of 10mm to 16mm is said to be an *ultra-wide-angle lens*; from about 16mm to 30mm is said to be a *wide-angle lens*. *Normal lenses* have a focal length roughly equivalent to the diagonal of the film or sensor, in millimeters, and so fall into the range of about 30mm to 40mm on a D300. *Short telephoto lenses* start at about 40mm to 70mm, with anything from 70mm to 250 mm qualifying as a conventional *telephoto*. For the Nikon D300, anything from about 300mm-400mm or longer can be considered a *super-telephoto*.

Using Wide-Angle and Wide-Zoom Lenses

To use wide-angle prime lenses and wide zooms, you need to understand how they affect your photography. Here's a quick summary of the things you need to know.

- **More depth-of-field.** Practically speaking, wide-angle lenses offer more depth-of-field at a particular subject distance and aperture. (But see the sidebar below for an important note.) You'll find that helpful when you want to maximize sharpness of a large zone, but not very useful when you'd rather isolate your subject using selective focus (telephoto lenses are better for that).

- **Stepping back.** Wide-angle lenses have the effect of making it seem that you are standing farther from your subject than you really are. They're helpful when you don't want to back up, or can't because there are impediments in your way.

- **Wider field of view.** While making your subject seem farther away, as implied above, a wide-angle lens also provides a larger field of view, including more of the subject in your photos. Table 8.1 shows the diagonal field of view offered by an assortment of lenses, taking into account the crop factor introduced by the Nikon D300's smaller-than-full-frame sensor.

- **More foreground.** As background objects retreat, more of the foreground is brought into view by a wide-angle lens. That gives you extra emphasis on the area that's closest to the camera. Photograph your home with a normal lens/normal zoom setting, and the front yard probably looks fairly conventional in your photo (that's why they're called "normal" lenses). Switch to a wider lens and you'll discover that your lawn now makes up much more of the photo. So, wide-angle lenses are great when you want to emphasize that lake in the foreground, but problematic when your intended subject is located farther in the distance.

- **Super-sized subjects.** The tendency of a wide-angle lens to emphasize objects in the foreground, while de-emphasizing objects in the background can lead to a kind of size distortion that may be more objectionable for some types of subjects than others. Shoot a bed of flowers up close with a wide angle, and you might like the distorted effect of the larger blossoms nearer the lens. Take a photo of a family member with the same lens from the same distance, and you're likely to get some complaints about that gigantic nose in the foreground.

- **Perspective distortion.** When you tilt the camera so the plane of the sensor is no longer perpendicular to the vertical plane of your subject, some parts of the subject are now closer to the sensor than they were before, while other parts are farther away. So, buildings, flagpoles, or NBA players appear to be falling backwards, as you can see in Figure 8.7. While this kind of apparent distortion (it's not caused by a defect in the lens) can happen with any lens, it's most apparent when a wide angle is used.

- **Steady cam.** You'll find that you can hand-hold a wide-angle lens at slower shutter speeds, without need for vibration reduction, than you can with a telephoto lens. The reduced magnification of the wide-lens or wide-zoom setting doesn't emphasize camera shake like a telephoto lens does.

- **Interesting angles.** Many of the factors already listed combine to produce more interesting angles when shooting with wide-angle lenses. Raising or lowering a telephoto lens a few feet probably will have little effect on the appearance of the distant subjects you're shooting. The same change in elevation can produce a dramatic effect for the much-closer subjects typically captured with a wide-angle lens or wide-zoom setting.

Table 8.1 turns the conventional "equivalent" listing on its head. Usually, you'll see a table that tells you that, say, a 100mm lens when used on a camera like the Nikon D300, will have an equivalent field of view of a 150mm lens on a full frame camera. That's actually not a difficult calculation, and might not be as useful as you think. If you're concerned about focal length equivalents, you probably have some experience using full-frame cameras.

So, what you really want to know is, if I want the same field-of-view that I got with my old 20mm lens on my film camera, what focal length lens do I need to use *now?* The fact that your 20mm lens is now the equivalent of a 30mm lens on the D300 isn't as important as the question, *"Do I own a lens that will provide the same field of view that I used to get with my trusty 20mm lens?"* That's what the table shows you. In the center column, you find a list of common focal lengths for prime lenses originally designed for full frame cameras. You can scan down the column to see that, if you want the same

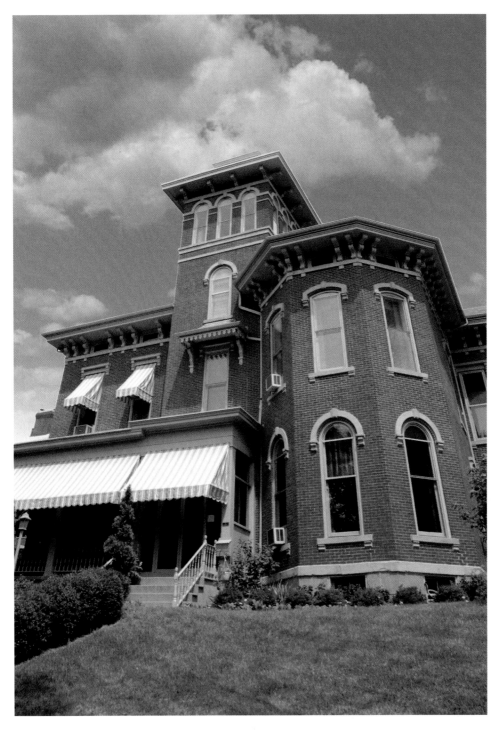

Figure 8.7
Tilting the camera back produces this "falling back" look in architectural photos.

field of view that you got with your 35mm lens, you'll need to use a 23mm focal length or zoom position when you're shooting the D300. Or, if you preferred 85mm as a focal length for portraits, then you'll need a 56mm focal length when the 1.5X crop factor is figured in. The left column shows the angle of the field of view of each lens focal length, because many old-timers sometimes think in those terms.

The crop factor strikes again! You can see from this table that wide-angle lenses provide a broader field of view, and that, because of the D300's 1.5X crop factor, lenses must have a shorter focal length to provide the same field of view. If you like working with a 28mm lens with your full-frame camera, you'll need a 19mm lens for your Nikon D300 to get the same field of view. (Some focal lengths have been rounded slightly for simplification.)

Table 8.1 Field of View at Various Focal Lengths

Diagonal Field of View	Focal Length at 1X Crop	Focal Length Needed to produce same Field of View at 1.5X Crop
107 degrees	16mm	10.5mm
94 degrees	20mm	13mm
84 degrees	24mm	16mm
75 degrees	28mm	19mm
63 degrees	35mm	23mm
47 degrees	50mm	33mm
28 degrees	85mm	56mm
18 degrees	135mm	90mm
12 degrees	200mm	133mm
8.2 degrees	300mm	200mm

DOF IN DEPTH

The DOF advantage of wide-angle lenses is diminished when you enlarge your picture; believe it or not, a wide-angle image enlarged and cropped to provide the same subject size as a telephoto shot would have the *same* depth-of-field. Try it: take a wide-angle photo of a friend from a fair distance, and then zoom in to duplicate the picture in a telephoto image. Then, enlarge the wide shot so your friend is the same size in both. The wide photo will have the same depth-of-field (and will have much less detail, too).

Avoiding Potential Wide-Angle Problems

Wide-angle lenses have a few quirks that you'll want to keep in mind when shooting so you can avoid falling into some common traps. Here's a checklist of tips for avoiding common problems:

- **Symptom: converging lines.** Unless you want to use wildly diverging lines as a creative effect, it's a good idea to keep horizontal and vertical lines in landscapes, architecture, and other subjects carefully aligned with the sides, top, and bottom of the frame. That will help you avoid undesired perspective distortion. Sometimes it helps to shoot from a slightly elevated position so you don't have to tilt the camera up or down.

- **Symptom: color fringes around objects.** Lenses are often plagued with fringes of color around backlit objects, produced by *chromatic aberration,* which comes in two forms: *longitudinal/axial,* in which all the colors of light don't focus in the same plane; and *lateral/transverse,* in which the colors are shifted to one side. Axial chromatic aberration can be reduced by stopping down the lens, but transverse CA cannot. Both can be reduced by using lenses with low diffraction index glass (or ED elements, in Nikon nomenclature) and by incorporating elements that cancel the chromatic aberration of other glass in the lens. For example, a strong positive lens made of low dispersion crown glass (made of a soda-lime-silica composite) may be mated with a weaker negative lens made of high-dispersion flint glass, which contains lead.

- **Symptom: lines that bow outward.** Some wide-angle lenses cause straight lines to bow outwards, with the strongest effect at the edges. In fisheye (or *curvilinear*) lenses, this defect is a feature, as you can see in Figure 8.8. When distortion is not desired, you'll need to use a lens that has corrected barrel distortion. Manufacturers like Nikon do their best to minimize or eliminate it (producing a *rectilinear* lens), often using *aspherical* lens elements (which are not cross-sections of a sphere). You can also minimize barrel distortion simply by framing your photo with some extra space all around, so the edges where the defect is most obvious can be cropped out of the picture. Some image editors, such as Photoshop and Photoshop Elements, have a lens distortion correction feature.

- **Symptom: dark corners and shadows in flash photos.** The Nikon D300's built-in electronic flash is designed to provide even coverage for lenses as wide as 17mm. If you use a wider lens, you can expect darkening, or *vignetting,* in the corners of the frame. At wider focal lengths, the lens hood of some lenses (my 18mm-70mm lens is a prime offender) can cast a semi-circular shadow in the lower portion of the frame when using the built-in flash. Sometimes removing the lens hood or zooming in a bit can eliminate the shadow. Mounting an external flash unit, such as the mighty Nikon SB-800 can solve both problems, as it has zoomable coverage up to as wide as the field of view of a 14mm lens when used with the included adapter. Its higher vantage point eliminates the problem of lens-hood shadow, too.

■ **Symptom: light and dark areas when using polarizing filter.** If you know that polarizers work best when the camera is pointed 90 degrees away from the sun and have the least effect when the camera is oriented 180 degrees from the sun, you know only half the story. With lenses having a focal length of 10mm to 18mm (the equivalent of 15mm-27mm lens on a full frame camera), the angle of view is extensive enough to cause problems. Think about it: when a 10mm lens is pointed at the proper 90-degree angle from the sun, objects at the edges of the frame will be oriented at 135 to 41 degrees, with only the center at exactly 90 degrees. Either edge will have much less of a polarized effect. The solution is to avoid using a polarizing filter with lenses having an actual focal length of less than 18mm (or 27mm equivalent).

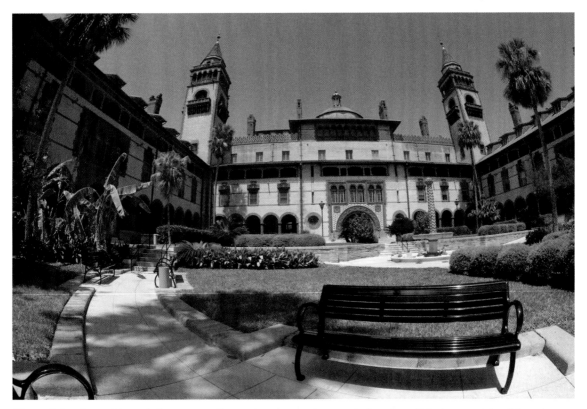

Figure 8.8 Many wide-angle lenses cause lines to bow outwards towards the edges of the image; with a fisheye lens, this tendency is considered an interesting feature.

Using Telephoto and Tele-Zoom Lenses

Telephoto lenses also can have a dramatic effect on your photography, and Nikon is especially strong in the long-lens arena, with lots of choices in many focal lengths and zoom ranges. You should be able to find an affordable telephoto or tele-zoom to enhance your photography in several different ways. Here are the most important things you need to know. In the next section, I'll concentrate on telephoto considerations that can be problematic—and how to avoid those problems.

- **Selective focus.** Long lenses have reduced depth-of-field within the frame, allowing you to use selective focus to isolate your subject. You can open the lens up wide to create shallow depth-of-field, or close it down a bit to allow more to be in focus. The flip side of the coin is that when you *want* to make a range of objects sharp, you'll need to use a smaller f/stop to get the depth-of-field you need. Like fire, the depth-of-field of a telephoto lens can be friend or foe. Figure 8.9 shows a photo of several blossoms of a plant photographed using a telephoto macro lens (a 105mm f/2.8 Micro-Nikkor) and wider f/stop to de-emphasize the other portions of the plant in the background.

- **Getting closer.** Telephoto lenses bring you closer to wildlife, sports action, and candid subjects. No one wants to get a reputation as a surreptitious or "sneaky" photographer (except for paparazzi), but when applied to candids in an open and honest way, a long lens can help you capture memorable moments while retaining enough distance to stay out of the way of events as they transpire.

- **Reduced foreground/increased compression.** Telephoto lenses have the opposite effect of wide angles: they reduce the importance of things in the foreground by squeezing everything together. This compression even makes distant objects appear to be closer to subjects in the foreground and middle ranges. You can use this effect as a creative tool to squeeze subjects together.

- **Accentuates camera shakiness.** Telephoto focal lengths hit you with a double-whammy in terms of camera/photographer shake. The lenses themselves are bulkier, more difficult to hold steady, and may even produce a barely perceptible see-saw rocking effect when you support them with one hand halfway down the lens barrel. Telephotos also magnify any camera shake. It's no wonder that vibration reduction is popular in longer lenses.

- **Interesting angles require creativity.** Telephoto lenses require more imagination in selecting interesting angles, because the "angle" you do get on your subjects is so narrow. Moving from side to side or a bit higher or lower can make a dramatic difference in a wide-angle shot, but raising or lowering a telephoto lens a few feet probably will have little effect on the appearance of the distant subjects you're shooting.

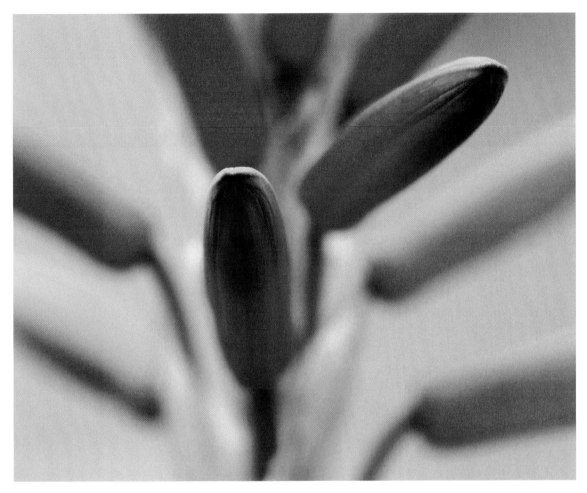

Figure 8.9 A wide f/stop helped isolate two blossoms while allowing the others to go out of focus.

Avoiding Telephoto Lens Problems

Many of the "problems" that telephoto lenses pose are really just challenges and not that difficult to overcome. Here is a list of the seven most common picture maladies and suggested solutions.

■ **Symptom: flat faces in portraits.** Head-and-shoulders portraits of humans tend to be more flattering when a focal length of 50mm to 85mm is used. Longer focal lengths compress the distance between features like noses and ears, making the face look wider and flat. A wide-angle might make noses look huge and ears tiny when you fill the frame with a face. So stick with 50mm to 85mm focal lengths, going longer only when you're forced to shoot from a greater distance, and wider only when shooting three-quarters/full-length portraits, or group shots.

- **Symptom: blur due to camera shake.** Use a higher shutter speed (boosting ISO if necessary), consider an image-stabilized lens, or mount your camera on a tripod, monopod, or brace it with some other support. Of those three solutions, only the first will reduce blur caused by *subject* motion; a VR lens or tripod won't help you freeze a racecar in mid-lap.

- **Symptom: color fringes.** Chromatic aberration is the most pernicious optical problem found in telephoto lenses. There are others, including spherical aberration, astigmatism, coma, curvature of field, and similarly scary-sounding phenomena. The best solution for any of these is to use a better lens that offers the proper degree of correction, or stop down the lens to minimize the problem. But that's not always possible. Your second-best choice may be to correct the fringing in your favorite RAW conversion tool or image editor. Photoshop CS3's Lens Correction filter (found in the Distort menu) offers sliders that minimize both red/cyan and blue/yellow fringing.

- **Symptom: lines that curve inwards.** Pincushion distortion is found in many telephoto lenses. You might find after a bit of testing that it is worse at certain focal lengths with your particular zoom lens. Like chromatic aberration, it can be partially corrected using tools like the correction tools built into Photoshop and Photoshop Elements. You can see an exaggerated example in Figure 8.10; pincushion distortion isn't always this obvious.

- **Symptom: low contrast from haze or fog.** When you're photographing distant objects, a long lens shoots through a lot more atmosphere, which generally is muddied up with extra haze and fog. That dirt or moisture in the atmosphere can reduce contrast and mute colors. Some feel that a skylight or UV filter can help, but this practice is mostly a holdover from the film days. Digital sensors are not sensitive enough to UV light for a UV filter to have much effect. So you should be prepared to boost contrast and color saturation in your Picture Controls menu or image editor if necessary.

- **Symptom: low contrast from flare.** Lenses are furnished with lens hoods for a good reason: to reduce flare from bright light sources at the periphery of the picture area, or completely outside it. Because telephoto lenses often create images that are lower in contrast in the first place, you'll want to be especially careful to use a lens hood to prevent further effects on your image (or shade the front of the lens with your hand).

- **Symptom: dark flash photos.** Edge-to-edge flash coverage isn't a problem with telephoto lenses as it is with wide angles. The shooting distance is. A long lens might make a subject that's 50 feet away look as if it's right next to you, but your camera's flash isn't fooled. You'll need extra power for distant flash shots, and probably more power than your D300's built-in flash provides. The Nikon SB-800 speedlight, for example, can automatically zoom its coverage down to that of a 105mm medium telephoto lens, providing a theoretical full-power shooting aperture of about f/11 at 30 feet and ISO 400. (Try *that* with the built-in flash!)

Figure 8.10
Pincushion distortion in telephoto lenses causes lines to bow inwards from the edges.

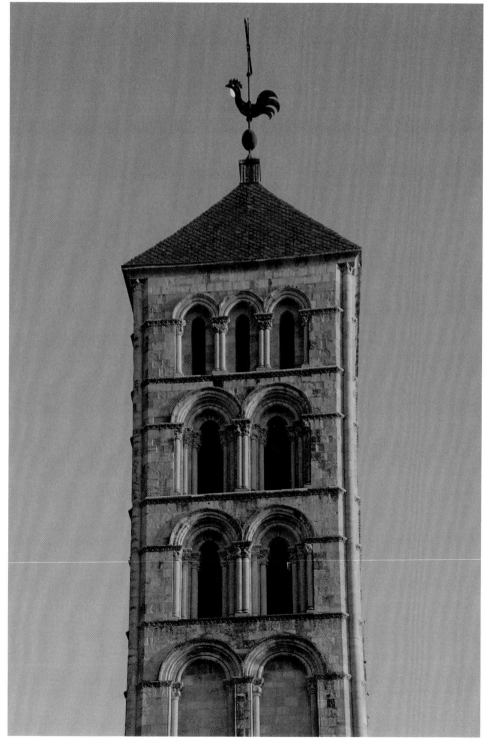

Telephotos and Bokeh

Bokeh describes the aesthetic qualities of the out-of-focus parts of an image and whether out-of-focus points of light—circles of confusion—are rendered as distracting fuzzy discs or smoothly fade into the background. *Boke* is a Japanese word for "blur," and the h was added to keep English speakers from rendering it monosyllabically to rhyme with *broke.* Although bokeh is visible in blurry portions of any image, it's of particular concern with telephoto lenses, which, thanks to the magic of reduced depth-of-field, produce more obviously out-of-focus areas.

Bokeh can vary from lens to lens, or even within a given lens depending on the f/stop in use. Bokeh becomes objectionable when the circles of confusion are evenly illuminated, making them stand out as distinct discs, or, worse, when these circles are darker in the center, producing an ugly "doughnut" effect. A lens defect called spherical aberration may produce out-of-focus discs that are brighter on the edges and darker in the center, because the lens doesn't focus light passing through the edges of the lens exactly as it does light going through the center. (Mirror or *catadioptric* lenses also produce this effect.)

Other kinds of spherical aberration generate circles of confusion that are brightest in the center and fade out at the edges, producing a smooth blending effect, as you can see at right in Figure 8.11. Ironically, when no spherical aberration is present at all, the discs

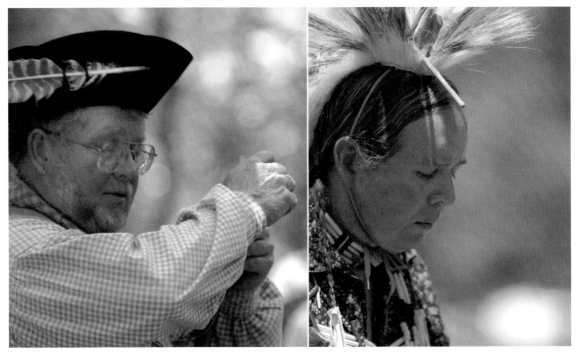

Figure 8.11 Bokeh is less pleasing when the discs are prominent (left), and less obtrusive when they blend into the background (right).

are a uniform shade, which, while better than the doughnut effect, is not as pleasing as the bright center/dark edge rendition. The shape of the disc also comes into play, with round smooth circles considered the best, and nonagonal or some other polygon (determined by the shape of the lens diaphragm) considered less desirable.

If you plan to use selective focus a lot, you should investigate the bokeh characteristics of a particular lens before you buy. Nikon user groups and forums will usually be full of comments and questions about bokeh, so the research is fairly easy.

Add-ons and Special Features

Once you've purchased your telephoto lens, you'll want to think about some appropriate accessories for it. There are some handy add-ons available that can be valuable. Here are a couple of them to think about.

Lens Hoods

Lens hoods are an important accessory for all lenses, but they're especially valuable with telephotos. As I mentioned earlier, lens hoods do a good job of preserving image contrast by keeping bright light sources outside the field of view from striking the lens and, potentially, bouncing around inside that long tube to generate flare that, when coupled with atmospheric haze, can rob your image of detail and snap. In addition, lens hoods serve as valuable protection for that large, vulnerable, front lens element. It's easy to forget that you've got that long tube sticking out in front of your camera and accidentally whack the front of your lens into something. It's cheaper to replace a lens hood than it is to have a lens repaired, so you might find that a good hood is valuable protection for your prized optics.

When choosing a lens hood, it's important to have the right hood for the lens, usually the one offered for that lens by Nikon or the third-party manufacturer. You want a hood that blocks precisely the right amount of light: neither too much light nor too little. A hood with a front diameter that is too small can show up in your pictures as vignetting. A hood that has a front diameter that's too large isn't stopping all the light it should. Generic lens hoods may not do the job.

When your telephoto is a zoom lens, it's even more important to get the right hood, because you need one that does what it is supposed to at both the wide-angle and telephoto ends of the zoom range. Lens hoods may be cylindrical, rectangular (shaped like the image frame), or petal shaped (that is, cylindrical, but with cut-out areas at the corners which correspond to the actual image area). Lens hoods should be mounted in the correct orientation (a bayonet mount for the hood usually takes care of this).

Telephoto Converters

Teleconverters (often called telephoto extenders outside the Nikon world) multiply the actual focal length of your lens, giving you a longer telephoto for much less than the price of a lens with that actual focal length. These converters fit between the lens and your camera and contain optical elements that magnify the image produced by the lens. Available in 1.4X, 1.7X, and 2.0X configurations from Nikon, a teleconverter transforms, say, a 200mm lens into a 280mm, 340mm, or 400mm optic, respectively. Given the D300's crop factor, your 200mm lens now has the same field of view as a 420mm, 510, or 600mm lens on a full-frame camera. At around $300-$400 each, converters are quite a bargain, aren't they?

Actually, there are some downsides. While extenders retain the closest focusing distance of your original lens, autofocus is maintained only if the lens's original maximum aperture is f/4 or larger (for the 1.4X extender) or f/2.8 or larger (for the 2X extender). The components reduce the effective aperture of any lens they are used with, by one f/stop with the 1.4X converter, 1.5 f/stops with the 1.7X converter, and 2 f/stops with the 2X extender. So, your 200mm f/2.8 lens becomes a 280mm f/4 or 400mm f/5.6 lens. Although Nikon converters are precision optical devices, they do cost you a little sharpness, but that improves when you reduce the aperture by a stop or two. Each of the converters is compatible only with a particular set of lenses greater, so you'll want to check Nikon's compatibility chart to see if the component can be used with the lens you want to attach to it.

If your lenses are compatible and you're shooting under bright lighting conditions, the Nikon extenders make handy accessories. I recommend the 1.4X version because it robs you of very little sharpness and only one f/stop. The 1.7X version also works well, too, but I've found the 2X teleconverter to exact too much of a sharpness and speed penalty to be of much use.

Macro Focusing

Some telephotos and telephoto zooms available for the Nikon D300 have particularly close focusing capabilities, making them *macro* lenses. Of course, the object is not necessarily to get close (get too close and you'll find it difficult to light your subject). What you're really looking for in a macro lens is to magnify the apparent size of the subject in the final image. Camera-to-subject distance is most important when you want to back up farther from your subject (say, to avoid spooking skittish insects or small animals). In that case, you'll want a macro lens with a longer focal length to allow that distance while retaining the desired magnification.

Nikon makes five lenses that are officially designated as macro lenses. They include:

- **AF-S Micro-Nikkor 60mm f/2.8G ED.** This new type G lens supposedly replaces the type D lens listed next, adding an internal Silent Wave autofocus motor that should operate faster, and which is also compatible with cameras lacking a body motor, such as the Nikon D40/D40x and D60. It also has ED lens elements for improved image quality. However, because it lacks an aperture ring, you can control the f/stop only when the lens is mounted directly on the camera or used with automatic extension tubes. Should you want to reverse a macro lens (which can improve image quality) or mount it on a bellows, you're better off with a lens having an aperture ring.

- **AF Micro-Nikkor 60mm f/2.8D.** This older lens's aperture ring gives it a little more versatility but, realistically, only fanatical close-up shooters actually use the Nikon BR-2a lens reversing ring or mount the lens on a bellows. I happen to belong in that camp, so I am hanging onto mine.

- **AF-S VR Micro-Nikkor 105mm f/2.8G IF-ED.** This G-series lens did replace a similar D-type, non-AF-S version that also lacked VR. I own the older lens, too, and am keeping it for the same reasons described above—but also because I find VR a rather specialized tool for macro work. Some 99 percent of the time, I shoot close-ups with my D300 mounted on a tripod or, at the very least, on a monopod, so camera vibration is not much of a concern. Indeed, *subject* movement is a more serious problem, especially when shooting plant life outdoors on days plagued with even slight breezes. Because my outdoor subjects are likely to move while I am composing my photo, I find both VR and autofocus not very useful. I end up focusing manually most of the time, too. This lens provides a little extra camera-to-subject distance, so you'll find it very useful, but consider the older non-G, non-VR version, too, if you're in the market.

- **AF Micro-Nikkor 200mm f/4D IF-ED.** With a price tag of about $1,300, you'd probably want this lens only if you planned a great deal of close-up shooting at greater distances. It focuses down to 1.6 feet, but provides enough magnification to allow interesting close-ups of subjects that are farther away. A specialized tool for specialized shooting.

- **PC Micro-Nikkor 85mm f/2.8D.** Priced about the same as the 200mm Micro-Nikkor, this is a manual focus lens that offers both tilt and shift capabilities, so you can adjust the perspective of the subject as you shoot. The tilt feature lets you "tilt" the plane of focus, providing the illusion of greater depth-of-field, while the shift capabilities make it possible to shoot down on a subject from an angle and still maintain its correct proportions. If you need one of these, you already know it; if you're still wondering how you'd use one, you probably have no need for these specialized capabilities.

You'll also find macro lenses, macro zooms, and other close-focusing lenses available from Sigma, Tamron, and Tokina. If you want to focus closer with a macro lens, or any other lens, you can add an accessory called an *extension tube*, like the one shown in Figure 8.12, or a *bellows extension*. These add-ons move the lens farther from the focal plane, allowing it to focus more closely. Nikon also sells add-on close-up lenses, which look like filters, and allow lenses to focus more closely.

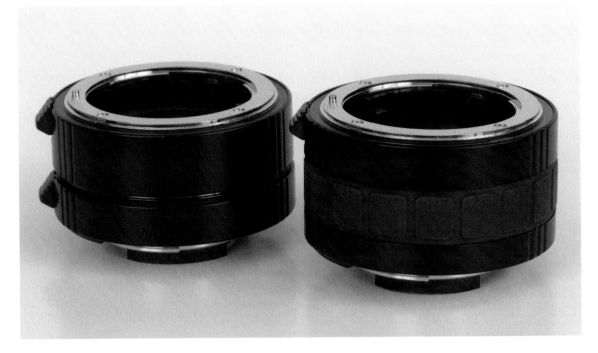

Figure 8.12 Extension tubes enable any lens to focus more closely to the subject.

Vibration Reduction

Nikon has a burgeoning line of more than 14 lenses with built-in vibration reduction (VR) capabilities. I probably shouldn't have mentioned a specific number, because I expect another half dozen or so new VR lenses to be introduced rather early in the life of this book.

The VR feature uses lens elements that are shifted internally in response to vertical or horizontal motion of the lens, which compensates for any camera shake in those directions. Vibration reduction is particularly effective when used with telephoto lenses, which magnify the effects of camera and photographer motion. However, VR can be useful for lenses of shorter focal lengths, such as Nikon's 16-85mm and 18-55mm VR lenses. Other Nikon VR lenses provide stabilization with zooms that are as wide as 24mm.

Vibration reduction offers two to three shutter speed increments' worth of shake reduction. (Nikon claims a four-stop gain, which I feel may be optimistic.) This extra margin can be invaluable when you're shooting under dim lighting conditions or handholding a lens for, say, wildlife photography. Perhaps that shot of a foraging deer would require a shutter speed of 1/2,000 second at f/5.6 with your AF-S VR Zoom-Nikkor 200-400mm f/4G IF-ED lens. Relax. You can shoot at 1/250 second at f/11 and get a photo that is just as sharp, as long as the deer doesn't decide to bound off. Or, perhaps you're shooting indoors and would prefer to shoot at 1/15 second at f/4. Your 16mm-85mm VR lens can grab the shot for you at its wide-angle position. However, consider these facts:

- **VR doesn't freeze subject motion.** Vibration reduction won't freeze moving subjects in their tracks, because it is effective only at compensating for *camera* motion. It's best used in reduced illumination, to steady the up-down swaying of telephoto lenses, and to improve close-up photography. If your subject is in motion, you'll still need a shutter speed that's fast enough to stop the action.

- **VR adds to shutter lag.** The process of adjusting the lens elements, like autofocus, takes time, so vibration reduction may contribute to a slight increase in shutter lag. If you're shooting sports, that delay may be annoying, but I still use my VR lenses for sports all the time!

- **Use when appropriate.** You may find that your results are worse when using VR while panning, although newer Nikon VR lenses work fine when the camera is deliberately moved from side to side during exposure. Older lenses can confuse the panning motion with camera wobble and provide too much compensation. You might want to switch off VR when panning or when your camera is mounted on a tripod.

- **Do you need VR at all?** Remember that an inexpensive monopod might be able to provide the same additional steadiness as a VR lens, at a much lower cost. If you're out in the field shooting wild animals or flowers and think a tripod isn't practical, try a monopod first.

The AF-S VR Zoom-Nikkor 70-200mm f/2.8G IF-ED, which I discuss next in terms of its role in the Nikon lens menagerie's ideal "Magic Three" is typical of the VR lenses Nikon offers. It has the basic controls shown in Figure 8.13, to adjust focus range (full, or limited to infinity down to 2.5 meters), VR On/Off, and Normal VR/Active VR (the latter an aggressive mode used in extreme situations, such as a moving car). Not visible (it's over the horizon, so to speak) is the M/A-M focus mode switch, which allows changing from autofocus (with manual override) to manual focus. There's also a focus lock button near the front of the lens (see Figure 8.14). I often use the rotating tripod mount collar as a grip for the lens when shooting hand-held, and, as you can see in Figure 8.15, I've replaced the factory tripod mounting foot with Kirk's Arca-Swiss-compatible quick release mount foot.

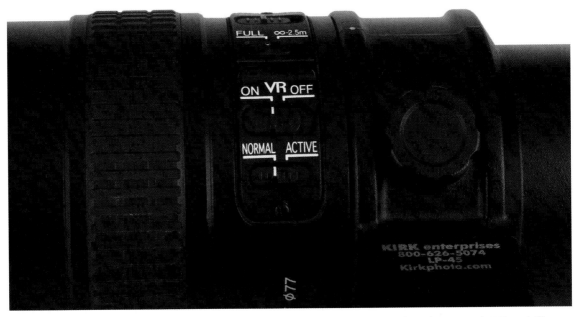

Figure 8.13 On the Nikon 70-200mm VR zoom you'll find (top to bottom): the focus limit switch, VR on/off switch, and Normal/Active VR adjustment.

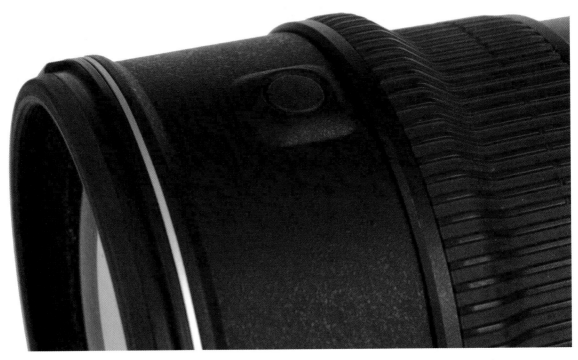

Figure 8.14 The lens also includes an autofocus lock button that can be activated while holding the lens.

Figure 8.15
The rotating collar allows mounting the lens/camera to a tripod in vertical or horizontal orientations— or anything in-between.

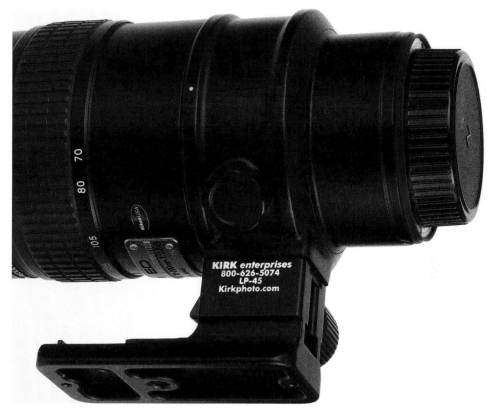

VIBRATION REDUCTION: IN THE CAMERA OR IN THE LENS?

Sony's acquisition of Konica Minolta's dSLR assets and the introduction of an improved in-camera image-stabilization system has revised an old debate about whether VR belongs in the camera or in the lens. Perhaps it's my Nikon bias showing, but I am quite happy not to have vibration reduction available in the body itself. Here are some reasons:

■ Should in-camera VR fail, you have to send the whole camera in for repair, and camera repairs are generally more expensive than lens repairs. I like being able to simply switch to another lens if I have a VR problem.

■ VR in the camera doesn't steady your view in the viewfinder, whereas a VR lens shows you a steadied image as you shoot.

■ You're stuck with the VR system built into your camera. If an improved system is incorporated into a lens and the improvements are important to you, just trade in your old lens for the new one.

Your Second (and Third...) Lens

There are really only two advantages to using just a single lens. One of them is creative. Keeping one set of optics mounted on your D300 all the time forces you to be especially imaginative in your approach to your subjects. I once visited Europe with only a single camera body and a 35mm f/2 lens. The experience was actually quite exciting, because I had to use a variety of techniques to allow that one lens to serve for landscapes, available light photos, action, close-ups, portraits, and other kinds of images.

Of course, it's more likely that your "single" lens is actually a zoom, which is, in truth, many lenses in one, taking you from, say, 16mm to 85mm (or some other range) with a rapid twist of the zoom ring. You'll still find some creative challenges when you stick to a single zoom lens's focal lengths.

The second advantage of the unilens camera is only a marginal technical benefit since the introduction of the Nikon D300. If you don't exchange lenses, the chances of dust and dirt getting inside your D300 and settling on the sensor is reduced (but *not* eliminated entirely). Although I've known some photographers who minimized the number of lens changes they made for this very reason, reducing the number of lenses you work with is not a productive or rewarding approach for most of us. The D300's automatic sensor cleaning feature has made this "advantage" much less significant than it was in the past.

It's more likely that you'll succumb to the malady known as *Lens Lust,* which is defined as an incurable disease marked by a significant yen for newer, better, longer, faster, sharper, anything-er optics for your camera. (And, it must be noted, this disease can *cost* you significant yen—or dollars, or whatever currency you use.) In its worst manifestations, sufferers find themselves with lenses that have overlapping zoom ranges or capabilities, because one or the other offers a slight margin in performance or suitability for specific tasks. When you find yourself already lusting after a new lens before you've really had a chance to put your latest purchase to the test, you'll know the disease has reached the terminal phase.

In this final part of the chapter, I'm going to discuss some specific Nikon lenses that I have experience with, and provide some recommendations. That's not to say that I use only Nikon lenses; I absolutely love my 10-17mm Tokina fisheye zoom lens, and couldn't afford a zoom that reaches all the way out to 500mm if I hadn't been able to pick up my 170-500mm Sigma zoom lens second-hand for an excellent price. But there are so many lens options available that it makes more sense to confine my comments to the true-blue Nikkors that I've had experience with.

The Magic Three

If you cruise the forums, you'll find the same three lenses mentioned over and over, often referred to as "The Trinity," "The Magic Three," or some other affectionate nickname. They are the three lenses you'll find in the kit of just about every serious Nikon photographer (including me). They're fast, expensive, heavier than you might expect, and provide such exquisite image quality that once you equip yourself with the Trinity, you'll never be happy with anything else.

Until, perhaps, now. Nikon has muddied the waters recently by introducing some new lenses that threaten to displace the magic trio. Moreover, D300 owners just might be happier with a triad-plus-one that I'm going to describe.

The Original Magic Three

For a significant number of years, the most commonly-cited "ideal" lenses for "serious" Nikon digital SLRs (meaning the D200 through D2xs) were the 17-35mm f/2.8, 28-70mm f/2.8, and 70-200 f/2.8 VR. The trio share a number of attributes. All three are non-DX lenses that work equally well on film cameras, the Nikon D3, and DX cameras like the D300, making for a sound investment in optics that could be used on any Nikon SLR, past or future. All three incorporate internal Silent Wave motors and focus incredibly fast. They all have f/2.8 maximum apertures that are *constant*; they don't change as the lens is zoomed in or out. All three are internal focusing (IF) models that don't change length as they focus, and include extra-low dispersion (ED) elements. And, all three are expensive, at $1,400-$1,600. But, as I discovered when I added this set, once you have them, you don't need any other lenses unless you're doing field sports like football or soccer, extreme wide-angle, or close-up photography. I generally take these three lenses with me everywhere, adding another lens or two as required for specialized needs.

- **AF-S Zoom-Nikkor 17-35mm f/2.8D IF-ED.** When I am shooting landscapes, doing street photography, or some types of indoor sports, this lens goes on my D300 and never comes off. It was my main lens on my last trip to Europe; I was traveling light and took this one, a 10-17mm Tokina fish-eye zoom, and my 28-200mm Nikkor G lens (in place of my humongous 70-200 VR lens), and didn't need anything else. It's one of the two or three sharpest lenses I own, and focuses down to about 1 foot, so I can use it for close-ups of flowers and other macro subjects. With the DX 1.5X crop factor, it serves as a highly versatile medium wide-angle to normal lens.

- **AF-S Zoom-Nikkor 28-70mm f/2.8D IF-ED.** Nicknamed "The Beast" because of its size and weight, this lens, too, is wonderfully sharp, and well-suited for anything from sports to portraiture that falls within its focal length lens. I know many photographers who aren't heavily into landscapes who use this lens as their main lens. With its impressive lens hood mounted, The Beast is useful for terrifying small children, too.

- **AF-S VR Zoom-Nikkor 70-200mm f/2.8G IF-ED.** This legendary lens is perfect for some indoor and many outdoor sports, on a monopod, or hand-held, and can be used for portraiture, street photography, wildlife (especially with the 1.4X tele-converter), and even distant scenics. I use it for concerts, too, alternating between this lens and my 85mm f/1.8. It takes me in close to the performer, and can be used wide-open or at f/4 with good image quality. The only time I leave it behind is when I need to travel light (although it's not really that huge). This is the only lens of the magic trio that lacks an aperture ring, but you probably won't be using it with a bellows extension, anyway.

To the Original Magic Trio, I often recommend adding one (or both) of these lenses:

- **AF Nikkor 85mm f/1.4D IF.** The nickname of this lens is "The Cream Machine" because of its remarkably smooth bokeh, which provides absolutely gorgeous out-of-focus backgrounds, especially when the lens is used with a wide aperture. It's incredibly sharp, and can definitely be used at f/1.4. The 85mm f/1.4 is the perfect portrait lens, and can be used wide-open without qualms. If you need this sort of lens, it's almost a bargain at its $1,000 price, and worth the extra $600 over its 85mm f/1.8 counterpart. Both Nikon 85mm lenses are D-series AF, rather than G-type AF-S lenses, and are becoming long in the tooth, so you might want to look for one now before they are replaced. I seriously doubt that the introduction of a newer lens will cause the used prices for this wonderful lens to plummet.

- **AF-S DX Zoom-Nikkor 12-24mm f/4G IF-ED.** If you need a slightly wider view than that provided by the Trio's 17-35mm f/2.8, this constant-aperture lens makes a good supplement. It could never replace my 17-35 fave in terms of sharpness and freedom from aberrations, but, since I already own one, I'm keeping it for those times when I want to capture something requiring the field of view of a 12-16mm (or slightly longer) lens. The overlap between this lens and the 17-35mm doesn't bother me; it just means I don't have to swap lenses quite as often. Each will do a little of what the other one is best at. One disadvantage of this lens is that it won't cover the full frame of an FX-format camera like the Nikon D3, so you can't use it effectively if you upgrade in the future.

The New Magic Three

When Nikon introduced the D3 and D300, it also debuted two new lenses, an AF-S Nikkor 14-24mm f/2.8G ED, and an AF-S Nikkor 24-70mm f/2.8G ED lens. Both are G-type lenses (they lack an aperture ring), have AF-S focusing, and have constant f/2.8 apertures. Until Nikon announces a replacement for the 70-200mm VR lens (perhaps one with "upgraded" VRII capabilities), the "old" lens remains in the Magic Trio. Like the original big three, these are all full-frame lenses that work with any DX or FX-format Nikon camera.

The chief advantage of the new lineup (if you can call it that) is that there is no overlap. You can go from 14-24mm to 24-70mm to 70-200mm with no gaps in coverage. I don't find that an overwhelming advantage, because there are lots of situations in which the 17-35mm range of my existing lens is exactly what I need; if I had the "new" trio, I'd find myself swapping lenses whenever I needed more than a 24mm focal length. Carefully consider the focal lengths you need before deciding which "magic" triad is best for you. The new lineup looks like this:

- **AF-S Nikkor 14-24mm f/2.8G ED.** I've shot with this lens, and its image quality is incredible, with very low barrel distortion (outward bowing at the edges) and very little of the chromatic aberrations common to lenses this wide. Because it has full-frame coverage, it's immune to obsolescence. It focuses down to 10.8 inches, allowing for some interesting close-up/wide-angle effects. The downside? The outward curving front element precludes the use of most filters, although I haven't tried this lens with add-on Cokin-style filter holders yet. Lack of filter compatibility isn't a fatal flaw for D300 users, as the use of polarizers would be problematic in any case. The polarizing effect would be highly variable because of this lens's extremely wide field of view.

- **AF-S Nikkor 24-70mm f/2.8G ED.** This lens seems to provide even better image quality than the legendary Beast, especially when used wide open or in flare-inducing environments. (You can credit the new internal Nano Crystal Coat treatment for that improvement.) My recommendation is that if you already own The Beast, or can get one used for a good price ($1,000 or less), you don't sacrifice much going with the older 28-70mm lens, and may find the overlap with the 14-24mm lens useful. But if you have the cash and opportunity to purchase this newer lens, you won't be making a mistake. Some were surprised when it was introduced without the VR feature, but Nikon has kept the size of this useful lens down, while maintaining a reasonable price for a "pro" level lens. Figure 8.16 shows the Beast side-by-side with the new upstart.

- **AF-S VR Zoom-Nikkor 70-200mm f/2.8G IF-ED.** Not a lot to be added about this lens, which is a worthy representative of the telephoto zoom range in this "ideal" trio of lenses.

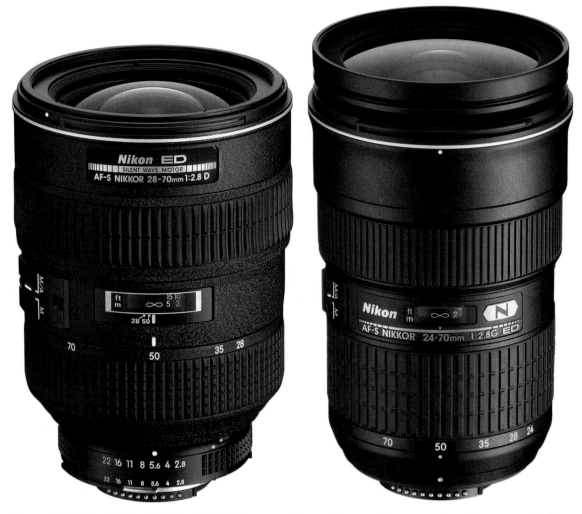

Figure 8.16 The old "Beast" (left), and (right) the newer, slimmer, longer, and just as weighty (about 2 pounds for each lens) 24-70mm f/2.8 zoom from Nikon.

9

Making Light
Work for You

All forms of visual art use light to shape the finished product. Sculptors don't have control over the light used to illuminate their finished work, so they must create shapes using planes and curved surfaces so that the form envisioned by the artist comes to life from a variety of viewing and lighting angles. Painters, in contrast, have absolute control over both shape and light in their work, as well as the viewing angle, so they can use both the contours of their two-dimensional subjects and the qualities of the "light" they use to illuminate those subjects to evoke the image they want to produce.

Photography is a third form of art. The photographer may have little or no control over the subject (other than posing human subjects) but can often adjust both viewing angle *and* the nature of the light source to create a particular compelling image. The direction and intensity of the light sources create the shapes and textures that we see. The distribution and proportions determine the contrast and tonal values: whether the image is stark or high key, or muted and low in contrast. The colors of the light (because even "white" light has a color balance that the sensor can detect), and how much of those colors the subject reflects or absorbs, paint the hues visible in the image.

As a Nikon D300 photographer, you must learn to be a painter and sculptor of light if you want to move from *taking* a picture to *making* a photograph. This chapter provides an introduction to using the two main types of illumination: *continuous* lighting (such as daylight, incandescent, or fluorescent sources) and the brief, but brilliant snippets of light we call *electronic flash*.

Continuous Illumination versus Electronic Flash

Continuous lighting is exactly what you might think: uninterrupted illumination that is available all the time during a shooting session. Daylight, moonlight, and the artificial lighting encountered both indoors and outdoors count as continuous light sources (although all of them can be "interrupted" by passing clouds, solar eclipses, a blown fuse, or simply by switching a lamp off). Indoor continuous illumination includes both the lights that are there already (such as incandescent lamps or overhead fluorescent lights indoors) and fixtures you supply yourself, including photoflood lamps or reflectors used to bounce existing light onto your subject.

The surge of light we call electronic flash is produced by a burst of photons generated by an electrical charge that is accumulated in a component called a *capacitor* and then directed through a glass tube containing xenon gas, which absorbs the energy and emits the brief flash. Electronic flash is notable because it can be much more intense than continuous lighting, lasts only a brief moment, and can be much more portable than supplementary incandescent sources. It's a light source you can carry with you and use anywhere.

Indeed, your Nikon D300 has a flip-up electronic flash unit built in, as shown in Figure 9.1. But you can also use an external flash, either mounted on the D300's accessory shoe or used off-camera and linked with a cable or triggered by the D300's wireless

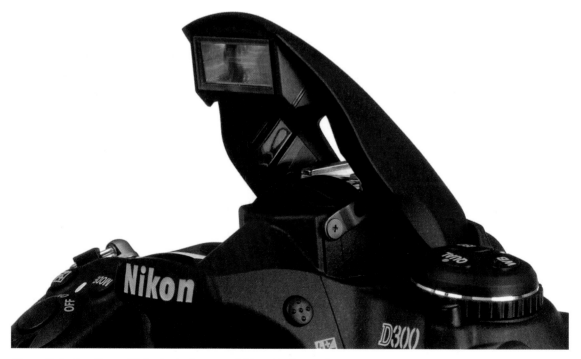

Figure 9.1 One form of light that's always available is the flip-up flash on your Nikon D300.

Commander mode. Studio flash units are electronic flash, too, and aren't limited to "professional" shooters, as there are economical "monolight" (one-piece flash/power supply) units available in the $200 price range. Anyone can buy a couple to store in a closet and use to set up a home studio, or use as supplementary lighting when traveling away from home.

There are advantages and disadvantages to each type of illumination. Here's a quick checklist of pros and cons:

- **Lighting preview—Pro: continuous lighting.** With continuous lighting, you always know exactly what kind of lighting effect you're going to get and, if multiple lights are used, how they will interact with each other. With electronic flash, the general effect you're going to see may be a mystery until you've built some experience, and you may need to review a shot on the LCD, make some adjustments, and then reshoot to get the look you want. (In this sense, a digital camera's review capabilities replace the Polaroid test shots pro photographers relied on in decades past.)

- **Lighting preview—Con: electronic flash.** While the D300's built-in flash and external units like the Nikon SB-800 have a modeling light function (consisting of a series of low-powered bursts that flash for a period of time), this feature is no substitute for continuous illumination, or an always-on modeling lamp like that found in studio flash. As the number of flash units increases, lighting previews, especially if you want to see the proportions of illumination provided by each flash, grows more complex.

- **Exposure calculation—Pro: continuous lighting.** Your D300 has no problem calculating exposure for continuous lighting, because it remains constant and can be measured through the 1005-segment sensor that interprets the light reaching the viewfinder. The amount of light available just before the exposure will, in almost all cases, be the same amount of light present when the shutter is released. The D300's Spot metering mode can be used to measure and compare the proportions of light in the highlights and shadows, so you can make an adjustment (such as using more or less fill light) if necessary. You can even use a hand-held light meter to measure the light yourself.

- **Exposure calculation—Con: electronic flash.** Electronic flash illumination doesn't exist until the flash fires and so can't be measured by the D300's 1005-segment sensor when the mirror is flipped up during the exposure. Instead, the light must be measured by metering the intensity of a preflash triggered an instant before the main flash, as it is reflected back to the camera and through the lens. An alternative is to use a sensor built into the flash itself (which is an option for the Nikon SB-800 unit) and measure reflected light that has not traveled through the lens. If you have a do-it-yourself bent, there are hand-held flash meters, too, including models that measure both flash and continuous light.

- **Evenness of illumination—Pro/con: continuous lighting.** Of continuous light sources, daylight, in particular, provides illumination that tends to fill an image completely, lighting up the foreground, background, and your subject almost equally. Shadows do come into play, of course, so you might need to use reflectors or fill-in light sources to even out the illumination further, but barring objects that block large sections of your image from daylight, the light is spread fairly evenly. Indoors, however, continuous lighting is commonly less evenly distributed. The average living room, for example, has hot spots and dark corners. But on the plus side, you can *see* this uneven illumination and compensate with additional lamps.

- **Evenness of illumination—Con: electronic flash.** Electronic flash units (like continuous light sources such as lamps that don't have the advantage of being located 93 million miles from the subject) suffer from the effects of their proximity. The *inverse square law*, first applied to both gravity and light by Sir Isaac Newton, dictates that as a light source's distance increases from the subject, the amount of light reaching the subject falls off proportionately to the square of the distance. In plain English, that means that a flash or lamp that's eight feet away from a subject provides only one-quarter as much illumination as a source that's four feet away (rather than half as much). This translates into relatively shallow "depth-of-light."

- **Action stopping—Con: continuous lighting.** Action stopping with continuous light sources is completely dependent on the shutter speed you've dialed in on the camera. And the speeds available are dependent on the amount of light available and your ISO sensitivity setting. Outdoors in daylight, there will probably be enough sunlight to let you shoot at 1/2,000 second and f/6.3 with a non-grainy sensitivity setting of ISO 400. That's a fairly useful combination of settings if you're not using a super-telephoto with a small maximum aperture. But inside, the reduced illumination quickly has you pushing your Nikon D300 to its limits. For example, if you're shooting indoor sports, there probably won't be enough available light to allow you to use a 1/2,000th second shutter speed (although I routinely shoot indoor basketball with my D300 at ISO 3200 and 1/1,000 second at f/4). In many indoor sports situations, you may find yourself limited to 1/500 second or slower due to the quality and quantity of the light available.

- **Action stopping—Pro: electronic flash.** When it comes to the ability to freeze moving objects in their tracks, the advantage goes to electronic flash. The brief duration of electronic flash serves as a very high "shutter speed" when the flash is the main or only source of illumination for the photo. Your Nikon D300's shutter speed may be set for 1/250th second during a flash exposure, but if the flash illumination predominates, the *effective* exposure time will be the 1/1,000 to 1/50,000 second or less duration of the flash, as you can see in Figure 9.2, because the flash unit reduces the amount of light released by cutting short the duration of the flash. The only fly in the ointment is that, if the ambient light is strong enough, it may produce a secondary "ghost" exposure, as I'll explain later in this chapter.

Figure 9.2
Electronic flash
can freeze
almost any
action.

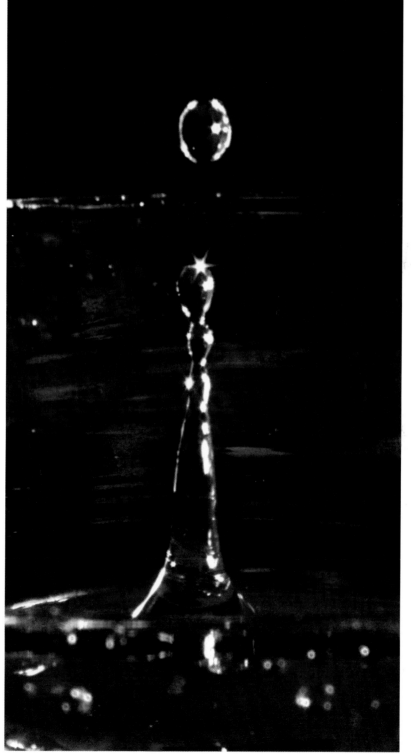

- **Cost—Pro: continuous lighting.** Incandescent or fluorescent lamps are generally much less expensive than electronic flash units, which can easily cost several hundred dollars. I've used everything from desktop hi-intensity lamps to reflector flood lights for continuous illumination at very little cost. There are lamps made especially for photographic purposes, too, priced up to $50 or so. Maintenance is economical, too: many incandescent or fluorescents use bulbs that cost only a few dollars.

- **Cost—Con: electronic flash.** Electronic flash units aren't particularly cheap. The lowest-cost dedicated flash designed specifically for the Nikon dSLRs is the Nikon SB-400 (about $110, plus about $18 for the almost-mandatory diffuser dome). It's limited in features, however, and intended for those with entry-level Nikon cameras. A D300 owner will probably want something like the more powerful and versatile SB-800 (about $315 including the diffuser dome and some filters). Studio flash are priced at $200-$500 and up, and you can also purchase third-party shoe-mount units at prices comparable to the Nikon brand. Plan on spending some money to get the features that electronic flash offers.

- **Flexibility—Con: continuous lighting.** Because incandescent and fluorescent lamps are not as bright as electronic flash, the slower shutter speeds required (see Action stopping, above) mean that you may have to use a tripod more often, especially when shooting portraits. The incandescent variety of continuous lighting gets hot, especially in the studio, and the side effects range from discomfort (for your human models) to disintegration (if you happen to be shooting perishable foods like ice cream). The heat also makes it more difficult to add filtration to incandescent sources.

- **Flexibility—Pro: electronic flash.** Electronic flash's action-freezing power allows you to work without a tripod in the studio (and elsewhere), adding flexibility and speed when choosing angles and positions. Flash units can be easily filtered, and, because the filtration is placed over the light source rather than the lens, you don't need to use high quality filter material. For example a couple sheets of unexposed, processed Ektachrome film can make a dandy infrared-pass filter for your flash unit. Roscoe or Lee lighting gels, which may be too flimsy to use in front of the lens, can be mounted or taped in front of your flash with ease.

Continuous Lighting Basics

While continuous lighting and its effects are generally much easier to visualize and use than electronic flash, there are some factors you need to take into account, particularly the color temperature of the light. (Color temperature concerns aren't exclusive to continuous light sources, of course, but the variations tend to be more extreme and less predictable than those of electronic flash, which output relatively consistent daylight-like illumination.)

Color temperature, in practical terms, is how "bluish" or how "reddish" the light appears to be to the digital camera's sensor. Indoor illumination is quite warm, comparatively, and appears reddish to the sensor. Daylight, in contrast, seems much bluer to the sensor. Our eyes (our brains, actually) are quite adaptable to these variations, so white objects don't appear to have an orange tinge when viewed indoors, nor do they seem excessively blue outdoors in full daylight. Yet, these color temperature variations are real and the sensor is not fooled. To capture the most accurate colors, we need to take the color temperature into account in setting the color balance (or *white balance*) of the D300—either automatically using the camera's smarts or manually using our own knowledge and experience.

The only time you need to think in terms of actual color temperature is when you're making adjustments using the **Choose color temp.** setting in the Shooting menu (which, as described in Chapter 3, allows you to dial in exact color temperatures, if known). So, those occasions are the only times you're likely to be confused by a seeming contradiction in how color temperatures are named: warmer (more reddish) color temperatures (measured in degrees Kelvin) are the *lower* numbers, while cooler (bluer) color temperatures are *higher* numbers. It might not make sense to say that 3,400K is warmer than 6,000K, but that's the way it is. If it helps, think of a glowing red ember contrasted with a white-hot welder's torch, rather than fire and ice.

The confusion comes from physics. Scientists calculate color temperature from the light emitted by a mythical object called a black body radiator, which absorbs all the radiant energy that strikes it, and reflects none at all. Such a black body not only *absorbs* light perfectly, but it *emits* it perfectly when heated (and since nothing in the universe is perfect, that makes it mythical).

At a particular physical temperature, this imaginary object always emits light of the same wavelength or color. That makes it possible to define color temperature in terms of actual temperature in degrees on the Kelvin scale that scientists use. Incandescent light, for example, typically has a color temperature of 3,200K to 3,400K. Daylight might range from 5,500K to 6,000K. Each type of illumination we use for photography has its own color temperature range—with some cautions. The next sections will summarize everything you need to know about the qualities of these light sources.

Daylight

Daylight is produced by the sun, and so is moonlight (which is just reflected sunlight). Daylight is present, of course, even when you can't see the sun. When sunlight is direct, it can be bright and harsh. If daylight is diffused by clouds, softened by bouncing off objects such as walls or your photo reflectors, or filtered by shade, it can be much dimmer and less contrasty.

Daylight's color temperature can vary quite widely. It is highest in temperature (most blue) at noon when the sun is directly overhead, because the light is traveling through a minimum amount of the filtering layer we call the atmosphere. The color temperature at high noon may be 6,000K. At other times of day, the sun is lower in the sky and the particles in the air provide a filtering effect that warms the illumination to about 5,500K for most of the day. Starting an hour before dusk and for an hour after sunrise, the warm appearance of the sunlight is even visible to our eyes when the color temperature may dip to 5,000-4,500K, as shown in Figure 9.3.

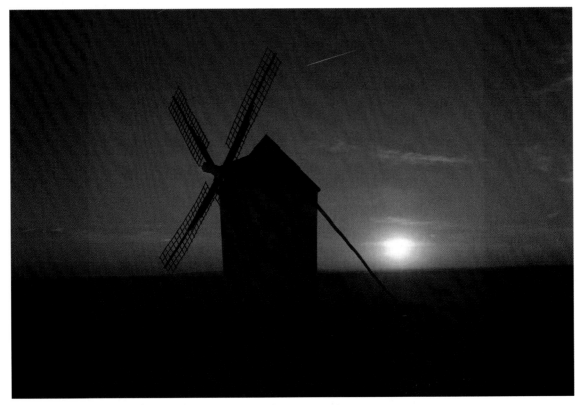

Figure 9.3 At dawn and dusk, the color temperature of daylight may dip as low as 4,500K.

Because you'll be taking so many photos in daylight, you'll want to learn how to use or compensate for the brightness and contrast of sunlight, as well as how to deal with its color temperature. I'll provide some hints later in this chapter.

Incandescent/Tungsten Light

The term incandescent or tungsten illumination is usually applied to the direct descendents of Thomas Edison's original electric lamp. Such lights consist of a glass bulb that contains a vacuum, or is filled with a halogen gas, and contains a tungsten filament that is heated by an electrical current, producing photons and heat. Tungsten-halogen lamps are a variation on the basic light bulb, using a more rugged (and longer-lasting) filament that can be heated to a higher temperature, housed in a thicker glass or quartz envelope, and filled with iodine or bromine ("halogen") gases. The higher temperature allows tungsten-halogen (or quartz-halogen/quartz-iodine, depending on their construction) lamps to burn "hotter" and whiter. Although popular for automobile headlamps today, they've also been used for photographic illumination.

Although incandescent illumination isn't a perfect black body radiator, it's close enough that the color temperature of such lamps can be precisely calculated and used for photography without concerns about color variation (at least, until the very end of the lamp's life).

The other qualities of this type of lighting, such as contrast, are dependent on the distance of the lamp from the subject, type of reflectors used, and other factors that I'll explain later in this chapter.

Fluorescent Light/Other Light Sources

Fluorescent light has some advantages in terms of illumination, but some disadvantages from a photographic standpoint. This type of lamp generates light through an electro-chemical reaction that emits most of its energy as visible light, rather than heat, which is why the bulbs don't get as hot. The type of light produced varies depending on the phosphor coatings and type of gas in the tube. So, the illumination fluorescent bulbs produce can vary widely in its characteristics.

That's not great news for photographers. Different types of lamps have different "color temperatures" that can't be precisely measured in degrees Kelvin, because the light isn't produced by heating. Worse, fluorescent lamps have a discontinuous spectrum of light that can have some colors missing entirely. A particular type of tube can lack certain shades of red or other colors (see Figure 9.4), which is why fluorescent lamps and other alternative technologies such as sodium-vapor illumination can produce ghastly looking human skin tones. Their spectra can lack the reddish tones we associate with healthy skin and emphasize the blues and greens popular in horror movies.

Adjusting White Balance

I showed you how to adjust white balance in Chapter 3, using the D300's built-in presets, white balance shift capabilities, setting exact color temperatures, and white balance bracketing (there's more on bracketing in Chapter 6, too).

In most cases, however, the Nikon D300 will do a good job of calculating white balance for you, so Auto can be used as your choice most of the time. Use the preset values or set a custom white balance that matches the current shooting conditions when you need to. The only really problematic light sources are likely to be fluorescents.

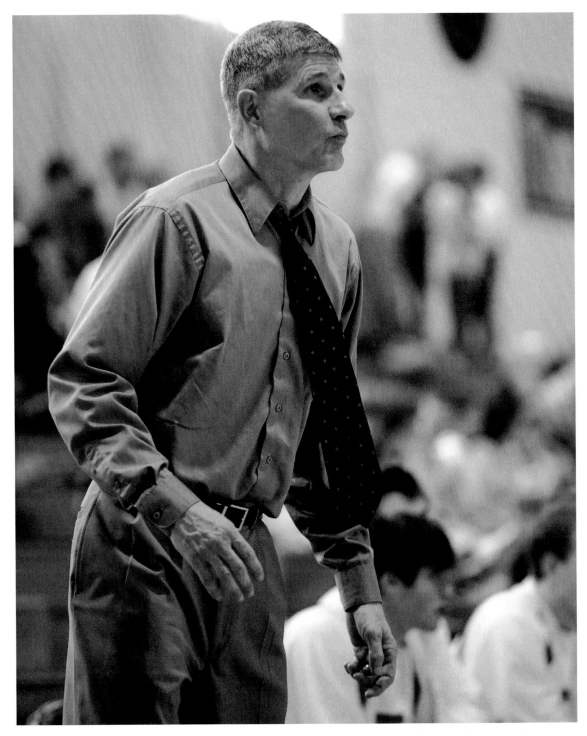

Figure 9.4 The uncorrected fluorescent lighting in the room added a distinct greenish cast to this image when exposed with a daylight white balance setting.

Vendors, such as GE and Sylvania, may actually provide a figure known as the *color rendering index* (or CRI), which is a measure of how accurately a particular light source represents standard colors, using a scale of 0 (some sodium-vapor lamps) to 100 (daylight and most incandescent lamps). Daylight fluorescents and deluxe cool white fluorescents might have a CRI of about 79 to 95, which is perfectly acceptable for most photographic applications. Warm white fluorescents might have a CRI of 55. White deluxe mercury vapor lights are less suitable with a CRI of 45, while low-pressure sodium lamps can vary from CRI 0-18.

Remember that if you shoot RAW, you can specify the white balance of your image when you import it into Photoshop, Photoshop Elements, or another image editor using Nikon Capture NX, Adobe Camera RAW, or your preferred RAW converter. While color-balancing filters that fit on the front of the lens exist, they are primarily useful for film cameras, because film's color balance can't be tweaked as extensively as that of a sensor.

Electronic Flash Basics

Until you delve into the situation deeply enough, it might appear that serious photographers have a love/hate relationship with electronic flash. You'll often hear that flash photography is less natural looking, and that the built-in flash in most cameras should never be used as the primary source of illumination because it provides a harsh, garish look. Indeed, the most advanced "pro" cameras like the Nikon D2xs and D3 don't have a built-in flash at all. Available ("continuous") lighting is praised, and built-in flash photography seems to be roundly denounced.

In truth, however, the bias is against *bad* flash photography. Indeed, flash has become the studio light source of choice for pro photographers, because it's more intense (and its intensity can be varied to order by the photographer), freezes action, frees you from using a tripod (unless you want to use one to lock down a composition), and has a snappy, consistent light quality that matches daylight. (While color balance changes as the flash duration shortens, some Nikon flash units can communicate to the camera the exact white balance provided for that shot.) And even pros will cede that the built-in flash of the Nikon D300 has some important uses as an adjunct to existing light, particularly to fill in dark shadows.

But electronic flash isn't as inherently easy to use as continuous lighting. As I noted earlier, electronic flash units are more expensive, don't show you exactly what the lighting effect will be (unless you use a second source or mode called a *modeling light* for a preview), and the exposure of electronic flash units is more difficult to calculate accurately.

For the pop-up flash built into the Nikon D300, the full burst of light lasts about 1/1,000th and provides enough illumination to shoot a subject 10 feet away at f/5.6

using the ISO 200 setting. As you can see, the built-in flash is somewhat limited in range; you'll realize why external flash units are often a good idea later in this chapter.

An electronic flash (whether built in or connected to the Nikon D300 through a cable or the hot shoe or fired wirelessly) is triggered at the instant of exposure, during a period when the sensor is fully exposed by the shutter. As I mentioned earlier in this book, the D300 has a vertically traveling shutter that consists of two curtains. The first curtain opens and moves to the opposite side of the frame, at which point the shutter is completely open. The flash can be triggered at this point (so-called *front-curtain sync*), making the flash exposure. Then, after a delay that can vary from 30 seconds to 1/250th second (with the Nikon D300; other cameras may sync at a faster or slower speed), a second curtain begins moving across the sensor plane, covering up the sensor again. If the flash is triggered just before the second curtain starts to close, then *second-curtain sync* is used. (I'll describe these in more detail later in this chapter.) In both cases, though, a shutter speed of 1/250th second is ordinarily the maximum that can be used to take a photo. If you use a faster shutter speed, you'll expose only the part of the sensor exposed by the gap between the shutter curtains when the flash fires.

Determining Exposure

Calculating the proper exposure for an electronic flash photograph is a bit more complicated than determining the settings for continuous light. The right exposure isn't simply a function of how far away your subject is (which the D300 can figure out based on the autofocus distance that's locked in just prior to taking the picture). Various objects reflect more or less light at the same distance so, obviously, the camera needs to measure the amount of light reflected back and through the lens. Yet, as the flash itself isn't available for measuring until it's triggered, the D300 has nothing to measure.

The solution is to fire the flash twice. The initial shot is a *monitor preflash* that can be analyzed, then followed virtually instantaneously by a main flash (to the eye the bursts appear to be a single flash) that's given exactly the calculated intensity needed to provide a correct exposure. As a result, the primary flash may be longer in duration for distant objects and shorter in duration for closer subjects, depending on the required intensity for exposure. This through-the-lens evaluative flash exposure system is called i-TTL (intelligent Through The Lens), and it operates whenever the pop-up internal flash is used, or you have attached a Nikon dedicated flash unit to the D300.

Guide Numbers

Guide numbers, usually abbreviated GN, are a way of specifying the power of an electronic flash in a way that can be used to determine the right f/stop to use at a particular shooting distance and ISO setting. In fact, before automatic flash units became prevalent, the GN was actually used to do just that. A GN is usually given as a pair of numbers for both feet and meters that represent the range at ISO 100. For example, the Nikon D300's built-in flash has a GN in i-TTL mode of 17/56 (meters/feet) at ISO 200. In Manual mode, the true guide number is a fraction higher: 18/59 meters/feet. To calculate the right exposure at that ISO setting, you'd divide the guide number by the distance to arrive at the appropriate f/stop.

Using the D300's built-in flash as an example, at ISO 200 with its GN of 56, if you wanted to shoot a subject at a distance of 10 feet, you'd use f/5.6 (56 divided by 10). At 5 feet, an f/stop of f/11 would be used. Some quick mental calculations with the GN will give you any particular electronic flash's range. You can easily see that the built-in flash would begin to peter out at about 20 feet, where you'd need an aperture of f/2.8 at ISO 200. Of course, in the real world you'd probably bump the sensitivity up to a setting of ISO 800 so you could use a more practical f/5.6 at that distance.

Today, guide numbers are most useful for comparing the power of various flash units, rather than actually calculating what exposure to use. You don't need to be a math genius to see that an electronic flash with a GN in feet of, say, 174 (like the SB-800) would be *a lot* more powerful than your built-in flash. At ISO 200, you could use f/9 instead of f/2.8 at 20 feet, an improvement of about 3.5 stops.

A Typical Electronic Flash Sequence

Here's what happens when you take a photo using electronic flash, either the unit built into the Nikon D300 or an external flash like the Nikon SB-800:

1. **Sync mode.** Choose the flash sync mode by holding down the Flash button and rotating the main command dial until the icon representing the choice you want is displayed in the top panel monochrome LCD. (See Figure 9.5.)

2. **Metering method.** Choose the metering method you want, from Matrix, Center-Weighted, or Spot metering.

3. **Activate flash.** Press the flash pop-up button to flip up the built-in flash, or mount (or connect with a cable) an external flash and turn it on. A ready light appears in the viewfinder and on the back of an external flash when the unit is ready to take a picture.

4. **Check exposure.** Select a shutter speed when using Manual, Program, or Shutter Priority modes; select an aperture when using Aperture Priority and Manual exposure modes.

5. **Preview lighting.** If you want to preview the lighting effect, press the depth-of-field button to produce a modeling flash burst (unless you've redefined this control in the Custom Setting menu as described in Chapter 4).

6. **Lock flash setting (if desired).** Optionally, if the main subject is located significantly off-center, you can frame so the subject is centered, lock the flash at the exposure needed to illuminate that subject, and then reframe using the composition you want. Lock the flash level using the Flash Value Lock button (which can be assigned to the Fn, Preview, or AE-L/AF-L buttons in **CSM #f4, CSM #f5,** or **CSM #f6**). Press the FV lock button, and the flash will emit a preflash to determine the correct flash level, and then the D300 will lock the flash at that level until you press the FV lock button again to release it. FV lock icons appear in the monochrome LCD status panel and the viewfinder.

7. **Take photo.** Press the shutter release down all the way.

8. **D300 receives distance data.** A D- or G-series lens now supplies focus distance to the D300.

9. **Preflash emitted.** The internal flash, if used, or external flash sends out one or two preflash bursts. One burst can be used to control additional wireless flash units in Commander mode, while one burst is used to determine exposure.

10. **Exposure calculated.** The preflash bounces back and is measured by the 1005-pixel RGB sensor in the viewfinder. It measures brightness and contrast of the image to calculate exposure. If you're using Matrix metering, the D300 evaluates the scene to determine whether the subject may be backlit (for fill flash), or a subject that requires extra ambient light exposure to balance the scene with the flash exposure, or classifies the scene in some other way. The camera to subject information as well as the degree of sharp focus of the subject matter is used to locate subject within the frame. If you've selected Spot metering, only standard i-TTL (without balanced fill-flash) is used.

11. **Mirror up.** The mirror flips up. At this point exposure and focus are locked in.

12. **Flash fired.** At the correct triggering moment (depending on whether front or rear sync is used), camera sends a signal to one or more flashes to start flash discharge. The flash is quenched as soon as the correct exposure has been achieved.

13. **Shutter closes.** The shutter closes and mirror flips down. You're ready to take another picture. Remember to press the FV lock button again to release the flash exposure if your next shot will use a different composition.

14. **Exposure confirmed.** Ordinarily, the full charge in the flash may not be required. If the flash indicator in the viewfinder blinks for about three seconds after the exposure, that means that the entire flash charge was required, and it *could* mean that the full charge wasn't enough for a proper exposure. Be sure to review your image on the LCD to make sure it's not underexposed, and, if it is, make adjustments (such as increasing the ISO setting of the D300) to remedy the situation.

Choosing a Flash Sync Mode

The Nikon D300 has five flash sync modes, selected by holding down the Flash button while rotating the main command dial. (See Figure 9.5 again for the icons.) Those modes (which I've listed in logical order, so the explanation will make more sense, rather than the order in which they appear during the selection cycle) are as follows:

■ **Front-curtain sync.** This setting should be your default setting. In this mode the flash fires as soon as the front curtain opens completely. The shutter then remains open for the duration of the exposure, until the rear curtain closes. If the subject is moving and ambient light levels are high enough, the movement will cause a secondary "ghost" exposure that appears in front of the flash exposure.

■ **Rear-curtain sync.** With this setting, which can be used with Shutter Priority, Aperture Priority, Program, or Manual exposure modes, the front curtain opens completely and remains open for the duration of the exposure. Then, the flash is fired and the rear curtain closes. If the subject is moving and ambient light levels are high enough, the movement will cause a secondary "ghost" exposure that appears behind the flash exposure (trailing it). You'll find more on "ghost" exposures next. In Program and Aperture Priority modes, the D300 will combine rear curtain sync with slow shutter speeds (just like slow sync, discussed below) to balance ambient light with flash illumination. (It's best to use a tripod to avoid blur at these slow shutter speeds.)

■ **Red-eye reduction.** In this mode, there is a one-second lag after pressing the shutter release before the picture is actually taken, during which the D300's red-eye reduction lamp lights, causing the subject's pupils to contract (assuming they are looking at the camera), and thus reducing potential red-eye effects. Don't use with moving subjects or when you can't abide the delay.

Figure 9.5
Icons for flash sync modes include front sync (top left), rear sync (top middle), red-eye reduction (top right), slow sync (lower left), and slow sync with red-eye reduction (lower right).

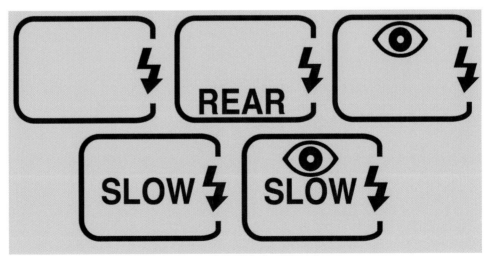

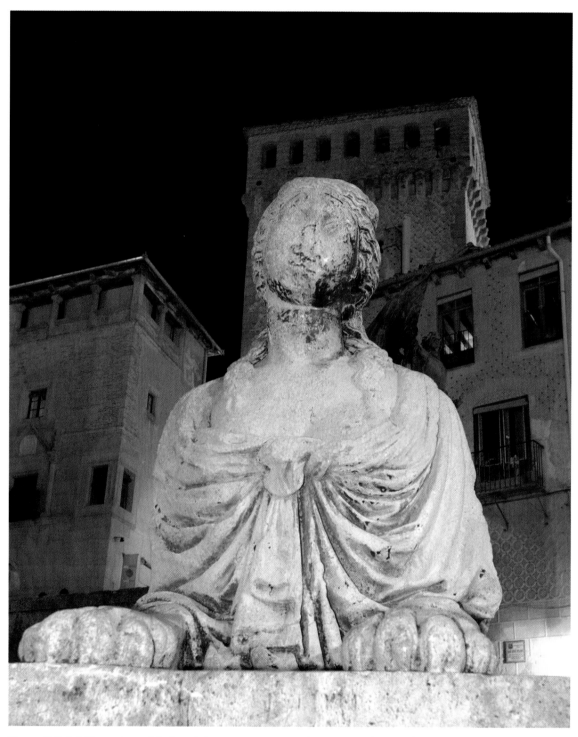

Figure 9.6 I deliberately used flash and slow-sync to separate this Roman sphinx sculpture (lined in bluish light from the flash) from the background illuminated by warmer incandescents.

- **Slow sync.** This setting allows the D300 in Program and Aperture Priority modes to use shutter speeds as slow as 30 seconds with the flash to help balance a background illuminated with ambient light with your main subject, which will be lit by the electronic flash. You'll want to use a tripod at slower shutter speeds, of course. As shown in Figure 9.6, it's common that the ambient light will be incandescent illumination that's much warmer than the electronic flash's "daylight" balance, so, if you want the two sources to match, you may want to use a warming filter on the flash. That can be done with a gel if you're using an external flash like the SB-800, or by taping an appropriate warm filter over the D300's built-in flash. (That's not a convenient approach, and many find the warm/cool mismatch unobjectionable and don't bother with filtration.)

- **Red-eye reduction with slow sync.** This mode combines slow sync with the D300's red-eye reduction behavior when using Program or Aperture Priority modes.

Ghost Images

The difference might not seem like much, but whether you use first-curtain sync (the default setting) or rear-curtain sync (an optional setting) can make a significant difference to your photograph *if the ambient light in your scene also contributes to the image.* At faster shutter speeds, particularly 1/250th second, there isn't much time for the ambient light to register, unless it is very bright. It's likely that the electronic flash will provide almost all the illumination, so first-curtain sync or second-curtain sync isn't very important.

However, at slower shutter speeds, or with very bright ambient light levels, there is a significant difference, particularly if your subject is moving, or the camera isn't steady. In any of those situations, the ambient light will register as a second image accompanying the flash exposure, and if there is movement (camera or subject), that additional image will not be in the same place as the flash exposure. It will show as a ghost image and, if the movement is significant enough, as a blurred ghost image trailing in front of or behind your subject in the direction of the movement.

As I mentioned earlier, when you're using first-curtain sync, the flash goes off the instant the shutter opens, producing an image of the subject on the sensor. Then, the shutter remains open for an additional period (which can be from 30 seconds to 1/250th second). If your subject is moving, say, towards the right side of the frame, the ghost image produced by the ambient light will produce a blur on the right side of the original subject image, making it look as if your sharp (flash-produced) image is chasing the ghost. For those of us who grew up with lightning-fast superheroes who always left a ghost trail *behind them*, that looks unnatural (see Figure 9.7).

So, Nikon provides rear (second) curtain sync to remedy the situation. In that mode, the shutter opens, as before. The shutter remains open for its designated duration, and

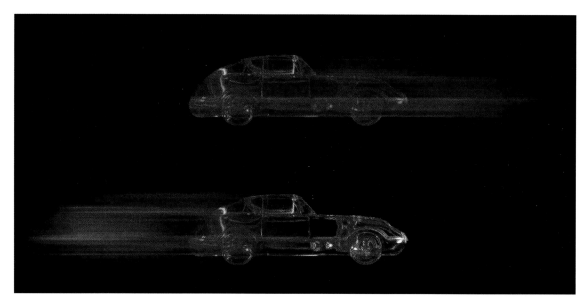

Figure 9.7 Front curtain sync produces an image that trails in front of the flash exposure (top), while rear-curtain sync creates a more "natural looking" trail behind the flash image (bottom).

the ghost image forms. If your subject moves from the left side of the frame to the right side, the ghost will move from left to right, too. *Then*, about 1.5 milliseconds before the second shutter curtain closes, the flash is triggered, producing a nice, sharp flash image *ahead* of the ghost image. Voilà! We have monsieur *le Flash* outrunning his own trailing image.

EVERY WHICH WAY, INCLUDING UP

Note that, although I describe the ghost effect in terms of subject matter that is moving left to right in a horizontally oriented composition, it can occur in any orientation, and with the subject moving in *any* direction. (Try photographing a falling rock, if you can, and you'll see the same effect.) Nor are the ghost images affected by the fact that modern shutters travel vertically rather than horizontally. Secondary images are caused between the time the first curtain fully opens, and the second curtain begins to close. The direction of travel of the shutter curtains, or the direction of your subject does not matter.

High-Speed (FP) Sync

Triggering the electronic flash only when the shutter is completely open makes a lot of sense if you think about what's going on. To obtain shutter speeds faster than 1/250th second, the D300 exposes only part of the sensor at one time, by starting the second curtain on its journey before the first curtain has completely opened. That effectively provides a briefer exposure as a slit of passes over the surface of the sensor. If the flash were to fire during the time when the first and second curtains partially obscured the sensor, only the area defined by the slit that was actually open would be exposed.

However, the D300 and certain Nikon flashes provide a partial solution, called *high-speed sync* or *FP sync* (focal plane sync). Those flash units can fire a series of flashes consecutively in rapid succession, producing the illusion of a longer continuous flash, although at reduced intensity. These multiple flashes have a duration long enough to allow exposing the area of the sensor revealed by the traveling slit as it makes its full pass. However, the reduced intensity means that your flash's range is greatly reduced.

This technique is most useful outdoors when you need fill-in flash, but find that 1/250 second is way too slow for the f/stop you want to use. For example, at ISO 200, an outdoors exposure is likely to be 1/250 second at, say, f/14, which is perfectly fine for an ambient/balanced fill-flash exposure if you don't mind the extreme depth-of-field offered by the small f/stop. But, what if you'd rather shoot at 1/1,600 second at f/5.6? High-speed sync will let you do that, and you probably won't mind the reduced flash power, because you're looking for fill flash, anyway. This sync mode offers more flexibility than, say, dropping down to L 1.0 (ISO 100 equivalent).

To use auto FP sync with units like the Nikon SB-800, SB-600, and SB-R200, there is no setting to make on the flash itself. You need to use **CSM #e1** to specify either **1/320 s (Auto FP)** or **1/250 s (Auto FP)**. When either of those settings is activated and a compatible external flash is attached, higher shutter speeds can be used with full synchronization, at reduced flash output.

Working with Nikon Flash Units

If you want to work with dedicated Nikon flash units, at this time you have five choices—the D300's built-in flash, the Nikon SB-800, SB-600, SB-400 on-camera flash units, and the SB-R200 wireless remote flash. These share certain features, which I'll discuss while pointing out differences among them. Nikon may introduce additional flash units during the life of this book, but the current batch and the Nikon Creative Lighting System ushered in with them were significant steps forward, so I don't expect any major changes in the near future.

Nikon D300 Built-in Flash

The built-in flash has a guide number of 17/56 (meters/feet) and must be activated by manually flipping it up (Nikon entry-level cameras have modes that will pop up the flash for you when it's needed.) This flash is powerful enough to provide primary direct flash illumination when required, but can't be angled up for diffuse bounce flash off the ceiling. It's useful for balanced fill flash (more on that later) and for use in Commander mode, which allows the built-in flash to trigger one or more off-camera flash units in up to four separate groups wirelessly. You can use **CSM #e3** to dial down the intensity of the built-in flash to 1/128 power so that, in Commander mode, it will activate off-camera flash units but not contribute much (if at all) to the exposure. The built-in flash also has useful modeling light and repeating flash modes, which will be described later in this chapter.

Because the built-in flash draws its power from the D300's battery, extensive use will reduce the power available to take pictures. For that reason alone, use of an external flash unit can be a good idea when you plan to take a lot of flash pictures.

Nikon SB-800

The Nikon SB-800 (see Figure 9.8) is currently the flagship of the Nikon flash line up, and has a guide number of 53/174 (meters/feet), which makes it about 3.5 times more powerful than the D300's built-in flash. It has all the features of the D300's flash unit, including Commander mode, repeating flash, modeling light, and selectable power output, along with some extra capabilities.

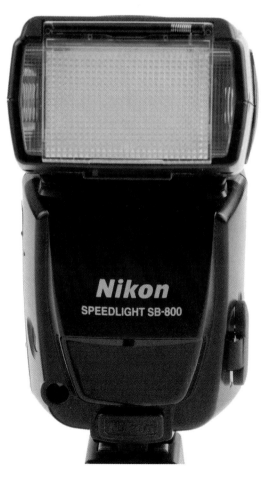

Figure 9.8
The Nikon SB-800 is currently the flagship of the Nikon electronic flash line up.

For example, you can angle the flash and rotate it to provide bounce flash. It includes additional, non-through-the lens exposure modes, thanks to its built-in light sensor, and can "zoom" and diffuse its coverage angle to illuminate the field of view of lenses from 16mm to 70mm on a D300 (24mm to 105mm on a full-frame camera), plus 14mm with an included diffuser. The SB-800 also has its own powerful focus assist lamp to aid autofocus in dim lighting, and has reduced red-eye effects simply because the unit, when attached to the D300, is mounted in a higher position that tends to eliminate reflections from the eye back to the camera lens. Other specifics include:

- **Multiple flash exposure modes.** In addition to i-TTL mode, the SB-800 has AA (auto aperture) exposure mode, in which the flash unit reads the light reflected back from the subject to a sensor on the flash. There is a Manual mode to allow you to set flash levels yourself. It also has D-TTL mode for use with older Nikon D1 and D100 cameras, a TTL Auto Flash mode for many Nikon film cameras, and an A (automatic) mode compatible with the Nikon N55/F55 and FM10 film cameras.

- **Flash groups.** In Advanced Wireless Lighting mode, you can use the SB-800 to control up to four groups of flash units (as you can with the built-in flash) and choose a flash exposure mode (i-TTL, AA, A, or M) individually for each of the four groups.

- **Bounce capability.** The SB-800's flash head tilts down –7 degrees or up 90 degrees, and rotates horizontally 180 degrees to the left and 90 degrees to the right for versatile bounce flash effects. There's a pop-up "white card" that reflects some fill light back to the subject to soften shadows or provide a catch light in the eye when the unit is bounced off the ceiling.

- **Distance Priority Manual mode.** Set the distance and aperture, and the SB-800 automatically adjusts the power output to a setting appropriate for that f/stop and subject distance.

- **Backlit illuminated LCD control panel.** Features of the SB-800 can be set using an array of buttons and a large, informative backlit LCD display.

- **Add Ons.** The SB-800 is furnished with a Sto-Fen-style clip on diffuser dome, and several gel filters to adjust the flash color output for tungsten and fluorescent illumination (so you don't accidentally mix the flash's "blue" lighting with the ambient incandescent or fluorescent lighting). There is also a battery holder for a fifth AA battery, which can speed up recycling time and extend battery life by about 20 percent.

Nikon SB-600

This lower-cost unit (see Figure 9.9) has a guide number of 42/138 (meters/feet) when set to the 35mm zoom position. It has many of the SB-800's features, including zoomable flash coverage equal to the field of view of a 16-56mm lens on the D300 (24-85mm settings with a full-frame camera), and 14mm with a built-in diffuser panel. It has a built-in modeling flash feature, but lacks repeating flash, accessory filters, and an included flash diffuser dome, which can be purchased separately. Other differences include:

■ **Multiple flash exposure modes.** The SB-600 does not offer AA or A automatic, non-TTL exposure modes, but does support i-TTL, D-TTL (for the Nikon D1 series and D100), TTL Auto Flash for many Nikon film cameras, and Manual flash modes. (Output can be varied only from 1/1 to 1/64 power.)

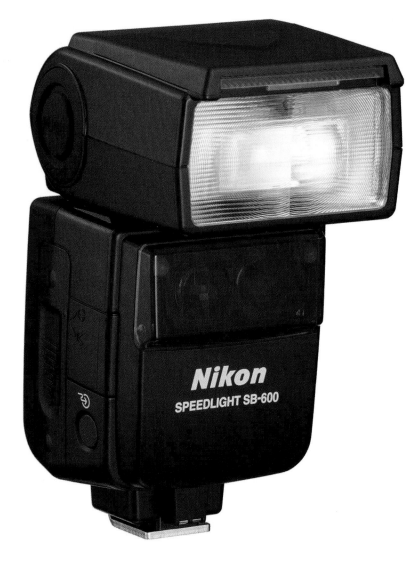

Figure 9.9
The Nikon SB-600 is a popular medium-priced electronic flash with most of the features of the SB-800, except for Commander mode to control remote units.

- **Flash groups.** The SB-600 cannot function in Commander mode to control other Nikon flash units, but it can serve as a slave unit triggered by a commander as part of a flash group.

- **Bounce capability.** The flash head tilts upwards up to 90 degrees, plus 180 degrees to the left or 90 degrees to the right.

Nikon SB-400

The entry-level SB-400 (see Figure 9.10) really isn't suitable for most Nikon D300 applications, but I am including it to round out the discussion. It's intended for entry-level Nikon cameras like the D40 or D60, and has limited features. While it does offer i-TTL exposure functions, it can be used in Manual mode only on the D40, and has a limited guide number of 30/98 at the 18mm zoom-head position. It tilts up for bounce flash to 90 degrees, with click detents at the 0, 60, 75, and 90 degree marks. Unless you feel the need for an emergency flash or fill-flash unit that's only slightly more powerful than the D300's built-in flash, you'll probably be happier with something more sophisticated.

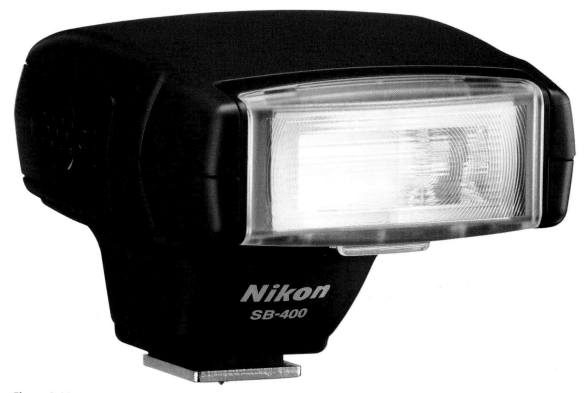

Figure 9.10 The Nikon SB-400 is an entry-level flash best suited for Nikon's entry-level dSLRs.

Nikon SB-R200

This is a specialized wireless-only flash (see Figure 9.11) that's especially useful for close-up photography, and is often purchased in pairs for use with the Nikon R1 and R1C1 Wireless Close-Up Speedlight systems. Its output power is low at 14/46 (meters/feet) as you might expect for a unit used to photograph subjects that are often inches from the camera. It has a fixed coverage angle of 78 degrees horizontal and 60 degrees vertical, but the flash head tilts down up to 60 degrees and up to 45 degrees (with detents every 15 degrees in both directions). In this case, "up" and "down" has a different meaning, because the SB-R200 can be mounted on the SX-1 Attachment Ring mounted around the lens, so the pair of flash units are on the sides and titled towards or away from the optical axis. It supports i-TTL, D-TTL, TTL (for film cameras), and Manual modes.

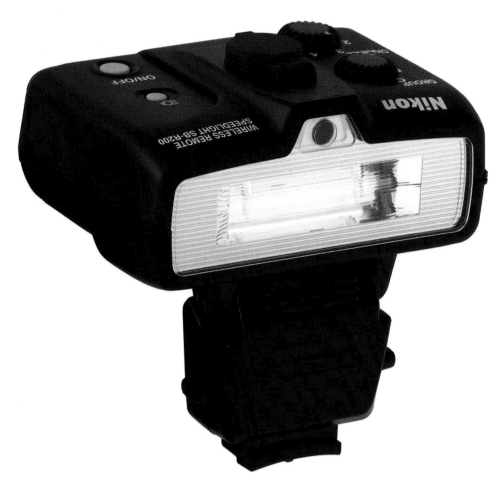

Figure 9.11

The Nikon SB-R200 is a wireless macro-only flash supplied with the Nikon R1 and R1C1 Wireless Close-Up Speedlight systems.

Flash Techniques

This next section will discuss using specific features of the Nikon D300's built-in flash, as well as those of the Nikon dedicated external flash units. It's not possible to discuss every possible feature and setting of the external flash units in this chapter (entire books have been written to do that), so I'll simply provide an overview here.

Using the Zoom Head

External flash zoom heads can adjust themselves automatically to match lens focal lengths in use reported by the D300 to the flash unit, or you can adjust the zoom head position manually. Automatic zoom adjustment wastes some of your flash's power, because the flash unit assumes that the focal length reported comes from a full-frame camera. Because of the 1.5X crop factor, the flash coverage when the flash is set to a particular focal length will be wider than is required by the D300's cropped image. You can manually adjust the zoom position yourself, using positions built into the flash unit that more closely correspond to your D300's field of view. Table 9.1 shows the actual focal length of a lens (or focal length position of a zoom lens) in the left column, with the closest zoom head position on the flash unit in the right column. Note that only the SB-800 has a 105mm zoom position, which is appropriate when using an 85mm lens on a Nikon D300.

Table 9.1 Zoom Head Equivalents for DX		
Lens Focal Length	**Zoom head position**	
14mm	20mm	
18mm	24mm	
20mm	28mm	
24mm	35mm	
28mm	50mm	
35mm	50mm	
50mm	50mm	
70mm	85mm	
85mm	105mm	*Available with SB-800 only.

To set the zoom position manually, follow one of these steps:

- **SB-800.** Press the Wide button on the selector pad (indicated by the "three trees" icon) to zoom wider, or the single tree icon to zoom to a more telephoto position. A small M appears above the Zoom indicator in the lower-left corner of the LCD. To cancel the manual zoom setting, press the buttons until the zoom setting corresponds to the actual focal length set on the lens. Figure 9.12 shows the controls on the back of the SB-800.

- **SB-600.** Press the Zoom button and adjust zoom position manually. M appears above Zoom in the LCD. To cancel manual zoom, press the zoom button until it matches the focal length set on the lens.

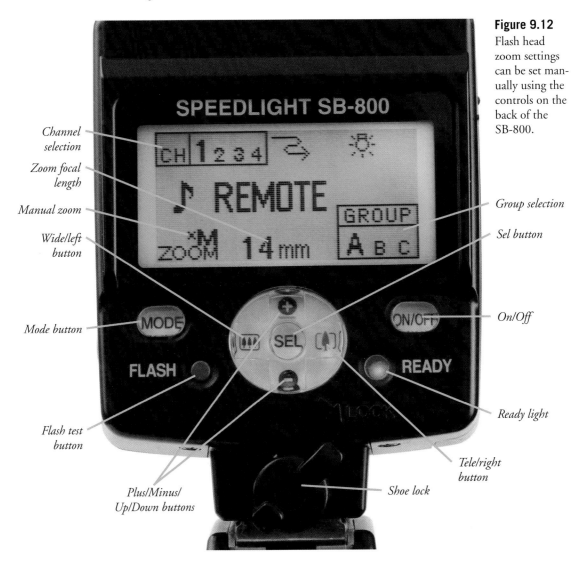

Figure 9.12
Flash head zoom settings can be set manually using the controls on the back of the SB-800.

Channel selection

Zoom focal length

Manual zoom

Wide/left button

Mode button

Flash test button

Plus/Minus/ Up/Down buttons

Group selection

Sel button

On/Off

Ready light

Tele/right button

Shoe lock

Flash Modes

The external flash units have various flash modes included, which are available or not available with different camera models, categorized into nine different groups. A table showing most of the groups is included in the manuals for the external flash units, but the table is irrelevant for D300 users (unless you happen to own an older digital or film SLR). For digital cameras, there are two main groups: digital cameras *not* compatible with the Nikon Creative Lighting System (Nikon D1-series cameras, and the Nikon D100), and digital cameras that *are* compatible with CLS (including the D300). Groups I through VII, which support various combinations of features, consist of various film SLRs.

The TTL automatic flash modes available for the SB-600 and SB-800 are as follows:

- **i-TTL.** This intelligent through the lens (i-TTL) mode provides all the features available with the Nikon Creative Lighting System for compatible cameras. Use i-TTL BL (shown on the flash unit as TTL BL) when you want a balanced exposure of the main subject and background. Use Standard i-TTL (shown on the flash unit as TTL) to expose only for the subject, regardless of the brightness of the background.

- **D-TTL.** This mode (Digital TTL) can be used with digital SLRs that are not compatible with CLS (Nikon D1-series and D100).

- **TTL.** This is a TTL mode for film cameras in camera groups 1 to VI (but balanced fill flash is not available with cameras in Groups III and IV).

The Nikon SB-800 also has non-TTL automatic modes, and manual modes not possible with the SB-600. The manual mode repeating flash modes listed below (the last two shown) are also available with the D300's built-in flash unit.

- **AA.** Auto Aperture flash. The SB-800 uses a built-in light sensor to measure the amount of flash illumination reflected back from the subject, and adjusts the output to produce an appropriate exposure based on the ISO, aperture, focal length, and flash compensation values set on the D300. This setting on the flash can be used with the D300 in Program or Aperture Priority modes.

- **A.** Non-TTL auto flash. The SB-800's sensor measures the flash illumination reflected back from the subject, and adjusts the output to provide an appropriate exposure. This setting on the flash can be used when the D300 is set to Aperture Priority or Manual modes. You can use this setting to manually "bracket" exposures, as adjusting the aperture value of the lens will produce more or less exposure.

- **GN.** Distance priority manual. You enter a distance value, and the SB-800 adjusts light output based on distance, ISO, and aperture to produce the right exposure in either Aperture Priority or Manual exposure modes. Press the Mode button on the flash until the GN indicator appears, then press the SEL button to highlight the distance display, using the plus and minus buttons to enter the distance value you want (from 1 to 65.6 feet, or 0.3 to 20 meters). The SB-800 will indicate a recommended aperture, which you then set on the lens mounted on the D300.

- **M.** Manual flash. The flash fires at a fixed output level. Press the MODE button until M appears on the SB-800's LCD panel. Press the SEL button and the plus or minus buttons to increase or decrease the output value of the flash. Use the table in the flash manual to determine a suggested aperture setting for a given distance. Then, set that aperture on the D300 in either Aperture Priority or Manual exposure modes. (You can also use manual flash with the D300's built-in unit by choosing a flash level in CSM #e3, as described in Chapter 4, and calculating the appropriate aperture.) (Good luck. I use test shots to calculate the f/stop, myself.)

- **RPT.** Repeating flash. The flash fires repeatedly to produce a multiple flash strobing effect. To use this mode, set the D300's exposure mode to Manual. Then set up the number of repeating flashes per frame, frequency, and flash output level, as described in Chapter 4. When using the D300's built-in flash, use CSM #e3; with the SB-800, press the MODE button to display RPT, then the SEL button to highlight the flash output level display. Use the plus and minus buttons to increase or decrease the flash output, and then press the SEL button again to use the plus/minus buttons to adjust the frequency and number of repeating flashes per frame.

BURN OUT

When using repeating flash with the built-in flash or the SB-800, or *any* large number of consecutive flashes in any mode (more than about 15 shots at full power), allow the flash to cool off (Nikon recommends a 10 minute time out) to avoid overheating the flash.

Working with Wireless Commander Mode

The D300's built-in flash can be set to Commander mode (as described in Chapter 4) and used to control other compatible flash units. The Nikon SB-800 can also be a flash "Commander" to communicate with and trigger other flash units. Nikon offers a unit called the SU-800, which is a commander unit that has no built-in visible flash, and which controls other units using infrared signals.

The SU-800 has several advantages. It's useful for cameras like the D3 and D2xs, which have no built-in flash to function in Commander mode, and could also be used with the D300 to function as a commander that doesn't have any effect on the exposure. However, you can achieve much the same effect by dialing down the D300's built-in flash to 1/128 power, or by setting the built-in flash to - - (flash cancelled) in

Commander mode to turn off the built-in flash during exposure. The real advantage the SU-800 has over the D300's built-in flash is its "reach." Because it uses IR illumination rather than visible light to communicate with remote flashes, the infrared burst can be much stronger, doubling its effective control range to 66 feet.

To use the D300 to control other flash units in Advanced Wireless Lighting mode, if you want the built-in flash as the commander, you need to set it to that mode using **CSM #e3**, as described next. Once you have set either the D300's built-in flash or the SB-800 as the Master/Commander, you can specify a shooting mode, either Manual with a power output setting you determine from 1/1 to 1/128, or for TTL automatic exposure. When using TTL, you can dial in from −1.0 to +3.0 flash exposure compensation for the master flash. You can also specify a channel (1, 2, 3, or 4) that all flashes will use to communicate among themselves. (If other Nikon photographers are present, choosing a different channel prevents your flash from triggering their remotes, and vice versa.)

Each remote flash unit can also be set to one of three groups (A, B, or C), so you can set the exposure compensation and exposure mode of each group separately. For example, one or more flashes in one group can be reduced in output compared to the flashes in the other group, to produce a particular lighting ratio of effect. You'll find instructions for setting exposure mode, channel, and compensation next (for the built-in flash).

Setting Commander Mode for the D300's Built-in Flash

Setting Commander mode for the built-in flash unit may seem complicated, but it's fairly easy once you've gone through it a few times. Here are the instructions you need.

1. Navigate to **CSM #e3**, and choose **Commander Mode** (see Figure 9.13).

2. Use the multi-selector left/right buttons to highlight **Mode** in the **Built-in** flash row, then press the up/down buttons to choose **TTL**, **M**, or **- -** (flash disabled). Then use the multi-selector right button to highlight the **Comp.** parameter in the third column. If you chose **TTL**, you can select exposure compensation from −1 to +3.0; choose **M,** and you can set flash output from 1/1 to 1/128; choose **- -** and the preflashes will still be used to control any remote units in use, but the built-in flash will not fire to contribute to the exposure.

3. Use the multi-selector right button to move down to **Group A** to select **TTL, Manual, AA**, or **- -** exposure (to deactivate that group), then highlight the **Comp.** column to set the exposure compensation/output power as above. Repeat for any additional groups you want to set up.

4. Use the multi-selector right button to highlight the Channel setting, and use the up/down buttons to select the channel that all the flash units will communicate over.

5. Press **OK** when finished.

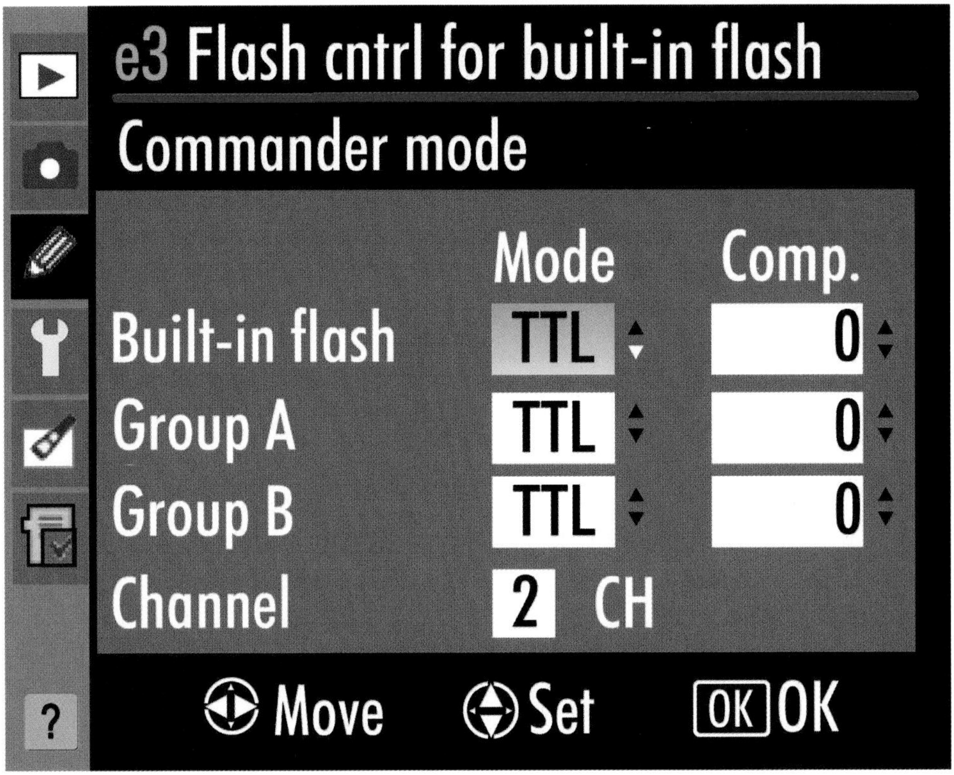

e3 Flash cntrl for built-in flash
Commander mode

	Mode	Comp.
Built-in flash	TTL	0
Group A	TTL	0
Group B	TTL	0
Channel	2 CH	

⊕ Move   ⊕ Set   [OK] OK

Figure 9.13
Commander mode for the built-in flash can be set in the Custom Settings menu.

Setting Commander and Remote Modes for the SB-800

Setting modes for the SB-800 are a little more complicated, but just as easy once you've done it once or twice. Here are the instructions you need. To set Commander mode, follow these steps:

1. To use the SB-800 as a commander, select the flash's Custom Settings mode (hold down the SEL button for about two seconds).

2. Use the left/right (Wide/Tele) and up/down (Plus/Minus) buttons on the multi-selector to choose the Wireless Flash custom settings (a flash icon with a curving arrow), and press the SEL button again to highlight the wireless options.

3. Use the up/down buttons and choose **MASTER**. Press the On/Off button to confirm your choice and exit the Custom Settings mode.

4. Press the SEL button to highlight M (Master) on the LCD.

5. Press the Mode button repeatedly to cycle among **TTL, AA, Manual**, and - - (flash disabled) modes for the master flash.

6. With your choice highlighted, press the up/down buttons to specify the Comp. amount (or to adjust flash output if you've selected Manual flash).

7. Press the SEL button again to highlight Groups A, B, or C, and press the Mode button to set a mode for each group you want to use.

8. While a group is highlighted, press the up/down button to specify a Comp amount for each group you want to use.

9. Press the SEL button when finished to highlight the CH (channel) setting. Use the up/down button to choose a channel for all the flashes to use for communication.

To set up the SB-800 as a remote, follow these steps:

1. To use the SB-800 as a remote, select the flash's custom settings mode (hold down the SEL button for about two seconds).

2. Use the left/right/up/down buttons on the multi-selector to choose the Wireless Flash custom settings, and press the SEL button again to highlight the wireless options.

3. Choose **REMOTE**.

4. Press the On/Off button to exit the Custom Settings mode.

5. To set the channels for the SB-800 as a remote, press the SEL button to highlight the CH display on the LCD (shown in Figure 9.12), and then press the up/down buttons to change the channel.

6. To specify the group, press the SEL button to highlight the GROUP display on the LCD, then press the up/down buttons to change the group.

Connecting External Flash

You have five basic choices for linking an external flash unit to your Nikon D300. They are as follows:

- **Mount on the accessory shoe.** Sliding a compatible flash unit into the Nikon D300's accessory shoe provides a direct connection. With a Nikon dedicated flash, all functions of the flash are supported.

- **Connect to the accessory shoe with a cable.** The Nikon SC-28 (see Figure 9.14) and SC-29 TTL coiled remote cords have an accessory shoe on one end of a nine-foot cable to accept a flash, and a foot that slides into the camera accessory shoe on the other end, providing a link that is the same as when the flash is mounted directly on the camera. The SC-29 version also includes a focus assist lamp, like that on the camera and SB-800. Figure 9.14 shows the SB-800 mounted on a Nikon SK-7 bracket and connected to a camera with the SC-28 coiled cable.

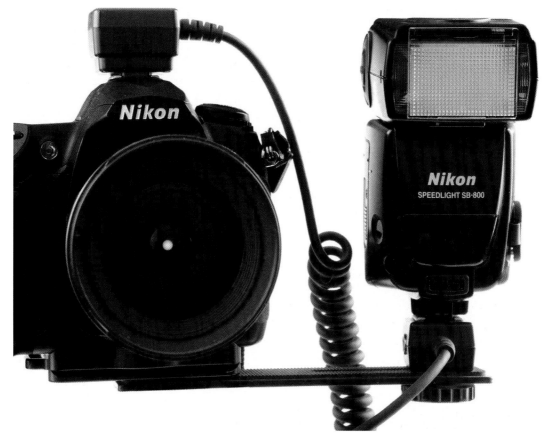

Figure 9.14 The Nikon SB-800 flash is connected for off-camera use with a Nikon SC-28 coiled cable.

- **Multi-flash cables.** The Nikon SC-27/SC-26 TTL Multi Flash Sync Cords can be used to connect TTL flash units to each other or through the AS-10 TTL Multi-Flash Adapter or SC-28 TTL Remote Cord for multi-flash operation. However, this three-pin connector does not support i-TTL or D-TTL operation. You may wish to use it with older Nikon flash units.

- **Connect to the PC/X connector.** Some external flash units, including studio units, can connect to the Nikon D300 through the PC connector on the front of the camera, above the 10-pin terminal. You also may find accessory shoe adapters with a PC connector on them, which can be specially useful if they are combined with a voltage limiter so you needn't fear frying your camera with an older flash unit that has a triggering voltage that's too high. I sometimes use a wireless flash trigger that plugs into the PC connector, and sets off flash units through radio waves.

- **Wireless link.** As described earlier in this chapter, a Nikon electronic flash can be triggered by another Master flash in Commander mode or by the RU-800 infrared unit.

Using Flash Exposure Compensation

You can manually add or subtract exposure to the flash exposure calculated by the D300. Just press the Flash button on the camera (just below the flash pop-up button) and rotate the sub-command dial until the amount of exposure compensation you want appears on the monochrome LCD and in the viewfinder. You can make adjustments from –3EV to +1EV in 1/3 EV increments. As with ordinary exposure compensation, the adjustment you make remains in effect until you zero it out by pressing the Flash button and rotating the sub-command dial until 0 appears on the monochrome control panel and in the viewfinder.

To view the current flash exposure compensation setting, press the Flash button. When compensation is being used, an icon will be displayed in the viewfinder and on the monochrome LCD.

More Advanced Lighting Techniques

As you advance in your Nikon D300 photography, you'll want to learn more sophisticated lighting techniques, using more than just straight-on flash, or using just a single flash unit. Entire books have been written on lighting techniques, and I've written multiple chapters on them in books of my own. I'm going to provide a quick introduction to some of the techniques you should be considering.

Diffusing and Softening the Light

Direct light can be harsh and glaring, especially if you're using the flash built into your camera, or an auxiliary flash mounted in the hot shoe and pointed directly at your subject. The first thing you should do is stop using direct light (unless you're looking for a stark, contrasty appearance as a creative effect). There are a number of simple things you can do with both continuous and flash illumination.

- **Use window light.** Light coming in a window can be soft and flattering, and a good choice for human subjects. Move your subject close enough to the window that its light provides the primary source of illumination. You might want to turn off other lights in the room, particularly to avoid mixing daylight and incandescent light. (See Figure 9.15.)

- **Use fill light.** Your D300's built-in flash makes a perfect fill-in light for the shadows, brightening inky depths with a kicker of illumination. (See Figure 9.16.)

- **Bounce the light.** External electronic flash units mounted on the D300 usually have a swivel that allows them to be pointed up at a ceiling for a bounce light effect. You can also bounce the light off a wall. You'll want the ceiling or wall to be white or have a neutral gray color to avoid a color cast.

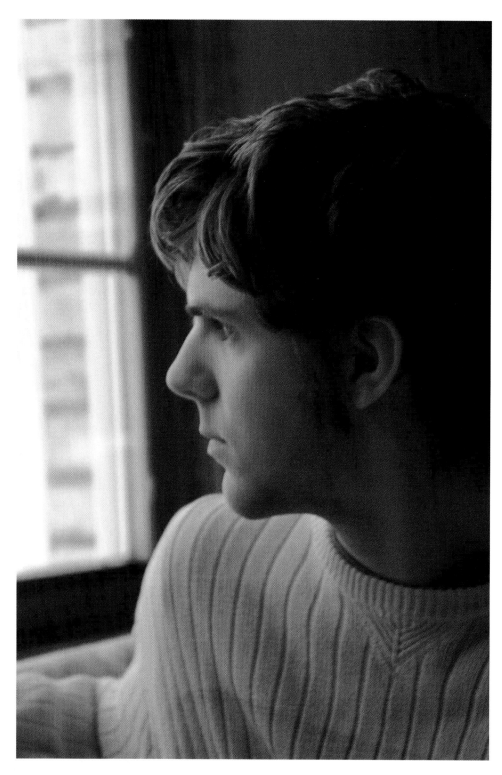

Figure 9.15
Window light makes the perfect diffuse illumination for informal soft-focus portraits like this one.

Figure 9.16
The flamingo (top) was in shadow. Fill flash (bottom) brightened up the bird, while adding a little catch light to its eye.

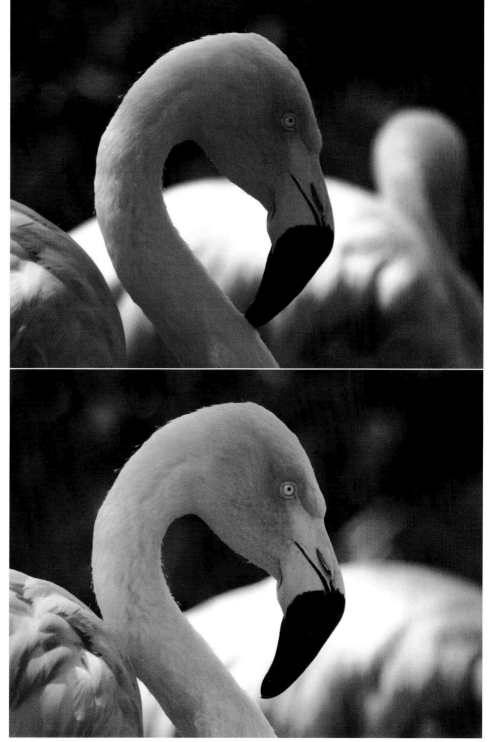

- **Use reflectors.** Another way to bounce the light is to use reflectors or umbrellas that you can position yourself to provide a greater degree of control over the quantity and direction of the bounced light. Good reflectors can be pieces of foamboard, Mylar, or a reflective disk held in place by a clamp and stand. Although some expensive umbrellas and reflectors are available, spending a lot isn't necessary. A simple piece of white foamboard does the job beautifully. Umbrellas have the advantage of being compact and foldable, while providing a soft, even kind of light. They're relatively cheap, too, with a good 40-inch umbrella available for as little as $20.

- **Use diffusers.** Nikon supplies a Sto-Fen-style diffuser dome with the SB-800 flash. You can purchase a similar diffuser for the SB-600 from Nikon, Sto-Fen, and some other vendors that offer clip-on diffusers. The two examples shown in Figures 9.17 and 9.18 fit over your electronic flash head and provide a soft, flattering light. These add-ons are more portable than umbrellas and other reflectors, yet provide a nice diffuse lighting effect.

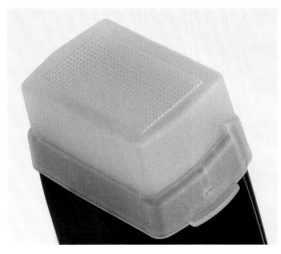

Figure 9.17 This diffuser dome is provided by Nikon with the SB-800, and softens the light of an external flash unit.

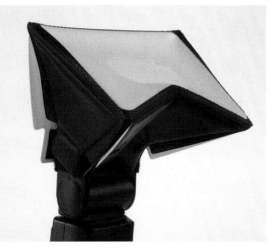

Figure 9.18 Softboxes use Velcro strips to attach them to just about any shoe-mount flash unit.

Using Multiple Light Sources

Once you gain control over the qualities and effects you get with a single light source, you'll want to graduate to using multiple light sources. Using several lights allows you to shape and mold the illumination of your subjects to provide a variety of effects, from backlighting to side lighting to more formal portrait lighting. You can start simply with several incandescent light sources, bounced off umbrellas or reflectors that you construct. Or you can use more flexible multiple electronic flash setups.

Effective lighting is the one element that differentiates great photography from candid or snapshot shooting. Lighting can make a mundane subject look a little more glamorous. Make subjects appear to be soft when you want a soft look, or bright and sparkly when you want a vivid look, or strong and dramatic if that's what you desire. As you might guess, having control over your lighting means that you probably can't use the lights that are already in the room. You'll need separate, discrete lighting fixtures that can be moved, aimed, brightened, and dimmed on command.

Selecting your lighting gear will depend on the type of photography you do, and the budget you have to support it. It's entirely possible for a beginning D300 photographer to create a basic, inexpensive lighting system capable of delivering high-quality results for a few hundred dollars, just as you can spend megabucks ($1,000 and up) for a sophisticated lighting system.

Basic Flash Setups

If you want to use multiple electronic flash units, the Nikon Speedlights described earlier will serve admirably. The higher-end models can be used with Nikon's wireless i-TTL features, which allows you to set up to three separate groups of flash units (several flashes can be included in each group) and trigger them using a master flash and the camera. Just set up one master unit, and arrange the compatible slave units around your subject. You can set the relative power of each unit separately, thereby controlling how much of the scene's illumination comes from the main flash, and how much from the auxiliary flash units, which can be used as fill flash, background lights, or, if you're careful, to illuminate the hair of portrait subjects.

Studio Flash

If you're serious about using multiple flash units, a studio flash setup might be more practical. The traditional studio flash is a multi-part unit, consisting of a flash head that mounts on your light stand, and is tethered to an AC (or sometimes battery) power supply. A single power supply can feed two or more flash heads at a time, with separate control over the output of each head.

When they are operating off AC power, studio flash don't have to be frugal with the juice, and are often powerful enough to illuminate very large subjects or to supply lots and lots of light to smaller subjects. The output of such units is measured in watt seconds (ws), so you could purchase a 200ws, 400ws, or 800ws unit, and a power pack to match.

Their advantages include greater power output, much faster recycling, built-in modeling lamps, multiple power levels, and ruggedness that can stand up to transport, because many photographers pack up these kits and tote them around as location lighting rigs. Studio lighting kits can range in price from a few hundred dollars for a set of lights, stands, and reflectors, to thousands for a high-end lighting system complete with all the necessary accessories.

A more practical choice these days are *monolights* (see Figure 9.19), which are "all-in-one" studio lights that sell for about $200-$400. They have the flash tube, modeling light, and power supply built into a single unit that can be mounted on a light stand. Monolights are available in AC-only and battery-pack versions, although an external battery eliminates some of the advantages of having a flash with everything in one unit. They are very portable, because all you need is a case for the monolight itself, plus the stands and other accessories you want to carry along. Because these units are so popular with photographers who are not full-time professionals, the lower-cost monolights are often designed more for lighter duty than professional studio flash. That doesn't mean they aren't rugged; you'll just need to handle them with a little more care, and, perhaps, not expect them to be used eight hours a day for weeks on end. In most other respects, however, monolights are the equal of traditional studio flash units in terms of fast recycling, built-in modeling lamps, adjustable power, and so forth.

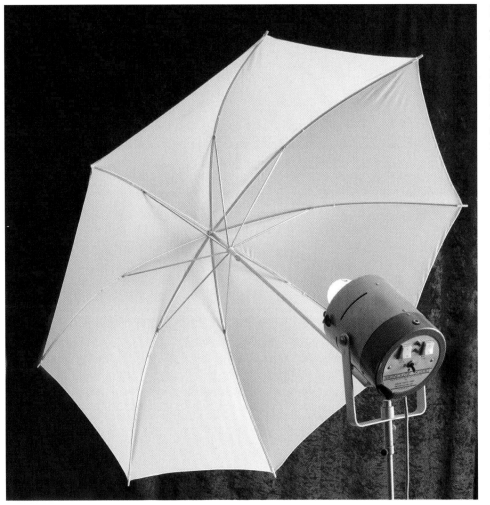

Figure 9.19
All-in-one "monolights" contain flash, power supply, and a modeling light in one compact package (umbrella not included).

Connecting Multiple Non-Dedicated Units to Your Nikon D300

Non-dedicated electronic flash units can't use the automated i-TTL features of your Nikon D300; you'll need to calculate exposure manually, through test shots evaluated on your camera's LCD, or by using an electronic flash meter. Moreover, you don't have to connect them to the accessory shoe on top of the camera. Instead, you can use the PC/X connector on the front of the camera under the rubber cover.

You should be aware that older electronic flash units sometimes use a triggering voltage that is too much for your D300 to handle. You can actually damage the camera's electronics if the voltage is too high. You won't need to worry about this if you purchase brand new units from Alien Bees, Adorama, or other vendors. But if you must connect an external flash with an unknown triggering voltage, I recommend using a Wein Safe Sync (see Figure 9.20), which isolates the flash's voltage from the camera triggering circuit.

Another safe way to connect external cameras is through a radio-control device, such as the transmitter/receiver set shown in Figure 9.21. It clips on the hot shoe and plugs into the D300's PC/X connector (see Figure 9.22) and transmits a signal to a matching receiver that's connected to your flash unit. The receiver has both a PC connector of its own as well as a "monoplug" connector (it looks like a headphone plug) that links to a matching port on compatible flash units.

Finally, some flash units have an optical slave trigger built in, or can be fitted with one, so that they fire automatically when another flash, including your camera's built-in unit, fires.

Figure 9.20

A voltage isolator can prevent frying your D300's flash circuits if you use an older electronic flash.

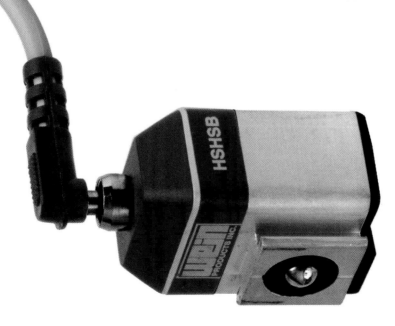

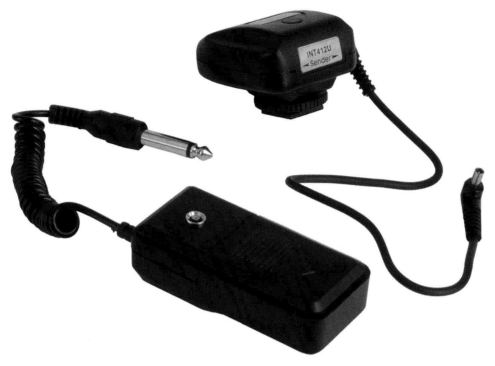

Figure 9.21 A radio-control device frees you from a sync cord tether between your flash and camera.

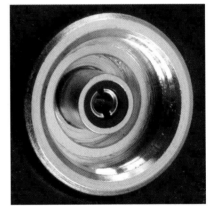

Figure 9.22 The PC/X connector allows attaching studio flash and non-dedicated flash units to the Nikon D300.

Other Lighting Accessories

Once you start working with light, you'll find there are plenty of useful accessories that can help you. Here are some of the most popular that you might want to consider.

Soft Boxes

Soft boxes are large square or rectangular devices that may resemble a square umbrella with a front cover, and produce a similar lighting effect. They can extend from a few feet square to massive boxes that stand five or six feet tall—virtually a wall of light. With a flash unit or two inside a soft box, you have a very large, semi-directional light source that's very diffuse and very flattering for portraiture and other people photography.

Soft boxes are also handy for photographing shiny objects. They not only provide a soft light, but if the box itself happens to reflect in the subject (say you're photographing a chromium toaster), the box will provide an interesting highlight that's indistinct and not distracting.

You can buy soft boxes or make your own. Some lengths of friction-fit plastic pipe and a lot of muslin cut and sewed just so may be all that you need.

Light Stands

Both electronic flash and incandescent lamps can benefit from light stands. These are lightweight, tripod-like devices (but without a swiveling or tilting head) that can be set on the floor, tabletops, or other elevated surfaces and positioned as needed. Light stands should be strong enough to support an external lighting unit, up to and including a relatively heavy flash with soft box or umbrella reflectors. You want the supports to be capable of raising the lights high enough to be effective. Look for light stands capable of extending six to seven feet high. The nine-foot units usually have larger, steadier bases, and extend high enough that you can use them as background supports. You'll be using these stands for a lifetime, so invest in good ones. I bought the light stand shown in Figure 9.23 when I was in college, and I have been using it for decades.

Figure 9.23
Light stands can hold lights, umbrellas, backdrops, and other equipment.

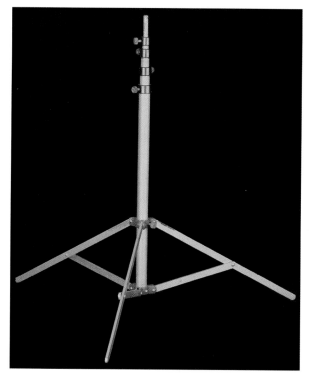

Backgrounds

Backgrounds can be backdrops of cloth, sheets of muslin you've painted yourself using a sponge dipped in paint, rolls of seamless paper, or any other suitable surface your mind can dream up. Backgrounds provide a complementary and non-distracting area behind subjects (especially portraits) and can be lit separately to provide contrast and separation that outlines the subject, or which helps set a mood.

I like to use plain-colored backgrounds for portraits, and white or gray seamless backgrounds for product photography. You can usually construct these yourself from cheap materials and tape them up on the wall behind your subject, or mount them on a pole stretched between a pair of light stands.

Snoots and Barn Doors

These fit over the flash unit and direct the light at your subject. Snoots are excellent for converting a flash unit into a hair light, while barn doors give you enough control over the illumination by opening and closing their flaps that you can use another flash as a background light, with the capability of feathering the light exactly where you want it on the background. Both are shown in Figure 9.24.

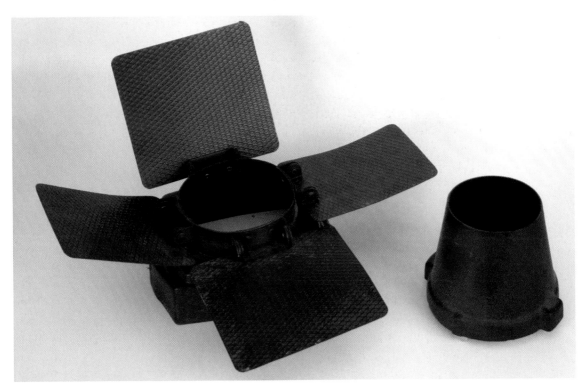

Figure 9.24 Snoots and barn doors allow you to modulate the light from a flash or lamp, and they are especially useful for hair lights and background lights.

10

Useful Software for the Nikon D300

Unless you only take pictures, and then immediately print them directly to a PictBridge-compatible printer, somewhere along the line you're going to need to make use of the broad array of software available for the Nikon D300. The picture-fixing options in the Retouch menu let you make only modest modifications to your carefully-crafted photos. If your needs involve more than fixing red-eye, cropping and trimming, and maybe adjusting tonal values with D-Lighting, you're definitely going to want to use a utility or editor of some sort to perfect your images. After you've captured some great images and have them safely stored on your Nikon D300's memory card, you'll need to transfer them from your camera and Compact Flash card to your computer, where they can be organized, fine-tuned in an image editor, and prepared for web display, printing, or some other final destination.

Fortunately, there are lots of software utilities and applications to help you do all these things. This chapter will introduce you to a few of them. Please note that this is *not* a "how-to-do-it" software chapter. This book has already expanded to more than twice the size of my previous camera guides, and I'm going to use every available page to offer advice on how to get the most from your D300. There's no space to explain how to use all the features of Nikon Capture NX, nor how to tweak RAW file settings in Adobe Camera Raw. Entire books have been written about both products. This chapter is intended solely to help you get your bearings among the large number of utilities and applications available, to help you better understand what each does, and how you might want to use them. At the very end of the chapter, however, I'm going to make an exception and provide some simple instructions for using Adobe Camera Raw, to help those who have been using Nikon's software exclusively get a feel for what you can do with the Adobe product.

The basic functions found in most of the programs discussed in this chapter include image transfer and management, camera control, and image editing. You'll find that many of the programs overlap several of these capabilities, so it's not always possible to categorize the discussions that follow by function. In fact, I'm going to start off by describing a few of the offerings available from Nikon.

Nikon's Applications and Utilities

If nothing else, Nikon has made sorting through the software for its digital cameras an interesting pursuit. Through the years, we've had various incarnations of programs with names like PictureProject, NikonView, and Nikon Capture. Some have been compatible with both the Nikon dSLR and amateur Coolpix product lines. Many of them have been furnished on disk with the cameras. Others, most notoriously Nikon Capture, have been an extra-cost option, which particularly infuriated those of us who had paid several thousand dollars for a Nikon dSLR, and found that we'd need to pay more to get the software needed for the camera.

Recently, Nikon has begun splitting their software offerings into separate programs that are sort-of stand-alone products, but which integrate with the others. For example, if you bought Nikon Capture NX (or received it for free with your D300) you found that the program didn't really capture anything, as the previous Nikon Capture 4 did. If you wanted to operate the camera remotely, you needed to buy the off-shoot program, Nikon Camera Control Pro, which cost even *more* money.

If Nikon software wasn't interesting enough already, some years back Nikon began *encrypting* the white balance information in image files, so that third-party utility programmers needed to use Nikon's software development kit or reverse-engineer the encryption to make their utilities work with Nikon NEF files. Even today, each time a new Nikon dSLR is introduced, you must upgrade your copy of most Nikon software products, as well as third-party products like Adobe Camera Raw, to ensure compatibility with the new camera's files. The fact that these upgrades often are not available until months after the camera is introduced is nothing short of frustrating.

The next few sections provide some descriptions of the Nikon software you'll want to use with your D300.

Nikon ViewNX

This latest incarnation of Nikon's basic file viewer is better than ever, making it easy to browse through images, convert RAW files to JPEG or TIFF, and make corrections to white balance and exposure, either on individual files or on batches of files. It works in tandem with Nikon Transfer and Nikon Capture NX, as you can open files inspected in ViewNX in one of the other programs—or within a third-party application you "register."

First and foremost, Nikon ViewNX is a great file viewer. There are three modes for looking at images: a Thumbnail Grid mode for checking out small previews of your images; an Image Viewer mode (see Figure 10.1) that shows a group of thumbnails along with an enlarged version of a selected image; and Full Screen mode, which allows you to examine an image in maximum detail.

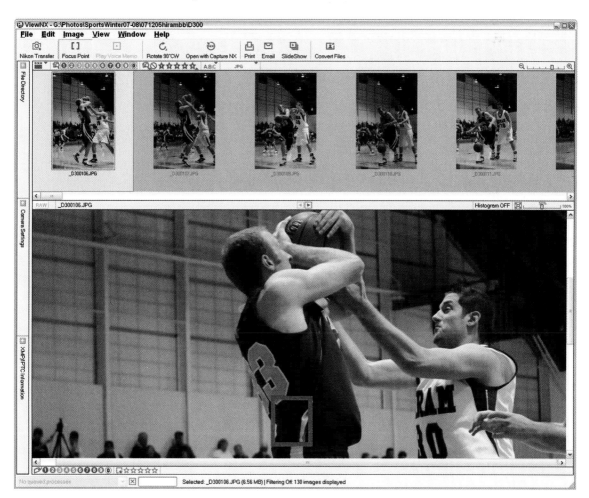

Figure 10.1 Nikon ViewNX is a great basic file viewing utility.

If you like to shoot RAW+JPEG, you can review image pairs as if they were a single image (rather than view the RAW and JPEG versions separately), and work with whichever version you need. The active focus area can be displayed in the image (see Figure 10.1 again), and there are histogram, highlight, and shadow displays to help you evaluate an image.

Should you want to organize your images, there are 10 labels available to classify images by criteria such as images printed, images copied, or images sent as e-mail, and you can mark your best shots for easier retrieval with a rating system of one to five stars. ViewNX also allows you to edit embedded XMP/IPTC Information in fields such as Creator, Origin, Image Title, and suitable keywords. The utility can be downloaded from the support/download pages of the Nikon website at **www.nikonusa.com**.

Nikon Transfer

It seems like everyone offers some sort of image transfer system that automatically recognizes when a memory card is inserted in a reader, or a digital camera like the Nikon D300 is attached to a computer using a USB cable. The most popular operating systems, from Mac OS X to Windows XP and Vista have their own built-in transfer programs, and Adobe Photoshop Elements 6.0 includes one in its suite of utilities.

Nikon Transfer is particularly well-suited for D300 owners, because it integrates easily with other Nikon software products, including ViewNX and Nikon Capture NX. You can download photos to your computer, and then continue to work on them in the Nikon application (or third-party utility) of your choice.

When a memory card is inserted into a card reader, or when the D300 is connected to your computer through a USB cable, Nikon Transfer recognizes the device, searches it for thumbnails, and provides a display like the one shown in Figure 10.2. You can preview the images and mark the ones you want to transfer with checks to create a Transfer Queue.

Then, click on the Primary Destination tab (see Figure 10.3) and choose a location for the photos that will be transferred. Nikon Transfer can create a new folder for each transfer based on a naming convention you set up (click the Edit button next to the box at top center in the figure), or copy to a folder named after the current folder in the D300's memory card. You can keep the current filename as the files are transferred, or assign a new name with a prefix you designate, such as Spain07_ . The program will add a number from 001 to 999 to the filename prefix you specify.

Figure 10.2
After Nikon Transfer displays thumbnails of the images on your memory card or camera, mark the ones you want to transfer.

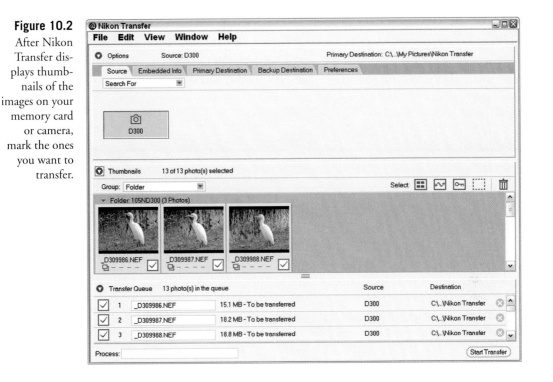

Figure 10.3
Copy files to a destination you specify using an optional file-name template you can define.

One neat feature is the ability to name a Backup Destination location, so that all transferred pictures can also be copied to a second folder, which can be located on a different hard disk drive or other media. You can embed information such as copyright data, star ratings, and labels in the images as they are transferred. When the file transfer is complete, Nikon Transfer can launch an application of your choice, set with a few clicks in the Preferences tab (see Figure 10.4).

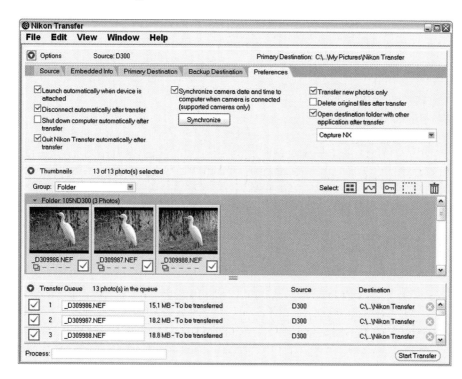

Figure 10.4
You can tell Nikon Transfer what to do after images are transferred in the Preferences tab.

Nikon Capture NX

Capture NX is a powerful image-editing program designed specifically to process Nikon's NEF-format RAW files (although this new edition has added the ability to manipulate JPEG and TIFF images as well). It includes an image browser (with labeling, sorting, and editing) that can be used to make many adjustments directly through the thumbnails. It also has advanced color management tools, impressive noise reduction capabilities, and batch processing features that allow you to apply sets of changes to collections of images. All the tools are arranged in dockable/expandable/collapsible palettes (see Figure 10.5) that tell you everything you need to know about an image, and provide the capabilities to push every pixel in interesting ways.

Figure 10.5
Capture NX's tools are arranged in dockable palettes.

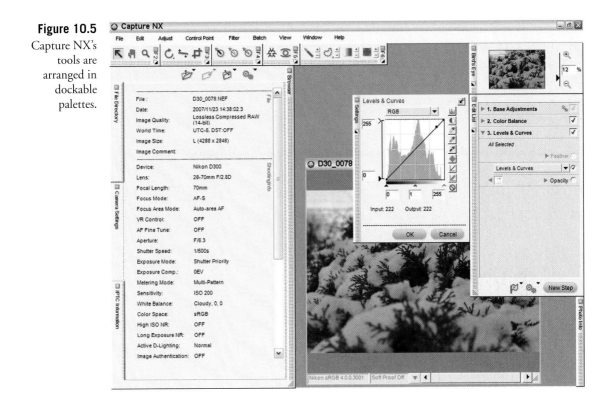

Photographers tend to love Capture NX or hate it, and it's easy to separate the fans from the furious. Those who are enamored of the program have invested a great deal of time in learning its quirky paradigm and now appreciate just how powerful Capture NX is. The detractors are usually those who are comfortable with another program, such as Photoshop or even Capture 4, this program's predecessor, and are upset that even the simplest functions can be confoundingly difficult for a new user to figure out. Capture NX's murky Help system isn't a lot of help; there's room for a huge book (or two) to explain how to use this program.

For example, instead of masks, Capture NX uses Nik Software's U Point technology, which applies Control Points to select and isolate parts of an image for manipulation. There are Color Control Points, with up to nine different sliders for each selected area. (See Figure 10.6.) There are also Black-and-White Control Points for setting dynamic range, Neutral Control Points for correcting color casts, and a Red-Eye Reduction Control Point that removes crimson glows from pupils.

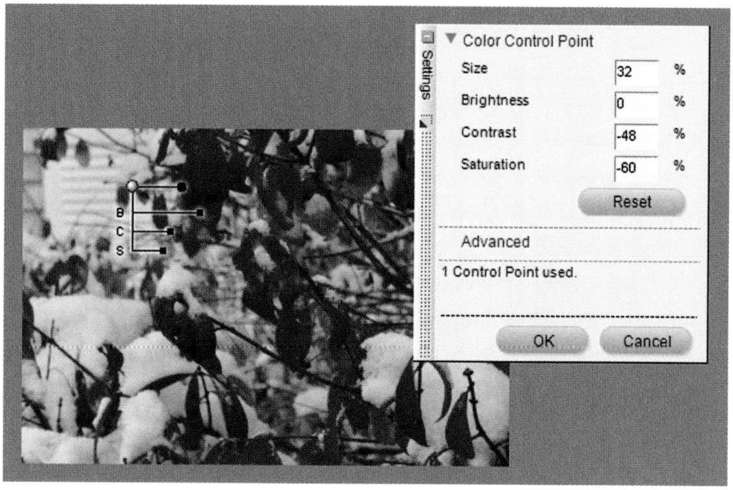

Figure 10.6
Up to nine different sliders can be adjusted for Color Control Points in Capture NX.

The workflow revolves around an Edit List, which contains a list of enhancements, including Camera Adjustments, RAW Adjustments, Light & Color Adjustments, Detail Adjustments, and Lens Adjustments, which can each be controlled separately. You can add steps of your own, cancel adjustments individually, and store steps in the Edit List as Settings that can be applied to individual images or batches.

There are also Color Aberration Controls, D-Lighting, Image Dust Off, Vignette Control, Fisheye-to-Rectilinear Image Transformation ("de-fishing"), and a Distortion Control to reduce pincushion and barrel distortion. One of the coolest features of Capture NX is the access it provides to the Picture Control Utility which allows changing the settings of Picture Controls used in the D300, and creating your own, such as the Snow Scene control I created for Figure 10.7.

Nikon Camera Control Pro

Nikon's Camera Control Pro is a versatile utility that allows you to communicate directly with your camera from your computer through a USB cable or wirelessly with a WT-4a accessory. Once the two are linked, you can perform a variety of functions:

- **Shoot remotely.** Just about any shooting function you can adjust on the camera can be performed remotely, as you can see from the cluster of tabbed dialog boxes shown at the top and right of Figure 10.8. Set exposure mode, adjust the aperture, add or subtract exposure compensation, choose a focus area, change ISO sensitivity or white balance, all are at your command through the software. You can even change Quality and Size settings, turn on auto bracketing, and change image optimization settings. You can optionally disable the controls on the camera, to prevent having settings you made at the computer changed accidentally. Best of all, in Live View mode, you can, for the first time, actually *preview* the image you will be shooting from the remote location!

Figure 10.7
The Picture Control Utility allows modifying the D300's Picture Controls and creating your own new controls.

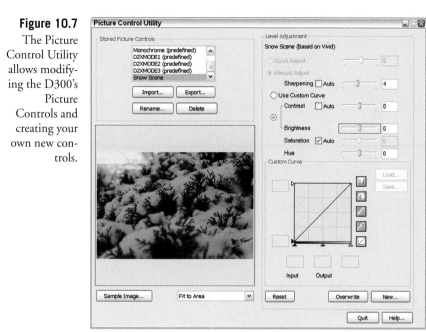

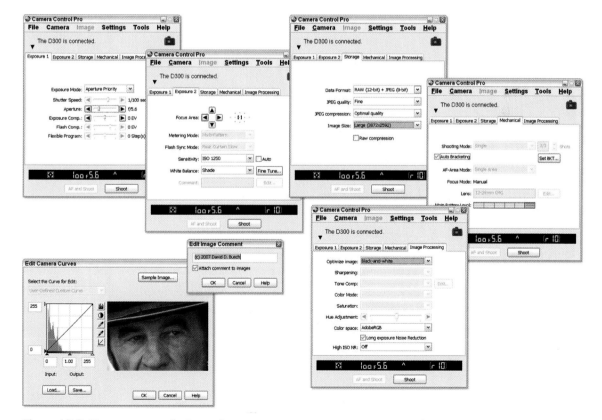

Figure 10.8 You can operate the D300 from your computer using Camera Control Pro.

- **Download directly to your computer.** When doing time-lapse photography, you can use Camera Control Pro to transfer the images you take directly to the computer.

- **Upload comments.** Frustrated by the Nikon D300's text entry screen? Edit your Image Comment and upload it directly to the camera from your computer keyboard. (Lower left in Figure 10.8.)

- **Create and save custom curves.** You can load a sample image and create a special tone compensation custom curve for that image using tools similar to those found in Photoshop.

- **View and change Custom Settings.** This is one of my favorite features. While changing the Custom Settings for any of the four Custom Setting Banks using the D300's menus isn't difficult (particularly after you've absorbed the information in Chapter 4), Camera Control Pro makes playing with these options a joy. You can use pull-down lists to select any of the four banks, change the name of the bank (without needing to use the D300's text entry screen), and then view and modify any of the entries in the submenus. Check out Figure 10.9 to see how much clearer Custom Settings options can be when presented in a traditional dialog box.

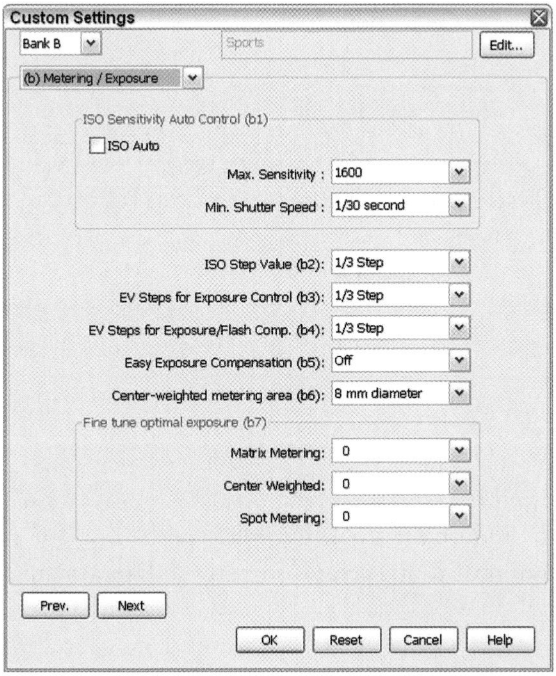

Figure 10.9
Custom Settings menu options can be quickly changed from your computer keyboard.

Other Software

Other useful software for your Nikon D300 falls into several categories. You might want to fine-tune your images, retouch them, change color balance, composite several images together, and perform other tasks we know as image editing, with a program like Adobe Photoshop, Photoshop Elements, or Corel Photo Paint.

You might want to play with the settings in RAW files, too, as you import them into an image editor. There are specialized tools expressly for tweaking RAW files, ranging from Adobe Camera Raw to PhaseOne's Capture One Pro (C1 Pro). A third type of manipulation is the specialized task of noise reduction, which can be performed within Photoshop, Adobe Camera Raw, or tools like Bibble Professional. There are also specialized tools just for noise reduction, such as Noise Ninja (also included with Bibble) and Neat Image. Some programs, like the incomparable DxO Optics Pro perform magical transformations that you can't achieve any other way.

Each of these utilities and applications deserves a chapter of its own, so I'm simply going to enumerate some of the most popular applications and utilities and tell you a little about what they do.

DxO Optics Pro

DxO Labs offers an incredibly useful program called Optics Pro that is unique in the range of functions it provides. Ostensibly an image quality enhancement utility that "cures" some of the ails that plague even the best lenses, the latest v5 release also features a new RAW conversion engine that uses a new demosaicing algorithm to translate your NEF files into images with more detail, less noise, and fewer artifacts. These features meld well with the program's original mission: fixing the optical "geometry" of images, using settings custom-tailored for each individual lens. (I'm not kidding: when you "assemble" the program, you specify each and every camera body you want to use with Optics Pro, and designate exactly which lenses are included in your repertoire.)

Once an image has been imported into Optics Pro, it can be manipulated within one of four main sections: Light, Color, Geometry, and Details. It's especially useful for correcting optical flaws, color, exposure, and dynamic range, while adjusting perspective, distortion, and tilting. If you own a fish-eye lens, Optics Pro will "de-fish" your images to produce a passable rectilinear photo from your curved image. A new Dust/Blemish Removal tool operates something like a manual version of the D300's Dust Off Reference Photo. The user creates a dust/blemish template, and the program removes dust from the marked area in multiple images. Figure 10.10 shows you DxO Optics Pro's clean user interface.

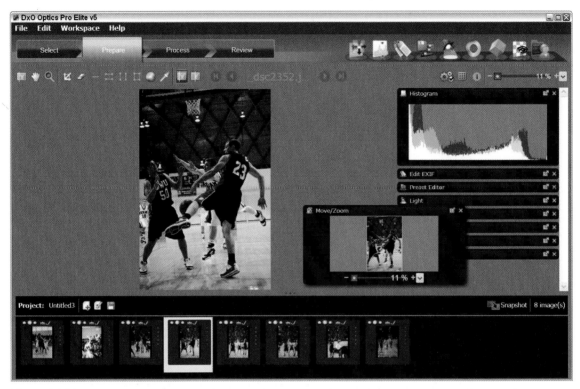

Figure 10.10 DxO Optics Pro fixes lens flaws, and functions as a high-tech RAW converter and noise reduction utility, too.

Phase One Capture One Pro (C1 Pro)

If there is a Cadillac of RAW converters for Nikon and Canon digital SLR cameras, C1 Pro has to be it. This premium-priced program does everything, does it well, and does it quickly. If you can't justify the price tag of this professional-level software, there are "lite" versions for serious amateurs and cash-challenged professionals called Capture One dSLR and Capture One dSLR SE.

Aimed at photographers with high-volume needs (that would include school and portrait photographers, as well as busy commercial photographers), C1 Pro is available for both Windows and Mac OS X, and supports a broad range of digital cameras. Phase One is a leading supplier of megabucks digital camera backs for medium and larger format cameras, so they really understand the needs of photographers.

The latest features include individual noise reduction controls for each image, automatic levels adjustment, a "quick develop" option that allows speedy conversion from RAW to TIFF or JPEG formats, dual-image side-by-side views for comparison purposes, and helpful grids and guides that can be superimposed over an image. Photographers concerned about copyright protection will appreciate the ability to add watermarks to the output images.

Bibble Pro

One of my personal favorites among third-party RAW converters is Bibble Pro. It supports one of the broadest ranges of RAW file formats available (which can be handy if you find yourself with the need to convert a file from a friend or colleague's non-Nikon camera), including NEF files from Nikon cameras dating as far back as the Nikon D1, D1x/h, D2H, and D100. It also supports .CRW files from the Canon C30/D60/10D/300D; .CR2 files from the Canon 20D and other newer models; .ORF files from the Olympus E10/E20/E1/C5050/C5060; .DCR files from the Kodak 720x/760/14n; .RAF files from the Fuji S2Pro; .PEF files from Pentax ISTD; .MRW files from the Minolta Maxxum; and .TIF from Canon 1D/1DS.

The utility supports lots of different platforms, too. It's available for Windows, Mac OS X, and, believe it or not, Linux.

Bibble works fast, which is important when you have to convert many images in a short time (event photographers will know what I am talking about!). Bibble's batch-processing capabilities also let you convert large numbers of files using settings you specify without further intervention. Its customizable interface lets you organize and edit images quickly and then output them in a variety of formats, including 16-bit TIFF and PNG. You can even create a web gallery from within Bibble. I often find myself disliking the generic filenames applied to digital images by cameras, so I really like Bibble's ability to rename batches of files using new names that you specify.

Bibble is fully color managed, which means it can support all the popular color spaces (Adobe sRGB and so forth) and use custom profiles generated by third-party color-management software. There are two editions of Bibble, a Pro version and a Lite version. Because the Pro version is reasonably priced at $129, I don't really see the need to save $60 with the Lite edition, which lacks the top-line's options for tethered shooting, embedding IPTC-compatible captions in images, and can also be used as a Photoshop plug-in (if you prefer not to work with the application in its stand-alone mode). Bibble Pro now incorporates Noise Ninja technology, so you can get double-duty from this valuable application.

Photoshop/Photoshop Elements

Photoshop is the high-end choice for image editing, and Photoshop Elements is a great alternative for those who need some of the features of Photoshop, but can do without the most sophisticated capabilities, including editing CMYK files. Both editors use the latest version of Adobe's Camera Raw plug-in, which makes it easy to adjust things like color space profiles, color depth (either 8 bits or 16 bits per color channel), image resolution, white balance, exposure, shadows, brightness, sharpness, luminance, and noise reduction. One plus with the Adobe products is that they are available in identical versions for both Windows and Macs (eventually!).

The latest version of Photoshop includes a built-in RAW plug-in that is compatible with the proprietary formats of a growing number of digital cameras, both new and old. This plug-in also works with Photoshop Elements, but with fewer features. Here's how easy it is to manipulate a RAW file using the Adobe converter:

1. Transfer the RAW images from your camera to your computer's hard drive.

2. In Photoshop, choose Open from the File menu, or use Bridge.

3. Select a RAW image file. The Adobe Camera Raw plug-in will pop up, showing a preview of the image, like the one shown in Figure 10.11.

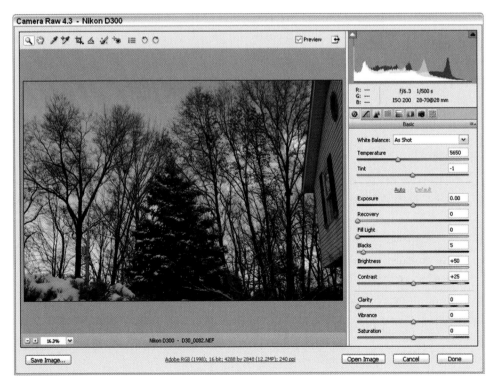

Figure 10.11
The basic ACR dialog box looks like this when processing a single image.

4. If you like, use one of the tools found in the toolbar at the top left of the dialog box. From left to right, they are:

- **Zoom.** Operates just like the Zoom tool in Photoshop.

- **Hand.** Use like the Hand tool in Photoshop.

- **White Balance.** Click an area in the image that should be neutral gray or white to set the white balance quickly.

- **Color Sampler.** Use to determine the RGB values of areas you click with this eyedropper.

- **Crop.** Pre-crops the image so that only the portion you specify is imported into Photoshop. This option saves time when you want to work on a section of a large image, and you don't need the entire file.

- **Straighten.** Drag in the preview image to define what should be a horizontal or vertical line, and ACR will realign the image to straighten it.

- **Retouch.** Used to heal or clone areas you define.

- **Red-Eye Removal.** Quickly zap red pupils in your human subjects.

- **ACR Preferences.** Produces a dialog box of Adobe Camera Raw preferences.

- **Rotate Counterclockwise.** Rotates counterclockwise in 90-degree increments with a click.

- **Rotate Clockwise.** Rotates clockwise in 90-degree increments with a click.

5. Using the Basic tab, you can have ACR show you red and blue highlights in the preview that indicate shadow areas that are clipped (too dark to show detail) and light areas that are blown out (too bright). Click the triangles in the upper-left corner of the histogram display (shadow clipping) and upper-right corner (highlight clipping) to toggle these indicators on or off.

6. Also in the Basic tab you can choose white balance, either from the drop-down list or by setting a color temperature and green/magenta color bias (tint) using the sliders.

7. Other sliders are available to control exposure, recovery, fill light, blacks, brightness, contrast, vibrance, and saturation. A checkbox can be marked to convert the image to grayscale.

8. Make other adjustments (described in more detail below).

9. ACR makes automatic adjustments for you. You can click **Default** and make the changes yourself, or click the **Auto** link (located just above the Exposure slider) to reapply the automatic adjustments after you've made your own modifications.

10. If you've marked more than one image to be opened, the additional images appear in a "filmstrip" at the left side of the screen. You can click on each thumbnail in the filmstrip in turn and apply different settings to each.

11. Click **Open Image/Open image(s)** into Photoshop using the settings you've made.

The Basic tab is displayed by default when the ACR dialog box opens, and it includes most of the sliders and controls you'll need to fine-tune your image as you import it into Photoshop. These include:

- **White Balance.** Leave it As Shot or change to a value such as Daylight, Cloudy, Shade, Tungsten, Fluorescent, or Flash. If you like, you can set a custom white balance using the Temperature and Tint sliders.

- **Exposure.** This slider adjusts the overall brightness and darkness of the image.

- **Recovery.** Restores detail in the red, green, and blue color channels.

- **Fill Light.** Reconstructs detail in shadows.

- **Blacks.** Increases the number of tones represented as black in the final image, emphasizing tones in the shadow areas of the image.

- **Brightness.** This slider adjusts the brightness and darkness of an image.

- **Contrast.** Manipulates the contrast of the midtones of your image.

- **Convert to Grayscale.** Mark this box to convert the image to black and white.

- **Vibrance.** Prevents over-saturation when enriching the colors of an image.

- **Saturation.** Manipulates the richness of all colors equally, from zero saturation (gray/black, no color) at the -100 setting to double the usual saturation at the +100 setting.

Additional controls are available on the Tone Curve, Detail, HSL/Grayscale, Split Toning, Lens Corrections, Camera Calibration, and Presets tabs, shown in Figure 10.12. The Tone Curve tab can change the tonal values of your image. The Detail tab lets you adjust sharpness, luminance smoothing, and apply color noise reduction. The HSL/Grayscale tab offers controls for adjusting hue, saturation, and lightness and converting an image to black and white. Split Toning helps you colorize an image with sepia or cyanotype (blue) shades. The Lens Corrections tab has sliders to adjust for chromatic aberrations and vignetting. The Camera Calibration tab provides a way for calibrating the color corrections made in the Camera Raw plug-in. The Presets tab (not shown) is used to load settings you've stored for reuse.

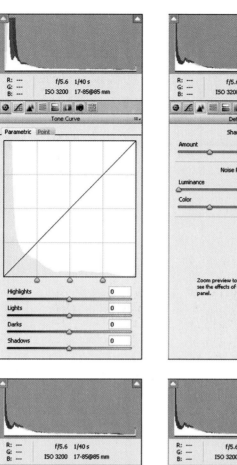
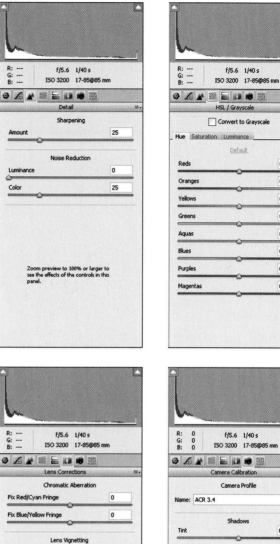

Figure 10.12 More controls are available within the additional tabbed dialog boxes in Adobe Camera Raw.

11

Nikon D300:
Troubleshooting and
Prevention

One of the nice things about modern electronic cameras like the Nikon D300 is that they have fewer mechanical moving parts to fail, so they are less likely to "wear out." No film transport mechanism, no wind lever or motor drive, no complicated mechanical linkages from camera to lens to physically stop down the lens aperture. Instead, tiny, reliable motors are built into each lens (and you lose the use of only that lens should something fail), and one of the few major moving parts in the camera itself is a lightweight mirror (its small size is one of the advantages of the D300's 1.5X crop factor) that flips up and down with each shot.

Of course, the camera also has a moving shutter that can fail, but the shutter is built rugged enough that you can expect it to last 100,000 shutter cycles or more. Unless you're shooting sports in continuous mode day in and day out, the shutter on your D300 is likely to last as long as you expect to use the camera.

The only other things on the camera that move are switches, dials, buttons, the flip-up electronic flash, and the door that slides open to allow you to remove and insert the Compact Flash card. Unless you're extraordinarily clumsy or unlucky and manage to bend the internal pins in the CF card slot, or give your built-in flash a good whack while it is in use, there's not a lot that can go wrong mechanically with your Nikon D300.

On the other hand, one of the chief drawbacks of modern electronic cameras is that they are modern *electronic* cameras. Your D300 is fully dependent on two different batteries. Without them, the camera can't be used. There are numerous other electrical and electronic connections in the camera (many connected to those mechanical switches and dials), and components like the color LCD and top-panel status LCD that can potentially fail or suffer damage. The camera also relies on its "operating system," or *firmware*, which can be plagued by bugs that cause unexpected behavior. Luckily, electronic components are generally more reliable and trouble-free, especially when compared to their mechanical counterparts from the pre-electronic film camera days. (Film cameras of the last 10 to 20 years have had almost as many electronic features as digital cameras, but, believe it or not, there were whole generations of film cameras that had *no* electronics or batteries.)

Digital cameras have problems unique to their breed, too; the most troublesome being the need to clean the sensor of dust and grime periodically. This chapter will show you how to diagnose problems, fix some common ills, and, importantly, learn how to avoid them in the future.

Update Your Firmware

As I said, the firmware in your Nikon D300 is the camera's operating system, which handles everything from menu display (including fonts, colors, and the actual entries themselves), what languages are available, and even support for specific devices and features. Upgrading the firmware to a new version makes it possible to add new features while fixing some of the bugs that sneak in.

Firmware upgrades are used most frequently to fix bugs in the software, and much less frequently to add or enhance features. For example, the D300's firmware Version 1.02A fixed a problem that could (in Nikon's words) "in rare cases" cause vertical bands (lines) to appear in images captured at shutter speeds slower than 8 seconds. The exact changes made to the firmware are generally spelled out in the firmware release announcement. You can examine the remedies provided and decide if a given firmware patch is important to you. If not, you can usually safely wait a while before going through the bother of upgrading your firmware—at least long enough for the early adopters to report whether the bug fixes have introduced new bugs of their own. Each new firmware release incorporates the changes from previous releases, so if you skip a minor upgrade you should have no problems.

How It Works

If you're computer savvy, you might wonder how your Nikon D300 is able to overwrite its own operating system—that is, how can the existing firmware be used to load the new version on top of itself? It's a little like lifting yourself by reaching down and pulling up on your bootstraps. Not ironically, that's almost exactly what happens: At your command (when you start the upgrade process), the D300 shifts into a special mode in which it is no longer operating from its firmware but, rather, from a small piece of software called a *bootstrap loader*, a separate, protected software program that functions only at startup or when upgrading firmware. The loader's function is to look for firmware to launch or, when directed, to copy new firmware from a Compact Flash card to the internal memory space where the old firmware is located. Once the new firmware has replaced the old, you can turn your camera off and then on again, and the updated operating system will be loaded.

Because the loader software is small in size and limited in function, there are some restrictions on what it can do. For one thing, it recognizes only Compact Flash cards that have been formatted using an organizational system called FAT16 (which again, you might be familiar with if you're comfortable with hard disk technology). To ensure that the Compact Flash card is formatted using FAT16, you must upgrade using a CF card at least 8MB in size and no larger than 2GB, and then format the card in your camera. Memory cards that are smaller or larger might be formatted using a different FAT system (FAT12 or FAT32, respectively).

In addition, the loader software isn't set up to go hunting through your Compact Flash card for the firmware file. It looks only in the top or root directory of your card, so that's where you must copy the firmware you download. Once you've determined that a new firmware update is available for your camera and that you want to install it, just follow these steps. (If you chicken out, any Nikon Service Center can install the firmware upgrade for you.)

WARNING

Use a fully charged EN-EL3e charged battery or a Nikon EH-5/EH-5a AC adapter to ensure that you'll have enough power to operate the camera for the entire upgrade. Moreover, you should not turn off the camera while your old firmware is being overwritten. Don't open the Compact Flash card door or do anything else that might disrupt operation of the D300 while the firmware is being installed.

Getting Ready

The first thing to do is determine whether you need the current firmware update. First, confirm the version number of your Nikon D300's current firmware:

1. Turn on the D300.

2. Press the Menu button and select **Firmware Version** from the Setup menu. The camera's firmware version will be displayed.

3. Write down the Version number for both Parts A and B.

4. Turn off the D300.

Next, go to the Nikon support site, locate, and download the firmware update. In the USA, the place to go is **http://support.nikontech.com/**, which will offer a list of choices, including one that says Current **Firmware Downloads available for Nikon Products**. Click that link, then click the **DSLR** link on the page displayed next. Scroll down to the D300 row in the table, and review the Version number for the current update.

If the version is later than the one you noted in your camera, click the firmware link in either the Windows or Macintosh columns (depending on your computer) to download the file. It will have a name like D300Update.zip (Windows) or D300update.sitx (Macintosh). Extract the file to a folder on your computer using the unzipping or unstuffing software of your choice.

The D300's firmware comes in two parts, A, and B, which can be updated individually. Indeed, the Version 1.02 firmware came only as the "A" file, because no changes were needed to the "B" part. The actual update file will be named something like:

A3000103.bin

B3000103.bin

The final preparation you need to make is to decide whether you'd like to upgrade your firmware using a memory card reader, or by transferring the software to the D300 using the UC-E4 USB cable. In either case, you'll need to format a memory card of 8MB to 2GB capacity in the D300. Then, perform one of the sets of steps in the sections that follow.

Updating from a Card Reader

To update from a card reader, use a reader connected to your computer with a USB cable. Then, follow these steps:

1. Insert a formatted memory card into the card reader. If you have been using Nikon Transfer or the "autoplay" features of your operating system to transfer images from your memory card to the computer, the automated transfer dialog box may appear. Close it.

2. The memory card will appear on your Macintosh desktop, or in the Computer/My Computer folders under Windows Vista/Windows XP.

3. Drag one of the firmware files to the memory card. You can install "A" first or "B" first; it doesn't matter. If your particular upgrade consists of only one of the two files, drag that to the memory card. Remember to copy the firmware to the *root* (top) directory of the memory card. The D300 will be unable to find it if you place it in a folder.

Updating with a USB Connection

You can also copy the firmware to the D300's memory card using a USB connection. Just follow these steps:

1. With the camera turned off, insert the formatted memory card. Then, turn the camera back on.

2. Press the Menu button and navigate to the Setup menu.

3. Choose USB and set the option to Mass Storage, as described in Chapter 5.

4. Turn the D300 off and connect it to your computer using the UC-E4 USB cable.

5. Turn the camera back on. If you have been using Nikon Transfer or the "autoplay" features of your operating system to transfer images from your memory card to the computer, the automated transfer dialog box may appear. Close it.

6. The camera will appear on the Macintosh desktop, or in the Computer/My Computer folders under Windows Vista/Windows XP.

7. Drag one of the firmware files to the memory card. It doesn't matter whether you install "A" or "B" first. If your particular upgrade consists of only one .bin file, drag that to the memory card. Remember to copy the firmware to the *root* (top) directory of the memory card. The D300 will be unable to find it if you place it in a folder.

8. Disconnect the camera from the computer.

Starting the Update

To perform the actual update, follow these steps:

1. With the memory card containing the firmware update software in the camera, turn the camera on.

2. Press the **Menu** button and select **Firmware version** in the Setup menu.

3. Select **Update** and press the multi-selector button to the right. (See Figure 11.1.)

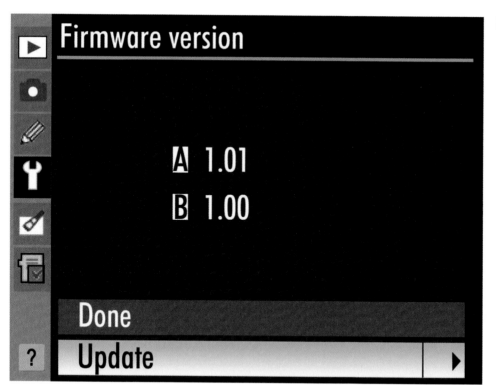

Figure 11.1

4. When the firmware update screen appears, highlight **Yes** and press **OK** to begin the update. (See Figure 11.2.)

5. The actual process may take a few minutes (from two to five). Be sure not to turn off the camera or perform any other operations while it is underway. (See Figure 11.3.)

6. When the update is completed, the screen shown in Figure 11.4 appears. Turn the camera off.

7. Turn the D300 back on to load the updated firmware.

8. Reformat the memory card.

9. Press the **Menu** button and select **Firmware version** in the Setup menu to view the current firmware number. If it matches the update, you've successfully upgraded that portion of the firmware.

10. If there is a second part to your firmware upgrade ("A" or "B"), then repeat all the steps for the additional firmware software.

11. If you transferred the firmware files to the memory card using USB transfer, then go back to the Setup menu, choose USB, and set the option to MTP/PTP, as described in Chapter 5.

Figure 11.2

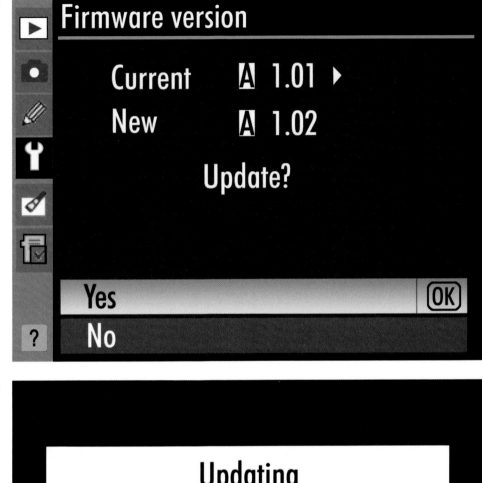

Figure 11.3

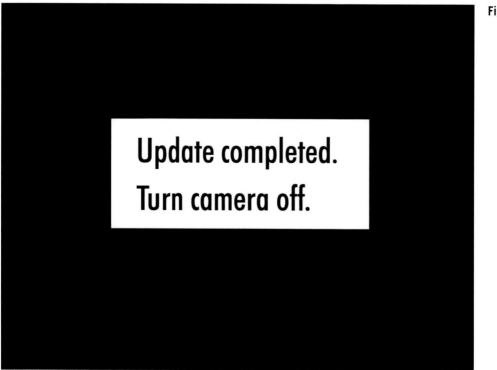

Figure 11.4

Protect Your LCD

The massive three-inch color LCD on the back of your Nikon D300 almost seems like a target for banging, scratching, and other abuse. The camera is furnished with the plastic Nikon BM-8 LCD protector, which I dislike strongly, as it tends to scratch easily and tends to fog up when you breathe on it while peering through the viewfinder. The LCD itself is quite rugged, and a few errant knocks are unlikely to shatter the protective cover over the LCD, and scratches won't easily mar its tempered glass surface. However, if you want to be on the safe side, there are a number of protective products you can purchase to keep your LCD safe—and, in some cases, make it a little easier to view. Here's a quick overview of your options.

- **Plastic overlays.** The simplest solution (although not always the cheapest), is to apply a plastic overlay sheet or "skin" cut to fit your LCD. These adhere either by static electricity or through a light adhesive coating that's even less clingy than stick-it notes. You can cut down overlays made for PDAs (although these can be pricey at up to $19.95 for a set of several sheets), or purchase overlays sold specifically for digital cameras. Vendors such as Hoodman (**www.hoodmanusa.com**), Delkin (**www.delkin.com**), and Belkin (**www.belkin.com**) offer overlays of this type. These products will do a good job of shielding your D300's LCD screen from scratches and minor impacts, but will not offer much protection from a good whack.

■ **Acrylic shields.** These scratch-resistant acrylic panels, laser cut to fit your camera perfectly, are my choice as the best protection solution, and what I use on my own D300. At about $6 each, they also happen to be the least expensive option as well. I get mine, shown in Figure 11.5, from a company called 'da Products (**www.daproducts.com**). They attach using strips of sticky adhesive that hold the panel flush and tight, but which allow the acrylic to be pried off and the adhesive removed easily if you want to remove or replace the shield. They don't attenuate your view of the LCD and are non-reflective enough for use under a variety of lighting conditions.

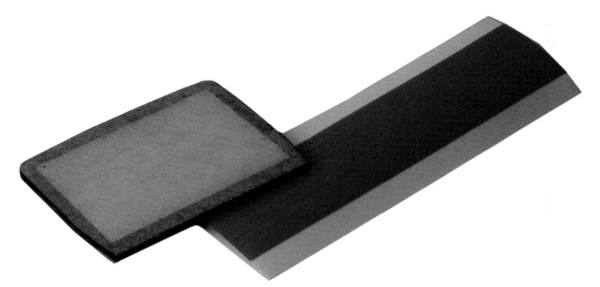

Figure 11.5 A tough acrylic shield, here shown with a piece of plastic containing a set of peel-off sticky strips to help it adhere to the camera, can protect your LCD from scratches.

■ **Flip-up hoods.** These protectors slip on using the flanges around your D300's eyepiece, and provide a cover that completely shields the LCD, but unfolds to provide a three-sided hood that allows viewing the LCD while minimizing the extraneous light falling on it and reducing contrast. They're sold for about $40 by Belkin and Hoodman. If you want to completely protect your LCD from hard knocks and need to view the screen outdoors in bright sunlight, there is nothing better. However, I have a couple problems with these devices. First, with the cover closed, you can't peek down after taking a shot to see what your image looks like during picture review. You must open the cap each time you want to look at the LCD.

Moreover, with the hood unfolded, it's difficult to look through the viewfinder: Don't count on being able to use the viewfinder *and* the LCD at the same time with one of these hoods in place.

■ **Magnifiers.** If you look hard enough, you should be able to find an LCD magnifier that fits over the monitor panel and provides a 2X magnification. These often strap on clumsily, and serve better as a way to get an enlarged view of the LCD than as protection. Hoodman, Photodon (**www.photodon.com**), and other suppliers offer these specialized devices.

Troubleshooting Memory Cards

Sometimes good memory cards go bad. Sometimes good photographers can treat their memory cards badly. It's possible that a memory card that works fine in one camera won't be recognized when inserted into another. In the worst case, you can have a card full of important photos and find that the card seems to be corrupted and you can't access any of them. Don't panic! If these scenarios sound horrific to you, there are lots of things you can do to prevent them from happening, and a variety of remedies available if they do occur. You'll want to take some time—before disaster strikes—to consider your options.

All Your Eggs in One Basket?

The debate about whether it's better to use one large memory card or several smaller ones has been going on since even before there were memory cards. I can remember when computer users wondered whether it was smarter to install a pair of 200MB (not *gigabyte*) hard drives in their computer, or if they should go for one of those new-fangled 500MB models. By the same token, a few years ago the user groups were full of proponents who insisted that you ought to use 128MB Compact Flash cards rather than the huge 512MB versions. Today, most of the arguments involve 8GB cards versus 4GB cards, and I expect that as prices for 16GB CF cards continue to drop, they'll find their way into the debate as well.

Why all the fuss? Are 8GB memory cards more likely to fail than 4GB cards? Are you risking all your photos if you trust your images to a larger card? Isn't it better to use several smaller cards, so that if one fails you lose only half as many photos? Or, isn't it wiser to put all your photos onto one larger card, because the more cards you use, the better your odds of misplacing or damaging one and losing at least some pictures?

In the end, the "eggs in one basket" argument boils down to statistics, and how you happen to use your D300. The rationales can go both ways. If you have multiple smaller cards, you do increase your chances of something happening to one of them, so, arguably, you might be boosting the odds of losing some pictures. If all your images are important, the fact that you've lost 100 rather than 200 pictures isn't very comforting.

Also consider that the eggs/basket scenario assumes that the cards that are lost or damaged are always full. It's actually likely that your 8GB card might suffer a mishap when it's less than half full (indeed, it's more likely that a large card won't be completely filled before it's offloaded to a computer), so you really might not lose any more shots with a single 8GB card than with multiple 4GB or 2GB cards.

If you shoot photojournalist-type pictures, you probably change memory cards when they're less than completely full in order to avoid the need to do so at a crucial moment. (When I shoot sports, my cards rarely reach 80 to 90 percent of capacity before I change them.) Using multiple smaller cards means you have to change them that more often, which can be a real pain when you're taking a lot of photos. As an example, if you use 1GB memory cards with a Nikon D300 and shoot RAW+JPEG FINE, you may get only a few dozen pictures on the card. That's not even twice the capacity of a 36-exposure roll of film (remember those?). In my book, I prefer keeping all my eggs in one basket, and then making very sure that nothing happens to that basket.

There are only two really good reasons to justify limiting yourself to smaller memory cards when larger ones can be purchased at the same cost per-gigabyte. One of them applies only to owners of older cameras that don't accept memory cards larger than 2GB. That rationale doesn't apply to you.

The other reason comes into play when every single picture is precious to you and the loss of any of them would be a disaster. If you're a wedding photographer, for example, and unlikely to be able to restage the nuptials if a memory card goes bad, you'll probably want to shoot no more pictures than you can afford to lose on a single card, and have an assistant ready to copy each card removed from the camera onto a backup hard drive or DVD onsite.

To be even more safe, you'd want to alternate cameras or have a second photographer at least partially duplicating your coverage so your shots are distributed over several memory cards simultaneously. Strictly speaking, the safest route of all is to spend some significant bucks on Nikon's Wireless Transmitter WT-4a, and beam the images over to a computer as you shoot them using the gadget's Image Transfer mode.

If none of these options are available to you, consider *interleaving* your shots. Say you don't shoot weddings, but you do go on vacation from time to time. Take 50 or so pictures on one card, or whatever number of images might fill about 25 percent of its capacity. Then, replace it with a different card and shoot about 25 percent of that card's available space. Repeat these steps with diligence (you'd have to be determined to go through this inconvenience), and, if you use four or more memory cards you'll find your pictures from each location scattered among the different Compact Flash cards. If you lose or damage one, you'll still have *some* pictures from all the various stops on your trip on the other cards. That's more work than I like to do (I usually tote around a portable hard disk and copy the files to the drive as I go), but it's an option.

What Can Go Wrong?

There are lots of things that can go wrong with your memory card, but the ones that aren't caused by human stupidity are statistically very rare. Yes, a Compact Flash card's internal bit bin or controller can suddenly fail due to a manufacturing error or some inexplicable event caused by old age. However, if your CF card works for the first week or two that you own it, it should work forever. There's really not a lot that can wear out.

The typical Compact Flash card is rated for a Mean Time Between Failures of 1,000,000 hours of use. That's constant use 24/7 for more than 100 years! According to the manufacturers, they are good for 10,000 insertions in your camera, and should be able to retain their data (and that's without an external power source) for something on the order of 11 years. Of course, with the millions of CF cards in use, there are bound to be a few lemons here or there.

Those mini-hard drives that have a Compact Flash form factor are a special case. Although these devices are practically extinct, some photographers continue to use them. They really are hard disk drives with moving parts and are subject to the same kinds of failure that their bigger siblings inside your computer can suffer. You'll find many, many happy users of mini-disks who have never had a problem, but anecdotal evidence suggests that they do fail significantly more often than solid-state memory cards. Mini-drives are slower and their price and capacity advantages faded, so I find little reason to use them for serious work.

Given the reliability of solid-state memory compared to magnetic memory, though, it's more likely that your Compact Flash problems will stem from something that you do. Although they're not as tiny as the SD and xD cards a few other digital SLRs use, CF cards are still small and easy to misplace if you're not careful. For that reason, it's a good idea to keep them in their original cases or a "card safe" offered by Gepe (**www.gepecardsafe.com**), Pelican (**www.pelican.com**), and others. Always placing your memory card in a case can provide protection from the second-most common mishap that befalls Compact Flash cards: the common household laundry. If you slip a memory card in a pocket, rather than a case or your camera bag often enough, sooner or later it's going to end up in the washing machine and probably the clothes dryer, too. There are plenty of reports of relieved digital camera owners who've laundered their memory cards and found they still worked fine, but it's not uncommon for such mistreatment to do some damage.

Memory cards can also be stomped on, accidentally bent, dropped into the ocean, chewed by pets, and otherwise rendered unusable in myriad ways. It's also possible to force a card into your D300's CF card slot incorrectly if you're diligent enough, doing little damage to the card itself, but bending the connector pins in the camera, eliminating its ability to read or write to any memory card. Or, if the card is formatted in your computer with a memory card reader, your D300 may fail to recognize it. Occasionally, I've found that a memory card used in one camera would fail if used in a different camera (until I reformatted it in Windows, and then again in the camera). Every once in awhile, a card goes completely bad and—seemingly—can't be salvaged.

Another way to lose images is to do commonplace things with your CF card at an inopportune time. If you remove the card from the D300 while the camera is writing images to the card, you'll lose any photos in the buffer and may damage the file structure of the card, making it difficult or impossible to retrieve the other pictures you've taken. The same thing can happen if you remove the CF card from your computer's card reader while the computer is writing to the card (say, to erase files you've already moved to your computer). You can avoid this by *not* using your computer to erase files on a Compact Flash card but, instead, always reformatting the card in your D300 before you use it again.

What Can You Do?

Pay attention: If you're having problems, the *first* thing you should do is *stop* using that memory card. Don't take any more pictures. Don't do anything with the card until you've figured out what's wrong. Your second line of defense (your first line is to be sufficiently careful with your cards that you avoid problems in the first place) is to *do no harm* that hasn't already been done. Read the rest of this section and then, if necessary, decide on a course of action (such as using a data recovery service or software described later) before you risk damaging the data on your card further.

Now that you've calmed down, the first thing to check is whether you've actually inserted a card in the camera. If you've set the camera so that **Enable Release** is activated in **CSM #9**, it's entirely possible (although not particularly plausible) that you've been snapping away with no memory card to store the pictures to, which can lead to massive disappointment later on. Of course, the **--E--** warning appears on the LCD when the camera is powered up, and the **Demo** message is superimposed on the review image after every shot (assuming you've enabled the D300 to take photos when a card is not inserted), but maybe you're inattentive, aren't using picture review, or have purchased one of those LCD fold-up hoods mentioned earlier in this chapter. You can avoid all this by setting the **No Memory Card?** (**CSM #f9**) feature to **Release locked**, and leaving it there.

Things get more exciting when the card itself is put in jeopardy. If you lose a card, there's not a lot you can do other than take a picture of a similar card and print up some Have You Seen This Lost Flash Memory? flyers to post on utility poles all around town.

If all you care about is reusing the card, and have resigned yourself to losing the pictures, try reformatting the card in your camera. You may find that reformatting removes the corrupted data and restores your card to health. Sometimes I've had success reformatting a card in my computer using a memory card reader (this is normally a no-no because your operating system doesn't understand the needs of your D300), and *then* reformatting again in the camera.

If your Compact Flash card is not behaving properly, and you *do* want to recover your images, things get a little more complicated. If your pictures are very valuable, either to you or to others (for example, a wedding), you can always turn to professional data recovery firms. Be prepared to pay hundreds of dollars to get your pictures back, but these pros often do an amazing job. You wouldn't want them working on your memory card on behalf of the police if you'd tried to erase some incriminating pictures. There are many firms of this type, and I've never used them myself, so I can't offer a recommendation. Use a Google search to turn up a ton of them.

THE ULTIMATE IRONY

I recently purchased an 8GB Kingston memory card that was furnished with some nifty OnTrack data recovery software. The first thing I did was format the card to make sure it was OK. Then I hunted around for the free software, only to discover it was preloaded onto the memory card. I was supposed to copy the software to my computer before using the memory card for the first time.

Fortunately, I had the OnTrack software that would reverse my dumb move, so I could retrieve the software. No, wait. I *didn't* have the software I needed to recover the software I erased. I'd reformatted it to oblivion. Chalk this one up as either the ultimate irony or Stupid Photographer Trick #523.

A more reasonable approach is to try special data recovery software you can install on your computer and use to attempt to resurrect your "lost" images yourself. They may not actually be gone completely. Perhaps your CF card's "table of contents" is jumbled, or only a few pictures are damaged in such a way that your camera and computer can't read some or any of the pictures on the card. Some of the available software was written specifically to reconstruct lost pictures, while other utilities are more general-purpose applications that can be used with any media, including floppy disks and hard disk drives. They have names like OnTrack, Photo Rescue 2, Digital Image Recovery, MediaRecover, Image Recall, and the aptly named Recover My Photos. You'll find a comprehensive list and links, as well as some picture-recovery tips at **www.ultimateslr.com/memory-card-recovery.php**.

DIMINISHING RETURNS

Usually, once you've recovered any images on a Compact Flash card, reformatted it, and returned it to service, it will function reliably for the rest of its useful life. However, if you find a particular card going bad more than once, you'll almost certainly want to stop using it forever. See if you can get it replaced by the manufacturer if you can, but, in the case of CF card failures, the third time is never the charm.

Clean Your Sensor

There's no avoiding dust. No matter how careful you are, some of it is going to settle on your camera and on the mounts of your lenses, eventually making its way inside your camera to settle in the mirror chamber. As you take photos, the mirror flipping up and down causes the dust to become airborne and eventually make its way past the shutter curtain to come to rest on the anti-aliasing filter atop your sensor. There, dust and particles can show up in every single picture you take at a small enough aperture to bring the foreign matter into sharp focus. No matter how careful you are and how cleanly you work, eventually you will get some of this dust on your camera's sensor. Some say that CMOS sensors, like the one found in the Nikon D300, "attract" less dust than CCD sensors found in cameras from other vendors. But even the cleanest-working photographers using the Nikon D300 are far from immune.

Fortunately, one of the Nikon D300's most useful new features is the automatic sensor cleaning system that reduces or eliminates the need to clean your camera's sensor manually. The sensor vibrates ultrasonically each time the D300 is powered either on or off (or both, at your option), shaking loose any dust.

Although the automatic sensor cleaning feature operates when you power the camera up or turn it off (depending on the behavior you specify in the Setup menu), you can activate it manually at any time. Choose **Clean image sensor** from the Setup menu, and select **Clean now**. If you'd rather specify when automatic cleaning occurs, choose **On** (clean at power up), **Off** (clean when the camera is switched off), **On/Off** (clean at both power up and power down), or **Cleaning off** (no automatic sensor cleaning will take place).

If some dust does collect on your sensor, you can often map it out of your images (making it invisible) using software techniques with the Dust off ref photo feature in the Shooting menu. Operation of this feature is described in Chapter 5.

Of course, even with the Nikon D300's automatic sensor cleaning/dust resistance features, you may still be required to manually clean your sensor from time to time. This section explains the phenomenon and provides some tips on minimizing dust and eliminating it when it begins to affect your shots. I also cover this subject in my book, *Digital SLR Pro Secrets*, with complete instructions for constructing your own sensor cleaning tools. However, I'll provide a condensed version here of some of the information in that book, because sensor dust and sensor cleaning are two of the most contentious subjects Nikon D300 owners have to deal with.

Dust the FAQs, Ma'am

Here are some of the most frequently asked questions about sensor dust issues.

Q. I see tiny specks in my viewfinder. Do I have dust on my sensor?

A. If you see sharp, well-defined specks, they are clinging to the underside of your focus screen and not on your sensor. They have absolutely no effect on your photographs, and are merely annoying or distracting.

Q. I can see dust on my mirror. How can I remove it?

A. Like focus-screen dust, any artifacts that have settled on your mirror won't affect your photos. You can often remove dust on the mirror or focus screen with a bulb air blower, which will loosen it and whisk it away. Stubborn dust on the focus screen can sometimes be gently flicked away with a soft brush designed for cleaning lenses. I don't recommend brushing the mirror or touching it in any way. The mirror is a special front-surface-silvered optical device (unlike conventional mirrors, which are silvered on the back side of a piece of glass or plastic) and can be easily scratched. If you can't blow mirror dust off, it's best to just forget about it. You can't see it in the viewfinder, anyway.

Q. I see a bright spot in the same place in all of my photos. Is that sensor dust?

A. You've probably got either a "hot" pixel or one that is permanently "stuck" due to a defect in the sensor. A hot pixel is one that shows up as a bright spot only during long exposures as the sensor warms. A pixel stuck in the "on" position always appears in the image. Both show up as bright red, green, or blue pixels, usually surrounded by a small cluster of other improperly illuminated pixels, caused by the camera's interpolating the hot or stuck pixel into its surroundings, as shown in Figure 11.6. A stuck pixel can also be permanently dark. Either kind is likely to show up when they contrast with plain, evenly colored areas of your image.

Finding one or two hot or stuck pixels in your sensor is unfortunately fairly common. They can be "removed" by telling the D300 to ignore them through a simple process called *pixel mapping*. If the bad pixels become bothersome, Nikon can remap your sensor's pixels with a quick trip to a service center.

Bad pixels can also show up on your camera's color LCD panel, but, unless they are abundant, the wisest course is to just ignore them.

Figure 11.6

A stuck pixel is surrounded by improperly interpolated pixels created by the D300's demosaicing algorithm.

Q. I see an irregular out-of-focus blob in the same place in my photos. Is that sensor dust?

A. Yes. Sensor contaminants can take the form of tiny spots, larger blobs, or even curvy lines if they are caused by minuscule fibers that have settled on the sensor. They'll appear out of focus because they aren't actually on the sensor surface but, rather, a fraction of a millimeter above it on the filter that covers the sensor. The smaller the f/stop used, the more in-focus the dust becomes. At large apertures, it may not be visible at all.

Q. I never see any dust on my sensor. What's all the fuss about?

A. Those who never have dust problems with their Nikon D300 fall into one of four categories: those for whom the camera's automatic dust removal features are working well; those who seldom change their lenses and have clean working habits that minimize the amount of dust that invades their cameras in the first place; those who simply don't notice the dust (often because they don't shoot many macro photos or other pictures using the small f/stops that makes dust evident in their images); and those who are very, very lucky.

Identifying and Dealing with Dust

Sensor dust is less of a problem than it might be because it shows up only under certain circumstances. Indeed, you might have dust on your sensor right now and not be aware if it. The dust doesn't actually settle on the sensor itself, but, rather, on a protective filter a very tiny distance above the sensor, subjecting it to the phenomenon of *depth-of-focus*. Depth-of-focus is the distance the focal plane can be moved and still render an object in sharp focus. At f/2.8 to f/5.6 or even smaller, sensor dust, particularly if small, is likely to be outside the range of depth-of-focus and blur into an unnoticeable dot.

However, if you're shooting at f/16 to f/22 or smaller, those dust motes suddenly pop into focus. Forget about trying to spot them by peering directly at your sensor with the shutter open and the lens removed. The period at the end of this sentence, about .33mm in diameter, could block a group of pixels measuring 40 x 40 pixels (160 pixels in all!). Dust spots that are even smaller than that can easily show up in your images if you're shooting large, empty areas that are light colored. Dust motes are most likely to show up in the sky, as in Figure 11.7, or in white backgrounds of your seamless product shots and are less likely to be a problem in images that contain lots of dark areas and detail.

To see if you have dust on your sensor, take a few test shots of a plain, blank surface (such as a piece of paper or a cloudless sky) at small f/stops, such as f/22, and a few wide open. Open Photoshop or another image editor, copy several shots into a single document in separate layers, then flip back and forth between layers to see if any spots you see are present in all layers. You may have to boost contrast and sharpness to make the dust easier to spot.

Avoiding Dust

Of course, the easiest way to protect your sensor from dust is to prevent it from settling on the sensor in the first place. Here are my stock tips for eliminating the problem before it begins.

- **Clean environment.** Avoid working in dusty areas if you can do so. Hah! Serious photographers will take this one with a grain of salt, because it usually makes sense to go where the pictures are. Only a few of us are so paranoid about sensor dust (considering that it is so easily removed) that we'll avoid moderately grimy locations just to protect something that is, when you get down to it, just a tool. If you find a great picture opportunity at a raging fire, during a sandstorm, or while surrounded by dust clouds, you might hesitate to take the picture, but, with a little caution (don't remove your lens in these situations, and clean the camera afterwards!) you can still shoot. However, it still makes sense to store your camera in a clean environment. One place cameras and lenses pick up a lot of dust is inside a camera bag. Clean your bag from time to time, and you can avoid problems.

- **Clean lenses.** There are a few paranoid types that avoid swapping lenses in order to minimize the chance of dust getting inside their cameras. It makes more sense just to use a blower or brush to dust off the rear lens mount of the replacement lens first, so you won't be introducing dust into your camera simply by attaching a new, dusty lens. Do this before you remove the current lens from your camera, and then avoid stirring up dust before making the exchange.

- **Work fast.** Minimize the time your camera is lens-less and exposed to dust. That means having your replacement lens ready and dusted off, and a place to set down the old lens as soon as it is removed, so you can quickly attach the new lens.

Figure 11.7
Only the dust
spots in the sky
are apparent in
this shot.

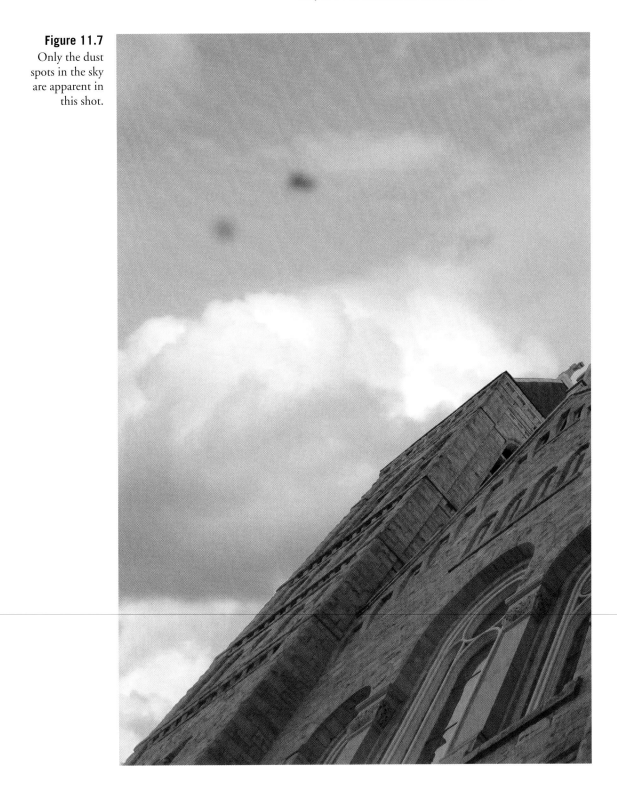

- **Let gravity help you.** Face the camera downward when the lens is detached so any dust in the mirror box will tend to fall away from the sensor. Turn your back to any breezes, indoor forced air vents, fans, or other sources of dust to minimize infiltration.

- **Protect the lens you just removed.** Once you've attached the new lens, quickly put the end cap on the one you just removed to reduce the dust that might fall on it.

- **Clean out the vestibule.** From time to time, remove the lens while in a relatively dust-free environment and use a blower bulb like the one shown in Figure 11.8 (*not* compressed air or a vacuum hose) to clean out the mirror box area. A blower bulb is generally safer than a can of compressed air, or a strong positive/negative airflow, which can tend to drive dust further into nooks and crannies.

- **Be prepared.** If you're embarking on an important shooting session, it's a good idea to clean your sensor *now*, rather than come home with hundreds or thousands of images with dust spots caused by flecks that were sitting on your sensor before you

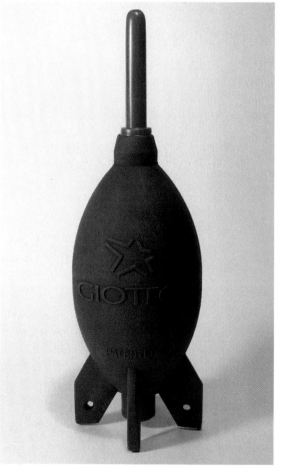

Figure 11.8
Use a robust air bulb like the Giottos Rocket for cleaning your sensor.

even started. Before I left on my recent trip to Spain, I put both cameras I was taking through a rigid cleaning regimen, figuring they could remain dust-free for a measly 10 days. I even left my bulky blower bulb at home, and took along a new, smaller version for emergencies.

■ **Clone out existing spots in your image editor.** Photoshop and other editors have a clone tool or healing brush you can use to copy pixels from surrounding areas over the dust spot or dead pixel. This process can be tedious, especially if you have lots of dust spots and/or lots of images to be corrected. The advantage is that this sort of manual fix-it probably will do the least damage to the rest of your photo. Only the damaged pixels will be affected.

■ **Use filtration in your image editor.** A semi-smart filter like Photoshop's Dust & Scratches filter can remove dust and other artifacts by selectively blurring areas that the plug-in decides represent dust spots. This method can work well if you have many dust spots, because you won't need to patch them manually. However, any automated method like this has the possibility of blurring areas of your image that you didn't intend to soften.

Sensor Cleaning

Those new to the concept of sensor dust actually hesitate before deciding to clean their camera themselves. Isn't it a better idea to pack up your D300 and send it to a Nikon service center so their crack technical staff can do the job for you? Or, at the very least, shouldn't you let the friendly folks at your local camera store do it?

Of course, if you choose to let someone else clean your sensor, they will be using methods that are more or less identical to the techniques you would use yourself. None of these techniques are difficult, and the only difference between their cleaning and your cleaning is that they might have done it dozens or hundreds of times. If you're careful, you can do just as good a job.

Of course vendors like Nikon won't tell you this, but it's not because they don't trust you. It's not that difficult for a real goofball to mess up their camera by hurrying or taking a shortcut. Perhaps the person uses the "Bulb" method of holding the shutter open and a finger slips, allowing the shutter curtain to close on top of a sensor cleaning brush. Or, someone tries to clean the sensor using masking tape, and ends up with goo all over its surface. If Nikon recommended *any* method that's mildly risky, someone would do it wrong, and then the company would face lawsuits from those who'd contend they did it exactly in the way the vendor suggested, so the ruined camera is not their fault.

You can see that vendors like Nikon tend to be conservative in their recommendations, and, in doing so, make it seem as if sensor cleaning is more daunting and dangerous than it really is. Some vendors recommend only dust-off cleaning, through the use of reasonably gentle blasts of air, while condemning more serious scrubbing with swabs and cleaning fluids. However, these cleaning kits for the exact types of cleaning they recommended against are for sale in Japan only, where, apparently, your average photographer is more dexterous than those of us in the rest of the world. These kits are similar to those used by official repair staff to clean your sensor if you decide to send your camera in for a dust-up.

As I noted, sensors can be affected by dust particles that are much smaller than you might be able to spot visually on the surface of your lens. The filters that cover sensors tend to be fairly hard compared to optical glass. Cleaning the 23.6mm x 15.8mm sensor in your Nikon D300 within the tight confines of the mirror box can call for a steady hand and careful touch. If your sensor's filter becomes scratched through inept cleaning, you can't simply remove it yourself and replace it with a new one.

There are four basic kinds of cleaning processes that can be used to remove dusty and sticky stuff that settles on your dSLR's sensor. All of these must be performed with the shutter locked open. I'll describe these methods and provide instructions for locking the shutter later in this section.

- **Air cleaning.** This process involves squirting blasts of air inside your camera with the shutter locked open. This works well for dust that's not clinging stubbornly to your sensor.

- **Brushing.** A soft, very fine brush is passed across the surface of the sensor's filter, dislodging mildly persistent dust particles and sweeping them off the imager.

- **Liquid cleaning.** A soft swab dipped in a cleaning solution such as ethanol is used to wipe the sensor filter, removing more obstinate particles.

- **Tape cleaning.** There are some who get good results by applying a special form of tape to the surface of their sensor. When the tape is peeled off, all the dust goes with it. Supposedly. I'd be remiss if I didn't point out right now that this form of cleaning is somewhat controversial; the other three methods are much more widely accepted.

Placing the Mirror/Shutter in the Locked and Fully Upright Position for Landing

Make sure you're using a fully charged battery or the Nikon EH-5/EH-5a AC adapter. Fortunately, the Nikon D300 is smart enough that it won't let you try to clean the sensor manually unless the battery has a sufficient charge.

1. Remove the lens from the camera and then turn the camera on.

2. You'll find the **Lock mirror up for cleaning** menu choice in the Setup menu. Select it.

3. Choose **Start**. The mirror will flip up and the shutter will open.

4. Use one of the methods described below to remove dust and grime from your sensor. Be careful not to accidentally switch the power off or open the Compact Flash card or battery compartment doors as you work. If that happens, the shutter may be damaged if it closes onto your cleaning tool.

5. When you're finished, turn the power off, replace your lens, and switch your camera back on.

Air Cleaning

Your first attempts at cleaning your sensor should always involve gentle blasts of air. Many times, you'll be able to dislodge dust spots, which will fall off the sensor and, with luck, out of the mirror box. Attempt one of the other methods only when you've already tried air cleaning and it didn't remove all the dust.

Here are some tips for doing air cleaning:

- **Use a clean, powerful air bulb.** Your best bet is bulb cleaners designed for the job, like the Giottos Rocket shown in Figure 11.8. Smaller bulbs, like those air bulbs with a brush attached sometimes sold for lens cleaning or weak nasal aspirators may not provide sufficient air or a strong enough blast to do much good.

- **Hold the Nikon D300 upside down.** Then look up into the mirror box as you squirt your air blasts, increasing the odds that gravity will help pull the expelled dust downward, away from the sensor. You may have to use some imagination in positioning yourself.

- **Never use air canisters.** The propellant inside these cans can permanently coat your sensor if you tilt the can while spraying. It's not worth taking a chance.

- **Avoid air compressors.** Super-strong blasts of air are likely to force dust under the sensor filter.

Brush Cleaning

If your dust is a little more stubborn and can't be dislodged by air alone, you may want to try a brush, charged with static electricity, which can pick off dust spots by electrical attraction. One good, but expensive, option is the Sensor Brush sold at **www.visible-dust.com**. A cheaper version can be purchased at **www.copperhillimages.com**. You need a 16mm version, like the one shown in Figure 11.9, which can be stroked across the short dimension of your D300's sensor.

Ordinary artist's brushes are much too coarse and stiff and have fibers that are tangled or can come loose and settle on your sensor. A good sensor brush's fibers are resilient and described as "thinner than a human hair." Moreover, the brush has a wooden handle that reduces the risk of static sparks. Check out my *Digital SLR Pro Secrets* book if you want to make a sensor brush (or sensor swabs) yourself.

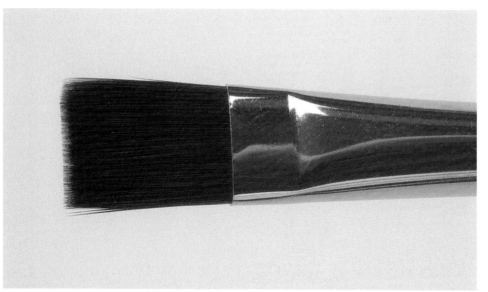

Figure 11.9
A proper brush
is required for
dusting off
your sensor.

Brush cleaning is done with a dry brush by gently swiping the surface of the sensor filter with the tip. The dust particles are attracted to the brush particles and cling to them. You should clean the brush with compressed air before and after each use, and store it in an appropriate air-tight container between applications to keep it clean and dust-free. Although these special brushes are expensive, one should last you a long time.

Liquid Cleaning

Unfortunately, you'll often encounter really stubborn dust spots that can't be removed with a blast of air or flick of a brush. These spots may be combined with some grease or a liquid that causes them to stick to the sensor filter's surface. In such cases, liquid cleaning with a swab may be necessary. During my first clumsy attempts to clean my own sensor, I accidentally got my blower bulb tip too close to the sensor, and some sort of deposit from the tip of the bulb ended up on the sensor. I panicked until I discovered that liquid cleaning did a good job of removing whatever it was that took up residence on my sensor.

You can make your own swabs out of pieces of plastic (some use fast food restaurant knives, with the tip cut at an angle to the proper size) covered with a soft cloth or Pec-Pad, as shown in Figures 11.10 and 11.11. However, if you've got the bucks to spend, you can't go wrong with good-quality commercial sensor cleaning swabs, such as those sold by Photographic Solutions, Inc. (**www.photosol.com/swabproduct.htm**).

You want a sturdy swab that won't bend or break so you can apply gentle pressure to the swab as you wipe the sensor surface. Use the swab with methanol (as pure as you can get it, particularly medical grade; other ingredients can leave a residue), or the Eclipse 2 solution also sold by Photographic Solutions. Eclipse 2 (see Figure 11.12) is

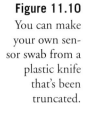

Figure 11.10
You can make your own sensor swab from a plastic knife that's been truncated.

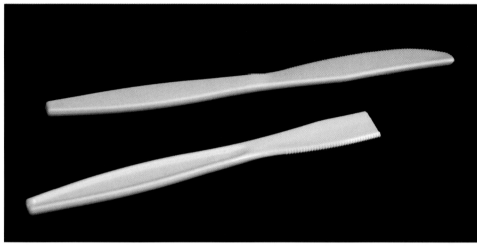

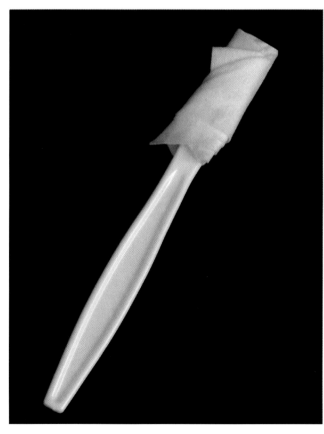

Figure 11.11 Carefully wrap a Pec-Pad around the swab.

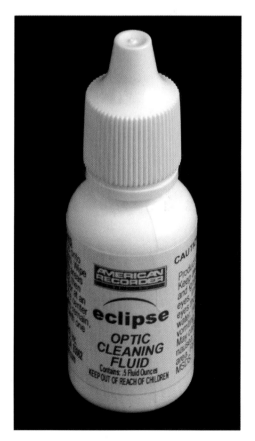

Figure 11.12 Pure Eclipse solution makes the best sensor cleaning liquid.

actually quite a bit purer than even medical-grade methanol. A couple drops of solution should be enough, unless you have a spot that's extremely difficult to remove. In that case, you may need to use extra solution on the swab to help "soak" the dirt off. Note: the E2 version of Eclipse is now recommended for cleaning what are termed "tin oxide" sensors, similar to the Nikon D300. If you have some of the older Eclipse solution, it's great for cleaning lenses! Buy the new stuff to be safe.

Once you overcome your nervousness at touching your D300's sensor, the process is easy. You'll wipe continuously with the swab in one direction, then flip it over and wipe in the other direction. You need to completely wipe the entire surface; otherwise, you may end up depositing the dust you collect at the far end of your stroke. Wipe; don't rub.

Tape Cleaning

There are people who absolutely swear by the tape method of sensor cleaning. The concept seems totally wacky, and I have never tried it personally, so I can't say with certainty that it either does or does not work. In the interest of completeness, I'm including it here. I can't give you a recommendation, so if you have problems, please don't blame me. The Nikon D300 is still too new to have generated any reports of users accidentally damaging the anti-dust coating on the sensor filter using this method.

Tape cleaning works by applying a layer of Scotch Brand Magic Tape to the sensor. This is a minimally sticky tape that some of the tape cleaning proponents claim contains no adhesive. I did check this out with 3M, and can say that Magic Tape certainly *does* contain an adhesive. The question is whether the adhesive comes off when you peel back the tape, taking any dust spots on your sensor with it. The folks who love this method claim there is no residue. There have been reports from those who don't like the method that residue is left behind. This is all anecdotal evidence, so you're pretty much on your own in making the decision whether to try out the tape cleaning method.

Glossary

It's always handy to have a single resource where you can look up various terms you'll encounter while working with your digital camera. Here is the latest update of a glossary I've compiled over the years, with some new additions specifically for the Nikon D300.

additive primary colors The red, green, and blue hues, which can be used by themselves or in combinations to create all other colors that you capture with a digital camera, view on a computer monitor, or work with in an image-editing program, such as Photoshop. *See also* CMYK color model.

Adobe RGB One of two color space choices offered by the Nikon D300. Adobe RGB is an expanded color space useful for commercial and professional printing, and it can reproduce a larger number of colors. Nikon recommends against using this color space if your images will be displayed primarily on your computer screen or output by your personal printer. *See also* sRGB.

AE-L/AF-L A button on the D300 that allows locking exposure and/or focus point prior to taking a photo.

ambient lighting Diffuse, non-directional lighting that doesn't appear to come from a specific source but, rather, bounces off walls, ceilings, and other objects in the scene when a picture is taken.

analog/digital converter The module in a camera that electronically converts the analog information captured by the D300's sensor into digital bits that can be stored as an image.

angle of view The area of a scene that a lens can capture, determined by the focal length of the lens. Lenses with a shorter focal length have a wider angle of view than lenses with a longer focal length.

anti-alias A process that smoothes the look of rough edges in images (called *jaggies* or *staircasing*) by adding partially transparent pixels along the boundaries of diagonal lines that are merged into a smoother line by our eyes. *See also* jaggies.

aperture The size of the opening in the iris or diaphragm of a lens, relative to the lens's focal length. Also called an *f/stop*. For example, with a lens having a focal length of 100mm, an f/stop with a diameter of 12.5mm would produce an aperture value of f/8.

Aperture Priority A camera setting that allows you to specify the lens opening or f/stop that you want to use, with the camera selecting the required shutter speed automatically based on its light-meter reading. *See also* Shutter Priority.

artifact A type of noise in an image, or an unintentional image component produced in error by a digital camera during processing, usually caused by the JPEG compression process in digital cameras.

aspect ratio The proportions of an image as printed, displayed on a monitor, or captured by a digital camera.

autofocus A camera setting that allows the Nikon D300 to choose the correct focus distance for you, based on the contrast of an image (the image will be at maximum contrast when in sharp focus). The camera can be set for *Single-Servo Autofocus (AF-S)*, (in which the lens is not focused until the shutter release is partially depressed), *Continuous-Servo Autofocus (AF-C)*, (in which the lens refocuses constantly as you frame and reframe the image), or *Manual* focus.

backlighting A lighting effect produced when the main light source is located behind the subject. Backlighting can be used to create a silhouette effect, or to illuminate translucent objects. *See also* front lighting and sidelighting.

barrel distortion A lens defect that causes straight lines at the top or side edges of an image to bow outward into a barrel shape. *See also* pincushion distortion.

blooming An image distortion caused when a photosite in an image sensor has absorbed all the photons it can handle so that additional photons reaching that pixel overflow to affect surrounding pixels, producing unwanted brightness and overexposure around the edges of objects.

blur To soften an image or part of an image by throwing it out of focus, or by allowing it to become soft due to subject or camera motion. Blur can also be applied in an image-editing program.

bokeh A term derived from the Japanese word for blur, which describes the aesthetic qualities of the out-of-focus parts of an image. Some lenses produce "good" bokeh and others offer "bad" bokeh. Some lenses produce uniformly illuminated out-of-focus discs. Others produce a disc that has a bright edge and a dark center, producing a "doughnut" effect, which is the worst from a bokeh standpoint. Lenses that generate a bright center that fades to a darker edge are favored, because their bokeh allows the circle of confusion to blend more smoothly with the surroundings. The bokeh characteristics of a lens are most important when you're using selective focus (say, when shooting a portrait) to deemphasize the background, or when shallow depth-of-field is a given because you're working with a macro lens, with a long telephoto, or with a wide-open aperture. *See also* circle of confusion.

bounce lighting Light bounced off a reflector, including ceiling and walls, to provide a soft, natural-looking light.

bracketing Taking a series of photographs of the same subject at different settings, including exposure and white balance, to help ensure that one setting will be the correct one. The Nikon D300 allows you to choose the order in which bracketed settings are applied, or bracket sequence.

buffer The digital camera's internal memory where an image is stored immediately after it is taken until it can be written to the camera's non-volatile (semi-permanent) memory card.

burst mode The digital camera's equivalent of the film camera's motor drive, used to take multiple shots within a short period of time, each stored in a memory buffer temporarily before writing them to the media.

calibration A process used to correct for the differences in the output of a printer or monitor when compared to the original image. Once you've calibrated your scanner, monitor, and/or your image editor, the images you see on the screen more closely represent what you'll get from your printer, even though calibration is never perfect.

Camera Raw A plug-in included with Photoshop and Photoshop Elements that can manipulate the unprocessed images captured by digital cameras, such as the Nikon D300's NEF files. The latest versions of this module can also work with JPEG and TIFF images.

camera shake Movement of the camera, aggravated by slower shutter speeds, which produces a blurred image.

CCD *See* charge-coupled device (CCD).

center-weighted meter A light-measuring device that emphasizes the area in the middle of the frame when calculating the correct exposure for an image. *See also* spot meter.

channel In an electronic flash, a channel is a protocol used to communicate between a master flash unit and the remote units slaved to that main flash. The ability to change channels allows several master flash units to operate in the same environment without interfering with each other.

charge-coupled device (CCD) A type of solid-state sensor that captures the image used in scanners and digital cameras.

chromatic aberration An image defect, often seen as green or purple fringing around the edges of an object, caused by a lens failing to focus all colors of a light source at the same point. *See also* fringing.

circle of confusion A term applied to the fuzzy discs produced when a point of light is out of focus. The circle of confusion is not a fixed size. The viewing distance and amount of enlargement of the image determine whether we see a particular spot on the image as a point or as a disc. *See also* bokeh.

close-up lens A lens add-on that allows you to take pictures at a distance that is less than the closest-focusing distance of the lens alone.

CMOS *See* complementary metal-oxide semiconductor (CMOS).

CMYK color model A way of defining all possible colors in percentages of cyan, magenta, yellow, and frequently, black. (K represents black, to differentiate it from blue in the RGB color model.) Black is added to improve rendition of shadow detail. CMYK is commonly used for printing (both on press and with your inkjet or laser color printer).

color correction Changing the relative amounts of color in an image to produce a desired effect, typically a more accurate representation of those colors. Color correction can fix faulty color balance in the original image, or compensate for the deficiencies of the inks used to reproduce the image.

complementary metal-oxide semiconductor (CMOS) A method for manufacturing a type of solid-state sensor that captures the image, used in scanners and digital cameras such as several of those from Nikon (including the Nikon D3, D300, and D2xs).

compression Reducing the size of a file by encoding using fewer bits of information to represent the original. Some compression schemes, such as JPEG, operate by discarding some image information, while others, such as RAW, preserve all the detail in the original, discarding only redundant data.

Continuous-Servo autofocus An automatic focusing setting (AF-C) in which the camera constantly refocuses the image as you frame the picture. This setting is often the best choice for moving subjects. *See also* Single-Servo autofocus.

contrast The range between the lightest and darkest tones in an image. A high-contrast image is one in which the shades fall at the extremes of the range between white and black. In a low-contrast image, the tones are closer together.

Creative Lighting System (CLS) Nikon's electronic flash system used to coordinate exposure, camera information, and timing between a camera's built-in flash (if present) and external flash units, which can be linked through direct electrical connections or wirelessly.

Custom Settings A group of different settings you can make to specify how the Nikon D300 behaves, such as the function of certain controls, electronic flash features, and other customizable attributes.

dedicated flash An electronic flash unit, such as the Nikon SB-800 Speedlight, designed to work with the automatic exposure features of a specific camera.

depth-of-field A distance range in a photograph in which all included portions of an image are at least acceptably sharp. With the Nikon D300, you can see the available depth-of-field at the taking aperture by pressing the Depth-of-Field Preview button, or estimate the range by viewing the depth-of-field scale found on some lenses.

diaphragm An adjustable component, similar to the iris in the human eye, which can open and close to provide specific-sized lens openings, or f/stops and thus control the amount of light reaching the sensor or film.

diffuse lighting Soft, low-contrast lighting.

digital processing chip A solid-state device found in digital cameras (such as the Nikon's EXSPEED module) that's in charge of applying the image algorithms to the raw picture data prior to storage on the memory card.

diopter A value used to represent the magnification power of a lens, calculated as the reciprocal of a lens's focal length (in meters). Diopters are most often used to represent the optical correction used in a viewfinder to adjust for limitations of the photographer's eyesight, and to describe the magnification of a close-up lens attachment.

equivalent focal length A digital camera's focal length translated into the corresponding values for a 35mm film camera. This value can be calculated for lenses used with the Nikon D300 by multiplying by 1.5.

exchangeable image file format (Exif) Developed to standardize the exchange of image data between hardware devices and software. A variation on JPEG, Exif is used by most digital cameras, and includes information such as the date and time a photo was taken, the camera settings, resolution, amount of compression, and other data.

Exif *See* exchangeable image file format (Exif).

exposure The amount of light allowed to reach the film or sensor, determined by the intensity of the light, the amount admitted by the iris of the lens, and the length of time determined by the shutter speed.

exposure compensation Exposure compensation, which uses exposure value (EV) settings, is a way of adding or decreasing exposure without the need to reference f/stops or shutter speeds. For example, if you tell your camera to add +1EV, it will provide twice as much exposure, either by using a larger f/stop or slower shutter speed, or both. The D300 offers both conventional exposure compensation and flash exposure compensation.

fill lighting In photography, lighting used to illuminate shadows. Reflectors or additional incandescent lighting or electronic flash can be used to brighten shadows. One common technique outdoors is to use the camera's flash as a fill.

filter In photography, a device that fits over the lens, changing the light in some way. In image editing, a feature that changes the pixels in an image to produce blurring, sharpening, and other special effects. Photoshop includes several interesting filter effects, including Lens Blur and Photo Filters.

flash sync The timing mechanism that ensures that an internal or external electronic flash fires at the correct time during the exposure cycle. A digital SLR's flash sync speed is the highest shutter speed that can be used with flash, ordinarily 1/250th of a second with the Nikon D300. *See also* front-curtain sync and rear-curtain sync.

focal length The distance between the film and the optical center of the lens when the lens is focused on infinity, usually measured in millimeters.

focal plane An imaginary line, perpendicular to the optical axis, which passes through the focal point forming a plane of sharp focus when the lens is set at infinity. A focal plane indicator is etched into the Nikon D300 on the top panel.

focus tracking The ability of the automatic focus feature of a camera to change focus as the distance between the subject and the camera changes. One type of focus tracking is *predictive,* in which the mechanism anticipates the motion of the object being focused on, and adjusts the focus to suit.

format To erase a memory card and prepare it to accept files.

fringing A chromatic aberration that produces fringes of color around the edges of subjects, caused by a lens's inability to focus the various wavelengths of light onto the same spot. Purple fringing is especially troublesome with backlit images.

front-curtain sync (first-curtain sync) The default kind of electronic flash synchronization technique, originally associated with focal plane shutters, which consists of a traveling set of curtains, including a *front curtain*, which opens to reveal the film or sensor, and a *rear curtain*, which follows at a distance determined by shutter speed to conceal the film or sensor at the conclusion of the exposure. For a flash picture to be taken, the entire sensor must be exposed at one time to the brief flash exposure, so the image is exposed after the front curtain has reached the other side of the focal plane, but before the rear curtain begins to move. Front-curtain sync causes the flash to fire at the beginning of this period when the shutter is completely open, in the instant that the first curtain of the focal plane shutter finishes its movement across the film or sensor plane. With slow shutter speeds, this feature can create a blur effect from the ambient light, showing as patterns that follow a moving subject with the subject shown sharply frozen at the beginning of the blur trail. *See also* rear-curtain sync.

front lighting Illumination that comes from the direction of the camera. *See also* backlighting and sidelighting.

f/stop The relative size of the lens aperture, which helps determine both exposure and depth-of-field. The larger the f/stop number, the smaller the f/stop itself.

graduated filter A lens attachment with variable density or color from one edge to another. A graduated neutral density filter, for example, can be oriented so the neutral density portion is concentrated at the top of the lens's view with the less dense or clear portion at the bottom, thus reducing the amount of light from a very bright sky while not interfering with the exposure of the landscape in the foreground. Graduated filters can also be split into several color sections to provide a color gradient between portions of the image.

gray card A piece of cardboard or other material with a standardized 18-percent reflectance. Gray cards can be used as a reference for determining correct exposure or for setting white balance.

group A way of bundling more than one wireless flash unit into a single cluster that all share the same flash output setting, as controlled by the master flash unit.

high contrast A wide range of density in a print, negative, or other image.

highlights The brightest parts of an image containing detail.

high-speed sync A method for syncing Nikon external flashes, like the SB-800, at shutter speeds higher than 1/250th second by increasing the flash duration through multiple bursts to match the speed of the focal plane shutter.

histogram A kind of chart showing the relationship of tones in an image using a series of 256 vertical bars, one for each brightness level. A histogram chart, such as the ones the Nikon D300 can display during picture review, typically looks like a curve with one or more slopes and peaks, depending on how many highlight, midtone, and shadow tones are present in the image. The D300 can also display separate histograms for the red, green, and blue channels of an image.

hot shoe A mount on top of a camera used to hold an electronic flash, while providing an electrical connection between the flash and the camera. Also called an accessory shoe.

hyperfocal distance A point of focus where everything from half that distance to infinity appears to be acceptably sharp. For example, if your lens has a hyperfocal distance of four feet, everything from two feet to infinity would be sharp. The hyperfocal distance varies by the lens and the aperture in use. If you know you'll be making a grab shot without warning, sometimes it is useful to turn off your camera's automatic focus, and set the lens to infinity, or, better yet, the hyperfocal distance. Then, you can snap off a quick picture without having to wait for the lag that occurs with most digital cameras as their autofocus locks in.

image rotation A feature that senses whether a picture was taken in horizontal or vertical orientation. That information is embedded in the picture file so that the camera and compatible software applications can automatically display the image in the correct orientation.

image stabilization A technology that compensates for camera shake, usually by adjusting the position of the camera sensor or lens elements in response to movements of the camera.

incident light Light falling on a surface.

International Organization for Standardization (ISO) A governing body that provides standards used to represent film speed, or the equivalent sensitivity of a digital camera's sensor. Digital camera sensitivity is expressed in ISO settings.

interpolation A technique digital cameras, scanners, and image editors use to create new pixels required whenever you resize or change the resolution of an image based on the values of surrounding pixels. Devices such as scanners and digital cameras can also use interpolation to create pixels in addition to those actually captured, thereby increasing the apparent resolution or color information in an image.

ISO *See* International Organization for Standardization (ISO).

i-TTL Nikon's intelligent through-the-lens flash metering system, which uses preflashes to calculate exposure and to communicate between flash units, using the camera's 1005-sensor viewfinder exposure meter.

jaggies Staircasing effect of lines that are not perfectly horizontal or vertical, caused by pixels that are too large to represent the line accurately. *See also* anti-alias.

JPEG A file "lossy" format (short for Joint Photographic Experts Group) that supports 24-bit color and reduces file sizes by selectively discarding image data. Digital cameras generally use JPEG compression to pack more images onto memory cards. You can select how much compression is used (and, therefore, how much information is thrown away) by selecting from among the Standard, Fine, Super Fine, or other quality settings offered by your camera. *See also* RAW.

Kelvin (K) A unit of measure based on the absolute temperature scale in which absolute zero is zero; it's used to describe the color of continuous-spectrum light sources and applied when setting white balance. For example, daylight has a color temperature of about 5,500K, and a tungsten lamp has a temperature of about 3,400K.

lag time The interval between when the shutter is pressed and when the picture is actually taken. During that span, the camera may be automatically focusing and calculating exposure. With digital SLRs like the Nikon D300, lag time is generally very short; with non-dSLRs, the elapsed time easily can be one second or more under certain conditions.

latitude The range of camera exposures that produces acceptable images with a particular digital sensor or film.

lens flare A feature of conventional photography that is both a bane and a creative outlet. It is an effect produced by the reflection of light internally among elements of an optical lens. Bright light sources within or just outside the field of view cause lens flare. Flare can be reduced by the use of coatings on the lens elements or with the use of lens hoods. Photographers sometimes use the effect as a creative technique, and Photoshop includes a filter that lets you add lens flare at your whim.

lighting ratio The proportional relationship between the amount of light falling on the subject from the main light and other lights, expressed in a ratio, such as 3:1.

Live View The ability of some Nikon cameras, including the D3 and D300, to provide a real-time preview image, as seen by the sensor, on the rear panel color LCD, achieved by flipping up the mirror and opening the shutter.

lossless compression An image-compression scheme, such as TIFF, that preserves all image detail. When the image is decompressed, it is identical to the original version.

lossy compression An image-compression scheme, such as JPEG, that creates smaller files by discarding image information, which can affect image quality.

macro lens A lens that provides continuous focusing from infinity to extreme close-ups, often to a reproduction ratio of 1:2 (half life-size) or 1:1 (life-size).

matrix metering A system of exposure calculation that looks at many different segments of an image to determine the brightest and darkest portions, and base f/stop and shutter speed on settings derived from a database of images.

maximum burst The number of frames that can be exposed at the current settings until the buffer fills.

midtones Parts of an image with tones of an intermediate value, usually in the 25 to 75 percent brightness range. Many image-editing features allow you to manipulate midtones independently from the highlights and shadows.

mirror lock-up The ability of the D300 to retract its mirror to reduce vibration prior to taking the photo and to allow access to the sensor for cleaning.

modeling light A secondary light used to provide a preview of the lighting effects of an electronic flash unit. A modeling light can be an incandescent or fluorescent bulb, or may be simulated by a series of low-power bursts lasting a few seconds.

neutral color A color in which red, green, and blue are present in equal amounts, producing a gray.

neutral density filter A gray camera filter that reduces the amount of light entering the camera without affecting the colors.

noise In an image, pixels with randomly distributed color values. Noise in digital photographs tends to be the product of low-light conditions and long exposures, particularly when you've set your camera to a higher ISO rating than normal.

noise reduction A technology used to cut down on the amount of random information in a digital picture, usually caused by long exposures at increased sensitivity ratings. In the Nikon D300, noise reduction is automatically applied for long exposures, and it involves the camera automatically taking a second blank/dark exposure at the same settings that contain only noise, and then using the blank photo's information to cancel out the noise in the original picture. Although the process is very quick, it does double the amount of time required to take the photo.

normal lens A lens that makes the image in a photograph appear in a perspective that is like that of the original scene, typically with a field of view of roughly 45 degrees.

overexposure A condition in which too much light reaches the film or sensor, producing a dense negative or a very bright/light print, slide, or digital image.

pincushion distortion A type of lens distortion in which lines at the top and side edges of an image are bent inward, producing an effect that looks like a pincushion. *See also* barrel distortion.

polarizing filter A filter that forces light, which normally vibrates in all directions, to vibrate only in a single plane, reducing or removing the specular reflections from the surface of objects.

RAW An image file format, such as the NEF format in the Nikon D300, which includes all the unprocessed information captured by the camera after conversion to digital form. RAW files are very large compared to JPEG files and must be processed by a special program such as Nikon Capture NX or Adobe's Camera RAW filter after being downloaded from the camera.

rear-curtain sync (second-curtain sync) An optional kind of electronic flash synchronization technique, originally associated with focal plane shutters, which consists of a traveling set of curtains, including a *front (first) curtain* (which opens to reveal the film or sensor) and a *rear (second) curtain* (which follows at a distance determined by shutter speed to conceal the film or sensor at the conclusion of the exposure). For a flash picture to be taken, the entire sensor must be exposed at one time to the brief flash exposure, so the image is exposed after the front curtain has reached the other side of the focal plane, but before the rear curtain begins to move. Rear-curtain sync causes the flash to fire at the end of the exposure, an instant before the second or rear curtain of the focal plane shutter begins to move. With slow shutter speeds, this feature can create a blur effect from the ambient light, showing as patterns that follow a moving subject with the subject shown sharply frozen at the end of the blur trail. If you were shooting a photo of The Flash, the superhero would appear sharp, with a ghostly trail behind him. *See also* front-curtain sync (first-curtain sync).

red-eye An effect from flash photography that appears to make a person's eyes glow red, or an animal's yellow or green. It's caused by light bouncing from the retina of the eye and is most pronounced in dim illumination (when the irises are wide open) and when the electronic flash is close to the lens and, therefore, prone to reflect directly back. Image editors can fix red-eye through cloning other pixels over the offending red or orange ones.

RGB color A color model that represents the three colors—red, green, and blue—used by devices such as scanners or monitors to reproduce color. Photoshop works in RGB mode by default, and even displays CMYK images by converting them to RGB.

saturation The purity of color; the amount by which a pure color is diluted with white or gray.

selective focus Choosing a lens opening that produces a shallow depth-of-field. Usually this is used to isolate a subject in portraits, close-ups, and other types of images, by causing most other elements in the scene to be blurred.

self-timer A mechanism that delays the opening of the shutter for some seconds after the release has been operated.

sensitivity A measure of the degree of response of a film or sensor to light, measured using the ISO setting.

shadow The darkest part of an image, represented on a digital image by pixels with low numeric values.

sharpening Increasing the apparent sharpness of an image by boosting the contrast between adjacent pixels that form an edge.

shutter In a conventional film camera, the shutter is a mechanism consisting of blades, a curtain, a plate, or some other movable cover that controls the time during which light reaches the film. Digital cameras, including the Nikon D300, use actual mechanical shutters for the slower shutter speeds (less than 1/250th second) and an electronic shutter for higher speeds.

shutter priority An exposure mode in which you set the shutter speed and the camera determines the appropriate f/stop. *See also* aperture priority.

sidelighting Applying illumination from the left or right sides of the camera. *See also* backlighting and front lighting.

slave unit An accessory flash unit that supplements the main flash, usually triggered electronically when the slave senses the light output by the main unit, or through radio waves.

slow sync An electronic flash synchronizing method that uses a slow shutter speed so that ambient light is recorded by the camera in addition to the electronic flash illumination. This allows the background to receive more exposure for a more realistic effect.

specular highlight Bright spots in an image caused by reflection of light sources.

spot meter An exposure system that concentrates on a small area in the image. *See also* center-weighted meter.

sRGB One of two color space choices available with the Nikon D300. The sRGB setting is recommended for images that will be output locally on the user's own printer, as this color space matches that of the typical inkjet printer and a properly calibrated monitor fairly closely. *See also* Adobe RGB.

subtractive primary colors Cyan, magenta, and yellow, which are the printing inks that theoretically absorb all color and produce black. In practice, however, they generate a muddy brown, so black is added to preserve detail (especially in shadows). The combination of the three colors and black is referred to as CMYK. (K represents black, to differentiate it from blue in the RGB model.)

through-the-lens (TTL) A system of providing viewing and exposure calculation through the actual lens taking the picture.

time exposure A picture taken by leaving the shutter open for a long period, usually more than one second. The camera is generally locked down with a tripod to prevent blur during the long exposure.

tungsten light Light from ordinary room lamps and ceiling fixtures, as opposed to fluorescent illumination.

underexposure A condition in which too little light reaches the film or sensor, producing a thin negative, a dark slide, a muddy-looking print, or a dark digital image.

unsharp masking The process for increasing the contrast between adjacent pixels in an image, increasing sharpness, especially around edges.

vignetting Dark corners of an image, often produced by using a lens hood that is too small for the field of view, a lens that does not completely fill the image frame, or generated artificially using image-editing techniques.

white balance The adjustment of a digital camera to the color temperature of the light source. Interior illumination is relatively red; outdoor light is relatively blue. Digital cameras like the Nikon D300 set correct white balance automatically or let you do it through menus. Image editors can often do some color correction of images that were exposed using the wrong white balance setting, especially when working with RAW files that contain the information originally captured by the camera before white balance was applied.

zoom head The capability of an electronic flash to change the area of its coverage to more closely match the focal length setting of a prime or zoom lens.

Index